EXPANDING REALISM

EXPANDING REALISM

The Historical Dimension of World Politics

George Liska

ROWMAN & LITTLEFIELD PUBLISHERS, INC.
Lanham • Boulder • New York • Oxford

ROWMAN & LITTLEFIELD PUBLISHERS, INC.

Published in the United States of America
by Rowman & Littlefield Publishers, Inc.
4720 Boston Way, Lanham, Maryland 20706

12 Hid's Copse Road
Cumnor Hill, Oxford OX2 9JJ, England

British Library Cataloguing in Publication Information Available

Library of Congress Cataloging-in-Publication Data

Liska, George.
    Expanding realism : the historical dimension of world politics /
George Liska.
        p.   cm.
    Includes bibliographical references and index.
    ISBN 0-8476-8679-5 (cloth : alk. paper).—ISBN 0-8476-8680-9 (pbk. :
alk. paper)
        1. World politics—20th century—Historiography.   2. Historicism.
I. Title.
D443.L4964   1998
909.82'07'2—dc21   97-22607
                                                                CIP

ISBN 0-8476-8679-5 (cloth : alk. paper)
ISBN 0-8476-8680-9 (pbk. : alk. paper)

Printed in the United States of America

∞ ™ The paper used in this publication meets the minimum requirements of
American National Standard for Information Sciences—Permanence of Paper
for Printed Library Materials, ANSI Z39.48—1984.

Contents

Preface

This book has two equally important objects: to present a speculative view of world politics intimately tied up with world history, while serving as a source and potential stimulus for the probing student of either subject; and to offer a guide to an imaginary anthology of my earlier works which amount to a discursively theorized contemporary interpretation of the Cold War, evolving from a historico-analogical method to its final geohistoricist formulation. Abstracting now the associated reflections into a more self-consciously systematic way of thinking about world politics exacts, in compensation for any possible gain, the unavoidable cost of omitting too much of the originally presented supporting material, to be found in the original writings listed (together with the footnoted abbreviations) at the end of this volume.

At the philosophical core of the proposed approach is a variety of realism that extends its traditional preoccupation with power-balancing interactions to encompass the inextricably associated problems of expansion and evolution. Making a range of qualitative and normative features equally explicit is another part of amplifying the scope of inquiry, while integrating domestic and economic factors and determinants into the external or systemic ones narrows the gap between real politics and genuinely political economy. Embedded in the empirically most accessible operational—as opposed to the philosophical and normative—core of this multifaceted design is realism's projection into a geohistoricism that combines space (or geography) with time (or history): the former's articulation by major powers differentiated principally but not only by their continental or oceanic settings and corresponding contentions; and the latter's by the cyclical recurrence of patterns and products of evolutionary progression poised between continuity and change. Successively schematizing the range of relevant facets and systematizing the associated patterns are the method for substituting a coherent system of thought for rigorous theory as the chosen way to understanding.

Were I to make a *pro domo* argument in favor of this approach, it would be that it fills some of the void between the two most ambitious approaches of recent years, neo-realism and poststructuralism: one conceived as a methodological advance on traditional realism and the other as a critique of that effort. Amplifying now the range of real-world referents means reversing neo-realism's restrictively quantitative view of structure and injecting policy-relevant substance into its essentially qualitative critique. While building on the foundation laid by conventional realism, I try to do what its post-World War II restorers did not, and could not, do when fulfilling the immediately pressing mandate to replace a discredited utopia with insight into the rationally explicable core of real politics and supply a pragmatically useful strategic rationale for the formulation of newly dominant America's national policies. This essential initial step is not necessarily a satisfactory terminus, least of all in an environment that has lost much of the articulation that traditional realism stripped bare before contributing to its management in a measure wholly exceptional for a scholarly effort. For the same reasons, the present task is to associate the study of world politics with a sufficiently wide range of intellectually challenging ideas and policy quandaries to make it worth pursuing independent of waxing and waning current issues and transient academic fashions. An attempt to do this cannot dispense with preliminary exploration of the peripheral lowlands of the subject before contemplating the more intriguing high points and have a fair chance to render the many connections at least partially discernible behind the fog of not only war but also peace, likely to persist as a continuing challenge despite anyone's best efforts.

References to my past works are arranged topically rather than chronologically by date of their appearance. This arrangement may deny insight into the evolution of my thought—which is possibly inconsistent with an evolutionary approach—reinforcing the impression of yet another inconsistency, that between anthologizing and systematizing previously published reflections. Both seeming deficiencies are removed if the present work exhibits sufficient internal coherence to permit equating evolution with elaboration of a seminal mindset traceable to the chronologically first of the sources. When *International Equilibrium* stated the power-normative essence of world politics, it left room only for its operational development in a range of processes widening from alliances to empires. So also the early work's subsequently continuing close association of contemporaneous processes and institutions with their historical antecedents and exemplars points unmistakably to the progressively developed historicization of world politics, integrating interactions into evolution of the state system. As a result, subordinating the consecutive order of publications to interlocking topics, far from distorting continuity in thinking, enables a kind of anthology to order formerly scattered ideas into a "system of thought" under part-aggregating and part-differentiating categories or mere headings.

As refinements ramify and extend to the textual medium of conveying the progressively fathomed complexities, a discontinuity external to the oeuvre itself surfaces in the division between two cultures or vocations peculiar to the scholarly enterprise. One is the culture of the creative effort at understanding for the sake of better informed action by the thinker himself if this proves to be his destiny. For this reason alone, an ultimately solitary undertaking is epitomized in the work of exiles from polity, authority, or both, reflecting on past errors of themselves or others. But, being originally self-regarding, the effort is pursued in the hope of passing on the understanding to equally motivated torchbearers in the grandest of relays or more favored aspirants to an active part in the still more dramatic encounter of a collective self with the makings of *its* destiny. Thinking and writing become thus not only a substitute for action, but action in and of itself. The other culture is the professionally academic culture with its rituals, servitudes, and occasional stimulations. These invest the genuine academic's efforts at least equally in defining and developing the field itself, conceived of as a collective undertaking. The choice is in kinds of engagement: in the work of one's peers at least as much or more than in one's own, producing corresponding kinds of alienation. One is from the discipline as a profession, while the field passes through conflicts of schools. The other estrangement is from an undeviating drive ever deeper down into the resistant mysteries of the subject matter itself.

More than in any other field or subject, a secondary or derived cleavage in world politics is between theory and practice, concepts and policies. It tends to discourage and, in fact, penalizes efforts to homogenize the two parts of a whole at unavoidable cost to the professionally more highly prized search for a conceptually unified, simplifying product. Aiming at the more important unity entails using concepts to inform policies and vice versa, while failing to satisfy the votaries of either theory or practice. Too much theory-construction for the policy addict is too great a preoccupation with policy-advising for the theoretical purist. The profession's preferred solution is to juxtapose ever more unreal theory with ever less speculative writing on policy. Yet mobilizing a form of philosophy of history for the sake of explicating strategy is the only available tradition, hallowed by connecting a Thucydides writing for all time with the late eighteenth-to-nineteenth century pamphleteer writing for his time. Renewing this nearly extinct tradition is now a condition of the discipline's survival as something of social and cultural, rather than only "academic," value.

When the necessary excisions from inadequately collected earlier works in matters of policy even more than history are allowed for, this quasi-anthology is an attempted celebration of this tradition. Its bequest is anything but betrayed by a caesura in underlying ideology that formed the works' progressive gestation more than any other evolutionary trait. A deepening conservatism was as much implicit in progressively developed historicism as it expresses a failure to be assimilated into American-style liberalism—or, in due course, neoconservatism. An ultimately failed effort to find a common ground with a uniquely hospitable civilization was enshrined in the very same previously mentioned doctoral dissertation, only to be dissipated at a moment of this country's defining foreign involvement in Southeast Asia by an equally ahistorical society's failure to live up to the East Central European's rapidly obsolescent innate predispositions. Yet again, just as the first published work contains the seed of all that was to follow intellectually, this last one—and one or two immediately preceding ones—reduces the ideological imbalance by counterposing a moderately "progressivist" variety of realism to the integrally "romantic" one. This partial redressal signifies less a discontinuity than a transition, from probing into a comprehensible past to speculating about a future capable of improving on an ambiguous present, sentimentally darkened further by the returning exile's inability to apply one-time capacity for *virtù* to the foreign policy of his ancient homeland any more effectively than in the land of his scholarly labors. Admitting to this not unprecedented disappointment is less a despairing than ultimately sustaining comment on the intellectual and cultural, as distinct from social, significance of scholarly engagement with world politics, placing it squarely in the realm of art worth preserving for use by enlightened statecraft through the ages.

Introduction: From Realism to a Theory of World Politics?

The critical half-century of world politics at its entry into the third mil-
lennium is not the chronological one from A.D. 1950 to 2000, but the
historically significant one from 1935 to 1985. It is critical because it covers the climax of the modern international system from its interwar pathology to its putative demise, following upon a two-part crisis: a feverish
climax marked by World War II and its continuance, shading off gradually
into mere simulation, by the subsequent Cold War. The specific events
bordering the era are the initial escalation of the Nazi German challenge
through military rearmament and the initiation of Soviet political disar-
mament, effectively calling off the second totalitarian challenge. The
transformations surfacing at an accelerating rate after 1985 mark instead
of a decennial, a millennial demarcation: of the impending future from
the thousand years-long development of the Eurocentric state system.
This system proceeded from its chaotically pluralist post-Roman Empire
beginnings (ready for a post-Carolingian takeoff by the second half of the
tenth century) to its current passing into a new, unevenly institutionalized, and chaotically primitive pluralism. Recalling at its chaotic extreme
the uncontrolled migrations toward antiquity's center of civilization, the
more orderly kind of pluralism is presently interspersed with elements of
variously vital and viable statism in different parts of the world. The state
system's consequent passing to its next centers in space and confusingly
anterior and posterior formats in time occurs in a world no longer centered on Europe or even on the two imperial combatants in a cold war
over succession to Europe's commanding position.

The actual historical processes entail more of cyclically moving progression than of linear progress, not only over the longer millennial, but
also the shorter, five times decennial time span. From attempts at appeasement with Germany in the 1930s, the oscillation progressed via an escalat-

1

ing world war to the next efforts at accommodation, with the Soviet co-belligerent, until the failure of concert projected the two principal Allied victors into the climax of a cold war which, absent its eruption into real war, could eventually only subside into a detente subject to regressive setbacks before finally resolving itself into a prelude to terminal pacification. While tensions rose and fell, stress on collective security-promising international institutions (first the League of Nations and subsequently the United Nations) alternated with undisguisedly assertive national power politics, competition in armaments with essays at their control, and emphasis on military power with concern for economic potential, depending on whether the imperatives of security actually did or seemed to yield to opportunities for stability. Just as the actual processes, so also analytical perspectives or preferences have alternated between projections from an immediately preceding situation and anticipations postulating the possibility of a radical break in the direction of melioration. Accordingly, both the actual and the analytic process would revolve around a split latent in any conceivable central norm: its aspirational part, pointing to a reformation of action-energizing mindsets as an avenue to conciliation and cooperation, and its referent to actuality, pointing to conflict and a mere possibility to appease it more than superficially by reevaluating the critical dynamic in a way permitting and promoting its possible consummation.

Alternative scientific and speculative perspectives and aspired-to panaceas of academic investigations

As always tributary to the real-world dynamic, the study of the unfolding and lately climaxing historical process has been taking place from several perspectives and with a view to alternate panaceas. The analytically process-ordering perspectives subdivided into those of international politics, international relations, and comparative foreign policies. The intended panaceas were methodologically shaped successive theories, reflective of the needs and potentials implicit in the perspectives. The essential target has been a constant: the dynamic, interactive, and evolution-prone process. It undergoes variations in relative salience of particular features or constituents, liable to being overrated and then mistaken for unprecedented novelties that alter the target sufficiently to warrant repositioning, instead of the target, the shooting range. As alternative shooting ranges, international politics overlapped with international relations, but differed from the comparative foreign policy approach as to key subject: overall action vs. particular agendas, interactor vs. intraactor processes. And whereas international relations would analyze and differentiate the functional components of the overall process, international politics would focus on the characteristics of the process itself, allowing the subsumed functional constituents to surface only at the point or level at which they visibly affected the process directly. In consequence, the key organizing tools and the would-be organizer's qualifying endowments have pertained, for the latter, to conceptually guided (re-)centralization of analytically disclosed facets; for the former, to (re-)combination of expertly mastered factors and related functions; and for the comparativist approach, to (re-)constitution of empirically establishable facts, amenable to differentiating description. Altogether, the range comprises ascending degrees of particularization (and differentiation by internal-domestic conditions) and descending degrees of systematization (and uniformization beyond internal differentials). The most recently dominant methodology aspiring to the status of theory has been structuralist neo-realism, reformulating the systemic approach, in relation to international politics; in relation to international relations, factor analyses strategic in intention, focusing on military security or political economy; and in relation to comparative foreign policy, mere frameworks, organizing the investigation of policy choices.

Aiming at the intrinsically constant target from a fundamentally altered angle of vision rather than from an unstable and therefore shifting shooting range is an approach that sets out to combine analytic dissection with the synthesizing integration of the facets, factors, and facts of the process, conducive to understanding. Such speculative theorizing is materially distinct from theory-making. But formally it not only can, but ultimately must, occur around a concept that is central because it unifies without congealing: unifies the process's dynamic and links it to the essence of pertinent reality; and, in addition, unifies the subject matter both temporally (in and over time) and spatially (in and across space).

In order to meet the requirement, the speculative approach shares with theory-making the concept of equilibrium, while subjecting it to less exacting tests of validity. Imaginatively applied, the concept expands into new dimensions the balance-of-power idea central to the most elementary and revealing, but technically deficient, realist theory of international politics. And it deepens the operational focus confined to geographical space (giving the name to geopolitics) by a systematic exploration of the formative effect of evolving historical time (allowing for its denotation as geohistorical). Methodologically strict theory-making aims at the discovery of a set of verifiable hypotheses capable of cumulation into a general theory; philosophically wide-ranging speculative theorizing aspires to the identification and articulation of historically revealed tendencies, transactions, and transformations, interlocking in a catholic understanding. However, both theory and theorizing are, like international politics- and international relations-emphasizing perspectives, linked through potentially complementary efforts at and approaches to generalization and systematization. By contrast, the comparative-foreign-policies methodology and conventional historiography place a similar emphasis on distinctive uniqueness. Their concern is with morphologically delineated particularity, even or especially when it is arrived at by a comparative method wedded to identifying and highlighting contrasts.

Insofar as the study of thus delimited international politics is divided between the scientific and the speculative approaches, one aiming at a theory and the other at mere understanding, secondary differences apply. A theory is the supreme achievement of the professional, while understanding is the domain of the philosopher. One is concerned with what can be demonstrated or at least represented, in the last resort mathematically. Cult of technique is supplanted for the other by "love of truth," searching for what can be reflected upon and reproduced meditatively. Related to this difference is that between academic study of politics and concern with its substance on the practical and policy-related level. Unevenly realistic perceptions and diversely intense melioristic predispositions disclose a corresponding tension between existential and normative facets, unevenly subject to preconceptions, preferences, and precepts that are mainly or only utilitarian. For the several facets and discrete levels to be integrated by a unifying concept, it must encompass both the dynamic and the evolutionary component of "compleat" politics—as equilibrium does through countervailance and adaptation respectively.

Realism vs. "idealism" in America and its kinds and formulations generally

The multifaceted unity of the substance of politics confronts any approach to its study with the mission to apprehend the essential attributes of underlying or environing reality even while articulating the circumstantial aspects of particular actualities. Hence the central—and contested—place of "realism" in the international relations discipline and its exposure to different forms of utopian idealism in actual relations. The attendant dialectic is all the more fundamental because it adjusts to its own, intellectually relatively low, plane the ever-recurring realist-nominalist or positivist-idealist dichotomy in philosophy, from antiquity through medieval scholastics to modern times.

Ending in the late 1960s, the post-World War II era witnessed the transfer of political realism to America and the subsequent quest for a more scientific approach by a more thoroughly institutionalized profession. If only because of America's uncontestable salience in world affairs and the needs attached to it during the long "heroic" decade, this era was dominated by realism as either the dominant (academic and bureaucratic) approach or the prime target of (academic) critique and opposition on primarily substantive grounds (idealism) or methodological grounds (behaviorism). Both kinds of critique were beside the point. For one thing, no one argued or (after the eclipse of Wilsonianism) could meaningfully argue for idealism pure and simple. Instead, so-called idealists sought to extend the more congenial "American" interest-group analysis of pluralist politics to foreign affairs in opposition to the continental-European statist national-interest approach. For another thing, realism neither was nor was it represented as being a theory of international politics in the social-scientific meaning of theory. It was and is much more a general conception or even philosophy of world politics embodying a central insight (about power) into, and a dominant (specifically rational or rationalist) perspective on, complex-to-shapeless phenomena and variable-to-volatile processes. Insofar as this commitment is being implemented with a view to facilitating the mastery of both the phenomena and the processes by practical policy, realism (and any other practically as well as intellectually valid approach to world politics) is a conceptual instrument of socially useful activity rather than a branch of social science strictly speaking.

Among the advantages of traditional or classic realism over its neorealist constriction in quantitatively conceived structuralism is its potential for speculatively embraced amplitude. Taking off from the exploration of the psychological—or "behavioral"—impulses that engender instrumentalities before being objectified into structures that can co-determine strategy, this amplitude accommodates variations in such crucial relationships as those between existential and normative determinants and between territorial or other material and formal status- or strategic role-related ideal, stakes constitutive of the prime agenda of different international systems and alternative orders. A consequent relaxation of theoretical rigor makes it possible to encompass and weight differentially the geopolitical and institutional facets or principles of world politics without abandoning conservative real politics wholesale for any of its opposites. It becomes possible to both comprise and differentiate such politics' varying prime subjects or actors—political and ethno-religious organisms as well as states and societies, functionally integrated regions and culturally discrete civilizations, and all such variously creative aggregate entities and informal groups and private individuals oriented unevenly to creation and consumption of material and immaterial assets.

In order to do this, the basic realist construct or model focuses on power as not only a means but also a proximate end, preconditional to the effective pursuit of both ulterior objectives and particular short-term interests. As such, conventional realism is sufficient in itself. But it is also the efficient basis for a romanticized variety that marries power more explicitly or elaborately to purposes, and interests to values. In thus expanding its field of vision, traditional realism conjugates the strategic with the structural constituents of policy while relating the former to the latter by means of a moderately reified polity. Both subsuming and representing individuals, a polity acts in an arena the configuration of which determines action more than any other single factor; this emphasis is expressed in corresponding neglect of, if not disdain for, domestic politics that deprives neo-realism of its principal claim to originality. An inclusive, qualitative as well as quantitative, view of structure differentiates conventional realism favorably from both the extreme reification of neo-realism and the extreme reductionism of behaviorism. The former absolutizes a narrowly defined structure acting from above, without mediating the determinative effect by psychologically or otherwise equipotent motivational impellents from below; the latter absolutizes such impellents, without mediating them through individual agents as role players in and for corporate entities such as states and alternative institutional actors with distinctive values and needs.

Conventional realism's combination of equally moderate reduction and reification necessarily entails a degree of diffuseness, responsible for there being no single, uniquely authentic, realism. Whereas the philosophical realist would mainly affirm the prime role of power in politics, he would also constrain its use, unlike the practitioner of power politics who aims at the creation of a radically novel configuration, but without sharing the prudent-to-timid concern with preserving the status quo peculiar to the practitioner of Realpolitik. The normatively reformist bend of the progressivist realist oriented toward institutions while conscious of power is in turn as much averse to incurring the taint of naively idealistic utopia as is the romantic realist concerned with adding a wider range of values to narrowly utilitarian motivations. Foundations for such differences and their association with different (liberal and conservative) social philosophies began to be laid at an early stage by subtle philosophical and theoretical differences between the "founding fathers" of realism in America, Hans J. Morgenthau and Arnold Wolfers. Juxtaposing the two highlights the difference between identification of a central insight or concept (Morgenthau) and a nuanced delineation of a principle's manifestations in political practice (Wolfers)—a lastingly more important difference than that between realism and idealism. Likewise more important are critical differences between essentially (central) European and typically American approaches, the difference between substantive values-related statist and societal-pluralist preferences overlapping with broadly speculative if not philosophical and self-consciously methodological and would-be rigorously theoretical ones. Whereas the substantive difference distinguished the realists from the so-called idealists, the methodological one was eventually to divide the would-be novel from the classic variety of realism that had meanwhile survived essentially unimpaired the assault of behaviorism combining the substantive with the methodological difference.

The continuing appeal of traditional realism for the policy maker reflects a commonality typical of all realists: absorbing concern with high policy questions—and thus with history in the making. This interest manifests the close connection between traditional realism and unevenly systematic and conceptually integrated "historicism," a fuller development of which is realism's unfinished agenda. Comparing and contrasting major representatives and subcategories of realism on the grounds of either "theory" or "history" and either criticizing or applauding realist analyses and prescriptions with respect to policy leave intact one conclusion about realism as a socially significant intellectual resource rather than rigorous social science: its persistent concern with policy in no way guarantees unity of views as to a correct policy, but it permits in compensation the principled critique of any policy as more or less consistent with the conception's basic presuppositions and precepts, regardless of the critic's approval or disapproval of the policy on the plane of evaluative judgment and/or the policy's success or failure on the plane of its results and consequences.[1]

From revolution to resignation in the search for realism-replacing theories

The same merit cannot be confidently attributed to the scientific impulse that—concerned more with method than subject matter and programmatically and prescriptively with peace than policy—has engendered in the more recent, post-heroic, decades a continuing proliferation of approaches, moving from revolution through retreat to a relapse followed by yet another attempt at regeneration, disguising a form of resignation.

The would-be revolutionary advance through the social scientism of the so-called behaviorism fell victim to smaller-than-anticipated professional accomplishments and deeper-than-foreseeable ideological revulsion, converging in the approach's focus on stability as the code word for peace. Even as the method failed to deliver a vigorous elucidation of its subject matter, the fixation on stability exposed the approach to the charge of crypto-imperialist support for U.S. hegemony. Thus, by the early 1970s, the would-be theoretical revolution had been delegitimized by ultimately no more effective social revolutionaries even before the immunity of the international political substance to its analytical assault techniques became fully manifest. Before fading, behaviorism had already faltered over its ultimate dependence on the applicability of individual and group behavior-elucidating insights and precepts to the "conduct" of institutional entities, actually altered when mediated through incumbents of pertinent roles. In a failed effort to bridge the gap between private and public conduct, proponents of behaviorism elevated the supposedly quantifiable formal and institutional features that realism had been so anxious to discount to undeserved causal efficacy. Finally, when trying to expand their database by a copious draft on history, the would-be revolutionaries fell back upon an eminently traditional mode of inquiry.

Behaviorism's retreat from social scientism to formalism and historicism was to be subsequently only slightly muted in a theory of cycles that proposed to correlate the incidence of wars rigorously with alternations of expansion and contraction in the world economy, bracketing out the wider range of less quantifiable real-political factors. The ability to formalize the latter differently in terms of determinant structures (confined to numbers and sizes of powers) has been so-called neo-realism's claim to originality over traditional realism. Even before its much-debated ascendancy was terminated by a genuine revolution in the real world (the dissipation of the bipolar power structure), this pretended upward revision and actual downsizing of the classic realist doctrine had actually represented a distracting disciplinary relapse—a terminologically modified and substantively impoverished return to tradition carried with it a radical cost to the latter's latent capacity to deal with evolutionary change (or time) and transcend association with any specific form of territoriality (or space) by assimilating the intra- to the interactor dimension.

The unsustainably self-limiting rigor and philosophical poverty of this culturally U.S.-bred revision of an old-world doctrine has meanwhile inspired a "critical theory" impugning its lack of historicity and its static territoriality. However, this latest attempt at the field's regeneration at its intellectual foundations has been accompanied by resignation of either will or ability to address real-world politics. The telltale substitution of "national identity" for "national interests" was only a part of the shift from construing sociopolitical actualities as a matter of interpretation to actually "constructing" them by means of their supposedly determinative perception and representation embodied in dominant discourse about them. The attendant shift has been from both scientific theoretical and speculatively theorizing investigation of reality, supposed to be knowable, to esoteric (epistemological and ontological) investigation of the problem of knowledge and reality as such, radically "problematizing" conventional understandings.

Over the decreasingly heroic five decades of professional effort, the initially productive shift from positing basic principles to probing processes has thus been veering downward into concern with procedure. This (de-)gradation applies to both social constructivism and liberal institutionalism when the latter favors "regimes" as procedural mechanisms over the substantive stakes relating political economy to real politics, and to theory-making as such when it selects subjects according to their fitness for available techniques of inquiry rather than their inquiry-worthiness to begin with.

When applied to international relations as a profession entrusting a collective purpose to identifiable specialized personnel, its three-step declension via attempted (behavioral) revolution through (neo-realist) relapse to the (poststructuralist) combination of regenerative purpose with practical resignation parallels a continuing search for a substitute for international law as a widely usable because intellectually readily accessible framework for interpreting and understanding international politics in its more elusive core aspects. Not unusually, the three-step declension coincided with a three-generational succession from the discipline's founders or restorers through second-generation developers to its virtual liquidators, before the sequence could recommence from a plane that has (or has not) assimilated usable antecedents. Second-generation epigoni typically elaborate on the original insights and findings of the founding fathers and refine them somewhat while staying within the original perspective and orientation. Their successors exceed both prior generations in technical sophistication and methodological commitment while inexorably reducing as a result the scope of phenomena susceptible of being fruitfully addressed. The casualty is the social utility and cultural value of an academic discipline inevitably dependent for its raison d'être upon not being only "academic."

Throughout, the successively dominant approaches have had one thing in common. They responded to wars: early institutionalism to the ending of World War I and last phases of World War II; traditional realism to the onset of the Cold War; anti-behaviorism and compensating liberal-institutionalist economism to America's defeat in the Vietnam War; and anti-neo-realist critical poststructuralism (or postpositivism) to the structurally and strategically indeterminate sequelae of the Cold War. The immediately posed question bears on the utility of replacing crudely applied economic theory with amateur epistemology, drawing on developments in academic political philosophy as a model (or only the prime source of metaphors) in theory construction. Can and will a respite from real politics during theoretically and practically unmanageable confusion in the real world help revitalize the discipline for a new beginning or developmental cycle? And do it in ways profitable also for speculative counter-theory?

Introduction

Beyond resignation to reconstruction
of conventional realism

If it is to justify itself as a viable alternative to scientifically rigorous theory, the speculative approach, while amplifying the substantive scope of
traditional realism, must reduce resulting diffuseness by successively dis-
and re-articulating the constituents of entailed processes of interaction
and evolution and their products. Moreover, it must do this sufficiently to
reach its ultimate object—intuitive understanding—by way of discernible
steps of analysis bound to retrace previously trodden ground at successive
levels of complexity. The means thereto is, with respect to interactions, a
combination of analytic descent (from phenomena to processes) and ascent (from essential form to its operative expressions), applied in a corresponding manner to evolutionary progression. In an approach
sympathetic to a dialectical view of social reality, the latter's political side
is perceived and structured in terms of interlocking dualities and triads.
Originating in drives and restraints expressive of power-normative essence, the dualistic structure of analysis appears in diversely paired values-
related schisms, organic and operational facets of the dynamics of real
politics and dilemmas of political economy, and progressions and regressions in evolution. Such complexities imply abdication of the ambition to
predict in favor of projecting from past to future the insights from successively schematizing, systematizing, and even more tentatively synthesizing the factors and processes capable of such a projection—a basis not
substantially firmer than outright prophecy for prescription of strategies
that would ideally reflect the time/space duality-and-unity of politics,
conveyed philosophically in a blend of romantic and progressivist realism
and expressed operationally in the two corresponding sides of geohistoricism.

Consequently, the speculative approach to understanding differs from
scientific theory in both method and objective. It is content with articulating observable phenomena into constitutive processes while probing beneath and beyond them for fundamental reality and its meaning for
international politics. A species of phenomenology connects in this fashion a peculiar epistemology of international politics to quasi-ontology
through a realism that borrows from historicism to extend beyond instrumental rationalism and construe the nature of reality. One related movement—the decomposition of observable phenomena in the shape of basic
givens or major events into processes that mediate their direct bearing on
politics—is within this reality an integral part of another: the processes'
derivation from the essential form or essence of politics, consisting of the
dialectical interplay between power and unevenly formal-legal and value-
cultural norms. This essence informs the interactional dynamic of world

politics as well as the evolution of the constituent polities when the form that shapes either determines their purpose or end—i.e., finality.

Notes

1. SR 5–11, WP 429 (4.par.)–431 (end 2.par.); MvM 104–111; AW 17 (3.par.)–33; RRA 243–252; BK 6–38.

Part I

Schematizing World Politics:
Facets and Factors

1

Constituents of World Politics: Analytical and Operational

Expanding geopolitical realism by investing it with a historicist dimension is inseparable from plumbing layers upon layers of the constituents of world politics. They need to be schematized in a way that points through their subsequent systemization to a final summation that rewards the intervening effort by revealing hitherto unsuspected features of both nature and culture. For this to happen, the narrowing tenets of theory must be betrayed for the larger allowances of speculation, only disciplined by an innate sense of propriety and standards of internal coherence subservient to the single purpose of understanding. The interweaving facets of perception are not the same as the discrete even though complementary levels of analysis such as individual actors and interactor systems. They are only analytically distinguishable avenues to apprehension of factors to be identified schematically before they can be systematized in a comprehensive view of world politics and serve as a basis for speculation aiming at, without achieving, a synthesis outside the realm of strategy.

Several relationships are basic to the inquiry: between structure and process via mediating strategy and propelling spirit (i.e., values and beliefs), and between successively "present" actuality and history represented by unevenly revealing slices of time within unevenly spacious and strategically crucial sectors of space. Such fundamental relationships inform the pragmatically salient ones between domestic and systemic, and political and economic, determinants of policies. The recurrence of clusters and configurations facilitates by way of significant correspondences the quest for causation that extends real politics toward political economy, without resolving the attendant dilemmas.

Basic distinctions and definitions of key dualities
shaping political reality

The specifically power-normative essence of international politics reflects the generic existential-normative duality of all politics and is embodied in the attitude to and apprehension of the state as the prototypical polity. The generic existential-normative duality is also in this connection methodologically replicated in the character of "norm." It is analytical when the state is reduced schematically to an ideal type, preceded by anterior proto- and followed by posterior post-statist deviations in both interaction and evolution. The norm is ethical when the state is speculatively enhanced to a normative facet of political reality—one stretched between the state's identity as transcendental mystique, a matter of spirit only rooted in basic function, and as implementing machinery, a matter of structure translating into a wide and widening range of functions. Reflecting more fundamental or universal dualities, both the mystique and the machinery are connected to a shared substratum of material and physical substance as conditions of survival, albeit both contrary in principle and in a mutually corrective fashion in practice. The mystique transcends the societally plural intergroup articulation of the state as it acquires the role and status of indispensable protector of physical security and provider of material sustenance for the members of society. The state forfeits much or all of this mystique when it ceases to be uniquely fit to act and becomes dispensable in a materially less deficient and physically either safer or effective defense-resistant environment. Paradoxically, the state may, and presently does, suffer this loss even while it continues to expand functionally as machinery and despite sharing the expanded functions with other and nominally superior agencies.

    In consequence, the difference between statism and pluralism is not primarily one of relative prominence of intergroup pluralism as opposed to unitary structure. Rather, it resides in subjective feeling at the psychologically motivated subsoil of world politics, shaping the relative salience of structure and structure-transcending spirit. This is evident when the two compounds of differently accented structure and spirit, reflected in machinery and mystique, overlap at the margins. They overlap when the ideal, communitarian form of pluralism co-opts statist features such as moral legitimacy and solidarity, while it functionally encroaches upon the state's sovereignty without necessarily acquiring the state's ultimately decisive disciplinary authority. As an aspect of power over society, this kind of authority constitutes the operationally critical negative but necessary side of the mystique as an aspect of "norm." This distinction matters because like the underlying dualities, the statist-pluralist ambiguity is also entrenched in the tension between humans' physical and metaphysical needs, transposed into the difference between the utilitarian criteria of material costs and benefits that predominate in societal pluralism and the ideal precepts of rights and duties peculiar to normative statism. It is this interplay that surfaces practically in contending perceptions of politics and expectations from politics. Moreover, the duality of power and norm is invariably interstate politics, but also superficially, intimated through geopolitical as opposed to institutional principles. This opposition permeates both realism and utopianism in their unevenly pragmatic and romantic variations. Associated tensions are manifested in political practice through revolution and attempts to defuse it with reform.[1]

Nothing illustrates the power-normative essence of politics more dramatically, while confirming its operational unity, than the apparent complementarity but actual conflict between revolution—from above on behalf of the affirmation of authority or from below for the sake of the transfer of power—and reform in the service of mere attenuation of either purpose. Less closely intertwined than revolution and reform, but pertinent to the existential-normative duality of real politics, are two distinct neo-medievalisms revolving around two kinds of nonrealistic utopia. One is represented by right-wing totalitarianism and looks backward to the darker side of the historical Middle Ages. It assumes the shape of a mytho-normative regression from pervasive duality to the cult of power qua violence under the cover of the principle of hierarchy and precepts of heroism. The other has, pursuant to the defeat of left-wing totalitarianism, been idealizing an imagined Middle Ages. It centers on the vision of achievable future perfection in a cooperatively pluralistic community misperceived as diametrically opposite to the power principle in the statist mode. Attendant mythologizing or conversely utopian revolutionary or reformist deformations are either regressivist or covertly materialist and ostensibly progressivist. Subject to either, the normative side of the pervasive duality has, with respect to values, ethical or purposive implications. It comprises, in contradistinction from pragmatic motivations implicit in the interest-related side of the power analysis, the broadly speaking emotive incentives distinct from either fundamentally irrational, mainly formally legalistic, or apolitically moralistic impulses. In the guise of beliefs and aspirations, these creedal incentives can originate in religious faith or its secular substitutes such as sociopolitical ideologies, national-tribal myths or statist mystiques, and cultural or civilizational predispositions. The most political of the creeds bear on the status and role of state-like actors that, as objects of concern, are separable from their material basis psychologically even though not indefinitely in fact. Although a comprehensive view of power includes the immaterial features, it reduces their impact when it relates power to interests too closely if not exclusively.

Nor does the nominal inclusion of immaterial factors and values in the definition of "power" automatically encourage the analyst of world politics to identify and explicate the changing balance and comparative incidence of material and immaterial constituents of either power or interests, despite the significance the mix has for the spirit as well as substance of a political order in crucial transitional periods such as the present.

Power qua material capability is also a psychological relationship that comprises intangibles such as morale, while pragmatic expediency invades the precincts of value-institutional norm. When these complexities are understood, the power-normative essence in action is recognized as a dialectical relationship. Complexity grows when the material-immaterial duality is extended from atemporal dialectic to its development over time. The two main material components, economic resource and territory, are apt to evolve contrarily in relation to the ideal ones of role and status, while the operationally salient ones remain implicitly representative of progressively updated forms of the primitive material ones. A species of historicist idealism (i.e., evolutionary statism, not to be confused with utopian idealism) is disclosed as the other side of historicist materialism (i.e., cyclically recurring pluralism, not to be confused with historical materialism) when evolution from narrowly material stakes (booty, ransom) to ideal stakes (role-status) coincides with the development of the state, and turns back to undisguised materialism with the reversion of statism to societal pluralism. Insofar as this re-materialization intersects with a concurrent but contrary trend away from territoriality in intra- and inter-unit relations, deterritorialization of politics coincides with desacralization of the state even before pluralism will have acquired or reacquired an ethos of its own as it evolves into regionalized communitarianism.

So viewed, the power-normative essence or form projects outward into, one, the interplay of drive with restraint at the core of real political (balance-of-power) dynamics and, two, the circular inter-determination of various factors that constitute the core dilemma of political economy. How much debased the statist-idealist norm is in societal materialism in the process depends on the specific kind of pluralism: is it primitively chaotic in confusedly gestating new or reviving failed (quasi-)states, or has it been institutionalized within a wider post- and supra-statist community? The attendant challenge of either is to the ethical dimension of classic statehood, embedded in tragedy as opposed to melodrama, and to statecraft's association with art susceptible of esthetic appreciation rather than a more exact science than is implicit in a politicized variety of physics. The individual standing and reciprocal relation of the two main tangible facets of statehood and statecraft—material sustenance and territorially defined physical security—are critical. Are they original and primary or derivative and secondary factors relative to the ideal attributes of role and status? Connections and priorities of the "material" and "ideal" factors change cyclically in the progression toward and regression from the religiously or mundanely sacralized state and, as a result, a territorially focused politics. The actual momentary situation is most significant when operational fading of the territorial imperative is combined with the emergence of regional community-type patriotism, provided the latter politicizes an otherwise only nominally or administratively "political" economy effectively within a corresponding political geometry: pluralist-circular attuned to integration, as against statist-linear associated with conflict.[2]

From dualities to equilibrium dynamic and associated triads

Only a flexibly centralizing concept can encompass a political reality conceived in terms of an existential-normative focus that ramifies widely and variably in spatio-temporally conditioned world politics. As such a concept, equilibrium is as much at the theoretical heart of the speculative approach as the power-normative essence defines its conceptual, realism its philosophical, and geohistoricism its operational or empirical facet. The reason is the concept's potential for unifying the interactive geopolitical (or spatial) with the historico-evolutionary (or temporal) dimension of politics. With respect to interactions, it accommodates the functional diversification and institutional formalization of the structural-and-strategic core of the real politics of countervailing forces, represented by the balance of power. That is to say, although reducible to this ultimately military-political operative focus, the equilibrium concept is just as readily extensible into a "multiple" or "complex" equilibrium comprising socio-political, cultural-political, and socioeconomic components. In either setting, the actual interactional dynamic is, just like the evolutionary one, centered on reciprocal adaptations as the way to reequilibration. However, as the statist shifts to the societal framework of action, analytical perspective and precepts of actual behavior shift from the militarily-politically accented geopolitical to the functionally more evenly inclusive institutional principle, made operational in organizations variably "in equilibrium" internally. A widened range of applications spans the societally slanted functional-institutional and state-centered structural-strategic model of politics. It is presently realized in the partial resurrection of the multilaterally institutionalized statist environment of the interwar era and the premodern pluralist environment. All the more significant, in addition to its varied expressions in interactional dynamics, is the role of equilibrium in adaptively restabilizing responses to breaks in and transi-

tions between stages of development within a particular system or between types of system or order. This temporal dimension does not
significantly affect the concept's own balance of strengths and weaknesses
bearing on the respective merits and demerits of narrowly empirical induction from specific facts and a deduction from a general principle
deemed to guide action that is, or is intended to be, at least minimally
rational by adjusting means to (objectively feasible) ends.[3]

Other distinctions and actual relations are pertinent in this connection.
Equilibrium as concept is a rational construct, abstracted from more variegated elements. When diversified beyond a balance of internally homogenized capabilities, the equilibrium concept translates operationally into
a strategic equation of attractions and revulsions exerted by the various
factors. Put differently, "equilibrium" as a dynamic engages values as well
as forces: cultural norms as well as economic or narrowly political interests, and institutional as well as geopolitical factors in actual interplays
among polities. To be rational, decision making will balance them all
against one another within a particular, strategic "equation" for purposes
of policy. Identifying distinctions and mediating between real differences
facilitates the necessary task of any inclusive approach: that of articulating
and schematizing the diffusely "soft" circumference of the "hard" core
of politics, reducible to the generation and projection of power. Doing so
matters practically, because equilibrium as a dynamic reflects most accurately the dialectic that, as a rhythm, permeates and, as a movement, actuates politically significant reality. It does this when it combines
countervailance in interactions focused on expansion with adaptation to
changes and disturbances in the context of evolution. In keeping with
this special affinity, countervailing a disturbance and adapting to it entail
absorption of some of the elements of the disturbing actor or factor in
the reestablished stability or developmental stage, which in turn will be
the seedbed of the next derangement to be contained. Any transient stability—provisional equilibrium—is thus the operational counterpart to a
temporary synthesis: the next-following thesis to be simultaneously negated by its antithesis and preserved, together with the latter, in the only
next or also higher state of the dialectical progression. The equivalent in
historical progression is the restabilized situation that is developmentally
more advanced as well as sequentially posterior to the antecedent one,
before being disrupted in turn.

This interplay is most graphically, but not exclusively, manifest in the
militarily enacted balance of power. It occurs when effective opposition to
a particularly empowered aspirant to preponderance or hegemony entails
adoption of at least some of the challenger's initial superior aptitudes or
advantages, before the defeated would-be hegemon can (because it must)
be affiliated with the coalition facing up to the next disturber (apt to have

been a member of the earlier combination). A similar dialectic applies to technological or other innovations that disturb anterior conditions, when adaptation to them entails—and to be effective necessitates—a counter-innovation that is qualitatively consonant with, and operationally contrary to, the source of the original disturbance. Much the same will apply to the less tangible or readily observable sources of a complex disequilibrium to be restabilized in either the interactional dynamics or evolutionary development of an international organization by adjusting legal norms to actual capabilities, commitments to obtainable compliance, and functions to real needs of actors or arena.

A speculatively inclined attempt to relate reality-defining essence to activity-directing equilibrium will associate the philosophical and conceptual with a comparatively empirical pathway to understanding. Philosophy is represented by crudely ontological and phenomenology-related epistemological facets. The former determines a view of reality and corresponding (qualifiedly romantic or progressivist) realism as the political expression of a social doctrine or ideology (predominantly conservative or liberal). The latter affects the pursuit and achievement of policy-relevant knowledge by means of (schematizing-to-systematizing) analysis that decomposes salient phenomena into processes of interaction and progression. Equilibrium as the central concept encompasses both kinds of processes in the ultimate unity of politics while the empirical dimension is provided for by geohistorical interpretation. The combination of philosophical, conceptual, and empirical facets is reflected in a range of more particular triads. To be analytically useful, the triads will articulate the three-step descent from phenomena via process to essence and ascent from essence through evolutionary transformations to an ideal or prospective finality, one that has translated the motion of dynamics into the momentum of development and fused them in meaning that has ceased being only putative. The trio of structure, stages of development, and strategies is actually operative, closely related to if not also loosely coterminous with the actor-arena-agenda triad. Their interplay projects into the three phases of development in conditions that either precede or follow an ideal-typical norm, identified with the territorial state and the system of such states, while their substantive expressions are conditioned by three principal schisms (sacral-secular, continental-maritime, and West-East). Closest to policy-related agenda is a triangular strategic perspective presenting any one actor with two principal other parties to be considered with a view to optimizing the net balance of costs and benefits or assets and liabilities. Conversely, the operational core of real politics is distilled into the two components of its inner economy—political physics relative to interactions and tragic poetics relative to their motivation—while the core itself is part of the dilemma of genuinely political economy when real politics competes with economics just as the external (or strategic/ systemic) determinants do with the internal (domestic) determinants in circular inter-determination.[4]

Interpenetrating processes and kinds of realism wihin the unity of politics

War and peace illustrate the peculiar epistemology befitting the phenome- nological mode of thinking about world politics better than anything else. Representing the conflict between reality and utopia, a revolutionary and a reformist approach to dealing with the power-normative essence, war and peace challenge with singular force the capacity to penetrate beyond observable phenomena to related states of consciousness and processes. Antagonization and appeasement are the processes linked to war and its absence or prevention most closely through those of expansion and coun- teraction, institutionalized in the formation, maintenance, and dissolution of alliances. When they undergo either process, alliances implement the ambiguously restraining-or-provocative effect of power balancing on war and peace. Resulting interplays are compounded in the wider than nar- rowly real political or geostrategic context, that of political economy, by the issues of stability and prosperity. Political, including domestic, stabil- ity and economic prosperity are themselves phenomena that, while subja- cent to those of war and peace causally and operationally, are likewise subject to decomposition into associated processes. Finally, to the extent that alliances are in themselves a kind of provisional ad hoc political asso- ciation or even community, they provide a link and constitute a bridge from primary manifestations of real politics to the basic kinds of polity, from the most minute and inchoate entities to the vastest empire. Such polities are another set of principal phenomena involved in a range of processes from formation through functional aggregation and institu- tional integration to internal erosion and supersession by alternative for- mations. Relatively most abstract as phenomena are agencies ranging from local or regional to global-universal organization, related to particular types of inter-polity order through interchangeably associative and com- petitive processes of interaction and evolutionary ones of origination, functional displacement, and dissolution.

Analytically the counterpart and operationally the complement of in- teraction, the process of evolution can be construed as resulting from two basic incentives. One resides in technological innovations mediated through the special processes of initiation and diffusion and contained by counter-innovation that limits the effect of the prior disruption while constituting the next-in-line link in the chain of functional revolutions.

The other incentive consists of real-political interactions when war as a phenomenon and antagonization as a process enter directly into evolution. They affect evolution as parts in its propellent motor and sustaining mechanism, thereby generating the manifest states or stages of progression.

The recurrence of such manifest states of evolution in several historical eras and geographic areas takes place in function of operational interlocks between micro- and macro-systems, differentiated by size, and developmental sequence-specific primitively pluralist "orders" (proto-systems) and institutionalized pluralist, imperial or communitarian, orders (meta-systems). The two categories flank the analytical norm of a moderate-sized territorial state and are connected by processes of immanence (of the macro- in the micro-system) and supersession (of the micro- by the macro- and the proto- by the meta-system). The interlock of interaction with evolution, processes with progression, is the intriguing object of progressively deepening apprehension to be pursued through the inter-determinative linkages between the factors that make up the political economy of world politics and the phenomena and processes that constitute the geohistorically created world of real politics. An apprehension resulting from an approach that inclines more to intuitively acquired cognition of the relation between phenomena and processes than to inductively ascertained causation of either is consistent with a preliminary assumption of capacity for developmental growth over time and across space toward a finality. Inasmuch as such finality is necessarily connected with a wager on the possibility of resolving or transcending the existential-normative tension that shapes politics as is, it constitutes together with the latter's essential form a key to the meaning of world politics-as-world history—the ultimate object of a quest for more than superficial understanding.

A reality conceived along these lines entails a peculiar kind of realism. In this connection particularly important for the speculative approach is how romantic realism relates to the other subcategories of conventional realism: in terms of its recognition of power to philosophical realism, its normative emphasis with utopian connotations to progressivist realism, and its residually passional commitment to extraordinary political creativity to realism's power-politics variety—while all these features raise the romantic vision above pragmatic Realpolitik. It matters less, for mainly formal purposes, whether the avenues to understanding—a species of epistemology—subdivide into the comparatively substantive concerns of ontology (i.e., reality/essence), phenomenology (phenomena/processes), and geohistoricism (space/time), to be unified by the concept of equilibrium (countervailance/adaptation). Or whether, alternatively, the equilibrium concept together with phenomenology and geohistoricism is viewed as the methodologically sharpened instrument for articulating the substantive diffuseness of realism in its conventionally broad and undifferentiated representation. All four avenues help clarify the actualities of world politics as they present themselves at any one time. But whereas equilibrium is central for relating the balance of power to the manifold processes that link what is manifest to what is meaningful, geohistoricism is central because relating interactions to evolution integrates world politics systematically with world history—an indispensable effort and possible achievement, the neglect of which reduces the social and nullifies the cultural interest and utility of any theory of international politics or relations.

A unified approach to world politics, reflective of the unity of politics itself, is observed when the several facets of interaction—the decomposition of phenomena into processes, the processes' abstraction into the essence of politics, and the distillation of the inner economy of real politics into its physics and poetics—are replicated in relation to progression. When that happens, the decomposition of evolution into its patterns and stages and the latter's abstraction into a relationship between continuity and change are analogous to the equally dialectical one between power and norm in the dynamics of interaction. Moreover, the connections between progression's propulsive motor, operative mechanism, external manifestations, and environmental matrix are as circular as the problematic inter-determination of factors in political economy. In fact, more than comparable, the inter-determination of factors responsible for the central dilemma of political economy is actually integrated into evolution when the circularity is straightened out into a regressive chain of causation—when, that is, each factor's apparent causal efficacy or primacy is correctly perceived as the effect of an antecedent factor: internal (domestic) of external (systemic/strategic) and economic of real political, and vice versa—and when this regressive causal chain is transposed from intricate dynamics into the interlocking sequences of stimuli to expansion and the still more complex stream of evolution. Exactly how similar the relationship between continuity and change in world politics is with that between power and norm or conflict and cooperation depends on a primacy issue that is subtly different from that of causal priority: which facet is primary in the continuity-change relationship and which incidental or derivative? The answer to this and related questions such as whether humans are social or antisocial, history meaningful or meaningless, will largely depend on an a priori "ideological" bias resistant to empirical confirmation. Conversely, the competitive or acquisitive drive that impels conflict and is identifiable with power seems to be clearly antecedent to the restraints, partaking of norm, requisite for cooperation. The power drive is, therefore, primary, and cooperation is incidental to conflict. Any such inherent logic or obtainable measure of empirical evidence does not apply to the space/time-related dilemma of continuity versus change.

Kinds of changes and continuity-favoring functional equivalents in historicist perspective

Decisive for analysis in the time category are lengths of intervals allowed for reequilibration of a disturbance that stands for significant break in continuity. The deeper an upheaval, such as a hegemonic war or a thoroughgoing revolution, the longer the time span available for restabilization, while the net change is likely to be something closer to conditions preceding the event than to the climactic alteration at the peak of turbulence. This difference will strengthen the impression of continuity, even though the net change is sufficient to set off a new cycle of escalating revolutionary disturbance and eventual conservative (if not reactionary) near-restoration. Within particular state systems, inessential alterations may occur mainly in the identities of the incumbents of principal roles, or the intensities of mediating transactions. Alternatively, near-imperceptible causal links between successively emergent or dominant state systems are consistent with alterations in their respective locations and spatial scopes while the agendas at identical stages of their evolution remain comparable. Or finally, the evolutionary process can overleap continuities both within and between state systems for the transformation of a statist into a societal-pluralist order or the other way round within an entire or only a part of an arena. When this happens, continuity consists in the demonstrable fact or a plausible presumption of an eventual return to the provisionally superseded framework of action.

Actual, or only perceived, primacy of continuity or change is thus contingent not only on the length of time that has been taken into account, but also on the size of the space that expands or restricts the range of potentially comparable conditions and occurrences. In addition, continuity prevails over the most dramatic instance of ostensible change, revolutionary technological (or organizational) innovations, whenever emphasis is transferred from the innovation to a political process certain to eventually absorb the innovation in the finite range of key political issues and associated transactions. A conversely change-friendly perception will be constricted in its time and space perspective. It disrupts the flow of evolution but incidentally accommodates if not actually favors the presumption of qualitative progress along an essentially linear pathway. The continuity-favoring perception leans by contrast toward a cyclical rhythm of qualitatively neutral progression. It accommodates truly significant transformations between statist and societal kinds of sociopolitical organization, organic and operational constituents and enhancements of national power, and functional and institutional or structural and strategic approaches to order and impediments to disorder. Since such transformations are basic, they are apt to be gradual and incremental while ostensible opposites are likely to be complementary and interpenetrate in changing combinations. What matters in the last resort is the ratio of persistence to permutations that determines the extent of real change and facilitates hypotheses as to its nature. A change is real when it actually alters fundamentals rather than being "logically" implicit in and plausibly inferable from mutations extraneous to the political dynamic, including technological and organizational alterations. A "real" change will manifest in action, rather than simplify interpretation, after surviving the acid test of functional equivalents: actions, agents, and agendas that perform identical or comparable functions at different levels of development despite differences in their outward form. It is only when changes in appearances, including disparate structures, have been discounted for functional equivalence that history can be effectively called upon to supply general and particular analogues of present and intimations of putative future phenomena and processes.

Continuity entails gradual development over time and comparability across discrete periods of time. Change is associated with more suddenly emergent differences that persist over a substantial length of time and engender significant contrasts between otherwise correspondent states of being. This said, it is easier to identify that which is not the source of significant change than to differentiate between degrees and kinds of change. To be downgraded, conjointly with technological innovations, are consequently also other functional (economic, military, organizational) and associated sociopolitical revolutions, and even combinations of them all in grand political revolutions enacted through major wars. When they come to be embedded and absorbed in the ongoing political process, these changes will corroborate rather than radically disrupt more fundamental continuities. Significant change is no more under way when the sundry upheavals or innovations cumulatively determine the identity of the incumbents of key positions and, implicitly, roles and particular interests. The change in incumbents and aspirants to incumbency is more disruptive than transformative even or especially when the late entrant's phase of development is at variance with the longer-lived state system's. Turnover in the system's great-power "elites" is actually additional evidence of the priority of continuity over change. So are the upheavals that attend if not engender those elites' "circulation" and represent adaptation to any of the major innovations in which the entire disturbance may originate. Consequently stressing what is only a superficial rather than substantial, a relative rather than radical, alteration does not identify "real" change—

i.e., change sufficiently significant to alter basic functions implicit in the structure of the arena and the attendant mindsets and motivations of the actors, converging in an altered momentum. Nor does it identify the comparative—and, in fact, diminishing—degrees of actual change or ranges of historically evidenced possible alteration across a spectrum from actors via the arena to the agenda. Greatest changes occur in actors themselves along a full evolutionary trajectory and lesser ones in alternative configurations of actor capabilities eliciting distinctive patterns of strategic responses. Least prone to constituting or exhibiting change is the pattern of evolutionary stages that succeed one another within comparable state systems in a manner that makes the particular stages themselves comparable across such systems.

If the range of historically evidenced change does decline from actors via agenda to arena, what is the identifiable "real" change within a state system proper? It consists of the gradual but at some point accelerating transfer of priority from external to internal functions and preoccupations of governments and, coincidentally, from operationally focused conduct to organic capabilities of polities. Changing concurrently with subjective dispositions are objective tendencies when they, though continuing, have ceased to be converted into transactions capable of accomplishing historically achieved or achievable transformations, whether intended by the parties or only implied in the process.

Finally, radical change is different from a real change within a state system. It occurs in transitions between such a system and a pluralist framework of action affecting, first, the identity of actors and consequent structures as either homogeneous or heterogeneous and, second, strategies as either rationally anticipatory or reactively haphazard. When pre-statist pluralism is primitive-to-chaotic, it anticipates (and when it is institutionalized into a post-statist pluralism it consummates) the attendant difference in political geometries: between a linear one that connects crystallized power centers along a straight line or axis of actual or potential conflict and a circular one that encompasses more inchoate aggregations of capabilities and functions in concentric or overlapping areas of actual or potential coalescence or all-out integration. The associated two basic models of politics, inherently statist structural-strategic and distinctively pluralist functional-institutional, are similarly different in principle and variably overlapping in practice. But even such radical change does not abolish fundamental continuity when the alternative frameworks of action alternate over definable periods of time in identifiably similar structures and other contexts. The attendant rebirths of arenas and returns to earlier agendas by actors will differ from exact repetitions and replications because of intervening changes—but, again, changes that are not essential, because they do not reverse or invert the cause-effect, means-end, or determinant-derivative status of key features of alternative frameworks of action. Most change-prone will tend to be organizational superstructures, less so functional priorities, and least changeable will tend to be the motivational mindsets affecting strategies within a progression that revolves cyclically along a line that connects developmentally climactic midpoints of either the statist or the pluralist frameworks of action.

The most important conclusion to draw is the rejection of two extremes: factually rigid periodization in regard to either operation or causation, and elimination of the evolutionary dimension in propositions about interactions. It is not useful to argue for instance that a precise point in time, say the French invasion of Italy in the late fifteenth century, differentiates the era of the formation of states from the subsequent onset of the balancing of power among states. The two evolve in continuous interstimulation and do so in ways and for reasons that may reverse commonsense assumptions, such as that actors determine the arena from the very beginning and equally at all times. Therefore, we shall wish to know other things than conventionally narrative historiography when theorizing history and politics conjointly. For example, we may need to know not when the balance of power began to function, but how its operation evolved; in other words, how it became more strategically rational rather than instinctual and how it was formally institutionalized in multiple-member coalitions or "collective security" organizations rather than depending on ad hoc countervailing reactions by one resistance-capable power after another. When rigid periodization is replaced by developmentally vacuous interaction, the historian averse to speculation is no more satisfactorily replaced by an ahistorical social scientist who gives up on changing balances in interactions completely in favor of temporally undifferentiated inter-determination. It is correct but not sufficient to affirm the mutually conditioning interplay of, say, the state, the interstate system, and the world economy—just as, going farther back in history, the church, the state, and society, because such entities are actually intergenerative before they can become interactive. A historicist perspective will suggest that, within the actor-centered triad, the church successively formed the state, and the state, society; while in the agenda-related spectrum, the state (when finally disengaged from the organized church) engendered the secular state system before the latter could impart the decisive impetus to the world economy. In each of these sequences, the creator will be dispossessed if not also devoured by the creature, the progenitor by its product, before a new configuration of elements pertaining to all can integrate their interaction into progression to a new phase. Proposing and substantiating such an articulation of historical developments can dispense with precise periodization because it allows for a combination of overall continuity with specific changes: continuity in terms of sequences, modes of transition between stages, and eventual transformation or mere trend or tendency with significant but not essential changes; specific changes in the shape of successively salient actors or agendas and the effect of each transitional phase on the real political process or, even, emergence of an alternative framework of action with overall continuity.

However artfully one may differentiate continuity and change in terms of definitions or articulate the way they interweave, in fact, truly critical because fundamental and thus underlying differences are located elsewhere: between function and form, structure and symbol, and process and particulars. Functions, performed in ways exhibiting greater or lesser conformity with structure while fostering its maintenance or alteration, differ substantially from the outward forms of either agents or their instruments. By the same token, if less conspicuously, a more or less rational implementation of functions in ways unevenly consistent with structure differs from rationalizing disguises that obscure or actually distort both structures and functions under deceptive symbols and legal or other fictions. As for the process, which joins functions to structures, it will be represented by the particulars it transcends, be they entities or events. But it is distinct from such particulars taken individually and will be lost sight of if they are overemphasized.

These distinctions, replete with real differences, ease the dilemma of continuity and change by providing the basis for the two continuity-favoring devices of analysis: functional equivalence and structural-processual analogy. Thus, the change from dynastic to democratic foreign policies, stressed by the liberal-progressivist interpreter, fades when the function of marriages in genealogically accented familistic politics, to aggregate capabilities and enhance cohesion, is with similarly uncertain and often counterproductive effects taken over by alliances in the ostensibly contrary, geopolitically driven format of largely impersonal politics. Connecting disparate stages of development, functional equivalence is enhanced further in a comparably personalist environment when extended from dynasts to nonaligned-to-neutralist leaders of the Third World. Similarly, ostensibly crucial functions such as conciliation and arbitration and, even, adjudication can be the province of differently elaborate universal agents standing in fact or fiction above the contending particular parties without disclosing substantive change in the kind of mandate or registering a marked increase in efficacy. It will make little difference whether the agents entrusted with the function are incumbents of the papacy or the Holy Roman Empire and at a later point in time a global organization such as the United Nations or a tribunal such as the International Court of Justice. Thus also, in the grey area between private and public, societal pluralist and formally statist arenas, contemporary nongovernmental organizations replicate the functions of great monastic orders and other subsequently evolving ecclesiastical organisms in the social domain, while in the economic sphere trading companies licensed by the Crown are replaced by multinational corporations in combining independence from and insubordination to governments. The principal change consists of the intervening organizational hypertrophy due to the advance of technical civilization and the growth of employable or to-be-employed personnel. This value-neutral progression may be credited with improving the ways of managing more substantive changes, albeit typically over a much longer period of time than posited by the advocates of the melioration or hoped for by its implementors, without any short-run effects cumulating into qualitative progress in the medium run.[5]

Continuity-friendly analogies and change-favoring revolutions and successions

Closely related to functional equivalence in kind, use, and utility is historical analogy directed to either structure or process. Analogy differs from functionally equivalent actions or structurally identical or comparable arenas and the resultant processes while drawing on all of these. It depends on them for validity in performing its several tasks of analysis, argumentation, and advocacy. For this reason, analogies are the very opposite of mere antecedents whenever these discredit or even controvert a proposed analogy because the focus of interpretation is on form over function and surface event over structure. Respecting this prerequisite, it becomes possible to specify the kind of analogies that are particularly valid in themselves and for strategy: link together relationships between more than two parties occurring (at least) three times, facilitating affirmative and authoritative anticipations by way of projection ascending problematically toward prediction and aspiring by way of prescription even more uncertainly toward prophecy. As we shall see, this demanding criterion validates analogies embracing three parties to three sequential realizations of the land-sea power schism, for instance, or three principal determinants of imperial expansion manifested comparably in as many instances.

Other analogies are differently compelling in terms of the structural-functional criteria. Thus, an analogy between external hostilities attending U.S.–Soviet relations in the periods following the end of World War I and the close of World War II is infinitely less valid than one between U.S.–Soviet (and –Chinese) relations during the Cold War and land–sea power conflicts in earlier centuries. That which is most recent is not necessarily, and will be rarely, most relevant for distinguishing continuity from change. However, the just-cited example also suggests that identities in functions and structures may be vastly more conducive to analogy and continuity than identical forms and symbols or fictions and slogans, but may still not suffice for a valid analogy. This happens when the actors' perceptions of crucial needs and roles, and the risks necessary to be assumed to meet the former and implement the latter, have changed to the point of evaporating within what is still a system of states on the face of it. Contrary to underestimating substantial continuity in features peculiar to strategy is overasserting discontinuity when "spirit"—a shorthand for the intangibles actuating strategies conjointly with the structure of power—is construed as nothing more than a conventional style of diplomatic procedure rather than what it is: the expression and consequence of the high value ascribed to the state as the indispensable agent in satisfying basic material as well as immaterial needs. Misapplying this distinction at the beginning of the Cold War led to postulating radical discontinuity between mid-eighteenth and mid-twentieth century statecraft. Doing so wholly subordinated basic continuities in strategy and statist spirit to an overemphasized difference between ideological and cultural homogeneity in the earlier and heterogeneity in the later era. Differently misleading in the post-Cold War setting has been the tendency to ignore the implications of the intervening depletion of the statist spirit for strategy, a discontinuity obscured by mistaking conventional diplomatic style for substantive foreign policy and reassociating the style with expanded normative consensus between the principal parties. This omission has been producing faulty propositions equating contemporary with late nineteenth-century contentions over regional "questions" and subcontinental "great games" on the strength of the controversial location of oil pipelines in, say, Central Asia replacing railway concessions.

Judgments responsible for falsely posited ostensible discontinuity or continuity misinterpret, while essential continuity absorbs, a complex of functionally specific as well as operationally general-to-universalist revolutions. The former can be normative-institutional, sociopolitical or -economic, and diversely functional-technological. The latter are either the gravitational revolutions that reconfigure centers of power or cyclical ones that produce rebirth of particular orders and types of polities over periods of time that are even longer than those that signal mere returns to preexistent types of policies. Whereas the returns are qualified by intervening procedural or institutional innovations, the rebirths are sustained by perennial givens and instincts. Mediating all such revolutions is another political universal, that of succession: likewise multifaceted between classes within and inter-actor between polities, and twice revolutionary as an event that recurs periodically and is directed to a major turnover. Although causing a major disruption, a bid for succession and the process itself do not basically alter the procedural mechanics and substantive causes and outcomes of consequently activated politics. A-not-too effective bid for succession to Europe as a prime stake of world politics by a new category of countries has recently illustrated a persistent problem: that of late entrants into the international system, of their internal maturation and external qualification for relaunching progression while challenging and potentially replacing receding protagonists. However, as shown in modern times by potent individual actors such as Germany and Russia among others as compared with the weaker groups of Third World countries, the disruption attendant on the late entry varies. It will grow when to be assimilated into the pre-crystallized international system are not only pretensions to role and status, but also internal social dynamics, exacerbated by external resistance to absorbing the new claimant to parity with incumbent protagonists. When it is a distinctive category of unevenly potent actors that intrudes into a pre-established order of things—presently the post-communist European and Asian polities after the postcolonial—the immediate priority of their assimilation only implies eventual claims to succession while instantly mobilizing previously latent differences in statist and pluralist structures and related strategies for the entire arena.

How far and how forcefully can or will the device of functional equivalence and historical analogy be applied to discount differences in form and symbols relative to function and structure, or particulars relative to process? This will depend, apart from the analyst's intellectual and other predispositions, on the basic purpose of the analysis itself. Is it intended to register history's variety reflected in world politics among other things? Or is the object to articulate the process of world politics as one revealed best in a history construed so as to highlight continuities?[6]

Kinds of historicism vs. rationalism and geohistoricism vs. geopolitics

When, rightly or wrongly, the emphasis is on change, the resulting variety of the record of the past can at best generate a wholly intuitive if not impressionistic sense of history as an unstructured and directionless flow of events in time. The resulting perception is valuable when it engenders a special kind of wisdom or instinct applicable to policy. However, having a sense of history is not the same as making sense of history with a view to allowing the past to have a direct effect on policy. One kind of effect is present when immediately preceding past impacts the present as one arising out of it immediately; another and more elusive, when a longer and more varied past is projected through the present into the future as one likely to continue being shaped by previously revealed patterns and processes. A discourse wedded to historicism construes the past without actually "constructing" either the present or future. It would make sense of history while incidentally fostering a sense of history as an extra dividend from the heightened intellectual investment. Consequently, systematizing history in a realistic, geostrategically informed or inquisitive, philosophy of history is a precondition to steering high policy away from its methodologically pluralist decomposition into tactical diplomatic and military-strategic or only -technological perspectives. When such a decomposition reproduces real-world anarchy, it prefigures anarchy's descent into chaos. The superior avenue from analysis to the most preliminary and partial synthesis is to schematize actuality by breaking it up into facets of a composite held together by internal coherence and intellectual consistency. The appropriate level of abstraction is one that permits reintegrating the facets into a system of thought that opens up a philosophical perspective for truly systemic thinking about particular policies, a form of thinking more often preached than practiced because more intuitive and instinctive than inductively contrived or achievable. Responding to this challenge is all the more urgent when a primitively quantitative structure is itself becoming indeterminate.[7]

History represents the dimension of time in both the actual course and analytic or other conceptualization of world politics. Integrating it fully into analysis and action permits supplementing rationality with intelligence: the strategic rationality responsive to momentary configuration of power-constituting capabilities in space, with historico-philosophically informed intelligence of the configurations' recurrent transformations and continuities over time. A thus solicited history can be a matter of scientifically established "facts" or imagined events converted into politically potent myths by immediate needs and desires. Either kind of history can produce or permit historical analogies. However, in order for analogies to rise above a technique to a component of philosophically grounded history, the relevant facts and events must be located genetically in their origin and subsequent development that constitute their historicity. Adopting this time-related perspective on actors and action, polities and politics, differentiates historicism favorably from narrating history for its own sake. However, theorizing world politics historically requires the right kind of historicism: not one portrayed as a vehicle for iron-clad determinism contrary to free choice in an "open society," but one consonant with the romantic variety of realism. Such realism is one that attenuates a form of rationalism peculiar to the Enlightenment with a range of strictly nonrational, primarily will-centered ethical, impulses for the sake of expanding the apparatus of interpretation to the totality of life-constituting acts and their motivations. Correcting for such a historicism's emphasis on discrete socio-cultural collectives as "historical individualities," the version of historicism most appropriate for the apprehension of world politics posits identifiable sequences of events or phenomena that reveal general trends and persistent patterns, while continuity in either allows for degrees of change ranging from modification to transformation.

This species of historicism avoids the pitfalls of both rigid determinism, which makes the inquiry into patterns of historical progression unnecessary, and unconditioned choice, which makes such an inquiry impossible. Nor does it celebrate either unqualified universality of a uniform process or radical uniqueness of particular events or entanglements. Qualities such as these extend usefully beyond historicity to geohistoricism, from time to its integration with space. This communion is inaccessible to a geopolitics that confines the interactional dynamic within too brief a time span to integrate the evolutionary dimension into strategy and qualify strategic rationality with the insights of historical intelligence. What kind of rationality—narrowly instrumental when relating means to ends, or the more inclusively strategic responsive to the environing configuration—is closer to historical intelligence? This is an easier question to answer than what conception of history is most appropriate for arbitrating between the contrary claims of uniqueness and uniformity. What weight can historical intelligence that makes sense of history for use by strategy legitimately assign to momentary ideological rationalizations and narrowly technocratic rationalism as opposed to a higher form of reason that can impart meaning to ongoing mutations? An intermediate, merely schematizing and systematizing, stance between synthesizing (Hegelian) metahistory and scaling the latter down to synthetic (Rankean) historic individualities provides a clue to such questions. It does so not least when schematizing and systematizing facilitates inferring continuities from comparisons of diverse entities at comparable stages of development—and when it simultaneously discloses regularities by allowing for a wide range of relativities to be factored into ostensibly absolute contrasts.[8]

Extrapolating in this manner from history into policy involves both backward- and forward-looking assumptions—premises and presuppositions—capable of engendering strategic precept as part of concept. Whereas precept implies strategic concept within a doctrine, such a doctrine differs as much from a visionary but static futuristic design as speculative theorizing differs from rigorously scientific theory. Since neither history-conscious statecraft nor historically intelligent scholarship need or can be scientific, both must be in large part intuitive if they are to be mutually sympathetic. The same latitude applies to history when its factually better documented core is productively supplemented by imaginative mytho-history—a history no less thoughtful for viewing the past more than usually in terms of present needs, and no less useful for failing to be proven by documentary or any other evidence. Such mytho-history is, together with both factual history and particulars-transcending meta-history, a source of a historical intelligence that is, in turn, best enlightened by the specific structures and law-like tendencies associated with a crystallized statist system, uniquely propitious to strategic rationality. Conversely, intuitions prompted by metahistory and imperatives mandated by mytho-history are peculiarly crucial in and with respect to a relatively indeterminate setting that consists, as does the present, of an uneasy balance between different kinds and degrees of statism and pluralism in regard to both time and space. However, a residual question remains to be addressed, albeit discursively and indirectly: how far beyond scientific rigor can a speculative approach proceed without crossing the line between disciplined reflection and dreamy meditation? Asking this question leads from the conceptual directly to the operational environment of world politics.[9]

From conceptual to operational, quantitative to qualitative, and structural to functional, constituents of the environment

A conceptually manifold approach corresponds precisely to a both structurally and operationally complex environment, beginning with a plurality of actors or agents within a structure diversely configured by balancing and aligning policies. This is so regardless of whether the units are politico-economically, ethnically, or otherwise pluralist societies or unitary states that are only plural in the sense of multiple within a spectrum of actors and arenas that comprises statist-pluralist hybrids such as empires or regional communities. The distinction made so far has, next to quantitative implications centered in numbers, also significant qualitative ones differentiating states from societies. The quantitative feature predominates in plural as opposed to pluralist structures, defined by the number of poles around and between which action takes place—i.e., the number of major powers, from two in a bipolar structure to three in a tripolar or triangular to several in a multipolar one. All of these structures have been exemplified historically in a more or less pure or modified, "tight" or "loose," form. Variations among them were more easily and prominently the subject of prospective anticipations and arguments about their differential bearing on system stability than of actual changes when extending beyond a triangular to a multipolar structure. The insufficiency of the quantitative dimension devoid of qualitative and procedural ones becomes manifest when the quantitative range orders actor sizes from questionably viable small polities to vast empires, and the former are the actual products of the statist bias of nationalism problematically legitimized by the principle of national self-determination and the latter a qualitatively distinct type of superior power oriented toward control within an expanded sphere while still exposed to the systemic norm of interactor conflict. The two extremes partake of the structurally critical processual dimension of fragmentation vs. aggregation or integration: the small states, as products of fragmentation from vaster ensembles and, via the denationalization of the state and depoliticization of nationality, candidates for pluralist regional integration in lieu of divisive statism; and the empires, as actual results of excessive prior fragmentation and the mere focus or outright enforcers of remedial aggregation.[10]

Suddenly reducing a plural into a "unipolar" situation, the collapse of the Soviet pole of power was contrary to both the habitual gestation of third parties by two-power contests and the automatically replenishable erosion of multi-power structures. The result is problematic operationally, because it bifurcates the political arena between an imperatively ordered and a chaotically disorderly segment, as well as conceptually, because a single pole is meaningless in the physical world. Both facts point to qualitatively accented revision of unipolarity into a mere "unifocality" and to the more generally time-limited value of parcelling geopolitical space into quanta of material capabilities while neglecting both qualitative features and dynamic attributes. Including them are motivating spirit vs. material substance; differently situated and evolved, ascendant and declining, polities vs. undifferentiated poles; and, contrary to particular conflicts, conflict-transcending schisms (sacral-secular, continental-maritime, and West-East) that more than any other qualifier affect structures without depending on the strategist's full awareness of their precise identity and thrust for influence. Modifying quantitatively uneven capabilities more conspicuously but not significantly than schisms is the uneven rise and decline of individual capabilities over time. This evolution-related organic factor complements the operationally more directly impacting qualitative components of a "total"—i.e., not only quantitatively or numerically differentiated—structure. The quantitative component of the two sides of a total structure, including the difference between smaller and greater powers, suggests a mere stratification only exceptionally endowed with the qualitative attributes of a hierarchy. By the same token, a qualitative dimension is latent in the difference between big powers and empires equipped with or claiming a distinctive role and status.

Tangibly functional rather than integrally qualitative modifiers apply by contrast when some poles of power are prominent militarily-politically and others economically as opposed to combining the two distinctive capabilities (and related attributes) about equally. When the several capabilities are fused in one power, the difference between one pole of power and a central focus of policies translates into one between dominance and mere prominence, supremacy and salience, associated with diverse kinds of authority and requisite supporting assets. Far-reaching immunity to immediately irreparable error on the part of the focus for the calculations of all others differs as much from capacity for complete and continuing control as access to all or most other parties differs from possessing overwhelming assets exceeding all the others'. Whereas a unifocal differs consequently from a unipolar structure, a bipolar structure is subject to modification into one either bifocal or bisegmental. A structure is bifocal when preeminence is divided between militarily-politically and economically preeminent actors and the conflicted balance of functionally integrated compact units of power is transformed into functionally diverse and only potentially complementary imbalances of, say, economic and military capabilities. On a broader basis, a structure is bisegmental when it comprises substantially diverse stages of political or economic or any other development and consequent efficacy. Different combinations of statism and pluralism or material prosperity and poverty will in such a setting replace confrontation of two actors endowed with quantitatively and qualitatively comparable capabilities.

The several qualitative differentiations point to a structure that is heterogeneous in terms of its components and tends to be heteropolar in terms of the functionally diverse poles around which the components cluster. This is a more complex, and perennially significant, articulation than one reduced to a particular capability, such as military, highlighted to distinguish (decreasingly valid) bipolarity on the nuclear-military plane from (prematurely posited) multipolarity on either the conventional-military or political-economic plane. However, just like homogeneity and any corresponding polarity, heterogeneity and heteropolarity help articulate structure into a configuration, associated in a cause-effect relationship with specific strategies responsive to the distribution of actors in space and their differentiation in kind. A configuration can and commonly will be institutionalized in diplomatic constellations and beyond in ways more or less consonant with the underlying structure and capable of sustaining its essential constituents.

All of the qualitative modifiers of quantitative structure are somehow connected with the several schisms (sacral-secular, continental-maritime, and West-East) that condition particular conflicts operationally and normatively. They impact structure with differently potent effect individually, and each with diversely salient consequences within actors-to-be and, typically at a later stage of their and the arena's evolution, between consolidated parties. In having this effect, the schisms supplement the features of structure that relate to size and evolutionary stage and are concentrated in the rise/decline dynamic as the (stage-related) process that generates provisionally stationary (size-related) products. Schematically, schisms complete the spectrum of dispositions that constitute the overall environment of world politics. Strategically, they condition the actions and reactions, drives and restraints, responsible for the power-balancing process that reflects as well as affects a particular configuration in terms of which world politics actually takes shape. In so doing, the schisms embody and illustrate the effects of the full range of socio- and cultural-politically crucial features of structure and structure-centered environment. As the pragmatically most conspicuous, the land-sea power schism also integrates the most autonomous technological factor directly with the political factor and plane through a wide range of innovations that add the oceanic to the continental arena of competition. The implied differentiation and sequential prominence of correspondingly defined and equipped types of power have affected structure, configuration, and environment more than any other of the many technologically or otherwise contrived innovations and changes confined to terra ferma, pending their geopolitically meaningful projection to outer space.

Extending schematization toward systematization of the several facets of the environment invests the statics inherent in the quantitative factor of number, ranging from uni- or bi- to multipolarity, with the dynamics implicit in the differently qualitative features. The most elementary qualifiers are categories of "power": nuclear- and conventional-military and political-economic, as alternative indices of actor salience. They diversify into unevenly functional—strategically rational and effective—behavior, contingent on the congruence of an actor's conduct with the configuration of the arena: the latter's basic quantitative structure impacted by a range of space/time qualifiers with relevance for strategy. Furthermore, a configuration of unevenly mobile or stalemated, mobilized or potential, capabilities conditions and is conditioned by a hierarchy of unevenly dominant global and subsidiary local conflicts. Their management and outcomes are constantly subject to behavioral deviations such as too-forward anticipation on prospective capability by actually weak powers and mere simulation of conflict by and between a number of currently potent poles of power. Likewise, dynamic implications pertain to the difference and potential sequence between unipolarity and unifocality, such as privileged access to allies in the "focal" setting and preponderant assets relative to clients in the "polar" one, predominating in both contexts over the relationship with an adversary or competitor. And finally, much the same applies to a functionally bi- to multifocal situation of militarily-politically, economically, and otherwise diversely favored or superior powers and a bi- to multisegmental structure of unevenly developed classes of actors. While a mixed-heterogeneous structure, such as the present, takes shape, it will foster premature projections gravitating between prospective multipolarity of a conventional (e.g., nineteenth-century) kind and diversely defined and modified ascendancy of one power, whose relation to regionally dominant powers in different parts of the world will inject culturally diverse qualitative features into the structure.[11]

Schisms vs. polarities and individual schisms vs. their connections over time

Interrelated throughout is the given of power, its configuration within the arena's core and periphery, with the ongoing process of reconfiguring migration of centers of power. Similarly, particular conflicts, their distribution in space and ranking in salience, are a given subject to power-balancing and a variable contingent on system development. Moreover, the foremost qualifiers of the quantitative structure are unevenly organic and operational: the moral and material vitality of actors reflecting their rise and decline is primarily organic and only incidentally and mostly indirectly operational; the several schisms (continental-maritime, West-East, and sacral-secular) impact operations more directly while being rooted in fundamentally organic basics including land and water, spatially differentiated cultures, and physical and metaphysical sides of human nature. Thus constituted, schism-like cleavages simultaneously pervade the power dynamic and rank above the particular conflicts that precipitate it. This combination of immanence and transcendence is reflected in the ambiguous character of the schisms themselves, inasmuch as the paired phenomena that constitute them lack a definite relationship reducible to either radical difference or positive fusion. The ensuing puzzles are reflected in the divergent historical developments and sequences of the several schisms as they emerge from primitive indifferentiation. Originally undifferentiable propitiative and administrative activities evolved first mainly within actors into sacral-secular (e.g., priestly-royal military or papal-imperial) schisms. Similarly overlapping trading, war-making, and piratical agendas crystallized into coastal and hinterland regions initiating the land-sea power schism. And, finally, more liberally societal and authoritatively statist features along the West-East spectrum completed the effect of all the schisms in configuring relations between the very actors they had helped fashion and in ever more refined forms and interlocking connections continued to activate.

The dilemmas ensuing for structure and, incidentally, statecraft can be partially clarified in terms of differentials in cultures and location (East–West schism), situation and capabilities (land–sea power schism), and creed and conventions (sacral–secular schism) that permeate a quantitatively conceived structure and condition a particular conflict and its immediate determinants. However, the differences are very much part of the overall setting or environment of the power-balancing process, which revolves around and is manifested through the particular conflicts. A wider- and deeper-reaching intelligence must, therefore, supplement strategic rationality, and a fusion of both constrains rationalizations based on conspicuously prominent "facts" or driven by a particular political or wider culture elevated into ideological rationales of strategies. The requisite of intelligent apprehension grows with the ambiguity defining the schisms themselves, implicit less in the contrast between schism and conflict than in the actual overlaps between the nominal contraries (e.g., West and East, etc.). These overlaps differentiate schisms from polarities and account for the tension between the paired terms. As these constituents strain simultaneously toward separation from one another and reciprocal subversion, they belie their actual dependence on each other for distinct identity and individual completeness.

This general characteristic is most significantly concretized in uneven mixes of politico-military and -economic power factors in parties to the operationally salient land-sea power schism. Matching this mix is the compound of (nominal) convergence and (effective) divergence between essentially Western and Eastern (or Northern and Southern) political and wider cultures and corresponding institutions. A potential positive becomes a negative when even unresisted diffusion and adoption of innovations from the originating side along either axis turn the potential improvements into their opposite in form or effect on the receiving side—a deformation of, say, liberalism and constitutionalism into anarchism inciting authoritarian-to-totalitarian reaction that, instead of attenuating, aggravates the West-to-East value-institutional schism. Whereas one of the mixes is primarily a matter of political economy and the other of cultural politics, a sacral–secular mix affects more immediately the normative side of politics. It entails not only interpenetration but also ever-changing, progressive and regressive interpretations of the sacral and secular constituents. They become reducible to increasingly value-neutral existential and normative if not also material and pragmatically construed immaterial factors along an evolutionary curve at one stage of which the state represents secularized sacrality and society deified materiality at another. The several "mixes" commingle in turn when, for instance, continental and maritime powers that are respectively also Eastern and Western are all at least formally state-like but substantively different-to-divergent societies.

Changing mixes within the schisms are projected outward into, or only manifested in, their changing prominence. Thus the continental–maritime schism has been intermittently (and is presently) subject to a dilution of its technological and other preconditions of efficacy and operational primacy. Such a dilution is translatable into a demotion apt to raise a de-ideologized, but culturally and institutionally intensified, East–West or North–South schism to compensating salience. That is to say, individual schisms will alternate operationally in primacy while they alternately aggravate and regenerate one another to make up for a temporary schism deficit apt to depress the qualitative level or disperse the operational core of world politics. When this happens, the schisms' imbrication translates into a sequential relation while the functional indifferentiation antecedent to the schismatization of the environment of politics is replaced by different degrees of isolation for individual schisms and interlock between then. Primitive indifferentiation can affect values and norms (sacral and secular), types of economic activities (agriculture and commerce, piracy and trade), and spatial situations and cultural orientations (East and West, North and South), to be eventually differentiated and interrelated in a corresponding schism. The sacral-secular schism is the most commonly isolated because it is mainly internally located at first. Its participation in the interlock of all three will be at its fullest when religiously or ideologically intensified instances of the land–sea power schisms are aggravated by West–East cultural differentials, as they were in the sixteenth and nineteenth-twentieth centuries. Conversely, the most prominently interlocked continental–maritime schism will be not so much isolated as dominant when, centered on the Anglo–French cleavage, it was relatively unaffected by the others in secularized and regionally delimited conditions of eighteenth century Western Europe.

All schisms supplement at all times in all their aspects the features of structure related to the size (magnitude) and the developmental stage (maturity) of either the progressively crystallized arena subject to expansion and contraction or individual actors and regions subject to rise and decline when articulating the arena. Schisms complete the range of basic attitudinal dispositions within the action-reaction dynamic by adding a variegated normative dimension to reflexes and rationales actuated by power-related specific interests. In that schisms inject subjective-passional next to narrowly pragmatic impellents into the definition of national interests and actual dynamics of world politics, they are an integral part not only of structure but also of the reality posited by normatively sensitive romantic realism.[12]

"Anarchy" vs. orderliness and "hierarchy" vs. stratification as part of actor-arena inter-determination

Affecting all aspects of structure is the question of the essential quality of actors and their relation to the arena. In any social nexus or activity, actors are ultimately people, individually or collectively. In conventional

analysis of world politics, they are "reified" entities such as (territorial-
or-national) states and (national-or-larger communal) societies, next to
arguably ascendant multi- or transnational corporations and inter- or
nongovernmental organizations. This attribution of thing-ness to actual
networks of relations and conceptual abstractions can be impugned for
empirical or ethical reasons, but unproductively as to its interpretative or
any other validity. Implicit in the critique is failure to appreciate that
human agents acting in institutional roles (e.g., on behalf of "France" or
the "United States") do and had better act in ways shaped by the institutional entity's position in time/space and the consequent needs and interests, reflected in traditions shaped by recurrent situations, rather than in
response to the agents' moods and humors as unevenly private individuals
or groups. This assertion is truest for unitary state-like actors firmly
placed in the physical environment ("space") and strongly imbued with
historical traditions ("time"), both of which create significant presumptions in regard to action. Reification is comparatively less valid for pluralistic societies, or regional communities, with insufficiently coherent
political or more inclusive culture to suggest strategically rational or historically intelligent external behavior. Finally, the presumption applies
least to indeterminate entities such as "multinational" corporations,
driven by mutually competing concerns of host countries and corporate
headquarters variably political and economic in kind while unfocused
spatially and focused on diversely short- or long-term perspectives temporally. Whatever may, therefore, be the case operationally in the real
world, supra-statist entities are descriptively intriguing but not very help-
ful analytically. Conversely, sub-state actors such as political parties, social classes, or unevenly autonomous provinces in a federative setup
become practically significant and analytically manageable only when
they act "as if" they are mini-states, emboldened or compelled to act
accordingly by a corresponding configuration of crises or opportunities.

The key distinction between states or quasi-states (including empires
and politicized religious or otherwise creedal entities) and societies (including proto-national sedentary tribes and "supranational" communities) is compatible with a more fluid differentiation in periods of
transition. More than commonly, complex interpenetration is then combined with volatility in the ranking of alternative collective actors in terms
of their role or status. However constituted and ranked, actors are both
products and protagonists of action just as polities are of politics. Since
they unavoidably partake of a shared essence, differences in the magnitudes of power interplay with variations pertaining to norm implicit in
the historically shifting attribution of relative—higher or highest—value
to diverse types of actor, extending across a range from individuals to
universal community while passing through territorially circumscribed

entities such as states. When norm and power coincide, stratification begins to figuratively shade into hierarchy as a condition at least as ambiguous as anarchy when the latter is confined to formal absence of a common authority—and implies thus a radical hiatus between power and norm. In fact, other than formal, actual anarchy is as absent from interstate relations as is ideal hierarchy, so long as law-like orderliness and, consequently, basic predictability of interactions among crystallized-and stratified states are enforced by instant or deferred sanctions for gross deviance from the unwritten rules and conventions of real politics. Such orderliness is paradoxically inseparable from the conflictual character of an "anarchic" state system and tends to fade with it unless replaced by an ordering agency such as empire or an exceptionally effective international organization.

No more descriptive of interstate relations than a formal definition of anarchy (as opposed to an actual one verging on chaos) is the ideal conception of hierarchy (as opposed to actual stratification) as an order of interlocking rights and duties among equally respected if differently dutiful incumbents of "hierarchically" graduated but equally necessary functions. The ideal norm of hierarchy being inadequately realized even in prototypical feudal society, its impact propels the stratification of an international system toward an international "society" more noticeably in a special case, such as that of a hegemonial alliance, than generally. However, contrary to the confusion wrought by the notion of anarchy, it can be profitable for both greater and lesser powers to borrow from the ideal of hierarchy in general, centered on reciprocal obligations of unevenly situated parties, and apply it to particular techniques such as great-power intervention. Both classes of actors will then manage better the relationship between pretension to influence and effective performance and between graduated formal status, as compared with formal-legal equality, and uneven physical substance. This is equally true within and outside both international (or confederative) institutions intended to reduce the impact of power inequalities and a power politics institutionalized in a great-power concert intended to simultaneously express and mute the disparities. Such diversely authoritative frameworks of action implement an ideal combination of apparent opposites in an institutionalized hierarchical equilibrium: hierarchy both conveying and constraining quintessential inequality of power, and balance of power or equilibrium pointing if not to equality then relative equalization as an attainable norm.[13]

Hierarchy qualifies quantitatively size-related stratification in the configuration of the arena more as a matter of elusive principle than of established practice. Somewhat similarly stretched between quantity and quality is the formation of two primitive classes of actors: small nuclear and large nebular. The larger, nebular entity—an aggregate such as the

Carolingian empire in medieval Europe and its Germanic successors—emerges sooner but is impermanent because premature, owing its loose conformation to a yet uncrystallized arena permissive of insufficiently backed short-lived expansion. In every respect contrary is the gradually evolving nuclear polity such as Capetian France that moves beyond its miniscule nucleus (the royal domain) only intermittently and incrementally because concurrently with the arena's evolution into a structured constraining one, but it does so with permanent results. The arena's intangible facets of structure will condition both elementary actor types in cooperation with its physical topography, affecting the distances between centers of potential actors and the radii of their possible outreach. Critical will be the configuration of flat and open or mountainous and intractable terrain and parallel or converging river flows—items of elementary geopolitics affecting the formation of actors before less narrowly physical and more extensively configured space can condition their interactions and, in cooperation with time, their evolution. From the beginning of the unevenly fluctuating inter-determinative relationship between actors and arena, the connection will evolve toward the critical one of proportionality between an actor's size and the scope of environmentally created opportunity or also imposed necessity for an actor's profitable or just necessary self-affirmation and -projection.

Not least in this connection, the relation between size and substance decisive for nuclear and nebular entities prefigures the relation between unevenly compact continental and maritime-mercantile states and relatively unitary states and pluralist communities. So long as the second type of polities exploits its greater immunity to environmental resistance to expansion and coincidentally manages better the relationship between its size and the scope of the environment, it will avoid similarities with the nebular antecedent. Specifically and representatively, the distinctive strengths and weaknesses of the continental and the oceanic powers are determined by their different settings—actual and perceptual arenas—and consequent constraints and impellents, necessities and opportunities. A maritime–mercantile power's relatively easy and abrupt rise, consequent on relatively unimpeded accumulation of resources and immunity to strategic constraints, will be matched by a correspondingly abrupt and typically irreversible decline consequent on an equally facile diffusion of material assets. This set of traits is not wholly different from an empire's alternating liability to dissolution in the wake of excessive concentration. Conversely, the course of a typical continental power is more even overall. Although or because subject to periodic-to-endemic crises, it will be as resistant to abrupt fall as incapable of meteoric rise within a commonly longer life span as a great power than that of either a commercially salient sea power or normatively ordered but functionally loosely assembled empire.[14]

Within this statist-pluralist spectrum and corresponding ranges of assets and liabilities, empires remain different from insular-maritime polities, and both of them contrast with the unitary bias of politico-militarily accented continental types of statehood. These differences are easily subsumed in a continuum of actor types, ranging from individuals and groups-in-primitive society to individuals-in-institutionalized micro/macro-regional communities or empires. This typological continuum manifests itself both normatively and existentially: normatively in the historically shifting hierarchy of values or, derivatively, status and role, ascribed to the diverse actors; and existentially in the historically likewise sequentially successive determinative role of either format in the emergence of another—church's of the state and the latter's of society or community. So long as an ultimately circular inter-determination shapes actors and arena into a complete environment, it implicitly determines both the role and the ranking of the manifest or hidden progenitors and their direct or indirect creations. It follows that the creation, prioritization, and reciprocal conditioning of the several actor types are complex processes susceptible of analytic dissection while inviting an increasingly speculative meditatation when relating state to society and individuals to world community. Juxtaposing pluralist societal and unitary statist actors and intergroup and interstate agendas as they stimulate one another before one supersedes the other or both are displaced by an alternative entity and process points directly to the next step: fathoming the relation between, and relative primacy of, domestic and international-or-systemic and economic and real political factors in the agenda of world politics. Variably slanted inter-determination of such factors extends via types of actors to the relation between actors and arena. This relation will be commonly shaped by the actually formative initial primacy of an arena structured spatially and materially rather than by settled conventions over incipient actors, to be eventually replaced by the intended normative ascendancy of developmentally most advanced actors over the arena after the mid-term state of evenly reciprocal conditioning. Primarily a facet of evolution, the less than obvious or "logical" relationship of reciprocally shaping influence between actors and the arena at the beginning and during their coexistence is nothing so much as the operational counterpart of the other paradoxical relationship: that between formal anarchy and essential orderliness of interstate politics. Both are, in a postmodern era, endangered by the state's and state system's temporal or only spatial passing—backward toward pre-statist pluralism reminiscent of the Middle Ages and eastward from the Occident to the Orient.[15]

Control vs. consent in empires and solidarity vs. subversion in inter-empire equilibrium dynamic

All the quantitative and qualitative facets of structure, some of which shape it into a particular configuration, converge in the issue of order, an object of human aspirations at least as profound and perennial as freedom. Both the aspiration and the resulting ambiguities are manifest in potentially universal and actually regionally delimited organizations over a wide spectrum of authority, efficacy, and legitimacy. This spectrum is bounded at one extreme by cooperative institutions that rank consent and conciliation above control in one kind of hierarchy as a matter of principle, and at the other extreme by institutionalized empires that reverse the order of priorities in favor of control when useful or necessary in practice. A historically most enduring format of control and cooperation for order, an empire is also the most awkward one. Combining regular statehood with engagement in the shaping of a larger order, it embodies the extreme of expansion intrinsic to statism but stands internally for inter-factional or -regional equilibrium necessitating a measure of restraint, characteristic of societal pluralism. However, propensity to control as a condition of order tempts empires to exceed constraint into coercion as a standing challenge to countervailance and thus to the balance of power. Yet inasmuch as containing cumulative disturbances can be at times preferable to unchecked liberties giving way to license, the contradictions empires represent are not sufficient to make this historically recurrent component of the environment irrevocably obsolete because presently anomalous or inherently illegitimate.

All the distinguishing features of empires will affect not only their specific identity but also their relations with other empires determined by an uneven contest between inter-empire solidarity and subversion. Whereas solidarity is hypothetically the ultimate expression of belonging to an identical class of polity exposed to qualitatively identical stresses and challenges and associated with a shared ideal mission, reciprocal subversion would comply with operationally proximate compulsion. Both are implicit in specific diversities and the empires' character as also territorially contiguous or only operationally interlocked actors. And whereas solidarity is predicated on a shared stake in control and opposition to uncontrollable disorder, efforts directed at subversion will aim at revising the existing terms of order. By the same token and with similarly indeterminate results, the physical distance between the governing centers of empires, translating into psychological distance, will free strategic rivalry of the emotional enmity peculiar to nation-states. But this conflict-muting effect will be offset by irritants from the empires' contentious interpenetration at their respective peripheries and spheres of actual or desired influence immediately beyond such orbits. Internal organization of individual empires and their external defense strategies will be interlocked in a dilemma comparable to the solidarity-or-subversion quandary: whether to tighten or relax controls, with consequences for an empire's liberalization, and opt for static peripheral or elastic in-depth defense, determining degrees and kinds of military mobilization. The constant danger is that of drifting beyond relative decline into outright dissolution or dispossession, apt to generate actual anarchy and with it, the problem of alternative organization.

All these and related issues have been conspicuous during the latest instance of empires and incidence of the empire formula, only thinly concealed by bipolarity as the more conspicuous and conventionally acceptable structural format. This fact corroborates the atemporal universality of empires as to kind, while the merely regional compass of any one empire does anything but negate its spatially wider ambitions or reverberations. Constructed to shield a vulnerable core polity within concentric circles of diminishing control and influence, the Soviet empire has been structurally a modified twentieth century reproduction of Sparta's in the fifth century B.C. and Spain's in the sixteenth-seventeenth centuries A.D. while reversing their conservative bias into revolutionary pretensions. So also the American kind of empire recalls the empires of Athens and Albion while presenting itself contrarily to their external dynamism as defensive and the obverse of expansionist.

Notes

1. WP 496 (2.par.)–499.

2. WP 427 (2.par.)–429 (end 1.par.); 431 (3.par.)–432 (end 1.par.); RR 130–132 (end 2. par.); 134–137 (end 1.par.).

3. IE 194 (3.par.)–201.

4. RUSR 7–17.

5. WPJ October 1963, 118–136; RWO 157–160 (end 2.par.); EA 143–155 (end 1.par.); RRA 79 (3.par.)–81 (end 3.par.), 83 (2.par.)–85 (end 1.par.), 86 (2.par.)–88 (end 2.par.); RWO 124 (4.par.)–125 (end 1.par.); RR 19 (first two pars.); 109–110 (end 2.par.).

6. RRA 90 (2.par.)–91 (end 2.par.); 39 (2.par.)–41 (end 2.par.); NIA 8 (2.par.)–11; WP 15 (2.par.)–22.

7. WP 476 (3.par.)–484.

8. RRA 15–17 (end 1.par.); 24 (2.par.–end 3.par.); 42–43 (end 1.par.).

9. RRA xi (3.par.)–xiii (end 2.par.), 91 (3.par.)–95 (end 4.par.), 97–98 (end 1.par.); RR 28 (2.par.)–32.

10. IE 119 (3.par.)–24 (end 1.par.); IA 10 (3.line from top)–12 (end 2.par.); NIA 161–167, 255–259 (end 2.par.).

11. IA 26–31 (end 1.par.); ATW 8 (2.par.)–12 (end 1.par.), 15 (3.par.)–18 (end 3.line from below).

12. WP 43 (3.par.)–52 (end 2.par.); RWO 57–64 (end 1.par.), 78 (2.par.)–82 (end 1. par.); WP 149 (2.par.)–155 (end 2.par.).

13. IE 23–33 (end 1. par.).

14. IA 9–10 (end 1.par.); WP 66 (last par.)–75 (end 1.par.), 78 (2.par.)–81 (end 2.par.).

15. RR 132 (3.par.)–133, 6 (4.par.)–9; RWO 153 (2.par.)–156.

2

Dynamics and Dilemmas of World Politics: Geopolitical and Geoeconomic

A mistake besetting the theory and practice of world politics is to project distribution directly into the balancing of power while omitting the consideration of both logically and actually antecedent expansion: to bypass drive to the advantage of restraint. The question whether the "drive" does not encompass being driven—in the sense of drawn into expansion by real or perceived compulsions built into the structure and including strategies of other—is suppressed as a result. This suppression engenders conceptual distortions in relation to "restraint," its necessity or legitimacy, thereby affecting such key problems of politics as (unprovoked) aggression and (warranted) appeasement. Ambiguous relations between the two are intertwined with like ones between equality and parity (involving the issue of equity in conditions of asymmetry between rival parties) and between hegemony and mere preeminence (involving the issue of proportionality between role and resources).

Facts and fallacies about expanding polities and balancing of power

Given the ambiguities, the problem of expansion is not resolved by attributing the drive to the very nature of power and of the state qua organized power, to an undifferentiated complex of functional stimuli, or to a culturally specific national or ideologically transnational predisposition embedded in a particular polity. Seriously misleading for the balancing of power, the consequent failure is to identify the international, or systemic, determinant of expansion with both offense and defense, predation and preclusion—in short, with pushing and being pulled forward by the configuration of external forces: either a vacuum or, more important, a

49

constellation potentially endangering or lastingly frustrating the "expansionist." When extreme expansion points to an empire, it is of secondary importance whether the stimulating constellation consists of qualitatively and quantitatively equal major powers or of small-scale peripheral forces endangering the outermost frontier of the expanded polity. Such systemic incentives to expansion demonstrably apply to a succession of empires both historical (including Roman and British) and contemporary (czarist-to-Soviet Russian and American). Consequently, their uniformity requires analyzing the reasons for expansion at least as intensely as, but more dispassionately than, the more immediate or specific reasons for competition when it comes to formulating and evaluating balance-of-power policies and their consequences for war and its absence.[1]

To the same extent that expansion oscillates between push and pull, radical self-aggrandizement and reactive entanglement, balancing of power is decomposed into, but actually aggregates, drives and restraints at the center of the dynamic that configures and reconfigures the structure over time while responding to it at any one moment. Because it is so central and so ambiguously omnipresent at different levels of action and social systems, the balance of power has been less steadily understood than impeached on analytical (as well as ethical) grounds and was repeatedly declared extinct in favor of a different but less determinate principle of action on ostensibly factual grounds.

The theoretical critique bears habitually on both of the terms involved: power and balance. It impugns "power" as a concept defined too broadly (or too narrowly) and an entity incapable of measurement. In fact, as the psychological relationship involved in asserting or withstanding control it actually is, power is either asserted or experienced without much reference to its precise volume or composition. Moreover, power had better not be practically measurable if counter-balancing opposition or resistance to ostensibly irresistible superior capabilities is to be forthcoming. Judged by "objective" criteria, this will be the case whenever an aspirant to the obverse of balance, hegemony, is actuated (as it commonly is) by initial superiority in some kind of resource and resource-based resolve when ascendant, or in strategic skills and urgency to deploy them in time when fending off impending decline. As for "balance," each party to a set of two- or three-power relationships is commonly indicted as striving for a margin of superiority or overbalance. However, everyone's doing so in a multi-member setting is in most circumstances the condition of, rather than a vitiating inhibition to, overall equilibrium as the unintended and (since power cannot be measured) deliberately unachievable outcome. Overall equilibrium will therefore normally emerge out of a network of no more than bi- or trilateral relationships, the greatest number that can be deliberately monitored and managed. Yet as a cumulatively achieved consequence, equilibrium's existence is even then more likely to be inferred from the actors' actually restrained conduct (reflecting a diffuse sense of hard-to-exploit equipoise) than established scientifically as a guide to conduct that is both right because constitutive and righteous because respectful of balanced power. Much the same is true for the allegedly requisite underlying consensus on fundamental rules. Such "rules" are in fact much more likely to emanate spontaneously from the process of progressively ever less blindly instinctual balancing than they are a codifiable procedural precondition to its smooth operation.

Conversely, when (and only when) inequality of power is massive and points to hard-to-reverse one-party preponderance, balancing will operate deliberately rather than incidentally and near-automatically, as it does most of the time. And it will do so without creating a warrant for positing either hegemony or equality as opposites to balance. Actually, hegemony qua empire merely depresses balance and balancing of power mechanics to relationships among factions or between center and periphery within an empire, and modifies the politics and psychology of balancing relative to another empire. Ultimately, actual parity as opposed to formal equality is just another word for, or implication of, balance.

In all these respects, it is essential to distinguish preponderance (a matter of weight) and hegemony (outright dominance) from mere preeminence (a matter of status and influence), just as it is to differentiate between equipoise (equal weight as a fact) and equilibrium (a process tending toward equalization). Preeminence connotes an actor's role and status as first among equals. In its authentically statist manifestations, it is a qualitative attribute co-acting with material factors to constitute the diplomatic focus for interactions among quantitatively unequal masses of capabilities gravitating around this particular reference point. Preeminence, being qualitative, is a matter of manipulable perceptions. Its most typical incumbent will be the offshore insular or oceanic power acting or posing as the much-acclaimed "balancer." The latter's likewise typical performance, when surfacing the ambiguities attendant on balancing, is to impute to a likewise merely preeminent continental state a hegemonic design in ways and with consequences apt to bring about the impugned ambition. The idealized function of an equalizing balancer, acting on behalf of weaker parties across the board, is then apt to be inextricably confounded with its actual role and effect: as the divider of the more problematic (continental) arena, if not also eventual disintegrator of the combined (continental-oceanic) core of the state system.

Absent such distortions, balancing as a process responds pragmatically to selfish concerns with commonly benign results. As a mechanism, it is a device for dealing rationally with intrinsically uncontrollable increase and decrease in the organic attributes of individual actors. These two aspects distinguish balance of power as a condition and balancing of power as process, encompassing equally drive and restraint, from formally institutionalized ways of constraining action and socializing actors—a valid distinction despite the institutions' dependence on power distribution for their efficacy. Aimed at achieving objectively positive consequences from constraining negative subjective impulses, these institutionalized ways themselves evolved historically and range conceptually from the concert of powers on the mildly reformist end of the spectrum of intended effect to a global organization of collective security at its would-be revolutionary end. In different ways and to different degrees, both can be mistakenly contrasted with the balance of power as frameworks of solidarity and cooperation rooted in only ultimate or already present identity or harmony of interests, implicitly discounting or only downgrading the difference between cooperation as an original event and cooperation as an incident to competition or conflict. Alternately and correctly, concert and collective security organization can be assimilated to the balance of power as institutions committed to achieving an identical result in that they too confront a "bad" agent with preponderant power advantage on the "good" side. One implied difference with primitive balancing of power is in such a case between actions responsive to a general principle of ultimately universal benefit and actions directed by specific ad hoc purposes of immediate urgency for individual parties. Another difference is between opposing an act, aggression or use of force, and remedying a condition, irreversible imbalance.

While new possibilities arise repeatedly, traditional problems remain for extending adversarial balancing and aligning beyond "mere" institutionalization in a concert to integration in an inter-regional community and global organization of collective security. To effectively modify raw power balancing, a concert of powers must combine competition with consensual orchestration of action. An organization of collective security must upgrade a "complex" inter-functional into "institutional" equilibrium by converting intra-societal into international solidarity. Institutionalization in a concert need not mean more than replacing military with diplomatic coalitions and substituting majority decisions for military defeats of the member challenging a consensus. Responsible for the latter will be temporarily shared fatigue from war, reorientation from external to internal problems and crises, lack of one polarizing dominant conflict, and presence of functionally or spatially peripheral outlets from tensions at the center of the system. Even thus minimally defined, the concert is the highest stage and maximum attainable modification of conflicted real politics and will be all the less imperfect and impermanent the more it is informal and contingent. The fragility of its external preconditions is compounded by inner contradictions: less between actual hierarchy favoring the great-power members and formal equality among states ruling out collective dictation than between the premises of cooperation at the apex of any hierarchy and the competitive implications of any, including an institutionalized, balance of power.[2]

Balanced power vs. collective security "in equilibrium"

In an informal concert of powers, the balance of power is still very much its core, much as its implementation shifts from military to diplomatic coalitions for managing the equilibrium process and accomplishing equipoised power distribution. By contrast, in a formalized organization of collective security, the attempted shift away from balanced power to normatively just equilibrium goes beyond a partial or relative to an absolute and total transfer of emphasis. Progressing beyond a balanced condition that rules out ascendancy to benign conduct that excludes aggression implies a radical elevation of deliberately pursued principle over self-regulating dynamic. The marriage of principle with process within the balancing of power is an uneasy but equal union in the case of either combined resistance to manifestly superior capabilities or the individually unintended result of diversely motivated bilateral relations. This marriage is dissolved in favor of rootless principle alone when power balancing is demoted from a coequal process to a subordinate or auxiliary mechanism, divorced from particular interests and circumstances and unresponsive to either organic (rise-decline) or situational (including schisms-related) disparities.

As with the concert of powers, collective security organization depends for efficacy on a relatively diffuse, i.e., nonpolarized, distribution of power. But this distribution is now one compliantly subject to an imperative compelling its coalescence into a special kind of imbalance, against an actual or potential aggressor. For the (collective security) principle to effectively control the dynamic and conduce to effective countervailance, an autonomous balancing of power would have to be dialectically *aufgehoben*: i.e., abolished in its original form, but preserved as an effective mechanism for raising the traditional into a novel and superior system of action within a normatively transformed reality. In fact, the interplay between a nominal principle and actual propensities in a collective security "system" is apt to be as counterproductive as that between only nominal hierarchy and actual anarchy would be in the concert system. As a result, the balance of power tends to devour collective security when the latter becomes a misnomer for a particular alliance, even as the balance is itself liable to dissolve into a functionally and institutionally diversified, "complex" or "multiple," equilibrium.

A functionally complex equilibrium is the most effective potential substitute for formally institutionalized collective security in a pluralist-societal setting. It replaces therein the balance of functionally homogenized capabilities, relegated henceforth from the status of fundamental law of action to the function of a residual mindset, surviving mainly as part of an unprincipled pragmatism responsive to an unfathomable dynamic. The virtually rescinded uses and requirements of the balance of power are then (in terms of the dialectical *Aufhebung*) still preserved for possible last-resort or later-stage reactivation in case of retrogressive developments. But they are not being raised by means of viable alternatives or adaptations into an actually operative formula and technique of here-and-now strategy.

Consequently, relegating power balancing to the background, beyond the complications wrought by the schism-related situational factors, achieves some of the expectations attached to its normative simplification by the radically escalated institutional formula. Pending more stable outcomes, the as-yet-unredressed initial failure of the organization of collective security has made it impossible to significantly relocate the point at which maximizing (or only "optimizing") national power destabilizes international politics. Achieving that feat requires an organization that is itself "in equilibrium" operationally (in terms of legal commitments relative to members' actual commitment and capacity to abide by them), spatially (in terms of regional or global scopes relative to their comparative operational efficacies), and functionally (in terms of useful-to-compelling tasks and needs relative to willing-and-able performance). What has actually happened has been the replacement of the commitment of all parties minus the guilty one by the effective command-and-control of a particular power willing and able to employ the formalities of the general system as a cover for the self-interested character of its own engagement. The field of hypothetically effective generalized action has consequently remained open to particular alliances for the time being.[3]

Continuing viability vs. problematic subtleties of power balancing

The balance of power had to withstand conditions translated readily into the facile polemics of its repudiation while it was being institutionalized in either a concert of all kinds of powers or a multilaterally camouflaged hegemony of the leading power, and well before it could be institutionally suppressed or supplanted in an organization of collective security. More difficult than to dismiss is to make the case for continued existence and relevance of the balance of power. But it is not impossible, given world politics' continuing identity as a mix of organic (rise/decline) and mechanistic (interactive) components, wholly operative in particular regions (such as the Middle East) and uncertainly modified (by nuclear weaponry) on the global plane, so long as continuing military-technological revolutions conventionalize both defense and offense, non-force (e.g., economic) inducements and sanctions substitute for force-dependent ones, and intra-polity sociopsychological or intra-alliance diplomatic mechanisms of disturbance and reequilibration substitute for interactor military-political ones. However, no continuity and substitutability removes questions about the need or occasion for power balancing in unpredictably revolutionary or conventional world politics. In principle, will or can revolutionary weaponry decisively and therefore lastingly constrain the political effects of the rise and decline of powers, and will or can unprecedented economic techniques eliminate the rise/decline dynamic completely? In practice, will another hegemony-seeking or only suspect power arise for whatever reason in the not only post-agricultural but also postindustrial age, one ordered less around a balance of power than a more complex equilibrium?

Absent dependable answers, the case for the balance of power remains sufficiently strong to preserve power balancing as the hard core of a more complex equilibrium, irrespective of any displacement of its center of gravity. No more does even a generally or regionally waning intensity of active geopolitics nullify the geopolitical mindset, which qualifies the most progressivist departures from or rejections of operative geopolitics so long as it preserves last-resort readiness to revert to form. This disposition is objectified in, and power balancing supplemented or replaced by, a strategic equation of power-political repellents, economic attractions, and neutral-to-ambivalent cultural-political affinities or animosities. Is the balance of power only disaggregated into its perennial components or modified beyond recognition when the various material and immaterial factors of power, compressed into capabilities for security against predominance, are relaxed into corresponding functions that have become diversely interwoven strands in the texture of policies keyed to stability and prosperity? Only when, and to the extent that, considerations are based on the diverse functions will it be certain that they will compete with and may ultimately supersede considerations determined wholly by spatial locations. Revulsion from a more proximate bigger power converts in the latter case into the attraction of a remoter and if possible still bigger or stronger power. The transition takes place when—or as the transition does take place—the circuit of military-political, economic, and administrative functions that has transformed inchoate social entities into states is projected outward into the functionally complex inter-societal equilibrium that transforms economics from instrument into determinant of

policies. Specific compounds of power factors have always formed generations of successively leading types of powers, most recently medieval continental-military and modern insular-economic, and their would-be or
potential successors. These generational types are in the more diversified
setting supplanted by variable compounds of corresponding generic traits
and propensities—communal or individualistic, creedal or pragmatic, culturally western or eastern, etc.—prone to or at least capable of reintegra-
tion in a radically pluralist national or regional setting.[4]

Both the continuities within and differences between the balance of
power and its institutionalization and functional disaggregation are compatible with a progressivist realism that balances liberal aspirations with
conservative reservations, if not also actually germane to this kind of realism. However, the latter will leave largely outside its purview the particular situational and consequent cultural and institutional disparities among
parties to the several schisms, significant for romantic realism. In thus
amplified perspective, reservations about the balance of power as either a
deliberately applied principle or precept (against preponderance) or self-
regulating process (of contrary drives for unilateral advantage) focalize a
wider set of qualifications on the role of the so-called balancer. In need
of prior correction is equating balance with equality of individual parties
or contending sides as part of confusing equilibrium with quantitative
equipoise as either the practically attainable state or a valid ideal-typical
(or purposively ethical) norm. One-actor preeminence that supplants the
false ideal of equality in tangible factors of power by actual inequality in
roles due to more varied situational and evolutionary conditions is the
historically common condition. However, preeminence as an ostensibly
contrary but actually complementary facet of actual balancing does not
override to the point of extinguishing the core principle—one of opposition to one-actor preponderance (in quantity of capability) or para-
mountcy (in authority) sufficient to suppress the equilibrium dynamic to
the detriment of, among other things, the beneficial effect of mere preeminence (in status and function). It only means that the more ominous, hegemonic contingency is less frequent than the other, while the difference
and its implications are in turn inseparable from that between "parity"
qua equivalence and equality. Closely related differentials are the organic
ones of rise and decline and the situational ones of continental and oceanic
locations, while the relationship between preeminence and the balance of
power is a persistent part of an equilibrium dynamic that comprises both
but makes their effective reconciliation contingent on a diplomatic practice attuned to the differentials.

The ubiquitous problem of parity is the issue most critically complicated by disparity in the situations, attitudes, and aspirations of primarily
continental and insular actors. So is the issue of one-actor preeminence

although, even more certainly than that of parity, it arises also among qualitatively identical—i.e., uniformly continental or insular—powers. However, the asymmetries implicit in the disparity do not merely derange, but actually distort interactions considered "normal" in a schism-indifferent setting. Thus, when preeminence in role and status falls to an insular power, as it frequently does, a hegemony that is either disowned (Britain's before World War I) or insufficiently supported (post-Cold War America's) is readily conceded as one that performs on the seas functions that are or can be plausibly represented as being useful for the prosperity of all without threatening any one's security on land. By contrast, when preeminence is vested in a continental state, it will be seen contrarily as useless for the growth of trade and perilous for the balance of power. Absent discrimination, preeminence merely circumscribes latitudes available to all parties while hegemony would abolish autonomy of all but its incumbent's, because preeminence avoids, while hegemony successfully implements, a revolt against a contradiction inherent in an anarchic state system: that between the requirement of effective self-help and the constraints imposed on its lastingly most effective form. Corresponding to the difference in process is one in protagonists: the self-assured and (still) ascendant incumbent of preeminence and the actual or pretended aspirant to hegemony, (already) fearful of decline and anxious to elude it through irreversibly consolidated ascendancy.[5]

Actual or would-be hegemony is at once the most radical denial of balance and, through hegemony's traumatizing connection with the rise and decline of powers, the most dramatic illustration of the basic stimulant of the equilibrium dynamic. Such a stimulus is not the protection of small states but preservation of a competitive international system, one that mediates between rising and declining powers as the system moves beyond the deadlock among actors, most of whom are ascending and expanding, to the more complex parity-approximating equipoise. Because the organic rise-decline factor is universally operative when it actuates the operational action-reaction facet of world politics, it affects both primarily continental and oceanic actors and arenas. However, this uniformity transcends only in principle a theoretically complicating and practically destabilizing actual difficulty-to-impossibility: to unify the equilibrium mechanics as one applicable—or, at least, historically applied—equally and (from the land powers' perspective) equitably to both of the disparate actors and arenas.

The land-sea power disparity negates the assumptions of a homogeneous interstate system of quasi-equal powers on at least two counts. First, a truly creative interplay of balancing with rise/decline would in such a system be institutionalized through alliances that anticipate the rise of actors and attenuate the consequences of their decline in power or role impartially—i.e., schism-neutrally. Instead, the land-sea power schism not only enhances the alliance potential of the insular power but also encourages both categories of powers to counterproductively support and seek alliance with third parties possessed of some maritime capability regardless of their being rising or declining. Second, in a homogeneous system several sets of conscious balancing between two powers, with reference to its effect on the situation or attitude of a third power, will unintentionally produce a multipower equilibrium through a process that bridges the gap between subjective intention and objective result. Instead, a maritime-mercantile balancer tends to create the hegemonic threat it claims to oppose for subjective reasons of its own immediate advantage and, when they apply, objective reasons of its smaller territorial base than the land power's. By the same token, the not-uncommon contrasting policy of the alleged balancer, to actually lean on a safely conservative continental power as a surrogate in upholding mainland stability, will foster its own overall hegemony—or, given its fragile foundation, phantom-hegemony. All such peculiarities make it impossible to evolve mutually acceptable and objectively equitable parity between the two types of powers. Nor can they implement for the sake of equality in security and prosperity the essential complementarity in resource and role implicit in the makeup of their diverse capabilities.[6]

Variably deliberate balancing of power and calculations of alliance making

When parties to the balance of power are disaggregated along with power itself, ultimately military balancing dissipates into functionally more complex equilibrium. By contrast, alliances—as the foremost mechanism for configuring and reconfiguring the arena—concentrate in themselves the calculations of costs and benefits characteristic for all power politics. Reflecting such calculations, the relationship betwen balance of power and alliances is most direct and conspicuous when alignments (and realignments) originate in stresses and strains in the arena. This relationship is less direct when stresses and strains beset the alliances themselves. Interallied competition conduces then to equilibrium (or, more typically, reequilibration) when the impulse directed against the initial target of the alliance has resulted in some kind of overperformance. The implementation of the two basic modalities is affected by the comparative "rise" and "decline" of actual adversaries in the first case and present allies and possible future adversaries in the second case. Being concerned with too much future ascendancy on the part of a too successful ally is, in its effects, comparable with employing alliance not so much to countervail an ascendant as to control a declining but compulsively self-asserting because previously preeminent power.

Wholly mistaking the short- and long-term equilibrating impulse shaping alliance politics is by contrast the theory of so-called "bandwaggoning." Imputed to Third World countries during the Cold War, this "theory" indicts the dominant group in a weak power that aligns for reasons of internal power balancing with rather than against the stronger, but potentially more supportive, greater power. Authentically bandwaggoning is instead a "jackal state" intent on satisfying its predatory ambition relative to another weak state by joining a great-power expansionist in hopes of sharing the benefits of victory without incurring the eventual greater cost of aggravated dependency. Ignoring the gradation of concern with balances and hierarchies of power within and between polities, the misapplied version of the deviance fails to understand that the less a polity is a genuine "state," the more likely are the internal balances to predominate over the external, implicitly negating the latter's effect on foreign policy. The influence or opportunity for influence of the stronger and more consolidated power or powers will be all the greater. Only when the domestic order is developed, i.e., constitutionalized or at least centralized, will the determinant efficacy of intergroup real politics recede to the same degree that the environment is crystallized and consequently crisis-prone and compelling. Conversely, it is the configurative effect or potential of alliances that will recede when a dominant conflict is present. Such a conflict's polarizing bias will tend to compel particular alignments compared with the more normal situation of a more complex conflict map allowing for, or actually encouraging, relatively "free" calculations and expanding them to include local, regional, and global external, along with compatible internal, interests and considerations.[7]

In general or in principle, the subjective rationale of cost-benefit calculations translates automatically into the objective criterion of the marginal utility of additions to an alliance: i.e., the net excess of benefit from associating one more party over the costs of alienating the latter's local antagonist while creating an overbalance apt to provoke more generalized counteraction. It will signify in this connection whether the interests involved in the calculations are wholly identical between the parties, compelling even an otherwise costly alignment, or constitute complexes of identical and contrary interests that are only potentially complementary, allowing for a more prudent or rational choice.

Only ostensibly contrary to alignment and the reasons for it are dealignment and, beyond it, realignment. Dealignment, due essentially to the inversion of reasons responsible for the original commitment, entails a "separate" peace and raises questions about its effect on generalized pacification depending on who accommodates first with whom. Logically consummating dealignment, realignment presents not so much a separate theoretical issue concerning interactions as a historical problem related to evolution: its frequency or facility in classic diplomacy is easy to exaggerate relative to the more recent situation, one presumptively more structurally rigid and ideologically polarized. Among the reasons for both de- and realignment will always be intraalliance stresses promoting disintegration as a result of discordant actual or putative gains and losses of allies, revealed by the alliance's success as often as by its failure. When the bias of the alliance institution and main purpose of most actual alliances increasingly favor restraint, the latter will in especially long-lasting peacetime alliances concentrate on "revisionist" or, still in the terminology of the period between the two world wars, radically "dissatisfied" allies. Such were in the post-World War II era parts of partitioned Germany in the West and (during the Sino–Soviet alliance) China in the East, just as post-1871 France before World War I. These countries highlight the always critical ratio between intraalliance stresses that strain, and outside pressures that intensify, alliance cohesion—a chronically unstable ratio fraught with the perpetual risk of an alliance's dissolution.[8]

Intraalliance stresses have the advantage of helping fill the conceptually puzzling gap between specific reasons for individual acts, inspired by instincts before they can develop into informed rationale, and the acts' systemic result. In an ostensibly self-regulating dynamic such as power balancing, the gap is between its individually not always fully intended outcome and the self-consciously anti-hegemonic purpose of the balance of power as a principle of action, contingent on the manifest (or sufficiently persuasively asserted) presence of a corresponding threat. Prominent in bridging the gap between subjective incentives and objective results through plausible strategic reflection rather than unintended consequences is precisely the concern of allies with intraalliance parity of gains and losses. Just as strains that pre-exist a war limit the size of alliances subject to marginal-utility considerations, so interallied disparities in costs and benefits revealed during a war or conflict short of war as it moves toward resolution will tend to limit the size of victory for the more successful side. This result is achieved or only sought by means of the either formal or merely tactical-operational de- or realignments of allies bent on keeping the most directly benefiting party "manageable" in the postwar period, with the help of reduced losses for the losing or defeated rival if possible and necessary.

This tactic and related tendency will incidentally contribute to meeting the regulatory function of alliances in regard to the quanta of capabilities to be aggregated on one side or balanced between sides. The moderating function of alliances relative to the qualitative dimensions is less certain of realization. It obtains with respect to the organic rise-decline fluctuations (and incidentally to the regulatory function) when, as an extra reward for a lesser power's assistance in the countervailing function, joining a defensive alliance legitimates (and in the process at least provisionally contains the implications of) the inferior ally's rise at the beginning of its ascent. Or inversely, when alliances soften or delay an ostensibly equipowerful ally's late-stage decline either directly by checking an adversary's assault on its waning strength or indirectly and more importantly through the exercise of control over such an ally's activities that exceed its remaining strength. Anything but moderating is the effect of alliances with respect to the schisms-related qualifier. Even the operationally most prominent, continental–maritime schism does not add new functions to alliances. It mainly exacerbates and rigidifies the operation of alliances when they fail to fundamentally alter the relationship between the schism and the balance of power advantageous to the sea powers, given the latter's privileged access to allies for war as well as to a weakening adversary for separate peace. Alliances obscure the schism symbolically and temporarily when mixed alignments cross the line of division between continental and oceanic powers because either of them fears a qualitatively cognate power more than the counterpart. However, alliances will actually aggravate the schism's war-prone tendencies when an encircling "grand coalition" of the insular with the rear-continental power drives the centrally located would-be amphibious power toward an only militant diplomatic response, embodied in an alliance for "continental duopoly" or co-hegemony with the rear-continental party to the triangle, if not to preemptively military counteraction. Or, the "condominial" alliance between the insular and the would-be amphibious continental power is conclusively shown to be too unequal to foster comprehensively continental-and-maritime parity as an avenue to appeasement, and too problematic in relation to third powers to come off at all or to last.[9]

As part of the successive land-sea power triangles, the grand coalition associated Britain successively with Austria (or, alternately, Prussia) against France and with Russia against Germany, just as the United States associated with China against Soviet Russia. The duopoly tied France to Austria at a somewhat later stage of the first triangle, while Germany came closer to an enduring alliance with Czarist Russia in the second than Soviet Russia to a permanent one with Communist China in the latest triangle. Finally, the condominial association had been briefly implemented between Britain and France once (after 1715) and adumbrated more often later, while an Anglo-German association was a serious possibility (in the late nineteenth century) and the United States moved toward a typically unequal "partnership" with Soviet Russia shortly before the latter's collapse—while its more equal expression was, as by all the other continentals previously, sooner and more persistently sought by the

Soviets at their apparent apogee. The fact that the insular power was, most of the time, Britain and its narrow home base militated against the kind of continental-and-oceanic parity or equilibrium aimed at successively by both France and Germany does weaken the persuasive power of the analogy in relation to the more equal U.S. and Soviet home bases. But it does so no more decisively than the fact that the progressively weakening tendencies toward a land-sea power condominium from the French to the German phase have not (despite the absence of the British metropolitan handicap) eventuated in either an actual transaction (U.S.-Soviet alliance) or the usual transformation (of militant diplomacy into a major war).

Even unconsummated tendencies are sufficiently significant to permit limiting the number of illustrations for the other linkages between balance of power and alliances to fewer than three cases prior to the total wars of the twentieth century, which had disrupted relevant continuities by instigating radical departures from strategic rationality. Thus Bourbon France's family pact with (post-Habsburg) Spain and Britain's several later "liberal" alliances with (differently Orleanist and Bonapartist) France in the early eighteenth and twice in the nineteenth century exemplify the conservative alliance aimed at moderating a restless revisionist partner, as does the Bismarck-initiated alliance of Imperial Germany with Austria-Hungary. Conversely, Prussia was successively lifted and legitimized en route to becoming Germany by alliance against the France of Louis XIV and with that of his successor, as was Sardinia en route to becoming Italy by membership in the Anglo–French alliance against Russia in the middle of the nineteenth century. Nor did America's quasi-alliance with China against the Soviet Union injure the former's diplomatic standing or fail to legitimate its rising might. Finally, there are repeated instances of a mere tendency to foster interallied parity and keep a forward ally manageable. Herein, post-Cold War European hesitancies to follow the American lead with regard to Cuba, Iraq, or Iran have not, despite their narrowly economic motivation, fundamentally differed from the diplomacy of Metternich's Austria during the last stages of the anti-Napoleonic grand coalition's advance in France. They merely did not duplicate Czarist Russia's role in the "miracle of the House of Hohenzollern" when saving the Prussia of Frederick the Great (and allowing Hitler to hope for the same from a separate peace) during the earliest and longest (seven years-long) global war of the modern age.

Antagonization and appeasement in relation to alliances and balance of power

The issue overarching all other alliance-related issues is the identity of supreme evil: war as such or the terminal supersession of a particular balance-of-power system, defeating its capacity for reequilibration within the existing boundary. Preventing both evils has become a more intricate task than it had been in the classic era of compact capability quanta vested in more than presently sovereign states. Only a small part of the growing complexity was intimated by the not so new statecraft of alliance-related foreign aid during the Cold War when, updating its antecedents, it injected the dilemmas of political economy into real politics more directly and materially than do alliance-forming strategic cost-benefit calculations. More than in kind, the novelty was in purpose compared to dynastic subsidies undertaken like alliances themselves in deliberate preparation of particular and oftentimes deliberately provoked wars or to the liberal-capitalist era's financial (including dollar) diplomacy employed for peacetime influence in anticipation of an alternately feared and desired war. When the economic-assistance programs have been designed to help deter at least one (the nuclear or central-systemic) kind of war, they addressed a special aggravation of conventional-military major or total war, increasingly apt to occur as a result of accumulating external pressures to be exorcised rather than anticipated external opportunities to exploit.[10]

Alliances neither provoke nor prevent wars by themselves, separately from radical innovations that disaggregate power, actors, and relations among actors. Instead, they have concentrated and augmented the mass of engaged capabilities while extending the intervals between incidences of armed violence—an effect that confirms everything that points to a constant sum of violence over finite stretches of time. Unevenly structured—officially declared and rationally managed and controlled—kinds of violence range from war to peacetime terrorism. Insofar as they are fungible, the issue of the causes of war as but one and not necessarily the basest or least manageable form of violence becomes normatively less compelling without ceasing to be of moment empirically. Moreover, if it is inconclusive to link war causation to the balance of power by way of alliances (and vice versa), it is problematic to assign chief culpability to either of the sides regarding the issue of hegemony: the party resisting its loss or opposing its retention by a weakened incumbent. Any attempt to adjudicate this academic controversy only enhances the critical importance of a generic relationship between an actor's actual or coveted status-conferring role and role-supporting material resources, and of a likewise generally operative mechanism for reconciling the two terms of the equation: assumption of extraordinary risks in either rigidly upholding the status quo (when asserted role exceeds resources) or forcefully rebelling against the status quo (when resource exceeds conceded role).

Steps taken or omitted, well-managed or mishandled, to accommodate the role-resource discrepancies, and risks-maximizing or -avoiding reactions to such disparities, will respectively conduce or be contrary to constructively appeasing the environment of crisis or conflict. Constructively appeasing the environment differs significantly from cravenly appeasing an expansionist at a prohibitive cost to balance—a difference implying many other distinctions in regard to the causation of wars. When a war is liable to degenerate into a thermonuclear confrontation, the question whether "deterrence" and "defense" and the difference between them are novel in kind or only in gravity itself comes to the fore. Its importance is overshadowed by—or is only part of—the query whether nuclear war is distinctively revolutionary itself or what is revolutionary is its anticipatory effect on the nature of international relations, with consequences for peace as merely a formally non-war situation or genuine appeasement in depth. If there is an indefinite propensity to conflict but only a limited absorptive capacity for violence in the international system, what about, first, the constant sum of different kinds of violence over definite periods of time? Sustaining this hypothesis is the progression from only seasonally articulated near-continuous low-intensity warlike activity in, say, early-medieval Europe (as mainly a condition of domestic tranquility), by way of limited wars recurring at short intervals (in response to alliances being entered into for a particular war), to lengthening intervals of formal peace and growing amount of informal violence between actual or prospective "total" wars (in accord with changing attitudes to alliances as primarily defensive or at least preemptive). An earlier implication of this hypothesis, to the effect that the end of the Vietnam War would be followed by dispersed but once again continuous turbulence, can now be transposed to a deepened degradation in the quality of force (including but not confined to state-supported terrorism) following the end of the bigger, if "colder," conflict.

The constant-sum hypothesis itself can be even more tentatively extended beyond the absorptive capacity of a system to its operational requirement of some form of violence to keep actors alert and the balancing of power operative—a requisite and resulting propensity that is confirmed administratively whenever foreign policy makers ration conflicts and attention to conflicts so as to avoid being overwhelmed by their cumulation or rendered irrelevant and in fact incapacitated by their absence. Such thoughts address directly or only by implication, but always negatively, simplistic theses regarding war causation or incidence. Just as the thesis that posits narrowly economic causation of wars is discredited by an analysis that differentiates between structural causes, functionally conditioned attitudinal predispositions, and operational precipitants, so is one that attributes wars to the link between the balance of power and alliances as such, projecting "eternal peace" into the time after their abolition. This connection is easily rendered more problematic by considering inequalities in the incidence and intensity of wars associated with or attributable to the different alignments and coalition politics implementing the successively Anglo/Dutch–Spanish–French, British–French–German, and Anglo–German–Russian land–sea power (progressively cum East–West) schisms and triangles culminating in the U.S.–Soviet–Chinese. Most war-inducing among the different alliance options and institutional formats of alliance associated with the continental–maritime schism is one resorted to most frequently: the grand coalition combining the insular sea power with the rear-continental power against the central amphibious (because would-be also maritime-mercantile) power. Whereas the parity-denying strategy of the sea power instigates the conflict, the rear-continental party actually regulates the configuration. It either represents an immediate threat to the centrally located continental power when strong or is the foremost party to be protected against the central power by the insulars when weak. The associated factors of resource and risk concerning the actors and the preemptive or provocative responses shaping the agenda are equally to blame in principle, while the individual parties are unequally responsible for the ensuing conflict in practice. Causing war less persistently will be the alliance for collusive duopoly (against the sea power's oceanic monopoly) between the two, central and peripheral, continental powers not only because it is less common. The central power will enter such an alliance to avoid encirclement and the rear-continental one to eschew entrapment by the sea power, a difference in motivation pointing to failure. The effort will founder and engender not so much war as such but instabilities prone to it because of the discrepancies in the potential partners' immediate interests and evolutionary stages or trends. The discrepancies will be reflected in the parties' objectives: the central power's is to neutralize (in effect demilitarize) the continental balance of power so as to release resources for its efforts overseas; the rear-continental power's, to avoid the continental hegemony of a central power that has successfully neutralized the sea power's capacity for continental projection before its own compensatory objectives and principally overland operations were consummated.

Most problematic—but potentially also most genuinely favorable to appeasement and least explosively polarization-prone—is the least frequent alliance between the maritime and the central-continental power. It replaces the potential of a continental duopoly for co-hegemony with the real possibility of an all-systemic condominium, apt to contain non-war-like violence while indefinitely deferring war-like conflict between not only parties to but also powers left out of the condominial association. Inhibiting the latter kind of alliance, next to disparities in evolutionary trends and between metropolitan and overseas resources of the potential parties, was the historical fear of the sea power, especially, lest the mere initiation of a far-reaching rapprochement expose either of them to pre-

emptive abandonment by possible or likely parties to the alternative alignment, producing isolation and with isolation exposure to the natural rival.
Thus, more than anything else in particular, it was Britain's fear of losing
a discouraged France to accommodation with Germany before assuring
itself of the latter within a "Teutonic alliance" (ideally comprising the
United States) that foredoomed the most on-again, off-again of pre-World
War I flirtations.

   Illustrating the categorical distinctions that invalidate any single-factor
or single-actor version of war causation, the implementation of the grand-
coalition scenario was the structurally occasioned or rooted and strategically activated direct cause of a series of major European wars including
the first and second global. Only short-lived realizations or approximations of the collusive duopoly-type combination (most recently Nazi–
Soviet) played mainly the role of a mere trigger or precipitant, as distinct
from determinant. Finally, failures to realize even a mutually desired or
attractive condominium-type association (most recently pre-World War
I Anglo–German) were only part of the preliminaries, as distinct from
precipitants. They contributed to war by creating together with functional (as distinct from the underlying structural) factors, such as economic and related colonial rivalry or armaments competition, popular
feelings of hostility and the policy makers' impression of the war's inevi-
tability. In such a case, the predisposition to embrace or endure armed
conflict will easily merge with the willingness to deliberately provoke war
while it is still winnable.[11]

Causes of war vs. abstention from war and prevention vs. resolution of warlike conflicts

Anything that points to the causal primacy of the geographically conditioned structure and strategies automatically downgrades the determinant
potency of any single factor or function, specifically the economic, much
as it may be prominent in crystallizing attitudinal predispositions. Because of its makeup, the maritime–mercantile power is the most likely
conduit for the economic factor. The interlock between the politico-economic agenda, which affects the resource base, and the military-political
agenda, affecting role and risks, is implemented for all parties through the
narrowly fiscal revenues-related side of the economy, as pertinent for the
concerned states' behavior as it was for their formation. So to hypothesize
war causation as part of real politics is merely to apply a distinction and
related propositions central to political economy concerning operational
and organic factors as proximately and ultimately determinant respectively. Their intertwining in particular situations accounts for the lack of

transparency of the causes of war, exculpates the balance of power and alliances per se, and relocates conventional attribution of guilt at least partially from continental to maritime powers. It also promotes serviceable analytic clarifications (structural vs. strategic determinants, determinants vs. precipitants, etc.) in lieu of ideologically determined rationalizations and obfuscations (exceeding if implicitly drawing on the identification of economic factors as determinant because in themselves seemingly more determinate than political factors). Illustrating the connection between types of determinants and organic and operational factors, the immediately "guilty" party will more than either of the principals be the formerly prominent but presently dependent-because-declining ally. Perceived as indispensable by the senior partner, it will—all the way from Corinth in the Peloponnesian to Austria–Hungary and to a lesser degree France in the first world war—be the only one desirous of war as the only means to restoring some antecedent loss and improving future prospects. Such a power will be the triggering precipitant of a war for which the ostensibly passive rear-continental regulator will from Persia to Russia be the critical background factor, the sea power from Athens to England the structurally and organically ultimate cause, and the continental power from Sparta to Germany the operationally proximate and when technically the initiator of hostilities also the ostensible cause.

Just as an incrementally aggravated structural or substantive divergence among parties is apt to propel them toward war, so the party suffering from asymmetrically adverse military-technological developments will incline toward preventive war rather than a separate peace. A preventive war as policy raises issues revolving less around its essential morality than the empirical possibility of projecting apparently adverse present trends reliably into the future and the ethical responsibility of a present generation for resolving hypothetical conditions on behalf of its successors. Leadership of the Soviet Union chose uncoerced capitulation over resort to a preventive war in that it failed to confront the United States with the prospect-to-certainty of war as the faltering party's sole remaining alternative to a peaceable recasting of the real political and military-technological state of things. This revolutionary change from classic statecraft was a signal of still more fundamental alterations in world politics, a deviance wholly at variance with the geohistorical authenticity of the Cold War as a conflict in the land–sea power tradition structurally and in terms of essayed strategies operationally. One reason for the disjunction—attenuating without annulling the deviance—is located within the framework of the schism itself. It points to the schism's imperfection on both economic grounds (the absence of politically manifested competition within a common type of economic system) and geostrategic grounds (insufficiently immediate threat from rear-continental China to the Soviet would-be amphibious central power and inadequately triggering potential of the Soviet Union's "last and indispensable" allies-satellites). Other and extraneous reasons were two and converging: first, the nuclear factor, not so much in and of itself but as impacting on, second, the institution of the state and quality of statecraft. An ideologically caused substitution of a particular social system for the state as the core stake or value on the part of the Soviet leadership exceeded in its consequences the historically undeveloped sense of statehood on the American side. A consequently weak statist ethos on both sides combined with restraint from the nuclear weaponry to produce at best a simulation of classic statecraft in regard to its tenets as well as operations. A thus doubly "as if" statecraft was consequently satisfied with reenacting tendencies when pretending to transformations traditionally pursued or achievable only by war. In the process, the imitative statecraft failed to exploit the restraining effect of the nuclear factor to recast—the American to concede even more than the Soviet to abandon—historically prohibitive objectives, such as supplementing military-technological with geopolitical parity, that used to be unacceptable for militarily-technologically obsolete demographic and other organic reasons. Thus, just as the continental military–maritime/mercantile schism, so also the power-normative essence was insufficiently operative to the extent that the nuclear factor stands for "power" and the statist spirit or mystique for "norm" without conclusively suggesting equivalent alternatives.[12]

Only contributory to in-depth appeasement other than one-sided renunciation are the techniques of conflict resolution, headed by negotiation, and the prerequisites of its efficacy headed by a two-sided conflict's at least tripartite dispersion or any deep-seated conflict's supersession by a more relevant contention. Over a still longer time span, a more hypothetical pathway to appeasement is a chain of comparable kinds of conflicts, such as the continental–maritime ones. For a chain of conflicts to have the effect of progressively easing the resolution of later conflicts, the earlier wars must be viewed as an agency co-responsible for changes converging in an altered moral-material environment because they extend from the specifics of (functionally diversified) structures and (diminishingly "real," resource- rather than role-centered) stakes to changed attitudes. Successive wars will then have provided less an unbreakable precedent for a repetition than a psychological impediment and covertly accumulating ultimate politico-military deterrent. The plausibility of the peace-through-wars scenario grows when the crucial events, compressed in both time and space, migrate from the global continental–maritime to the regional theater such as the post-World War II Middle East. It becomes a matter of emphasis whether the terminal phase of the Middle Eastern pacifications, following the cumulative effects of the several rounds of anterior local wars, is assigned to the deactivation of the Cold War or to the consequences of another regional and real (the Persian Gulf) war. In any event, neither supersession of the conflict by another more "relevant" one nor its dispersion among three or more distinct participants would have significantly accelerated the timetable of peace through war-making in this most classic of the contemporary balance-of-power theaters, were it not for the changes in the balance of (actually available or prospectively anticipated) resources and risks (to be incurred by war or assumed for peace) that has resulted from the repeal of the larger conflict.[13]

A special and controversial place in conflict resolution belongs to neutrality—or, during the Cold War, nonalignment and neutralism, ostensibly aimed at preventing nuclear war between the two alliance systems. The question whether either variety significantly contributed to this objective is one that can be usefully generalized into that of an optimum pro-peace distribution of alliance-saturated and alliance-free space. This query had commonly been attributed an answer hostile to alliance-wrought polarization in connection with World War I before engendering the opposite speculation in the practice of the Cold War while encountering unusual difficulties with respect to the period's brands of neutrality. Minimizing the practical result of the difference between the politically relatively passive stance of the nonaligned and the more active one of the neutralists with respect to their pacificatory intentions or only platforms was the feature common to both: radical inferiority in material assets to be thrown into the contest or annexed by either of the principal contestants with sufficiently conclusive effect to raise the real political weight of the neutrals above an occasional diplomatic salience that was only tolerated or also promoted by the principals for their own particular reasons. Lastingly more important is the consequence of the progressive diminution of interstate wars among both neutral and aligned Third World countries after decolonization and before the subsidence of also the central contention. This particular "appeasement" is relevant for the constant-sum-of-violence hypothesis and the related minimum or optimum of structured interactor conflict. The first part of the thesis is validated to the extent that the successive diminutions were being ever more manifestly offset by growing inter-factional turmoil within many of the one-time neutrals in particular. The second part achieves plausibility when ostensibly substituting concerns with domestic political stability and economic prosperity—i.e., political economy—for the real politically primary, war-peace issue caused a developmental arrest in the systemic crystallization of the relevant parts of the arena.[14]

Unlike termination of conflict by capitulation, resolution, or neutralist interposition, a deliberate strategy for in-depth appeasement of the environment shifts the focus from termination of war to its prevention by rethinking the phenomenon and reshaping the process of expansion. Subordinating perceptions of unprovoked expansionism of an adversary to a deliberate expansion of the strategy-relevant arena and agenda will introduce new factors and forces apt to engender additional countervailing assets or new common concerns into the strategic calculation. This expansion will be sufficient if it allows for satisfying the legitimate part of the rival's urge for parity while incidentally impeding any residual urge for predominance. It will simultaneously extend the relevant time span for realizing the measure of convergence in foreign policy techniques and domestic political orders that are usual between parties to a prolonged contention short of war. Such a strategy will compound the benefits accruing during a war from either dispersion of participants or supersession of the casus belli by new concerns in a restructured balance of power, always provided that an unconventional approach to appeasement can reverse the conventional view of the conflict. For a land–sea power conflict or any comparable contention, such a reversal will mean, first, assigning at least as much responsibility for the rivalry to the insular or otherwise more favored actor because of what it represents, a generally desirable combination of assets and attributes, rather than what it actually does or did. And second, allocating a large part of guilt on the part of the continental or any other comparably disadvantaged protagonist to what it fears from the eastern rear-continental or any other immediately threatening third power than what it covets from the conspicuously adversarial party. It is this combination of guilt and innocence that makes for the authentically tragic nature of great wars, wholly distinct from the human suffering they engender.

Replacing countervailance of a presumptively unprovoked and insatiable expansionist at the right point in time (e.g., more suitably before 1914 than 1939 relative to Germany, and in the 1980s rather than early 1950s relative to the Soviet Union) with expanding the environment of strategies so as to deliberately target foreign policies at domestic consequences is more than an adventurous or also unprincipled diplomatic sleight of hand: it is a way of exiting a fatal entanglement through the door of a broadly defined political economy of world politics that encompasses real politics but is not exhausted by its dynamics.[15]

Conflictual dynamics in geopolitics vs. dilemmas of causality and their resolutions in geoeconomics

Real politics is a matter of equilibration among more antagonistic than accommodating actors concerned directly with war and peace. Political economy is made up of inter-determination of more complementary than discordant external/systemic, economic, and internal/domestic factors, in keeping with its less direct and determinate relation to stability and prosperity. Given the ambiguous relationship between war-and-peace and stability-and-prosperity phenomena, the inter-determining factors are unequally real political. Real politics being manifest in intense and ultimately violent conflict, it can also occur among warring states or militant social groups over economic stakes. Therefore, it can pertain to not only the systemic, or external, but also the domestic, or internal, factors and arena, provided this arena operates and is analyzed in terms of societal actors engaged in competition capable of escalating into revolution just as states are of conflict climaxing in war. When domestic politics is less crystallized in terms of group or class structure and less antagonistic in terms of goals and strategies, routine interplays of various, including economic, interests can impact political economy through a domestic factor as diffuse and indeterminate as public opinion. It is this less real-political domestic factor that differs most from the systemic, or international, factor as one habitually or typically conflictual. In terms of another fundamental distinction, the economic factor subdivides into material sustenance as a matter of organically constituted capability, usable in war, and operational transactions involving economic interests and relating to prosperity as a degree of material well-being exceeding the sustenance minimum in peacetime.

When connecting the several factors with the war-and-peace and stability-and-prosperity phenomena, the essentially formal process of causation or, more appropriately, causal inter-determination arbitrates between the substantively real political processes of antagonization and stabilization for or against peace and prosperity. Inter-determination means that all the factors affect one another in overall causation. The more indistinguishable is the individual impact of the several factors and the less distinguishable is cause from effect, the more circular is the causation. To disentangle this circularity, practically significant distinctions are as important for political economy as those between preeminence and hegemony and parity and equality are for real politics.

Foremost is the essentialist distinction between organic and operational facets of reality, translating respectively into ultimate and proximate causation. "Organic" is the cumulatively integrated material and sociopolitical substance—material capability and domestic order—representing an actualized or only latent potential; "operational" relates to competitive action and reaction centered on interests and transactions to be managed in the relatively short run but with corresponding urgency. The organic dimension is ultimately determinant positively and negatively: positively because action will reflect and aim to promote, while its efficacy depends on, the integrated sum of the organic entity's constituents; negatively because these constituents need to be at least residually assured against irreparable damage as a condition of continuing capacity to resume action in due course. The operational determinant is by contrast proximate insofar as, subject to these reservations, immediate circumstances will compel and shape instant responses. They will do so to optimize longer-range capacity to shield the organic potential against direct threats and challenges while foreign policy success will have a benign, failure a malignant, short- or medium-term effect on either material capability or domestic order.

Another and directly related key distinction is between spatial and temporal aspects of causation. Empirically identifiable location of principal crisis in this or that factor and on this or that plane of politics is a quasi-spatial determinant. This schematic approach to and potential resolution of the causal dilemma relate readily to a systemic perspective, applied when determinative primacy is attributed to, or inferred from, the kind of system or order, presumed as it were a priori to entail causal primacy: a state system of the external/systemic and a pluralist-societal order of domestic and economic factors. Unlike the figuratively spatial differentiation of determinants in terms of the "location" of crisis, the temporal one disarticulates circular into consecutive causal primacy or at least operational salience. As part of this temporalization, antecedent and immediate causation supplements ultimate organic and proximate operational determination. The conceptually most abstract or generic aspect of this dimension is the regressive chain of causation, wherein the causal efficacy of any one factor is the consequence of another factor's prior primacy. More specific is the consecutively materializing circuit of military, economic, and administrative functions in forming actors. Finally, most conspicuous is the sequentially graduated interlock of systemic, domestic, and economic determinants, each primary or salient at different moments in a prolonged career of expansion of major actors. Actor formation relates more closely to the organic dimension in terms of both object and product of the process; expansion is linked more directly to the process's operational procedure, though not so equally for all the determinants. By the same token, the cumulative creation of an organic determinant over the long run differs in degree only from the operational one unfolding consecutively over the short or medium term.

Not unlike what is the case in the other relationships of the several factors, including the domestic and systemic, no simplifying formulation will resolve the complex inter-determination of economics and real politics affecting their relative operational salience. Not if the simplification occurs in terms of the actual role of either as the instrument or the determinant of the other, or in terms of however plausible an analogy contrasting (conservatively) mercantilistic from (liberally) progressivist principles, applicable to both real politics and economics.

When salient crisis revolves around prosperity as the condition of domestic political stability, economic capability as something "organic"—an incrementally evolved and internally coherent momentary given—is in its determinative impact exceeded by economic transactions engaging immediate group interests. When external security is at stake, the contrary causal hierarchy favors material capability as the geographically or situationally conditioned economic basis of power, reducing economic interests and particular transactions to derivative or auxiliary status and secondary if not peripheral agenda. Much the same applies to the distinction betwen determinant and instrument that defines the actual, as opposed to the analogical, relation of politics and economics. Economics is a means to and instrument of political ends in the context—and perceptual prism—favoring the statist principle. This relationship is reversed in favor of the economic determinant in a context or conceptual prisms favorable to the societal principle. In terms of peace- and wartime means and ends, however, maximizing economic capability is in itself the proximate end, antecedent to advancing effectively a variety of political objectives in peacetime. It is more clearly only the means to one paramount end in wartime. Overarching these differences is one between two contrasting states or tendencies: in the real political statist setting toward an ultimately inescapable link between the (political-)economic and (military-)political object of policy, and toward their disconnection in the societal-pluralist setting centered on stability and prosperity. Societal pluralism lacks, or aims to abolish, the critical war/peace-related linkage between material resource/sustenance and political role/status that compels self-interested strategies of risk assumption or avoidance designed to correct insufficient coincidence and contrive coherence between the essentially economic (resource) and political (role) dimensions.

Interconnections such as these are sufficiently intractable to encourage deceptively simplified ideologies and doctrines to elevate analogical similarities between (mercantilistic vs. liberal progressivist) economics and comparable politics into law-like causal priorities: replace mutual determination with one-sided determinism in a "solution" of the dilemmas, on a par with the cruder forms of political/systemic determinism in radical structuralism. Applying economic determinism to the war-peace issue is not content with tentative hypotheses concerning causation of wars in function of alternating expansion and contraction in long economic cycles or with structural discrepancy between economic core and periphery as opposed to the politicized economics-relevant land–sea power schism. It escalates to the dogmatic certainties of ideologies when the free market capitalist attributes war to economic underdevelopment of weak states in particular, while the Marxist–Leninist collectivist blames monopolistic overdevelopment of especially the greater powers. Proponents of both ideologies would eliminate war among parties that have realized the economic theories and applied the policies peculiar to them in correspondingly "liberal" or "socialist" sociopolitical orders and institutions.

Such simplicities contrast with the highly mixed historical record of recurrent postwar designs for a "new" international politics or diplomacy, starting with the early-eighteenth century Peace of Utrecht if not earlier, to rest on a combination of reformed national and international economics and upgraded interstate organization. It is no more reliable to postulate a necessary connection between economic development (i.e., prosperity) and political democracy (i.e., stability). This kind of simplification, too, ignores the historical counter-example of connections between industrialization (and stabilization) and authoritarian political (and mercantilistic economic) order from seventeenth century England through nineteenth-twentieth century Germany and Japan to today's Singapore. Simplifying the relationship implicitly downgrades the theoretically crucial difference between eventual (or long-term) positive consequences—presumptively of the liberal-progressivist kind—and intervening (middle-term) extra-economic, including cultural and sociopolitical, complications with often negative real political implications. The problem of political-economic inter-determination is solved least when Marxist–Leninist "socialism" attributes imperial expansion narrowly to economic stimuli (of overproduction and underconsumption) and anti-Marxist liberal capitalism to wholly political or at least sociopolitical incentives (ranging from quest for statist prestige to ex-ruling class atavisms). More to the point are alternations of systemic and domestic political determinants variably fused with and disconnected from economic incentives at different stages of expansion. Thus also, when both ideologies equate evolution with their version of either linear or dialectically achieved progress, they stand opposed to value-neutral sequential progression. This progression does allow for, but does not necessarily entail, a progressively escalating shift from power to plenty and warfare to welfare, implicit in the increase of domestic over external functions of government and, concurrently, organic over operational dimensions of interactor real politics. Such "real" changes are directly or indirectly favorable to economics in a reversible trend not to be confused with the transformation of warring into trading states, conceived of as typologically contrary developmental extremes.

An analogical is preferable to the ideological approach if the economic is to be doctrinally related to the political factor but retain operational relevance—i.e., concern not only or mainly ideal purposes but also patterns of actual policies. A close connection between analogy and actuality exists when mercantilistic politics operates on the assumption of a constant and therefore only conflictually divisible sum of security, incapable of the expansion and equal distribution by cooperative organization posited by the political counterpart to free-trading liberal economics. Mercantilistic politics in a fully developed state system corresponds to the historical role of economic mercantilism in the creation of internally unified post-medieval/pluralist polities and to the subsequent diversion of their strategic interactions into those between post-mercantilist liberal sea powers and still-mercantilist pre-liberal continental powers. Integrating the mercantilistic variety of politics together with the economic factor as such into the political economy of world politics favors its non-ideologically "realistic" over a purposively "utopian" representation. Accommodating thus the existential dimension preserves the normative one by allowing for the injection of communitarian solidarity into the pragmatic-economic norm of utility within a broadly ethical perspective on real politics. The obverse is counterposing societal materialism, a degeneration of societal-pluralist and economic-utilitarian pragmatism diametrically opposed to the romantic variety of realism, with a form of moralism that partakes less of political realism of any, including the philosophical and progressivist, kind than of politicized religiosity of a pietist-pacifist kind.[16]

Real political and economic factors coalesce readily in the statist context while gravitating asunder in the model of politics standing for plenty and stability rather than power and security. Whereas the latter vision centers on functions and institutions, the former emphasizes structures and strategy. The two ideal-typical models or visions actually overlap at the edges in the distinctive role they assign to economics as instrument (material capability) as opposed to objective (prosperity), while each of them composes a set of rationally construed and comprehensible features into a coherent representation of a distinctive political geometry. A purely interstate conflict is propelled in one of them by or will likely result in a polarity along a linear axis, prone to strategy-wrought triangular configuration, in the political geometry corresponding to the structural-strategic statist model. Conversely, different degrees of integration respond to or implement a tendency to concentricity within contiguous or overlapping circular areas. These are prone to a more fundamental triadic interplay, that of state, society, and different types of economy, in a political geometry germane to the functional-institutional pluralist as opposed to the structural-strategic statist model or vision. Conjointly, the ideal of solidarity within the orbit of integrative association, implicit in community (or mere confederation), modifies to some extent the pragmatic utilitarian bias peculiar to societal pluralism. The balance between drives and restraints along the power-normative continuum is most strik-

ingly revised in the functional-institutional model. Institutional constraints on the newly surfacing economic drives, mediated through
expanded functions, replace therein restraints from countervailing power
(which implement state autonomy as the supreme value in a setting of
physical insecurity) with checks from integration (which translate ultimate interdependence for socioeconomic stability into the value of solidarity). But the fact of ultimate interdependence does not, or not
immediately or necessarily, raise the solidarity ideal to the level attained
by the state idea when, mediated through self-sacrificial patriotism, it ele-
vates the existential instinct of self-preservation to the status of moral
inspiration.

Within an altered drive-restraint interplay, the operational unity and
primacy of politics as the coordinating agency can be reestablished only
through political economy acquiring increased salience over real politics.
Consequently, the economic factor is integrated into the newly complex
equilibrium via the attraction of more prosperous to less well-endowed
actors, potentially muting the revulsion superior power causes in politico-
militarily weaker agents. World political dynamic comprises henceforth
the economic factor not only as a factor of power, usable for politico-
military balancing in a field of forces. Through its relative deficiency in
the less prosperous country, the economic factor will coincidentally reinforce the attractive effect of a power vacuum on the more prosperous and
therefore powerful actor, favoring its expansion. This powerful attraction
will offset such an actor's attractiveness as a source of prosperity for the
weaker party to a degree that will calibrate its response in terms of
narrowly construed power politics. A multi-functionally interlocking
action-reaction agenda takes place within the henceforth only loosely
constraining formal mold of a revised, circular-cum-concentric as opposed to linear-cum-polar, political geometry.[17]

Control aims and circuitous effects vs. actual correspondences in causal determination of domestic and systemic factors

Central to integrating the economic factor through the domestic one into
world politics is reducing domestic to a common denominator with foreign politics. This reduction implies qualitatively identical motivation of
actors, social groups as much as states, involved in comparable power-
and interest-centered dynamics decisive for degrees of political stability
cum economic prosperity—and enacted operationally by interplays
among such actors rather than engendered organically by integration of
the several factors. As a matter of structure-related fact rather than principle, the domestic plane affects action on the external plane most in a
loosely articulated permissive—societal pluralist—environment. Determi-

native is the interplay among social classes or political factions engaged in competition for dominance over, or at least participation in, the political process. The implied contest over succession, peculiar to all politics, concerns the role or status of the contending groups within a developmentally changing configuration of their strengths and weaknesses, societal utility or redundance if not dysfunctionality. The external determinant is conversely stronger than the domestic in statist actors and grows for both unitary and pluralist polities as the structure of the environment crystallizes and its propensity to crisis increases. In the particular case of statist-pluralist hybrids such as empires, relatively insulated from systemic impact at their height, the balance of determinative weight will return to the environment only with the empire's relative weakening that stops short of the empire's dissolution.

In a statist environment, circular inter-determination between the domestic and systemic, internal and external, factors is conspicuous in medium-intensity contentions among near-equal powers allowing for pragmatic-to-opportunistic manipulation of either interclass or interactor balances of power. Circularity achieves a maximum of complexity when it interweaves domestic and systemic with economic factors between unequal powers, interacting on a relatively low level of crisis intensity over diverse or diffuse stakes. To the extent that efficient causality migrates inward, this is in keeping with the general tendency attending more routine than revolutionary processes and transactions. They typically engage economic or cultural or similarly directly nonstrategic stakes and issues transacted managerially rather than strategically over periods of time that are not dramatically compressed by acute crisis. The resulting state of the overall environment will have little direct or immediate effect on actor security or interactor succession, and only an indirect and unpredictable effect on domestic stability.

A significant instance of this type of activity is the international politics of economic assistance, engaging major powers with actual or potential clients in a complex of interactor alliance and intraactor coalition agendas. In the relatively contentious external setting of a cold war at its peak, the international or systemic determinant intruded on the domestic stimulant more—or more directly and instantly—than would be the case in conditions conducive to a purely apolitical economic assistance for development and stability. By the same token, the outside environment impacted more forcefully the actions and attitudes of the imperial-to-"imperialistic" donors and the domestic environment of most of the "neo-colonized" recipients. Such and comparable conditions will be constrained by military-political alliances as a primarily real political/systemic factor, but only loosely. Entering into and managing alliances with a view to fairly rigorous if not necessarily precise or reliable calculations of both material and immaterial, internal and external, costs and benefits or gains and losses, is formally part of the political economy of world politics. Though associated with the security-driven statist framework, alliances actually only crystallize the perceptual prism of participants in a much wider network of politico-economic intra- and cross-country coalitions, intended to foster domestic stability favorable to either and more commonly the stronger (i.e., the donor's) party to the uneven relationship. The associated issue of comparative degrees of one-sided or reciprocal control revolve not least—i.e., do ultimately—around interclass succession. Accordingly, the complex circularity of domestic and systemic determinants is expressed operationally in unevenly reciprocal manipulation of the relationship by two unequally independent and interdependent parties across two distinct but closely overlapping (domestic and external) spheres.

Determining the balance of domestic and external determinants for the weaker (specifically the recipient) party and the potency of the external impetus acting on the stronger (specifically donor) side are the two parties' comparative levels of external security concerns and the preponderant bias—tendency or purpose—of the horizontal (inter-elite) and vertical (elite-mass) coalitions to either support or overthrow the weaker party's established order convergently with or divergently from the intent and interest of the stronger side. At issue is the consonance or dissonance of external or "other-directed" and internal or "inner-directed" impulses acting within domestic and external balances of power and associated with security, stability, and succession. The more the perceived importance of the interclass or -elite succession issue exceeds that of external security on the part of the weak party (actual/potential recipient), the more will the domestic determinant overshadow the external on its part, enhancing the control potential of the stronger party (actual/potential donor). The stronger is the security-related external incentive and policy determinant of the stronger party, the lower will be its control potential and ability to discriminate between ideologically or otherwise more or less congenial or acceptable cross-country domestic allies. The determinant leans, conversely, toward the domestic, while the stronger party's control potential decreases further, when inter-country affinities of a cultural or ideological kind have grown in importance. Control by the stronger party vanishes and migrates toward the weaker side when impulses and incentives originating in external security and intercountry affinity coincide and reinforce one another.

Involving various kinds of alliances and coalitions in the effort of constraining circular inter-determination of factors pertaining to political economy has a paradoxical effect. It surfaces real complexities from the deceptively straightforward formulations centered on the only metaphorically quasi-economic strategic gains and losses pertaining to the abstractly generic political economy of alliances themselves.

A comparatively tense or relaxed alliance situation reflects the level of international security crisis. It will determine on the substantive-to-material and primarily interactor plane the proportions of political-military pressures and economic payments (inducements) emanating from the alliance- or coalition-builder that are necessary and sufficient for first originating and subsequently maintaining a particular alliance. Similarly conditioned—or determined—will be alliance readiness, i.e., the capacity for entering and disposition to enter a particular alliance, and the alliance value of especially the lesser party or parties. On the less substantive than symbolic level and less inter- than intraactor plane, the economic payments and military-political pressures and the readiness for and value of an alliance are only supplemented or actually supplanted by pressures toward malformations or deformations originated from within or without. One malformation results from premature entry into an alliance or inducement to enter it before a sufficiently well-defined internal identity has conferred the capacity for extending the self externally; another is due to unduly delayed—i.e., too long denied—access or admission to alliance in general or a specific alliance in particular. The former deformation scenario has conduced to chaotic domestic political fragmentation of many a weak or less developed country; the latter contributed to authoritative-to-authoritarian domestic political concentration of several politically and economically more fully developed and larger parties (such as Japan and Germany in modern times). One of the deformations will not be fully compensated by even superior economic payments, the other not completely undone by superior economic performance. Intimately related in the first instance is the extent of economic development, including the efficacy of the political elite in bringing it about, and in the second the nature of political change, including its toleration by the ruling class. The efficacy or the tolerance will decide whether relatively conservative (and defensive) or revolutionary (or offensive) mindsets and procedures will shape horizontal-and-equal inter-elite and vertical-and-unequal elite-mass domestic coalitions and condition their overlaps and interactions with interactor alignments.

Finally, formal differences and actual overlaps can extend—or be speculatively extended—to types of alliances differentiated less by their internal political economy of strategic costs and benefits and more by their relation to more substantive global political economy. One such alliance type aggregates multiple and changing functions within a consensus-fostering political coalition characteristic of economically developed pluralist societies. Another type is that of real politically combative and unstable alliances. These confine functional plurality to functionally mobile disparate elites—civilian, military, and technocratic—unevenly capable or uniformly incapable of stabilizing polities that are economically only incipiently developing and only primitively pluralist.[18]

When the interplay between domestic/economic and systemic factors gravitates to relations among more equal great powers, intensifying correspondingly is the strategic modifier of the structural and functional basis of inter-determination. Strategy-dependent alternatives correct for the limitations of the simplistic liberal-ideological extrapolation of foreign from domestic politics if not also interactor from intraactor structures, while potentially embracing the extrapolation's positive thrust toward in-depth appeasement. Just as real political relative to economic, so systemic relative to domestic determinants are compelling in proportion to the degree of crystallization of the environment in terms of the predominant type of actors (states vs. societies) in general and schismatically related land and sea powers specifically. They "act"—affect the agenda—via the consequently uneven impact from the interactor structures, and their "effects" are incidental to the constraining vs. permissive, schism-bound or -indifferent, state of such structures. Lowest in the scale of "determined" connections between domestic and foreign politics is a substantive foreign policy strategy calculated to achieve particular domestic consequences in another powerful polity without recourse to direct intervention—i.e., circuitously. This external-internal linkage ranks below not only the causal priority or primacy of domestic politics, but also the correspondence between domestic structures and basic foreign policy postures. It surpasses only a formally analogical link, such as one between the contest over nonaligned countries by two major antagonists and the electoral competition over the floating vote by two major political parties.

In the circuitous variety of strategic as opposed to structural determination or mere conditioning, policies replace polities, influence replaces impact, and intentions take the place of incidence while deliberate coordination between domestic and foreign policies or politics substitutes for either one-sided causation or coincidental correspondence. Setting the stage for its peculiar relevance in relations between equal powers, the circuitous approach is intimated when a stronger power affects or tries to affect the domestic politics, including intergroup coalitions, and consequently foreign policies of weaker polities inaccessible to more direct forms of control. In such a case, "remote" control in country A is the possible result of demonstrating sufficient consistency in comparable countries B and C to compel inference as an alternative to open interference in the target state. This type of "control" differs not only from direct control via virtual or actual coercion, but also and more significantly from indirect control via attempted cooptation of an actually governing or a favored oppositional clique. Whereas direct control is most certain but may end up being most costly, indirect control is less reliable when a favored foreign policy is to be elicited via revising a domestic political structure and hierarchy, because of the insufficient transparency and consequent manageability of the targeted societal pluralism. Remote control is, if anything, still more unreliable in either a pluralist or a statist context due to two equally potent difficulties: to maintain strict consistency with respect to any one country because of changing circumstances and variety of specific objectives, and to cultivate inferences across countries inevitably different in particulars unrelated to or irrelevant for the control effort's principal purpose.[19]

Differently problematic and even less often intentional will be the effort to shape the domestic consequences of foreign policies among great powers, typically equal in capabilities if likewise commonly differentiated situationally along the West–East and corresponding maritime–continental axes. The circuitous approach is historically as rare as is the strategy of in-depth appeasement it might implement, because it is contingent on extraordinary historical intelligence ostensibly contrary to although ideally always complementary with strategic rationality and occasionally corrective of its rationales. Wholly deliberately aimed at internal effects would be the permissive strategy of a preeminent (Western-maritime) power, as distinct from structure of the environment, that conceded geopolitical parity to its (Eastern-continental) rival. In such a strategy, actual concessions replace potential control as part of detente, devolution substitutes for denial, and co-optation substitutes for confrontation. As opposed to containment of the presumptive expansionist, decompression of the environment is the means of producing a corresponding relaxation of domestic structures and consequent foreign strategies of the target state. The latter is encouraged to pursue functional efficacy within a perceptually, functionally, and (relative to a third party) strategically expanded space under the impetus of political liberalization and societal pluralization. Even when offset by this potential reward, the speculative real political risk attaching to the strategy of geopolitical concessions cannot be ruled out. The risk will be commonly lessened by the reluctance of a possessor to concede incrementally more than a safe margin of advantage to a claimant in exchange for either legitimating or stabilizing what it retains, for fear of emboldening the rival to seek more at once and enabling it to usurp everything eventually.[20]

The hypothesis of circuitous determination of domestic politics by foreign policies postulates a connection between the legitimate domestic order and successful foreign policy while drawing on the conceptually fundamental distinction between proximate operational and ultimate organic determinants. In so doing, the hypothesis touches on both the salient and the subjacent phenomena crucial to world politics. It bears directly on the phenomenon of war and peace (including responsibility for war and its avoidance) and the associated processes of antagonization and appeasement. It bears indirectly on the phenomena of domestic stability and prosperity and the corresponding processes of stabilization and destabilization (entailing societal materialization and statist immaterialization of politics). Implicit is a two-fold expansion and disarticulation of the real-political balance of power. The first expansion is into a tripartite balance structurally and strategically by including the consideration of a third party, the mere existence of which may encourage and ascendancy impel conciliation through concessions to the second party. The second expansion is into a dual-to-plural balance functionally and institutionally by explicitly including the domestic in the systemic perspective and adding a societal and economic to the military-political statist dimension. Moreover, as if relations between domestic and systemic determinants were insufficiently subject to specific crises, structures, or strategies directing them toward causation, correspondences, or circuitous interactions, these relations are complicated further by distinctive value-institutional or cultural factors and orders. Associated with ways of integrating or malintegrating structure and evolutionary stage with "spirit" along the West–East or North–South axis, conservative and liberal emphases point to differently realist or utopian extrapolations of the power-normative essence of politics within its operational unity. In its many manifestations that are easier to dissect or categorize analytically than convincingly apprehend and describe in concrete instances, the internal-external relationship asserts itself also in this connection as an elusive but crucial focus around which to order world politics and an opaque but inescapable prism through which to perceive its political economy.[21]

Correspondences between structures and foreign policy postures

Reciprocal causation of domestic and systemic factors in the shaping of particular foreign policies differs from parallel international and internal/domestic structures that jointly condition more basic foreign policy postures. Articulating interactive dynamics in terms of the location of crises and related concerns yields simultaneously to the both easier and more difficult task of identifying the (structural) patterns and the (policy) postures, whose temporal coincidences and substantive correspondences permit no more than plausible correlations. Moving thus from ambiguously reciprocal determination to correlation-capable correspondences displaces open-ended empirical analysis to a special kind of schematic approach centered on crises. The approach is "special" because it substantiates the abstractly spatial location of crisis in any one of the factors and levels of inter-determination by historically recurrent concrete situations that also add the temporal facet of a patterned evolutionary progression to the peripatetic migration of crisis from factor to factor and level to level. Consequently, the approach projects inter-determinative circularity one step toward consecutive causal priorities most prominent in the determinants of expansion.

Unevenly centralized and pluralist domestic and systemic structures coincide with a historically evidenced multi-stage cycle of unevenly expansive and conservative foreign policy postures over an entire evolutionary trajectory. A consequence follows: the location and intensity of particular crises in either the domestic or the international arena forfeit some of the policy-determinative primacy they have in the scenario concerned with particular foreign policies. Moreover, since the process attends the different phases of actor formation, the domestic and related systemic structures corresponding to the successive external postures conform necessarily with a continuum comprising unitary statist and pluralist societal forms in both evolutionary directions: from a rudimentary kind of pluralism to statism and beyond statism to institutionalized forms of pluralism, parallel to the emergence, prominence, and decay of central and centralizing authority.

Providential-to-transcendent precepts impart fictitious coherence to inchoate societal pluralism in the initially unfocused expansive foreign policy posture before the statist feature can assert itself, in the next-following commitment of strategy to consolidation of a viable polity, and mend a chronic disparity between vast ends and limited means that, accentuating the tendency to dissolution, substitutes for the external restraints of an operative balance of power. Thereafter, a statist management of an incipiently enterprising sociopolitical and -economic pluralism substitutes legal fictions such as sovereignty and concepts such as reason of state for the transcendental precepts, while thus supplementing a still fragile institutional structure and narrow sociopolitical basis of stability. An initial crystallization of the systemic structure allows for permeability around consolidation-capable parties, stimulated to mutual balancing by the conspicuous ascent of one among them within a region. A thus internationally reinforced structure and legitimacy of internal authority constrains a newly exuberant sociopolitical pluralism, impelling it toward a more efficiently focused expansionist phase than was the incipiently expansive one. A self-sustaining balance of power dynamic that has evolved at the core of the emergent system supplements the domestic incentives to diverting typically paraofficial and private energies and activities

toward the less-crystallized periphery. Coincidental with the next-following, conservative balance-of-power, foreign policy posture is internally a statist-pluralist mix biased toward authoritative-to-authoritarian
statism in continental powers and increasingly toward societal pluralism
in the sea powers. This developmentally climactic midpoint posture is
more congenial to the maritime polities, precisely because they are by
now endowed with sufficiently developed internal pluralism capable of
engendering simultaneously or alternately (material) resources and (political) restraints: the former for external balancing as well as expanding, the
latter against its various possible perversions and malapplications. Both
will be at a premium in a widening international/systemic structure that
combines declining founders—apt to ideologize the balance of power in
favor of the legitimacy of static incumbents—with rising founders because
previously slower-developing peripheral actors are anxious to reactivate
competitive balancing before institutionalizing it within a more open and
dynamic concert of powers.

A reformist-to-revolutionary domestic authority reasserts-to-overex-
tends the statist formula coincidentally with a final expansionist foreign
policy posture, compulsive rather than the spontaneously expansive initial
or exuberantly climactic ones. On the part of continental powers, this
posture reacts typically to a provocatively denial-oriented balancing/con-
taining strategy of a maritime-mercantile power and, on the latter's more
typically than the continentals' part, to indications of impending decline.
Contributing will be either the antecedent inability to evolve domestic
pluralism, typically by a continental state, or consolidate it sufficiently to
ensure domestic stability and prosperity on the part of a sea power in
particular.

The international structure, biased toward polarization along several
axes, affects the foreign policy posture significantly for the last time at this
point, after alternating between one decreasingly permissive (congenial to
expansive and exuberant foreign policy postures) and one increasingly
constraining (reflected in consolidative, conservative, and compulsive
postures). Characteristic of the subsequent and terminal foreign policy
posture, that of withdrawal from self-dependent policies, is an indifferent-
to-supportive international structure and situation, depending on the self-
help requirements of still-active powers. The structure is indifferent, when
it is stalemated between two or more such powers; supportive, when it is
represented by one preeminent power. A withdrawal posture coincides
with inter-factionally particularist domestic structure that subordinates
"ideal" statism on the elite level to societal materialism on the vertical
interclass level and an effective foreign policy oriented to security to a
simulated one oriented to stability.[22]

Economic and domestic vs. systemic determinants in war-peace cycles and consecutively protracted expansion

The tendency for domestic politics to bestow prominence upon the economic factor will only modify or virtually nullify "pure" real politics of interacting forces. It is most graphically evidenced by a continental state when, engaged in the foreign policy posture of the withdrawal stage, it perversely approximates the naturally insulated and protected stance of an oceanic-insular polity. As strands of policies and constituents of polities, domestic political and functionally economic factors will in both instances be most intimately linked within the materially and value-institutionally organic dimension. Operationally, by contrast, real politics is linked more consistently and balanced more evenly with economics in domestic than in an interstate politics that is more insistently subject to instantly compelling geostrategic requisites of its "anarchic" makeup. On the latter plane, the economic factor as a matter of basic material sustenance (rather than politically stabilizing prosperity) within actors and material capability (rather than economic transactions or even systems) among them is prominent only variably, but is always present in the multi-phase coincidences of foreign policy postures with extensively construed domestic structures. By contrast, the domestic factor is at best implied as a mediating mechanism when domestic stresses from economic contraction are militantly projected outward.

Although equally broadly conceptualized, this set of processes is, despite its limitations, operationally more focused than one supposed to relate major foreign policy alternatives of war and peace identifiably to long-term cycles of expansion and contraction in the world economy, without explicit mediation through the full range of real political factors including the domestic. The domestic facet is, finally, bracketed out wholly in a self-consciously anti-reductionist structuralism, while the economic component, only implied in the attribution of superior stability to bipolarity rather than multipolarity, is kept in reserve for fuller integration into a post-bipolar multipolar situation as the one and only acceptable qualitative nuance in a decreasingly illuminating quantitative definition of structure. By contrast, no less than the economic, the domestic factor is explicitly included together with the economic in a qualitatively differentiated analysis centered on the continental–maritime and the historically associated East–West schism. Beyond the generic coincidences between structures and postures, the parties to the schisms are causally related to distinctive forms of domestic regimes and politics (conservative-authoritarian vs. liberal-representative), peculiar (external vs. internal) priorities, (centralizing vs. decentralized) procedures in both politics and economics, and principal (security- vs. prosperity-centered) preoccupations. Covering the corresponding spectra, these differences are projected directly into external politics that feed back into the domestic agenda as the mediating factor.

All the factors—systemic/strategic, domestic, and economic—must be released from atemporal circularity and "spatial" migration of crises into consecutively manifested priorities if the domestic factor is to be disclosed as actually causally determining in sequence with the other factors. The time dimension ascends to this end from an abstract status in a chain of causation to its opposite. In the former, depending on the extent of regression into the past, the domestic factor like all the others appears alternately as cause and consequence of the systemic or economic and vice versa. Such a chain's concrete opposite are the cumulatively fashioned actors, arenas, and agendas: actors as part of successively crystallizing outward-turned military, supportive economic, and internally integrating administrative functions; arenas and agendas when, unlike a self-isolating universal empire intent on ensuring internal stability, the several members' focus on individual security in a competitive interstatist system stimulates the successive emergence of enterprising national mercantile and worldwide free market economies.

The domestic factor realizes its potential to exercise causal primacy consecutively for the sake of a cumulatively produced organic result in the form of an enlarged (imperial) community when it acts as the primary determinant of expansion. Its temporary salience as the primary determinant is consistent with its functioning as a secondary determinant when the economic and systemic factors are primary—and the other way around, while chronologically first primary systemic determinant is the original one to which the domestic is, like the economic one, subsidiary. The domestic factor assumes determinant primacy relative to the international when the latter recedes at the point of passage from its push-related predatory and "offensive" to the pull-related preclusive and "defensive" phase, and from a limited-regional to a vaster global or grand empire in need of protection of its frontier. When predation and protection are replaced by projection of interclass stresses into the expansionary effect, the domestic factor can be primary relative to the economic factor, which blends with the international-systemic and domestic stimuli most intimately on two occasions. First is in the initial stage of forming, as part of resistance to a mortal threat to survival, a core polity that is viable in terms of both security and sustenance. Second is in the terminal phase of preserving the enlarged imperial polity as one capable of adaptation and survival. A "formative war imperialism" conjugates, concurrently with the initial stage, real political imperatives with economically productive instrumentalities in a war setting. At the later stage, "protective formalized imperialism" trades previously accumulated real political assets against economic concessions by weaker-to-dependent parties for the sake of buttressing an endangered domestic political stability and economic prosperity. The two similarly aggregated developmental opposites enframe a climactic "free-trading imperialism" as one causally primary for mainly informal expansion because it is inherently separable even when not actually separated from connection with its strategic framework and domestic basis. Throughout, the overall systemic environment functions critically as a source of either attraction (stimulating predation) or anxiety (compelling preclusion), and of opportunities for intervention to expand control in other countries—an inversely domestic incentive complementing preclusion.

When functioning as primary, the internal incentive to expansion reflects the universal concern of politics with succession within hierarchically modified equilibria—in the domestic context among social groups as an aspect of intergroup stabilization or destabilization coincidentally with processes of interfactor integration or disaggregation. The associated agenda revolves—as do all organizations in search of internal equilibrium—around (more or less pressing) needs, (more or less feasible) functions, and (more or less effective or efficacious) agencies for meeting the needs by performing the functions. In a perspective that embraces three major modalities and stages of intergroup or -class dynamics, the domestic determinant is alternately unitary statist and pluralist societal. It is the former when a relatively united will of a dominant social group (or society as a whole) is expressed in a strategy rationally responsive to outside conditions. It is the latter when competition among particular interest groups is projected abroad and the foreign (or imperial) policy represents either a dynamic equilibrium or a stalemated deadlock among such interests, unevenly or even erratically responsive to outside opportunities and constraints.

The prototype of the statist format of a domestic determinant is the "trusteeship" of an empire-constituent ruling class, exerting near-hegemony internally. Frequent actual coincidences do occur in particular times and places between a quasi-hegemonic political class position and a wider order-upholding hegemony of the polity it rules. Conceptually, however, the relation between the two kinds of hegemony is either one of merely a formal analogy or one of functional equivalence bridging two distinct spheres of activity. By the same token, the societal principle manifested through "transactions" between declining ruling and ascendant middle classes (a later-stage domestic determinant) matches an embattled interstate struggle over balance of power or hegemony. The ambiguously or alternately statist-and-societal expression and inspiration of the ruling class's terminal "trauma" (the third and last internal incentive) propels it toward alliance with the mass against the middle class challenger. It re-

sembles and will coincide with the predicament of a power facing imminent decline at the tail end of a hegemonic posture or on the verge of one
more bid for supremacy as part of a last-ditch defense against irreversible
loss of rank and role. Sharply different from either societal groups or
state-like actors are individuals, however prominent sociopolitically and
influential real-politically. Intergroup dynamic relegates them to a media-
tory role, as either the socially marginal "new men" whose co-optation
eases the midterm transactions between a receding ruling and the rising
middle class, or the politically marginal aristo-demagogues who exploit
their membership in the original ruling class to mediate its last-ditch defensive alliance with the populus. Just as the naked individual will not
effectively connect with the world community in politics without assistance from an intermediate form of social organization, so even an individual vested with extraordinary qualifying attributes will effectively
relate to the statist or societal whole only when mediating between its
subsidiary components.

Expansion into empire reveals the causal efficacy of the dynamic of
intergroup or -class succession best because an imperial polity connotes
an exceptionally dynamic unit of power, apt to insulate internal events
and their external effects most from outside influences in the form of
countervailing balance-of-power interactions. Incidentally upgraded is
the organic over the operational dimension in shaping ascent and decline
of any one actor relative to others. The inter-determinative circularity
between domestic and foreign politics is consequently least at the empire's
peak, only to reappear as it descends therefrom.[23]

Ordering the various determinants around the economic factor will
show that the conquest of a materially and psychopolitically viable habitat occurs typically for coequal and indistinguishable, or fused, objectives
of elementary security and sustenance. Thereafter, the economic factor
becomes gradually incidental to the concern with strategic security at the
center of the relevant system or space. Even aggressively pursued economic goods become a means to political power at home or abroad, and
the product or consequence of superior military power and skill. In historically recorded instances of the correspondingly denoted first stage,
that of formative war imperialism, an authoritative ruling class acted as a
trustee for the body politic and exercised a largely unfettered command
and control over community resources. In the second phase, identifiable
as one of informal free-trade or free-enterprise imperialism, the strategic
and economic factors are largely separate even while being variably interdependent. The strategic factors are more than ever autonomous in the
considerations of governmental policy makers responsible for the security
and coherence of the established order in a technologically or otherwise
changing environment. Economic concerns affect state policies and impe-

rial expansion principally by way of evolving interclass transactions within an internal political system that has become more pluralistic and competitive. A thus-mediated economic motive remains largely incidental, but now to the pursuit of internal political stability of the imperial body politic. The shift from external security to domestic stability as the key concern occurs while the imperial frontier continues to be locally endangered even though the imperial polity is at its most secure in the central balance of power. Continuing expansion is therefore only intermittently and marginally impelled for strategic reasons and is alternately undesired by and imposed on policy makers for reasons of political economy in the broadest sense of the term.

The final phase of expansion is associated with formalized protective imperialism. The economic factor emerges—or, looking back to the conquest of the initial viable habitat, reemerges—as a direct and coequal or even primary stimulus to expansion. As such, it is subsidiary when viewed in relation to the original stimuli that actuated early large-scale expansion for security and sustenance; but it has ceased being secondary to the previously ascending strategic and political determinants with which it is integrally re-fused. As a matter of fact, it is the concern with strategic factors that tends to become ancillary to the continued enjoyment of critical economic goods, endangered by growing incoherence within the empire and its subsequent decline relative to outside forces. Increasingly precarious internal transactions by a weakening and deteriorating ruling class shift from voluntary efforts to compensate rising social groups for their self-restraint in the political domain to enforced attempts to appease ever more assertive challengers. The more or less original empire-founding ruling class undergoes final trauma in economic corruption or social dilution and political division or dispossession, as part of a drift toward civil strife, demagogy, or autocracy. They may, but do not necessarily, reinfuse the empire with one more period of dynamism before it subsides into a terminal phase within protective economic or military barriers and either effectively centralizing or only nominally unifying institutions.[24]

Illustrating consecutive causal primacy of disparate factors on expansion has the policy-neutral purpose of disentangling the analytically opaque inter-determinative circularity characteristic of political economy, pending resort to the analytic potential of the land–sea power schism. Thus also the systemic/strategic incentives to expansion had to be clarified as ambiguously offensive-defensive and predatory-preclusive to correct the adverse policy implications of too one-sided conceptions, besetting the analytically easy or simple balance of power interactions at the core of real politics. Finally, inter-determination relates to the analytically even more difficult problem of evolution, substantively via the correspondences between successive domestic/environmental structures and foreign policy postures and formally through circularity's decomposition into consecutive determinants in expansion.

Notes

1. IA 4 (2.par.)–7 (end 1.par.); CE 7–30, 108–157, 338 (2.par.)–346 (end 3.par.) on international determinant of Roman, British, and American expansion; RRA 17 (2.par.)–21, 51–57, 108 (2.par.)–113 (end 3.par.) on Russian expansion.

2. IE 33 (2.par.)–44 (end 1.par.), 46 (2.par.)–56; EA 33 (2.par.)–46 (end 1.par.); SIE 162 (2.par.)–165 (end 1.par.).

3. IE 81 (beg. last par.)–87 (end 1.par.), 187 (2.par.)–194 (end 3.par.); WP 8 (2.par.)–15 (end 3.par.).

4. SIE 155 (2.par.)–162 (end 1.par.); RR 11 (2.par.)–13 (end 1.par.).

5. RUSR 168 (3.par.)–170; QE 21–38.

6. IA 36 (2.par.)–40 (end 1.par.); RUSR 95 (2.par.)–96 (end 2.par.); WP 276 ("The organic . . ." in 2.par.)–278 (". . . autonomy" in last par.),130 (2.par.)–138.

7. NIA 12 (2.par.)–26 (end 1.par.); ATW 4 (2.par.)–7 (end 1.par.).

8. NIA 26 (2.par.)–60, 175 (2.par.)–177 (end 1.par.), 185 (3.par.)–187.

9. QE 5 (2.par.)–20; WP 139 (2.par.)–149 (end 1.par.).

10. NS 36–64.

11. WO 18 (2.par.)–22 (end 2.par.); WP 155 (3.par.)–167, 319 (2.par.)–326 (end 1.par.).

12. RUSR 39–44 (end 1.par.), 49 (2.par.)–51, 54 (2.par.)–59 with deletion of 55 (last par.)–57 (end 2.par.), 145 (3.par.)–151, 174 (2.par.)–178; RRA 101 (5.par.)–103 (end 3.par.); RR 3 (2.par.)–6 (end 2.par.).

13. RRA 203 (2.par.)–210 (end 3.par.); QE 218–247.

14. RUSR 21 (3.par.)–38, 63 (3.par.)–83; NIA 202–219 (end 1.par.); AW2 343–423; RE 279–343.

15. RRA 43 (2.par.)–46 (end 2.par.), 48 (2.par.)–50 (end 1.par.); WP 174 (3.par.)–181.

16. RWO 46 (3. par.)–50 (end 3.par.); NS 5 (4.par.)–8 (middle of 2.par.); WP 4–7 (5.line from top of page), 464 (2.par.)–470 (end 2.par.).

17. RR 25 (2.par.)–28 (end 1.par.), 122 (2.par.)–125 (end 1.par.).

18. NS 74 (4.par.)–80 (3.par.), 148 (3.par.)–154 (2.par.); NS 2 (last par.)–5 (end 2.par.), 19 (2.par.)–23 (end 2.par.).

19. NS 176 (2.par.)–183, 156 (2.par.)–163 (end 1.par.).

20. RUSR 191 (last par.)–194 (end 1.par.), 123 (1.par.)–127 (end 4.par.); RRA 129–130 (end 3.par.), 173 (4.par.)–182.

21. RRA 165 (3.par.)–169 (end 1.par.), 58–59 (end 1.par.).

22. WP 280 (2. par.)–288 (end 1.par.), 296 (2.par.)–302 (end 1.par.), 309 (2.par.)–319 (end 1.par.). See chapter 3 for historical illustrations.

23. CE 31–51 for the Roman and British and 158–207 for the American empires' domestic stimuli.

24. CE 105 (2.par.)–106 for above slightly amended excerpt, 3–6 for concatenation of stimuli, and 52–72 and 208–268 for economic determinants in Roman-and-British and American empires.

Part II

Historicizing Geopolitics:
Past and Prospects

3

Progression Contra Progress:
Evolution through Adaptation

Two imponderables haunt world politics and, when omitted, hinder understanding. One concerns the reasons for expansion that precede the restraints administered on behalf of the balance of power. The other bears on the impulsions behind the evolution of a framework of action that determine the balance between continuity and change. The energy that keeps the balancing-of-power interactions in motion for the sake of progression can be traced back to a variety of structural and functional crises that upset normal routines sufficiently to compel adaptations propelling interactions and evolution toward a new equilibrium. Thus also with respect to expansion, before the domestic facet of its functional determinants can involve the economic one directly through the transactions between a founding ruling class and a commercial middle class, the largely structural "original" determinant of a systemic kind will have realized its potential and allowed the "subsidiary" ones to become successively primary. Such a staging of incentives is part of the temporally evolutionary character of world politics. Historicizing the latter translates into the possibility of operationalizing it differently in matters of policy. This is so because revealing the ambiguously offensive-defensive and anything but unquestionably "aggressive" character of expansion, as a precondition to accommodation in interactive equilibrium, will moderate the process of adaptation within equilibrium's evolutionary dimension.

Push and pull in exemplary Roman and British
expansion into empires

The differences between the Roman and the British empires span the gulf between the primarily military and the primarily mercantile systems: one oriented chiefly to land-based power and one based mainly on sea power; one bestriding the central arena and one gravitating toward the colonial periphery; and one evolving toward institutional centralization and one tending toward diffusion of self-government. The differences were most closely reflected in the external—or systemic—determinants of expansion; they also matter for America's as the intermediate type of empire and Russia's as another instance of a generic type of expansion.

The acute feeling of insecurity resulting from an early threat to physical survival occurs historically as the traceable primitive impetus to expansion on a relatively large scale. Like the wrestler who has been thrown off balance by the sudden yielding of a taxing counterforce, a body politic that has overcome a mortal threat will rush forward to regain its equilibrium within an enlarged habitat. Being both strategically located and well-protected by natural configuration, Rome was situated to both attract and successfully resist threats from greater aggressive peoples. Next to the Etruscans and the Gauls, these included also the Volscians and the Aequians, acting in alliances. Initially a reaction to such assaults and a consequence of withstanding them, Rome's gradual expansion turned into an ascent to supremacy extending to southern Italy through Rome's increasingly successful contest for leadership in an alliance, the Latin League. After failing in the first attempt, England had to wait for reconsolidating Tudor despotism and a withstood threat from Spain before bringing forth a full, defensive-offensive thrust outward on anything like the Roman scale.

If seafaring Britons would in time replicate the Roman empire on a global scale from a crystallizing balancer position in Europe, Rome itself had avoided being bogged down in a position of equal or, at best, balancer among coastal Mediterranean powers. When, instead, Rome managed early to transcend the peninsular Italian base into the adjoining North African and Spanish land masses via conflicts with Carthage and into the Dalmatian coast via contests with local pirates and Macedon, the Romans were able to continue perceiving their expansion as defensive for plausible reasons. In particular, any extension of the Carthaginian sway in Sicily threatened to complete the strategic encirclement of southern Italy and facilitate tactical access across the Messinian "bridge" to Italy proper. Thereafter, at the peak of the Hannibalic threat in the second Punic war, Rome ran anew the risk of reverting from being also a first-class naval power, a status acquired in the first Punic war, to a marginal land power threatened from the north Italian rear—the latter an equivalent of hostile Scotland ever-ready to ally with a weakened England's French enemy. Instead, survival in great-power status sustained further expansion by a narrow margin under the trusteeship of a consequently legitimized ruling class while Rome, fending off Macedonian and Syrian designs on enfeebled Egypt and divided Greeks, was drawn ever more deeply into the multipolar all-Mediterranean system of states.

A Roman world empire comprising two discrete and problematically related western and eastern wings emerged thus from initial expansion in two distinguishable phases. A largely predatory drive of variable scope and intensity, originating in an expansive reaction to a direct and positive threat to physical substance, had accounted for the first phase. Next came further and then preclusive expansion into which a power is drawn to avert or anticipate more or less hypothetical threats to the congenial makeup of a larger system of security transcending mere physical integrity. Both motives combine elements of defense and offense. But whereas the predatory drive does so sequentially, the preclusive involvement commingles the two inextricably as self-preservation merges with self-propagation. While the objects and objectives are analytically distinguishable, they are not different enough in their potency as determinants of policy to be sharply differentiated by policy makers.

The extension of Roman ascendancy into the three-power-plus Hellenistic state system (consisting of Macedon, Syria or "Asia," Egypt and the aggregate half-power of the Greek leagues and city-states) displayed some of the most basic tendencies of interstate relations responsible for transforming an equilibrium system into empire. Uncertainties implicit in a conflict among apparently but not really equal powers will compound the tensions that always attend the quest for parity in status among such states and be aggravated by the inherent instability of mere preeminence in favor of one of them. Rome could hardly rest satisfied with a provisionally peaceful preeminence in the Western Mediterranean so long as there remained the risk of an adverse imbalance separating an all-Mediterranean theater incapable of lasting segregation into two separate halves. Just as the intermediate Dalmatian coast had come to represent a physical nexus between contending East and West, so the policy link was forged by Macedon's two-faced orientation: friendly toward Rome's enemy in the West (Carthage), and hostile to Rome's potential allies for counterpoise (the Greek Aetolian League and Egypt) in the East. The expansion-stimulating possibility was that Rome might become permanently excluded from access to the Eastern Mediterranean by a firm alliance between Macedon and Syria, consolidated and enlarged by predatory sharing of weakened Egypt and its replication at the expense of European Greeks. The reality, which facilitated the expansion, was the lack of coordination between the two major Eastern powers, permitting Rome to conquer each in succession.

Long before Lord Palmerston was able to equate the status of the British subject with that of the Roman citizen, Elizabeth's aid to the Dutch estates struggling for independence from Catholic Spain in the name of common religious values performed some of the functions of Rome's one-time pro-Greek proclivities that were to draw the Italian Hellenistic polity ever more deeply and, once the process of involvement began, near-irresistibly into Greece proper. Incidentally but crucially, the Virgin Queen's assistance to the rebels could not but intensify Anglo-Spanish antagonism that played a key role in projecting England into empire, not least by covering rapine overseas with the prestige of resistance to the Habsburgs' continental hegemony. And ironically but no less significantly, in return for England's countervailing Spain on behalf of faltering France, a recovered French monarchy was eventually to supply ascendant England with alternative stimuli to expansion by reengaging the insular power in the secular contention over Europe and all the world's Indies. In conformity with the norm, England's overseas expansion had by then capitalized on the successful overcoming of a tangible threat to survival from a Spain that had been still earlier propelled forward by a threat from both land- and sea-based Ottoman power, while the results of eschewing encirclement by way of Scotland and outright invasion by the Armada compensated retroactively for the ultimately sterile failure of an earlier England's feudal-type expansion into France in the Hundred Years' War.

Prior to the early eighteenth century, England's essentially predatory drive westward was fueled by material needs of survival and was manned by more or less lawful traders with willing Spanish colonies and uniformly land-hungry colonizers in mostly unoccupied territories in North America. It entailed no major conflicts as a result. By marked contrast, worldwide wars attended British expansion in the eighteenth and the early nineteenth centuries, while motivation became increasingly preclusive. Unlike the earlier and real threat from Spain, the much-advertised later menace of French hegemony for Europe was itself in large part a response to the equations of world power shaped largely by Dutch and British material advances outside Europe. Although the critical Anglo-French contentions provoked by colonial issues and overseas incidents tended to be decided militarily in Europe, a strategic link supplemented the causal nexus whenever British naval superiority produced enough precautionary conquests of France's or Bourbon Spain's colonies to permit their exchange for typically insufficient French territorial gains on the Continent. When as part of this equation a delayed, because reluctant, conquest of Canada had released the American colonists from British rule for imitation of British-type expansion in North America, a mere coincidence between European and local contests replaced in relation to the India-centered second empire the closer interconnection of European and American balances and events that had first made and then unmade Britain's Atlantic-centered empire.

However, when British expansion was resumed on a major scale in the late nineteenth century, the strictly European balance of power, now tilted eastward in favor of the new German and the expanding Russian land empires, became once again stimulative, not least because devoid of the means of compensation traditionally offered by Europe's quasi-colonial southern and southeastern segments. In the ensuing final scramble for colonial possessions, Britain acted even more than the other powers preclusively to earmark and subsequently to effectively occupy previously only informally accessed assets in advance of anticipated occupation by a rival. Following upon the likewise unwillingly permanent occupation of Egypt, this late expansion comprised territories chiefly in East Africa under viceregal impulsion from New Delhi, a sphere of influence in China, and island positions in the Pacific Ocean. Reservation or effective occupation could be preemptive (in Africa, with respect to French and German designs) or countervailing (in China, with respect also to Russian ambitions), as new colonies or spheres of influence replaced strategic support points and zones of commercial interest.

The antecedent mid-Victorian lull in imperial enthusiasm had its Roman parallel in the mid-Republican period in the second century B.C. Whereas the lulls corroborated the defensive inspiration of much of preclusive expansionism, infractions of it denoted the activist implications of that peculiarly ambivalent posture. The Roman senate merely rolled defeated Syria back to a new line in Asia, sparing that country for the time being as it had twice-defeated Carthage and Macedon; and it had resisted local invitations to annex other rich eastern realms. Similarly, the British had returned most of Napoleon-era colonial conquests to the French and the Dutch before subsequently experimenting with military disengagement from the dominions-to-be. Surcease from expansion reflected decrease of systemic pressure on Rome as it became clearly supreme on land and (barring pirates) on sea; on Britain, after it had acquired the naval predominance it was to retain until late in the nineteenth century. With preeminence assured, the material need was not central to Rome's midterm condition until it reappeared in the late-empire period, while British dependence on colonial control was likewise temporarily lessened by the progressive dismantling of the mercantilistic system in trade and shipping.

When it nonetheless occurs, intermittent reexpansion during the lull period involves next to the self-perpetuating concern for the security of the imperial frontier also the special needs of and tensions within a matured ruling class. Continuing and compounding the expansionist potential of transactions between the landed Roman ruling class and a rising (chiefly non-Roman Italian) commercial middle class, the internal strains implicit in the senatorial class's traumatic phase relaunched the second wave of major Roman expansionism in the first century B.C. on the strength of defensive reasoning due to become fully valid only in the third century A.D. Nor was the later British empire immune to internal strains and resulting pressures for compensatory territorial extension or institutional tightening as the hold of the likewise land-owning original ruling class on trusteeship-type authority slackened and the need for compensating commercial interests in the privileged imperial-policy area grew as a result. Moreover, an essentially defensive expansion will be encouraged at all times by the risks inherent in avoiding action to ensure future access while present unlike future capabilities and power equations are known. Although the strategic interests and the threats may appear or will eventually prove to have been imaginary, doing more rather than less will try to preserve earlier achievements in less spectacular but often more difficult conditions.

The various kinds of threats that stimulated the protective expansion of the two empires along their strategic frontiers comprised assaults by more or less primitive warlike tribes on the imperial power's prior presence; regional counterimperialism of lesser states, stimulated often by a greater past; and contrary advance or pressures by one or more major powers. Political or military warfare occurred on all of the three levels, and was more perfidious or brutal as the scale and status of the empire's adversary diminished. Yet even while reacting to only imagined threats, neither empire rushed into remedial action against local disorder or anarchy that clearly lacked the potential for endangering frontier security. Thus Rome continued the delays in taking charge of Syria and Egypt despite chaos in both and the latter being bequeathed to the Roman people by the last of the Ptolemies, until growing local disorders meshed with intensified political struggles in Rome proper to produce action. Similarly, late British imperialists preferred a mere protectorate in Malaya, while local disorders in East and West Africa, the Nile and Niger rivers area, failed to produce annexations before the final scramble got under way.

As the threats moved to the imperial frontier, so did the two kinds of sub-imperial originators of expansion: alternately defensive and acquisitive viceregal or proconsular governors, British in India and Roman in the East, and mainly acquisitive local settlers. Only the longer-term consequences differed. Starting with Canada, settler imperialism evolved soon into colonial nationalism and carried the British empire toward dissolution by way of progressive disengagement from the white dependencies. The closer link between proconsular policies and metropolitan politics in Rome progressively undermined the Republican system itself. Whereas the British process was eventually to turn an empire into a commonwealth, the Roman type of evolution altered a free commonwealth with an *imperium* into an autocratic empire pure and simple.

America's imperial expansion viewed against the Roman–British background

Insofar as the fundamental choice for a major power between equilibrium and empire was also America's, its implicit and still less free choice has been between preclusive responses to pressures and predatory incentives, while an early contention over the fundamental strategy options, overland westward and southeastward or mainly overseas, would be as usual appeased by alternating between the directions before ultimately combining all.

Before this happened, it was initially possible in principle to consolidate a well-defined coastal realm within and with the aid of a dynamic North American balance of power. Won in the War of Independence, this realm depended for economic viability and strategic security on only marginal enlargements in the St. Lawrence–Newfoundland area in the north and in the lower Mississippi and, possibly, Cuba in the south. Thus also a Rome confined to Latium would have had to be safeguarded in the Adriatic, and an England juxtaposed with independent Wales and Scotland in the Irish sea and the Channel. A both shielding and stimulating regional balance of power would have comprised other autochthonous entities, progressively emancipated from European control by way of asserted independence from Spain or consented imperial devolution by Britain. This possibility was for all practical purposes abrogated when the fledgling United States acquired Louisiana as an outright dependency. Once annexation foreclosed an autonomous course for that huge area, while loose confederation had been discarded for the American political system, further expansion became inevitable. American pretensions and encroachments bred enough impotent opposition to engender as many stimuli, and gave rise to sufficiently irritating resentment to create a reliable supply of pretexts for further expansion.

Effective countervailing power to America's could be found henceforth only outside the North American continent. And for the growing United States to cope with the potentially counterpoising great powers in the long run on the basis of parity as the minimum, the necessary strategic resource and next possible resting place was a two-regional empire extending through insular positions into the Atlantic toward Europe and into the Pacific toward Asia. A purely continental United States, whether including or excluding Canada, was by the same token neither a sufficient compass nor a logical terminus for expansion despite cultural, constitutional, and economic coherence-related arguments for the continental solution. All ran afoul of the vital criterion of strategic security within a viable global balance of power comprising the world policy-minded Europeans and Japanese and conditioned by the existing military—chiefly coaling stations-dependent naval—technology and society's economic expectations.

American expansion could have stopped thereafter indefinitely within the bounds of the two-regional empire and interregional world equilibrium. But just as Louisiana had materially linked the Atlantic coastal realm with the core empire by making the former obsolete and a scope narrower than the latter impractical, so the Philippine annexation linked the regional empire to a global one—though at first only symbolically. Responding to a combination of domestic and economic determinants, the acquisition advertised periodically surfacing material incentives while anticipating future strategic vulnerabilities. If the latter reasons for the annexation gave a preview of the deteriorating strategic balances reducible to the central one in Europe, the circumstances attending the conquest testified inside the United States to reviving ruling-class biases relative to ascendant lower-class challengers and the increasingly attractive British as a social as well as strategic ally. Both sets of incentives made the regional Asian empire appear unstable, or hard to stabilize, within its limited scope and released intermittently activated pressures for global expansion.

Bypassing transient opportunities for self-limitation, the American polity was willy-nilly pulled into progression from an inchoate regional state system of the original colonies within an empire toward a world empire within an inchoate global system of states. On the functional plane, the preindependence period had been one of fused maritime and mercantile American "empire" within a protective real British empire. There was no concurrent shift to an essentially military empire, not least because the early predatory expansion's direction was away from the then central system. The emphasis on land was reminiscent of Rome, to the point of involving the issue of plantation slaves; the mercantile emphasis was more like that of Britain. British-type reliance on sea power for both trade and triumph in war and peacetime diplomacy resurfaced only when the United States extended itself, like Britain as well as Rome before, into the central balance of power after first extending itself marginally into the Pacific–Asian arena. The subsequent involvements in the Euro–Atlantic arena carried with them a fitful shift from mercantile to military emphasis culminating in World War II and its outgrowth in preclusive response to similarly motivated or rationalizable Soviet counter-imperialism.

Like Great Britain before, the basic capacity of the United States to involve itself effectively in the central system had taken shape during a period of self-isolation from the European balance of power. Thereafter, America asserted itself from a continental basis closely analogous to that of Rome in Italy and in the Western Mediterranean. The directors of American statecraft were neither able nor willing, however, to consum-

mate the resulting drives and pulls, similar to the incentives and impera-
tives that had led Rome from preeminence to imperium in the Eastern
Mediterranean Hellenistic system, by transforming Europe as a whole. If
Germany was twice America's Macedon in Europe, an also Asiatic Soviet
Russia seemed to be more effective than had been one-time "Asia" in the
shape of Syria and less passive than the then Persia in the guise of Parthia.
Consequently, the American experience of empire could not but gravitate
toward the British model as American expansion bypassed the but half-
dominated and consequently polarized center of the global state system
into its peripheries. However, while economic considerations had been
salient, albeit within strict limits, in the Spanish–American War and the
American entry into World War I, economic consequences of strategic
considerations were more important than were economic incentives in the
origins, the course, and the sequelae of World War II, before inspiring
efforts to move past the Cold War toward an essentially economic worldwide ascendancy. Throughout, oscillation in emphases on land-based and
sea-based military and economic power was thus a function of America's
relation to the changing character of the European, or Eurasian, balance
of power. Land-power emphasis having initially reflected America's immunity to a stalemated central balance before direct involvement in an
either deadlocked or fatally lopsided balance activated the sea-power factor, lack of stress on any kind of effective power reflected repeatedly a
more marginal relationship to a relatively dynamic and autonomous Eurocentric balance largely impervious to impact by an either only rising or
provisionally receding American empire.

   While it underwent alternating strategic and economic emphases, the
American experience evolved even more markedly than had the British
from the empire of settlement to an empire of diversely indirect or informal control. Beyond that very broad similarity in fundamental technique,
the geostrategic pattern of American expansion resembled the Roman
model more closely than the British. In terms of kind if not weight, and
less perhaps than the harshness of the land itself, European colonial powers and Indian tribes on the North American continent equaled Rome's
early threat to survival in Italy just as Rome's subsequent progression to
mastery over the Western Mediterranean was matched by America's in
the Western Hemisphere. If the price had been paid by Carthaginian sea
power in one case, it was charged against Great Britain and secondarily
Chile in the other. Roman power had been extended toward the adjoining
Dalmatian coast into Illyria as the strategic link and counter to Macedon;
mainly Cuba in the Atlantic and Hawaii and the Philippines in the Pacific
were to play the same roles in relation to Germany and Japan. If Rome
was to be drawn, as a result of earlier expansion, into first the Hellenistic
balance-of-power system and subsequently the Greek political system,

so was the United States pulled in two installments ever deeper into the European states and political system and, via Japan the second time around, the Eurasian system. And if, finally, Roman dominion had advanced by dint of both external and internal political dynamics and in response to peripheral disturbances ever farther east into Asia and into the barbarian West, so did America's involvement ramify into the Afro–Asian world while periodically veering back to Latin America.

Although anchored in a comparable configuration though not necessarily in equal weights of outside power and pressures, the structural parallels between the paths and patterns of American and Roman expansion were not necessarily matched in either style or spirit any more than was to be eventually the U.S.–Soviet–Chinese land-sea power triangle compared with its antecedents. The greater similarity with Britain's pragmatic mentality reduced therefore the practical bearing of the similarity with Rome and may have nullified it in ultimate effect. The common denominator of the differences was the responsibility of external threats for internal trends. The comparative weakness of threats to America's initial survival and subsequent security or sustenance was, as a result, responsible for the no more than broadly comparable and functionally equivalent role of Anglo-Roman style interclass dynamics and determinants in the United States. Regarding the external threats, America's geopolitical distance from a constraining international system comprised both her physical remoteness and the ineffectiveness of the European powers other than Britain initially present on the North American continent. America's initial advantage was to become a major drawback in the longer view, however, insofar as it ruled out a full equivalent of what Carthage had been for Rome in the critical phase forming American values and attitudes. That the deficiency was vaguely felt showed whenever the young American statecraft exaggerated beyond reason the post-independence British threat from the Caribbean south to the northern Canadian rear as well as the Spanish threat and the more or less associated Indian or Mexico-related threats from France.

Failing the Civil War and its international implications, it consequently took Pearl Harbor and the Cold War to present the American Rome at a late stage in its development with Carthage-like, fear-inspiring counterweight to complacency in the variously ill-fitting shapes of Asia's Japan and Soviet "Asia." The major consequence of insufficient prior environmental constraints was by then the insufficient consolidation of an original ruling class.

Only a prolonged, and in the end successful, testing by external dangers could have helped overcome the geographically and economically conditioned cleavages within an increasingly heterogeneous political class. Only a protracted ordeal could have been capable of entrenching the more martially qualified and politically stable landed Southern aristocracy in a likewise prolonged trusteeship position, giving that semi-feudal element the strength and the time to assimilate members of the mercantile wing in terms of both interests and values. Instead, transactions between ruling-class segments and among geographic sections projected domestic power plays into a precipitate expansionary process that may have been initially premature when compared with the Anglo–Roman model. Especially after the Founding Fathers who had masterminded the ascension to independence had become an increasingly mythical ruling-class substitute, the subsequent approximations related the American domestic scene only loosely, if still suggestively, to the classic ruling-class and interclass transactional pattern that bears significantly on expansion and maintenance of empire in the aftermath of the original systemic determinant. Therefore, anything comparable to an imperial ruling-class ethos in American history was both transient and insubstantial because either imitative or derivative: imitative of nonrepresentative early native, Hamiltonian, or contemporaneous foreign, British, values in the first empire wave; and derivative from the actual process of acquiring a publicly unacknowledged empire after World War II, albeit now in the image of a predominantly corporate or bureaucratic elite and only intermittently of a triumphant warrior (Eisenhower) or aristo-demagogic type politician (after the Roosevelts, the Kennedys).

Stressing material incentives was plausible in a setting inimical to a self-sustaining imperial ethos. This emphasis remained likewise problematic, however, not least because the ambiguous economic factor itself is commonly both an incentive and an incident to otherwise constituted aims and achievements. The economic factor will positively impact expansion into empire and its maintenance only if the political class is able to compensate via empire-created opportunities the domestic self-restraint of the middle class (e.g., Britain in the late nineteenth century and intermittently in a modified fashion also the United States); if the populace can be appeased by establishing a credible link between expansion abroad and controlled material prosperity or progress at home (Republican Rome extensively and briefly also the post-World War II United States); if empire managers erect a sufficient strategic framework to serve as the direct safeguard of, and an indirect impetus to, private economic initiatives (Britain in and past the mid-nineteenth century and the United States past the mid-twentieth century); or if supporting the strategic framework elicits public commitment to and support of the use of economic instruments for externally and internally rewarding ends (the United States during the Cold War globally after "dollar diplomacy" before and after World War I regionally).

Without such political mediation or strategic matrix, economic expansionism will not lead to an authentic empire when occurring from strength (e.g., interwar United States) any more than late-empire economism from weakness replacing predatory with protective imperialism will alone sustain past accomplishments in empire-building for long (interwar and post-World War II Britain) or indefinitely (post-Vietnam War United States). Economic causation will plausibly appear to predominate throughout only if an essentially materialistic view narrows power to its material component as the ultimately controlling incentive to self-assertion and reduces power to wealth as its ultimate object; if an idealistic view equates empire with corruption in the last analysis and reduces corruption to economic temptations and manifestations; or if a practical necessity reduces a polity to seeking constantly on the outside an always precarious access to the wherewithals of material existence.

The American course of expansion and empire could be properly understood by resorting to either form of reduction less than the British but more than the Roman. Unlike the primarily politico-military and economically relatively undeveloped if not dysfunctional Roman imperialism, Britain's imperial expansion, climax, and decline were readily subdivisible on material grounds into differently mercantilistic (or war-imperialistic) and liberally free-trading phases. The dialectic between and within the two basic economic doctrines and practices has been more nuanced in the economically more self-sufficient American case despite evidence of the earliest (1812) and subsequent war-related impetus for the economic determinant, the post-World War II free-trading bias, and the mid- and late-Cold War symptoms of protective imperialism trading strategic assets for economic concessions by allies. However, on balance, the reinforcing normative aspects of empire-related expansion were more important than the economic conjointly with the structurally systemic ones. An initiating illusion of innocence, not uncommonly sustaining predation and vindicating preclusion, allowed for projecting all doubt about self into imaginary as well as real hostile threats as evidence of innately aggressive expansionism by others.

Russia's expansion compared with others' and America's

Just as Spain or England or France and, up to a point, America, so also Russia expanded from a core in a series of responses to life-threatening intrusions from the outside. Any differences merely reinforce the continuity. Thus the inroads from the outside into England were few, feeble, and far between since the last formative one by the assimilable Normans; only incursions by the Moors into Spain and by the Anglo–Normans into France were comparable in quality or function with the Mongol inroads into Russia. Likewise, Russia's growth beyond Muscovy proceeded in a sequence from a predatory drive by trappers, peasants, and tradesmen to increasingly defensive, but expansive, preclusion of threats to the physical security or economic access of an emergent empire. The main direction of expansion was from the beginnings determined by the need to protect the geostrategic, economic, and racially vital core against threats from south, north, and west—to wit, to the land from marauding Tartars, to approaches to the sea from militaristic Swedes, and to the seat of national faith and power from Catholic Poles. The Russian impulse behind the either sequential or near-simultaneous thrusts northward (toward the Baltic Sea) and southward (toward the Caspian and Black seas) was on balance defensive, while the drive eastward (toward the Pacific Ocean) was more acquisitive—if, eventually, also preclusive of the economically more efficacious British and Japanese. Likewise comparable was the protection of a receding imperial frontier by subimperial predators, the Cossacks, or military proconsuls. This early close connection between political economy and military conflicts was not unusual, but did not give way at a later stage to conditions permitting freer trade or more informal imperialism either before or after the collapse of the tsarist regime despite some progress just before this regime's collapse.

Regardless of whether the Russians expanded in response to threat or to temptation, the core never ceased feeling vulnerable to hostile invasion or isolation. Whereas invasions came alternately from west and east, isolation was invariably initiated by the West when the purpose was to bar Russian action in the Near or the Far East.

Similarities apply to the size of Russian expansion as well as to its stimuli. By the close of the age of Peter the Great, its scope was certainly more than matched in the north by Britain's expansion into that nation's first empire in the Atlantic. By the time of Catherine the Great, the expansion southward was more than equaled by Britain's into its second empire in India. As Russia's horizons had expanded from the Crimea and the Caucasus to Korea, the same was true for Russia's and England's drives eastward: toward the more northern parts of China by the former and southern ones by the latter. No different conclusion would follow from comparing the rates and termini of American and Russian overland expansion any more than from measuring Russia's growth against the first multiplying and then shrinking number of major power centers in the system at large.

On the whole, method differed more than did matter, style than substance, and even that mainly in degree. Warfare was more barbarous and civilization more backward in the East than in the West, also because much of the soil was more barren and the climate brutal. And the strain of Russia's role as buffer between Europe and Asia was of some account

in a part of the world where space became more tempting as it grew pro-
hibitively dear in the European West. For this reason alone, much of the
Russian setting displayed the most salient feature of the American expansion: an underpopulated continent open to a predatory drive. Yet, in such
matters as the role of the state and the military, Russian expansion was
closer to the Roman antecedent than to the American pattern. It even
resembled British expansion of the seventeenth and eighteenth centuries
inasmuch as the landed ruling class predominated over the commercial
middle class in the actually completed phase of Russia's expansion, much
as it was itself subject to the state.

Critically similar to all other instances was the pull exercised by a progressively crystallized state system when supplanting the more or less
predatory drive or push, although the pressures exerted on Russia were
again more stressful when they elicited strictly defensive reactions and
less rewarding when the responses were only ultimately preemptive and
meanwhile auxiliary on behalf of other more directly pressed major
actors. The several interacting pulls from the West that drew historical
Russia into late entry and partial integration into the European state system can, when reduced to power terms, be found in the advantages, needs,
and failures of the West-centered complex of states. Threats and opportunities for Russian statecraft were combined in the West's need for Russia
in coping with its own socio- or military-political instabilities, while Russian assistance in legitimist reactions or diplomatic revolutions was
matched by Russia's own needs and dilemmas originating in the West's
technological revolutions.

At first, Russian rulers rejected requests for aid against both the expanding Ottomans in the early sixteenth century and the Holy Roman
Empire in the early seventeenth century. The later intermittent, but often
decisive, Russian engagement took place first in the Germanic balance of
power (the Seven Years' War) and then in the all-European balance of
power (the Napoleonic wars). An earlier, directly defensive thrust to the
sea against Sweden under Peter the Great had previously compelled a radical acceleration in Russia's functional westernization; involvement in old-
regime and postrevolutionary continental warfare and diplomacy drew
governmental and social elites ever deeper into cultural Europeanization.
The engagement escalated as Russia evolved through the eighteenth century from an auxiliary into a patron of older states or dynasties, earning
if not necessarily winning a full European identity when the eastern
power was called upon in the mid-nineteenth century to repress the socio-
ethnic upheaval filtered from the west into central Europe. This kind and
degree of Russia's assimilation were confirmed geostrategically when
partnership with old-regime France against Prussia and with Britain
against Napoleonic France-in-Poland, initiating the series of Russia's out-

flanking alliances with remote western against overassertive nearer-western powers, reappeared in alliances with France and Britain and, eventually, also the United States against Germany in two world wars.

If essentially "European" or "Western" standards can be applied with qualifications to both the stimuli and the scope of Russian expansion, is this also the case for the temporally articulated phases of its evolution? One related question relevant for policy is whether and at what point the evolutionary trajectory of Russian foreign policy under the tsars intersected with its replication under their successors. In what phase have the Soviets caught up with the tsarist sequence in Russia's essential national foreign policy and chiefly overland-military expansiveness?

As in the foreign policies of all major and historic powers, also in Russia's has a greater inclination to expand alternated with interest in consolidation and conservation. One possibility is to view Soviet foreign policy as having been poised, following the second German invasion, at an evolutionary midpoint. When their initial expansion into the combination of a power vacuum with a spontaneous-or-countervailing American expansive thrust into it toward East-Central Europe was followed by a policy oriented toward a balance of power on henceforth global scale, the Soviets rejoined the overall Russian trajectory at its middle-to-late nineteenth century point. This point had in the longer perspective been preceded by the usual array of phases and postures beginning with unfocused early expansiveness, associated with pre-Mongol Kiev's north- and eastward expansion for chiefly economic stakes, and continuing through the policy of post-Mongol consolidation of a viable habitat under the two Ivans (III and IV) and Peter the Great. A thus assured basis set the habitual stage for an exuberant expansionism, territorial and other, spearheaded by Catherine the Great and extending to the early reign of the first of the nineteenth-century Alexanders. Following the next conservative spell within an enlarged balance-of-power theater typified by Nicholas I, terminal tsarist expansion took place once again typically in a compulsively defensive reaction to threatening decline, associated with frontier turbulence, to be terminated in east Asia under Nicholas II.

Russia did not then and has not reached since the stage of self-isolation as part of withdrawal into passive dependence on the environing power balance, except for a brief approximation during the revolution. The Soviets' initial unfocused expansionism was motivated ideologically rather than economically while occupying the formative phase of Trotsky-type world revolution. The race to catch up with the pre-decline tsarist trajectory continued by reenacting Ivans- and Peter-like consolidation under Stalin. Logically and actually next was the expansive exuberance of Khrushchev's world policy, more like Catherine's than Peter's because more Europeanist in diplomacy as well as westernizing in techniques. In-

curred setbacks prepared the ground for the last Soviet posture of a measured pursuit of balance with the United States that extended internal
conservatism under Brezhnev into the world at large by means of peripheral forays for geopolitical as complement to strategic parity for the sake
of tactical leverages on America's own expansiveness toward the Soviet
European domain.

It is part of the problematic nature of expansion that the question of
"whither" overlaps with the question of "why." A land power's elite may
feel it necessary to expand in order to make up for pressing deficiency in
essential (including security) assets, or it may choose to expand in order
to inflict a crippling deficiency or abridge the surplus of another, and
typically insular, party. The difference between the two "whys" is especially telling for the risks the expansionist is prepared to run: they will
be much greater in the instance of felt necessity than in that of fancied
opportunity. By the same token, it matters whether the rationale behind
expansion is the desire to achieve a major or qualitative new strategic advantage—i.e., the expansion is offensive—or merely to offset a threatened
disadvantage, making the expansion intrinsically even if not procedurally
defensive. A move does not necessarily cease being primarily defensive or
preclusively preemptive if it also marginally improves the expanding power's preexisting situation when the counteracting adversary's response is
too drastic for fear of appearing supine, too prohibitive lest it be interpreted as unqualifiedly permissive.

Choosing the right, intermediate, response is especially important in
relation to an authoritarian-to-totalitarian power that negotiates an awkward exit from its condition and status. Any lessening of internationally
induced tensions will in such a political system highlight the often perverse relationship between short- and long-term effects, between tightening up internal controls or opting for a longer-term relaxing and
appeasing effect of an accommodation entailing a measure of foreign policy success. Because no reliable empirical judgment can be made within a
narrowly operational frame of reference, assumptions have to be made
about the essential character of the regime and the polity in a dual perspective associating interaction with evolution. Directly related to the balance-of-power dimension is the critical difference between hegemony and
mere preeminence, regional or global, as the real and more or less assimilable objective. It extends to the distinction and difference between impos-
sibly simple equality of differently constituted parties and necessarily
complex parity. Likewise if still more intricately related to the evolutionary dimension is the differently but complementarily shaped dialectical
interlock, one between past and present pointing to the future that extends the perspective from expansionary push and pull to the evolution-

ary stage of a particular polity and from the latter to that of the environment itself.[1]

Evolution's parallels with expansion vs. its fundamental properties and propelling crises

A potentially fatal particular threat that triggers the initial predatory drive for a viable habitat is one of the body of threats that in themselves constitute a primitive arena and which, when faced effectively by a potential polity, convert it into an actual power. While it commingles expansion with evolution, this transformation is part of the "original" structural crisis occurring at the very outset of an evolution. So also the processual kind of crises attending succession can be on the plane of "subsidiary" stimuli equated with the interclass transactions when they have taken over from ruling-class trusteeship as the primary domestic stimulant of a temporarily becalmed expansion. Finally, is not the evolutionary crystallization of the economically accented schism between continental-agricultural/industrial and maritime-mercantile powers germane to the economic stimulus to expansion subdivided into the three kinds and phases of imperialism? Which phase and what specific kind of crisis applies will depend on whether the economically more dynamic party to the schism is only beginning to acquire its advantage in connection with wars, has driven the less dynamic party to challenge its free trading near-monopoly overseas, or is itself forced into attempts to convert strategic assets into offsets to rising economic vulnerability.

The parallels between expansion and evolution confirm connections in the operations that merge the high drama of world politics with its agents' destinies. At their very heart, the dilemmas of continuity and change impact the conflictual dynamics of international politics, interspersed with designs for cooperation, through the problematic relationship between mere repetitions and evolution as meaningful progression or also moral progress. Does evolution imply pattern-less turbulence (change for the sake of change) or progress for the better (qualitatively ascendant continuity)? It signifies neither of the extremes and stands for the middle term of a sequentially articulable but normatively neutral or inconclusive progression. This progression constitutes the temporal facet of space/time geohistoricism when it points to distinctively modified recurrences of modal structures and strategies materializing through discernible stages of development of both actors and arenas. Introducing this kind of development systematically into dynamics connects political realism with history beyond ad hoc illustrations of presumptively immemorial principles through past practices.

Insofar as the dynamics with which evolution is inextricably linked entails conflicts, evolution will be catastrophic. And insofar as equilibrium and reequilibration are a coequal part of the dynamics, evolution will be also conservative—i.e., be punctuated by spells of regression from high points of revolutionary impulses and upheavals. Comprised in these interconnected existential features and attributes of evolution are two analytic requisites of any theory of evolution, which is the necessary complement of dynamics in any total understanding of world politics: evolution's motor and mechanism, which, while distinguishable, can be no more separated from each other than from their actual consequences and analytic complements, evolution's manifestations and matrix.

A motor is anything that impels motion by generating some form of previously nonexistent propulsive energy. In human terms, such extra energy will be typically connected with extraordinary tension, reducible to or identifiable with a crisis. It will then be of both practical and analytical importance whether the crisis is generated—and the stimuli to it are located—within the interactive political process that makes up the dynamic or outside the abstractly defined and delimited boundaries of the system or order. Given the distinctive constituents and characteristics of a true system as a whole of interconnected parts, the crises will in the first (endogenous) case be embedded in state-like actors or arena, in the latter's structure and the former's strategies, and—given the character of an interstate system—in the finite range of the conventional ways structures and strategies can or do relate (or fail to relate) to one another. By the same token, the range of possible incentives is wider when the impetus originates outside the system's analytical boundary (is exogenous), but within its environment—i.e., in processes and phenomena that are at bottom functional rather than structural in kind and substantively or procedurally innovative if not also revolutionary in their effect. Such functional revolutions spill over easily into sociopolitical ones because technological or organizational advances will incite struggles over succession to control over the innovation's benefits. The structural and functional impulses will commingle in actuating spatial or operational expansion or contraction of an arena of action. As a self-sufficient constituent of crisis as well as its setting, the consequent internationalization of sociopolitical revolution will be also subject, through the medium of adaptive grand strategies, to the tempo of any revolution—its initial escalation and eventual subsidence into at least partial restoration of its antecedents.

In fact the different (intra- and extra-systemic) stimuli, processed through the crises that constitute the nearest thing to a motor of evolution, will tend to converge in and with the dynamics. They do so in conflicts of distinctive kinds and magnitudes, which constitute the mechanism of evolution. This happens as the diffuse crises are sufficiently canalized in and through particular conflicts to connect with the interactive dynamic directly, without the conflicts' mediation between interaction and evolution depriving the crises of their distinctively initiating role in the progression's propulsion. The special contribution of the conflictual mechanism and the conflicts themselves will be to translate propulsion into the patterns, and the stimuli into the sequences, through which evolution becomes manifest. Evolutionary progression is manifested through patterned sequences—or sequentially succeeding patterns—of different or differently evolved or decayed identities of actors, structures of arenas, and attendant interactions. All change more conspicuously than the pattern of evolution itself. A "pattern" connotes some regularity in the incidence of definable attributes or identities, just as it entails some symmetry in regard to form. However, the close relation between evolution and interaction is itself asymmetrical in regard to both sequences of events and their relation to stability.

A matter of urges and drives, the sequence in balance-of-power dynamics is the logical and necessary one of action and reaction: the latter is literally unthinkable without the former, and on its actually following will depend instant (rather than circuitously achieved eventual) restabilization. A matter of crises and conflicts, the formally corresponding sequence in evolution is from the anterior or antecedent to the posterior or subsequent state or stage via a midterm analytical norm approximating an actual condition. This proven or postulated sequence is less logically necessary or implicit than commonsensically plausible, and the alterations that attend it will require description and explanation rather than demonstration or explication. Making the explanation plausible in terms of a meaningfully conceptualized systemic context becomes the substitute for deferring to a phenomenon's or process's innate necessity. The difficulty of doing so convincingly increases when the sequence involves, in lieu of highly visible actions and reactions, incrementally changing norms of behavior, basic foreign policy postures, and transiently dominant types of actors.

Not being intrinsically necessary, the sequence of distinct identities is nonetheless compatible with the identities' substantive interpenetration and operational interdependence. But it would be less certainly resolved in predictable stability than absorbed in shapeless fluidity were it not for the notion and actual motions of adaptation. As a mode or variety of reequilibration—or its absence—adaptation affects general tendencies and mentalities operating within or among actors across different stages of development or boundaries of discrete systems. Within the family of the equilibrium construct, adaptation is a vaguer concept and more complex process than countervailance. But their similarity is reestablished by counter-innovations following nearly as infallibly upon innovations, and restoration on revolutions, as reaction upon action and restraint upon drive in power balancing. Adaptations are intensified together with interactions in response to actors' consolidation into states and a system's contraction or polarization just as they become less intense even when more frequent with the arena's expansion or dispersal and the states' reversion into pluralist societies. A particular failure to countervail will not stop balancing; neither will a failure to adapt arrest evolution, but will instead advance the terminal crisis of a state system. Such a system's ensuing supersession and replacement by a successor framework of action or type of order are not categorically or qualitatively different from transfers of primacy (or independence, or existence) from an actor inadequately responsive to changes in power distribution. Ill-considered counterbalancing and misconceived adaptations are similarly parallel in kind and effect when they derange stability immediately or, at least, indefinitely defer the correction of destabilization.

When, propelled by crises and mediated by conflicts, equilibration-prone balancing and evolution-promoting adaptation engender sequentially patterned manifestations of progression, they constitute at any time the momentary though not static matrix of the ongoing evolutionary process. This continuity-supporting circularity of the "causes" and "consequences" of evolution survives when cyclical progression alternates between radically different kinds of order—statist and pluralist—subject to significant primary and secondary alterations. Primary changes are those in assets defining capabilities, in motivating mindsets, and in implementing strategies. These primary changes will derivatively invert the standing of conflictual interaction and associative integration as original impellents or secondary incidents, and do the same for direct interactor compulsions and environmental constraints. When institutionalized socialization predominates over incentives to self-assertion, the political physics of interaction and expansion gives ground in a revised geometry of politics, and its poetics of tragic necessity is muted by the imperatives of pragmatic utility.

The various factors and facets, processes and patterns, interlock dynamically against the backgrounds of three generic phases or static snapshots of progression embracing unevenly state-like actors, system-like arena, and authentically political agents. An analytic norm flanked by a pre- and a post-norm is associated with the consolidated territorial state whose agenda exhibits precise congruence between means and ends within a particularistic system revolving around the universalistic principle of equilibrium under impulse from essentially political man, one strategically rational and normatively-ethically disposed to match rights with obligations. Such a norm-like condition is schematically different from the pre-norm state, characterized by actors identifiable only indeterminately as units of actual or potential power disposed to pursue ends that vastly exceed their material-technological means. Accidental social aggregations are prone to dissolution while responding to a myth-saturated pre-political mentality prone to confound the particular with the universal and the transcendental with the mundane. A matter of near-logical reversal from the pre-norm and projection of the norm's propensity to deteriorate is the post-norm of a neo-feudally disaggregating state, exposed less to external security threats than to internal societal distempers. The reversal of key scarcity from physical assets to psychological attributes of will causes material means to exceed politically feasible ends on the part of post-political individuals sufficiently submerged in their economic substratum to confuse particular interests with ostensibly universal values and goals. In fact, the ideal-typically discrete states of being are activated and linked through variously moral and real-politically significant revolutions that supply the energizing motor and conflictual mechanism, while converting the distinctive outward shapes into successive manifestations of evolution and facets of its matrix.[2]

Actor-arena and structure-strategy relations in propelling evolution

Just as the energizing response to a mortal threat sets off the expansionist drive of a policy destined to become an empire, so the primeval energetic impulse to evolution reaches out to an inchoate actor-to-be from a preexistent arena. A consequently generating "arena" is not yet a fully structured field of forces constituted into territorially consolidated and mutually contiguous powers. However, it is already a pattern of competitive interaction among a plurality of agents responding to the scarcity of universally coveted requisites of short-run self-preservation and long-term self-perpetuation. The primitive kinetic impulses from the arena combine pressures on the potential actor to assume viable shape or to perish before being really born with more concrete or even material assets from affiliations that define pre-geopolitically genealogical (familistic and dynastic) politics. In either case, the impulses will be mediated into the formation of actors through the circuit of functions taking off (in keeping with the nature of the primordial arena) typically from the force-related military function and necessarily ramifying into supportive resource-creative economic and -coordinating administrative ones before they can be sublimated into an ethos. This circuit forms actors via the initially decisive impact of the material assets and mythical or broadly moral-psychological challenges present in the arena and arousing creative fears and ambitions.

The evolutionary midterm of the actor-arena relationship is that of a

balance between comparably crystallized, mutually stimulating and restraining, actors and arena. It will have preceded in due course the opposite of the original imbalance, one favoring the determinant primacy of
major actors over the arena for two interconnected reasons. While the
essential characteristic of the arena as a set of interactions coterminous
with the arena's progressively defined and redefined spatial scope is in
effect prenatal to the actors-to-be, the actors have on their side a wider
potential and a longer growth span of evolution. And, as part of this
asymmetry, the actor-formative functional circuit will have evolved concurrently to the advantage of the economic, administrative, and even the
integrating normative or creedal function over the initially salient military. The determinative primacy will therefore eventually migrate from
the arena to matured major actors, but in a comparatively less effective
(because not so much operational as normative) manner. It is exerted to
moderate if not restrain or suppress the conflictual interactions, originally
responsible for the same actors' emergence, in opposition to later-entering because slower-developing actors holding on to the primitive urges.
In so ambiguous a situation, it is normatively attractive to postulate the
improving influence of satiated actors adverse to the continuance of forcible and armed balancing, presentable as progress. It is at least equally
significant empirically to merely posit, as having a comparable moderating consequence in and for mere progression, particular relationships
conditioning equilibrium: e.g., between sizes or scales of the main actors
and the scope of the arena, or between ends that are sought and means
that are actually available at the high point to which evolution ascends
and from which it recedes.

At each point of evolution, the specific source and kind of released
energies will be consistent with the changing "balance" in the actor-arena
relationship. Thus at the approach to the evolutionary midterm (closest
to if somewhat past an actual actor-arena balance), conflicts among the
actors themselves will be critically affected by their congruence with the
arena in terms of their respective sizes and, definitely past the midpoint,
their stages of development. Size-related disproportionality energizes
evolution when a sudden enlargement of the arena (e.g., seventeenth-century Europe) is more readily responded and adapted to—in fact exploited
by—some actors (the Dutch and the English) than others (the French
after the Spaniards). Evolutionary stage-related disparity will eventually
confront overmature-pacific original, or system-founding, members
(Britain and France) with not yet fully satisfied or saturated late-entering
parties (Germany), each class disposing of different kinds of material and
psychic surpluses and scarcities with uneven potential to preserve and
generate energy. Thus unevenly inter-generative functional aggregation of
actors and structuration of arenas can occur in an either actually operative

manner—when one actually shapes the other—or a merely normatively suggestive manner—when the mature-declining members aspire to change the rules of the game without necessarily succeeding. The process is in either case sufficiently intricate to rule out any specific date of the actual transfer and transformation taking place and the effort succeeding. However, this particular kind of periodization, being as futile in this as in any other significant respect, does not mean that interpenetration of actors and arenas in the shaping of their respective structures is in and of itself a sufficient source and explanation of evolution-energizing crises: i.e., if "interpenetration" is conceived atemporally as a given devoid of sequentially different priorities, and "structure" itself is conceived narrowly quantitatively with respect to capabilities and value-neutrally with respect to instrumentalities.

For instance, the several schisms that transcend interactive or adaptive transactions because no actor can individually control the schism-constituents are as much the modifying-qualifying components of a "total" structure as they are impellents of maximum energy-releasing crises. Yet, in keeping with their ambiguous relation to particular conflicts, which they subsume without supplanting, the schisms are less independent sources of crises than emotive or normative intensifiers. The effect is normative when the sacral–secular schism migrates from location within to that between actors, and to the highest degree emotive when the relatively pragmatic-empirical land–sea power schism engenders or only intensifies creedal differences—e.g., when it interlocked after the religio-political Protestant–Catholic with the value-institutional East–West schism. When an occurrence of this kind anticipates and eventually accelerates a particular state system's terminal catastrophe, a crisis-constitutive interlock illustrates incidentally the all-pervading tension between an ideal and the actual, a potential and the manifest, state of actors-arena interaction, contingent on the schism-related evolutionary sequences. An effectively integrating rather than only nominal convergence and actually estranging divergence of West and East in Europe, and the depolarization of continental and oceanic powers in an actual condominium globally, might have progressed more effectively and with profit for the autonomy of the European arena. The condition is that the corner from antagonization to appeasement had been turned before either of the schisms was entangled with the other and burdened with its peculiar crisis potential. It is equally or more likely, however, that the crisis potential of either schism will subside only briefly when it has been relieved of the aggravating effect of the other. For example, after the Cold War, the globally extended East–West schism has been relieved of the land-sea power schism for possibly no longer than the European East–West had been of the wide Islam–Christianity cleavage and the continental–maritime of both the Catholic–

Protestant and the East–West cleavage in the eighteeenth century. The current respite is apt to last only until the value-institutional divisions that always originally defined the East–West schism have reacquired the capacity to engender or, if present, intensify real-political corollaries.[3]

Whereas speculation is only controversially grafted on "fact," the most conspicuous structural source of crisis is one fittingly transitional to the latter's functional and procedural sources: the mismatch between structure and strategies that objectifies crises-engendering disparities between sought ends and either applied or only available means, i.e., between intentions and capabilities. At its most basic, this mismatch is connected with strategic tripartism: the requisite in any structure of more than two powers for A to act in such a way as not to pay for advantage relative to power B with still greater cost relative to power C. The potential for misjudgment and, consequently, mismatch grows with the number of "third" parties in a multipolar structure, but is not substantially less when an ostensibly bipolar conflict (from the Athenian–Spartan via the Ottoman–Spanish to the U.S.–Soviet) is waged by one or both parties without reference to an unperceived or not fully appreciated third party (Persia or Thebes for the Hellenic protagonists; France for Spain and contemporaneous incarnation of Persia for the Ottomans; and China or Japan for either or both of the two superpowers).

Independently of the numbers, mismatch is virtually ensured and the crisis will be deferred only at the cost of deepening when the structure taken into account by the strategist is devoid of the qualitative modifiers headed by the other party's basic foreign policy posture reflective of its rise or decline if not also its position in the several schisms. Introducing the modifiers does not add new basic strategies to the three strategic variations on the tripartite (power A with B against C, A with C against B, and B with C against A). Quite to the contrary, qualitatively amplified structure paradoxically simplifies strategic decisions insofar as awareness of the modifiers reduces misperceptions by, say, the insular of the continental rather than another maritime-mercantile power as the primary long-term threat. If ignoring the qualifiers makes for structural-strategic mismatch, so does structuring the qualifying phenomena in terms of attributes and categories that are properly not relevant for policy. Since marrying strategic rationality with historical intelligence is a rare feat of supreme statecraft, crises due to either kind of mismatch will proliferate sufficiently to divert progression from either progress or evolutionary arrest.[4]

Functional innovations and sociopolitical revolutions over succession as the motor of progression

Strategic behavior is dysfunctional when action fails to perform its function relative to structure on behalf of a constructive mutual adaptation.

Dysfunctionality of this kind is more than nominally close to functional revolutions as a source of motor energy. Such revolutions shape the instrumental side of action, readjusting means to ends rather than assimilating trends to a newly perceived potential as do—or try to do—sociopolitical revolutions. Instrumental innovations constitute the most ostentatiously manifest motor behind evolutionary change. They are both the consequence of past crises acting as the impetus to invention and the cause of present-to-future crises born of either counter-innovations or the original innovations' liability to diffusion, before their absorption in the political process at large reaffirms continuity on the plane of evolution.

Conjointly prominent with the economics-related commercial and industrial revolutions shaping the means of production are the military-strategic revolutions shaping the means of destruction by way of radically new clusters of technological and related operational innovations. Economic and military revolutions converge in the possible choice and actual alternation between two types of politico-military economy: one based on barter and another on purchase. In the first, military service is exchanged for political participation and vice versa on the strength of either privately financed armaments (limited antique democracy, medieval feudalism) or voluntary engagement (populist or mass democracy). Or fighting men are paid together with the armaments by a central authority free to withhold the political reward of participation (ancient or modern, including enlightened, despotism). In either format, military safety via the capacity to destroy and material sustenance via the ability to produce are sufficiently problematic and interdependent to impel development. Prominent innovations combining economic with military effects range from the stirrup and the plow—occasioning feudalism, via high seas-capable maritime and differently mechanized overland transport, expanding localism into globalism—to corresponding administrative revolutions. Closely related to functional revolutions are disruptive alternations between centers of gravity in terms of preeminent power, between authoritarian (or only authoritative) and relatively representative forms of governance, and between inclusively large-scale imperial and more compact and cohesive small- or medium-sized polities, as optimally efficacious. When either of the principal instrumental and closely related dimensions undergoes a revolutionary transformation, the consequent disruption and pressures for adaptation will set off a sociopolitical revolution that implements a contest over who receives the principal benefits from the new situation.

Functionally induced and structurally occasioned crises combine with those born of sociopolitical upheavals to converge at a system's major turning point or terminus in a grand political revolution. This supreme kind of mostly ideologically rationalized crisis comprises intra- and interactor turbulence, attends bids for and struggles over primacy among actors or geographic segments of the arena, and is manifest in conjunctions of domestic revolutions with major wars before subsiding into a restabilized equilibrium as the basis for equally system-wide restoration. Following upon the worldwide conflicts preceding the French Revolution and the two world wars of the twentieth century, the Cold War was the most recent of the modern examples of such a grand political revolution. The connection between revolution and war—more specifically, defeat in war—will impel evolution all the more intensely at its midpoint when an advanced crystallization of structure propels energy flows through correspondingly narrowed channels rather than constraining the generation of energy. Combining transmission with compression will transmute diffuse crises into conflicts, while projecting this compression into war-related revolutions of the continental type will be only questionably or eventually translated into a progression that is beneficially progressive. Conversely, when the perturbation originates in the typically less violent politico-economic quasi-revolutions of the maritime mercantile polities, these simulacra and the more or less directly connected diffusion of assets will paradoxically impact the state system more significantly and lastingly than the continental prototypes. The succession crisis implicit in the connection between revolution and war will escalate when receding system-founding polities attempt to block the ascent of late-entering actors. Rather than mobilize their depleted energy in order to countervail the latecomers, the founders will erect formal-normative restraints so as to condemn them, intensifying the crisis further. Identical with the latecomers less in kind than in effect are intrusions by peripheral-to-barbarian agents announcing, now at the very end rather than the middle of evolution, the transition to the next type of system or order in conjunction with a consequently hybridized or newly re-homogenized political culture and ethos.

Succession is the single most important source of evolution-propelling energy because it combines an inclusive process and a climactic predicament. It aggregates structure with function while, as both an internally interclass and externally interactor issue, it cumulates the generation of energy in either revolutions or wars, or in the two combined. Moreover, succession is the clearest single expression of the constant sum of energy in a political order over a broadly definable finite period of time in that the bid to supersede would compensate for and resistance to it would reverse the depletion of energy on the part of the incumbent. Illustrating thus a law of political physics, succession is also a token of the ultimate unity of the real politics this particular physics reduces to its essence when it engages the most disparate parties to the political process and types of political order. The special intensity of a succession crisis and, therefore, its potency as a source of energy are due to its concentration. It is limited in the time normally available for its decisive resolution after an indefinite period of incremental preparation. It is confined in the space wherein it is resolved given the importance of capital cities for revolutions and related interclass and key battlefields for war-related interactor succession. And it traumatizes the psyche when dispossession inevitably precedes the vacancy's gratifying repossession. Moreover, the real political stakes will by then have been accentuated by ideological rationalizations of the stakes, keyed to the moral-political legitimation of newly acquired status and role.

In substantive terms, succession-related crises reach their maximum when repairing a prior disjunction between structure and functions interweaves schisms between actors with scissions within them. Thus early on in evolution, the normally original emplacement of the secular-spiritual schism inside polities will be projected outward from the primitively consensual formative division of administrative and military functions between ecclesiastical and secular agents. Subsequent contentions over the primacy of the psychological and physical facets of subsequent progression and their representatives are illustrated by, but not confined to, the many-sided external ramifications of the papal-imperial conflict over the investiture of bishops in the European Middle Ages. Each of the progressively secularized revolutions, ranging from the religio-political ones of investiture and subsequently Reformation to the only sociopolitical ones headed by the French Revolution or also ethnocultural in the guise of the eastern European revolutions, will, conjointly with highlighting a particular schism, produce an unevenly succession-capable new salient class capable of only nominal or also effective participation in the political process.

By contrast, assuredly effective was the new type of polities emerging when the increasingly less sacral and more military monarchial polity was being challenged and eventually supplanted by the mercantile-maritime type as dominant. The role and significance of economic factors rise concurrently over military assets, not least in relation to war. Ever less the original source of material gain concretized in tangible booty, war and its connection with commerce become progressively only one of the processes incidental to engendering prosperity. The related difference is in the kinds of unevenly authentic because violent revolutions that precede and follow wars. A largely political and institutional (or constitutional) revision initiated from above by a moderately altered and moderate alteration-seeking subgroup of the ruling class characterized revolutions that, engineering success in warfare, prepared the succession of the maritime-mercantile to the continental type of polity as preeminent. Conversely, differentiating the chain from Dutch and English to American from that of French to German and Russian revolutions is a more thoroughgoing sociopolitical revolution. It reaches beyond initial attempts at reform from above to full-scale revolution from below, and escalates externally in function of rising pressures to exchange inferiority for parity in relations with the more efficacious oceanic power type. This continental- or also Eastern-type revolution will be less preparatory to ascent than compensatory for relative regression and will typically follow defeat or defeats of the state in war. Conjointly with the revolutions they trigger, the defeats give rise to attempts at a totalitarian synthesis of disparate creedal attributes of the two historical prototypes in secularized quasi-religions sustained materially by a combination of the first generation's military and the second one's maritime capabilities. A plausible alternative to this third-generation power type has after its defeat become a developmentally post-state systemic, regional pluralist framework of order. This would-be energy-replenishing succession is less a product of defeats in climactic antagonism than of the desire to avert incipient attrition of the victorious mercantile-maritime power type. It is also less a matter of only constitutional revolution from above or actually sociopolitical domestic revolution from below than of an organizational and managerial transformation induced from the outside by substantively "revolutionary" changes in the environment.[5]

Arena expansion-and-contraction and cycles-and-circularities as processual impellents of evolution

More or less directly related to succession, but unquestionably part of crises related to process, are different forms of expansion and contraction of the environment, transactional in terms of the rate of interactions or temporal depending on the requisite speed of reactions, as well as spatial and functionally specific. This is so regardless of whether either kind of expansion and contraction is an independent source of energy or an incident to its increase and decrease, and the different kinds of expansion and contraction are related to one another contrarily. Thus, spatial contraction of the arena will not uncommonly cause the rate of transactions to expand and the reaction time to contract while spatial expansion has, depending on the reasons for it, differently untoward consequences. Moreover, the resulting crises have a differently problematical relation to conflicts in generating the impulse to evolution. Crises of whatever kind and origin, while closely intertwined with specific conflicts, differ from them more in origins and outward expression than in analytically significant roles in evolution. This problem is only partially alleviated by reducing the motor of evolution, associated with variously diffuse crises, to its mechanism, mediated by particular conflicts.

Both asymmetries affected the structural and functional sources of crises when, in the period between the fifteenth and the onset of the seventeenth centuries, a sudden and substantial spatial constriction of the European arena by the Ottoman advance intensified conjointly with the Spanish–Ottoman confrontation both the religio-political crisis centered in Germany and the Franco–Spanish conflict over Italy. A functional revolution in seafaring redrew simultaneously the pathways of commerce, relocating them from overland central to coastal-maritime western segments of the foreshortened Europe. This relocation permitted the overseas explorations that extended the rump arena spatially across the Atlantic, preparing with a new economic system the rise of a new class for eventual successional bid inside the primary (Dutch or English) beneficiary of a new order that was to change the medieval sociopolitical landscape into one essentially modern. A constant sum of energy and conflict was maintained also when at first only temporary appeasement of the Franco–Spanish contention, due more to France's defeats in Italy than to a shared concern with the rise of Protestantism in Germany, intensified religio-dynastic upheavals within France itself, setting off convulsions which, once brought under control, set a reinvigorated France on the road of succession to Spanish hegemony in Europe. Escalating religio-political contentions were in the advancing seventeenth century entangled ever more closely with the revolutionary economic consequences of the spatial projection of activities into the Western Hemisphere. These events transformed a spatially restricted Europe into the center of a Euroglobal system, but also delayed the relaxation of competitive transactions and a slowdown in requisite reaction time that can be plausibly anticipated from areal expansion. Conversely, a similar confinement of Europe in the mid-twentieth century, replicating the Ottoman inroads, accelerated the tempo of cooperative transactions in rump Europe while reenacting its economically profitable extension toward and across the Atlantic.

Thus and similarly interpenetrating impulses to evolution, combined in a grand political revolution, conjugate politico-militarily and -economically constituted expansion or contraction in the evolutionary facet of genuinely political economy. Consummating the related dilemmas, these impulses raise a special question regarding war causation: is war—or what kind of war (e.g., within or between civilizations)—apt to be associated with what kind of expansion or contraction in what functionally substantive (economic or other) terms and with what phase (beginning or end) of either? It is probable that economic contraction-or-expansion affects the war-peace issue more directly subjectively (via a feeling of buoyancy or depression) than objectively (by statistically evidenced economic trends, supposing these are available or actually followed and sufficiently understood by major policy makers at any time). But again, from the fallibility of one aspect of the "objective" approach can be salvaged some relief to the dilemmas implicit in another and more sweeping objectivity. Just as economic expansion-contraction reflects a cycle responsive automatically to the laws of economics that anchor expansion in contraction and vice versa, so the politico-military war-peace cycle is subject to a comparable law-like tendency. This tendency keeps transferring the evolution-propelling interlock of crisis with conflict between the two communicating, internal-domestic and external-strategic, vessels of politics—and does so in function of alternating exhaustion and replenishment of energy supply and consequent conflict-readiness in either. Energy implies in this context pressures and tensions attendant on immediately pressing tasks and ostensibly feasible goals to be relieved in the momentarily overstressed arena pending their reaccumulation in the provisionally neglected arena. As the war-peace or domestic-external priority cycles overlap with either functionally substantive (e.g., economic) or spatio-temporally/transactionally procedural ones of contraction and expansion, they incidentally determine one another causally. This happens not only in the realm of real politics but also in regard to economics when economic expansion is alternately due to the onset of war after a slump, giving rise to intensified arms production, or to a war's successful conclusion, followed by the surge of previously suppressed civilian consumption. However, for the inflows and outflows of energy attendant on either flattening or steepening cycles to translate into sequentially articulable progression, they must be canalized by particular conflicts so as to acquire not only direction from a conflict's course as a conduit but also thrust from the resulting compression.[6]

The causal ambiguities surrounding crises, the amplitude of their functional, structural, and processual sources, and the diffuse nature of the resulting energy combine to make for an indeterminate effect on the evolution they make happen. It is the role of particular conflicts to focalize the energy stream, operationalize the latent impulse, and exteriorize its effect on the manifest surface of the evolutionary currents—and do all this with the effect of creating new crises. Connecting the motor with the mechanism of evolution, this major circularity between crisis and conflict encloses the lesser one between structure, function, and process in the conflicts themselves. Responding to structurally conditioned discrepancies between role and resource, actors' deliberate self-help performs incidentally a function for the system by revising it into one constituted less disparately and therefore one more stable. By the same token, the attendant conflict is a medium for adaptation by actors and readjustment of structure as the converging parts of reequilibration. The latter finally completes one and restarts the ensuing two-faceted process of interlinking crises with conflicts and structures with functions, which produces the manifest outcomes of evolution. Circular processes make up an evolution that is modifiably cyclical—i.e., returns only to the neighborhoods of its structurally-functionally construed beginning in each phase—while conflicts fluctuate in intensity when revolving around different kinds of scarcities and surpluses. Conflicts do this with more certain and direct particular effects on the fortunes of contestants through their course and outcomes they are intended to shape. Their effect on an evolution whose wide range of determinants they merely mediate as part of their performance as the canalizing conduit of energy is correspondingly less certain and direct.

Organizing the stakes of conflict around material and immaterial scarcities and surpluses makes sense because they co-determine a strategically rational relating of means to ends, subject to anterior and posterior deviations from the ideal-typical norm: combination of psychological surplus and material scarcity leading to excess of ends over means at the beginning of evolution and the other way around at its end. This connection is reflected in the dual character of readiness to engage in conflict: material capability and psychopolitical disposition. Material capability plays a dominant role when material (including geostrategically significant territorial) scarcity as something to correct makes a routine conflict desirable to at least one party; a hegemonial conflict will be more ambiguously related to a substantial material surplus, as something to be preserved by the defender when accumulated over a considerable length of time, or consolidated through territorial expansion by the challenger when nonterritorial material assets have been acquired only recently and are in danger of being possessed only transiently. The more ambiguous is the materially conditioned readiness at any one time, the more critical will be the psychological disposition to conflict. Over time, the latter will ascend in importance as the ideal attributes of crystallizing states and stakes of interstate conflicts come to represent their material substratum, before the latter reacquires its original potency and reascends to prominence conjointly with economic crisis or the crisis of the state as an institution.

With respect to another dyadic range in the actual origination of specific conflicts, the incentive will also be concentrated at the evolutionary midterm in frictions due to sheer contact between or among territorially consolidated and contiguous actors. As part of this range, the trend toward contact proceeds from religio-ideological or other concept at the unformed beginning and reverts to concept at the differently rationalization-needy late stage of an actor's or both rivals' evolution, because it will have been caught up in an obversely unbalanced means-end relationship. Similarly, the enactment of conflicts will be catalytic at the evolutionary climax—i.e., be aimed at specific and concrete objectives to achieve (e.g., territory to acquire)—as opposed to the cathartic kind at either evolutionary extreme, when conduct reflects a different object. Such an object is psychopolitical purgation through a warlike effort undertaken for the sake of affirming some form of authority and legitimacy (mainly domestic for a primitive and yet untested ruling class at its early stage of evolution) or international standing and viability (for a declining polity engaging in compulsively preemptive expansionism toward its evolutionary terminus). Finally, as regards resolution of conflicts, the supersession of a major conflict or conflict series by a more timely or pertinent one will leave the deeper and longer-lasting effect on the evolution of the arena as a whole rather than the subduing of a particular party or a negotiated ratification of stalemate, whatever may be the differential impact on the actors themselves at their different stages of development.

Whatever its main source, the developmental effect of conflicts is less conspicuous but ultimately more important than their immediate consequence when these conflicts reveal particular discrepancies (between claimed role and disposable resource, for instance), or compel functional innovation or counter-innovation, while structures narrow into stakes of contention and individual motives expand into the overall momentum of evolution. The outward manifestation and inner depth of the cumulative impact of particular contentions on evolution can be in either case observed only after the event and be anticipated only by inference from the outcomes or residues of earlier conflicts of a kind likely to recur. The probable depth and scope of the impact is least problematic when it relates to the magnitude or intensity of the conflicts themselves. The conflicts will be all the more intense, the wider the range of the basic (differently expansion- and consolidation-related) foreign policy postures and the steeper the rise or decline and, consequently, the greater the disparity and more inverse the relationship between roles and resources of incumbent founding and insurgent late-entering participants in the system. The more asymmetrical the configuration and disparate the postures, the more probable the hegemonic character of the attendant conflicts will be. Moreover, it will be less plausible to assign responsibility for the conflict's origination unequivocally to parties resisting or seeking radical change.

When enactment of the conflict overshadows its origination, the corresponding dyad migrates from contact and concept to catalyst and catharsis: one designed to produce specific results, the other keyed to securing psychopolitical relief. Most clearly differentiated in conflicts involving fully developed and only developing parties to relatively small-scale routine conflicts, the two objects will be unevenly combined in a hegemonic confrontation. The challenger's approach is likely to be primarily catalytic with a view to consolidating an impregnable material reserve for an indefinite future, but to be secondarily cathartic with a view to reserving a claim by conspicuous action in the perspective of eventual decline. By the same token, the defender's primarily psychological impetus and partially normative purpose of affirming the legitimacy of the hegemony irrespective of the means of its original acquisition are reinforced by the real politically focused effort to reconfigure the arena into a balance of power disabling the present and prohibiting a future challenge. However "caused," even hegemonic conflicts will not ensure the outward forms and expressions of evolution. But they will expedite the rate of change and amplify oscillation between peaks of revolution and troughs of subsequent restoration. Finally, the ensuing evolution is apt to ensue from the urge to avoid the worst-case scenario for one or both of the contending parties rather than transform an indeterminate actual into a latent or normatively preferable environment yet to be created by a deliberate strategy.[7]

It is in this circuitous fashion that conflicts channel energies engendered by diverse crises into substantive manifestations of evolution. They do this through strategies engaged in a circular relation with the environmental matrix that issues out of and feeds back into the conflictual mechanics of evolution. It is this inter-determinative circularity that transmutes patterns in the sequential manifestations of evolution into a process that is sufficiently long-lasting and continuous to incline toward being cyclical. It differs thus from the only consecutive process that extends over briefer periods of time the inter-determination of factors subsumed in the political economy of world politics that only affect evolution. The short-, medium-, and long-term dimensions are at any time analytically reducible to the momentary matrix or environment of interactions and evolution, while the contents of the matrix represent nothing additional to their interpenetration. So also the manifestations can be analytically disaggregated over time and in kind from their complex totality into those pertaining more (though never solely) to the actors, the arena, and the agenda and as, respectively, cognitive, structural, and operational. Likewise mainly analytical is the distinction between evolutionary manifestations within a particular framework of action and between the corresponding "orders."

All of these not differing very much in actuality is immediately apparent with respect to the cognitive dimension. Apprehension as an antecedent to action begins from a mere instinct or reflex awakened by the agent's confrontation with the correspondingly inchoate arena well before the next steps toward instrumental means-ends rationality and beyond can take place by both responding to and acting upon the arena's structure as it itself takes shape. At this evolutionary midpoint, the instinctually reflexive behavioral pre-norm (exhibiting excess of goals over means, compensated by unrestrained surplus of energy) will have been carried forward by the actors' progressive acquisition of rudimentary knowledge of both geographic space beyond the reach of the naked eye and policy-relevant time beyond the immediate present but this side of extra-territorially located eternity. Only when this basic knowledge is forthcoming will cause-and-effect reasoning be in a position to substitute for the belief in magic or other forms of arbitrary intervention in human affairs. While means can consequently begin to be adjusted to immediate ends, the policy-related horizons will gradually expand spatially beyond the reach of instrumental to strategic rationality, embracing a more comprehensive configuration and tapping into incipient historical intelligence. This superior understanding may encompass only the antagonist and its position on the rise/decline curve as well as along the action-reaction axis. Or it can expand to include the larger environment and agenda and their condition relative to the past, comprising but exceeding precedents as part of strategic rationality, and to future portents, implicit in previously disclosed trends combining change with continuity.

Like everything else, manifestations are subject to deformations of the positive ideal-typical norm and deviations from a straight line of progression through the cyclical pattern of evolution. Ideally, cognition climbs from instinct via instrumental to strategic rationality and on to historical intelligence, each higher comprising the lower level of cognition, provided a loss of footing in the vital soil of political instincts does no more to sever historical intelligence from reality than strategic rationality is paralyzed by reduction to its down-to-earth instrumental core. Actually, deviations in behavior favoring the analytical post-norm state or condition will entail a distortion of the means-ends relationship toward excess of material and insufficiency of motivational means relative to objectively feasible or normatively valuable ends. A consequently deformed instrumental rationality will exhibit a tendency to substitute ideological rationalizations for strategic rationality in lieu of enriching the latter with historical intelligence. When the rationalizations point ideologically leftward and developmentally "forward" to progressivist utopias, or rightward and developmentally "backwards" to mytho-normatively nostalgic regressions, one displaces cooperation and the other conflict from a means of statecraft into self-purposive object. Both of these deformations are inimical to historical intelligence as the supplement to strategic rationality but also its substantial modifier. Integrating awareness of both continuity and change and of the rise/decline developmental curves of actors into the instantaneous action-reaction mode of strategic rationality, historical intelligence is uniquely capable of muting the conflictual dynamic at any one time while mediating over time the transition from primitive through climactic to terminal manifestations of evolution.[8]

A like displacement of means into ends will affect the structural and operational alongside the cognitive manifestations when administration becomes an end in itself on the part of the territorial state, if not in effect coterminous with it, coincidentally with loss of statist ethos or spirit. This is likely to happen after the state has superseded the variously church-like earliest provider of rudimentary rational organization and pre-rational reassurance, pending a wholly secular pseudo-church's promotion of radically mythologized politics. Similarly the economy becomes the end in itself for society when the latter, holding forth the conversely utopian promise of materially founded communal solidarity, has devoured its statist progenitor to whom a viable economy was a means to power and status implemented through the alliance of strategic with economic rationality. In either case, the pathology of a differently slanted "concept" pushes out "contact" in the origination of conflicts and a psychopolitically oriented "cathartic" overshadows the real politically slanted "catalytic" purpose in their enactment, with negative consequences for the cognitive compound able to identify and implement the "reason of state" necessary and sufficient to consolidate and subsequently interrelate polities.

From evolution within to evolutionary interlocks between types of systems or orders

Actors, arena, and agenda condition each other's evolution incessantly even when not at all stages equally. The formation of actors is manifested primarily though not solely through progressive aggregation of the key functions, the arena's by virtue of its structuration by major power centers, and the agenda's by connecting actors with the arena through the former's progressive socialization—until such time as the evolutionary cycle turns downward to the mutually reinforcing unraveling of its constituents. Declension terminates in final crisis for actors and agenda and supersession for the arena. Since the terminus of one stage or system is also the takeoff point for the next, the sequences constitute both a pattern and a process. In evidence across the ages are links between micro- and macro-systems determined by the size of actors and arenas and between differently pluralistic and unevenly evolved proto- and meta-systems surrounding the unitary statist norm. While both the micro- and the macro-systems are subject to this state-centered evolutionary range, they are linked not only chronologically but also causally through reciprocal effects.

Because the inchoate larger actors and arenas were taking shape

through contentions over earlier-crystallized smaller ones, the pre-Alex-
andrine Near Eastern, post-Alexandrine Mediterranean, European, and
global macro-systems were in effect immanent in the antecedent Sumerian, Greek, Italian, and, relative to the global, progressively dwarfed or
micro-systemized late-modern European, micro-systems. The micro-
will in turn survive posthumously in the macro-system when the former's
distinctive value-institutional innovations are systematically codified but
also devitalized in the latter, which consequently becomes a Babylonic or
Hammurabian Near Eastern, Hellenistic Mediterranean, Italic or Italianate European, and Europeanist global macro-system. Having superseded
the antecedent micro-systems structurally and operationally, the subsequent macro-systems comprise them normatively or only doctrinally and,
in consequence, procedurally. Such inter-systemic links will extend to less
manifest developmental ones when a primitively pluralist proto-system is
immediately latent in the deficiencies of anterior transition to the meta-
stage format of institutionalized pluralism. Thus the receding dominant
member or members of the intervening statist system hinder the potential
of a disruptively ascendent party to revitalize or reform this system. In
either the dynamic or the developmental form, the links and the transitions they imply have enough of a relation to the balance of power to be
mediated by organic (rise/decline) transformations and operational (ac-
tion/reaction) transaction. Even when not explicitly related to economic
and domestic determinants, the mediation will be sufficiently determinate
to raise consecutive sequences into cyclically unfolding process.[9]

Embedded in the inter-systemic linkage, a historic (micro-) system—be
it Sumerian, Greek, Italian, or European—takes off from radically pluralist functional indifferentiation combining structural heterogeneity with
related heteropolarity. That is to say, no manifest difference between the
sacral and secular or, say, trade and war on land and piracy on the sea will
coincide with territorially bounded sedentary (typically agriculturalist),
migratory (typically pastoralist), and other predatory societal units and
correspondingly differentiated "poles" of capabilities and activities. Both
the functional and structural features foster the emergence of hybrid entities coexisting around the vaguest of a common stake in physical survival.
And statist homogeneity and operational uniformity only begin to
emerge out of localism and fictitious universalism converging into territorial entities of intermediate scale and size. These will be eventually consolidated from primitively overlarge, organizationally invertebrate, and
consequently chronically dissolution-prone (nebular) polities into viable
polities around a (nuclear) core capable of sustained countervailance en
route to cumulative enlargement for some. Concurrently with this particular transition, say in Europe between the eighth and the fifteenth centu-

ries, structuration proceeds via primitive stratification if not hierarchization of actors. The sustainable scope of the arena is being concurrently defined and redefined as part of the multiform expansion-contraction dynamic and, within the progressively stabilized boundary, the by now emergent "system" of (quasi-)states undergoes segmentation. Regional subdivisions take shape in function of the emergence of a relatively stable map of dominant conflicts and associated "traditional" alignments. Supplementing these operational factors, the organic ones contribute uneven rates of development as between areas and actors favored unequally by their size and geoeconomic situation in relation to total space or locally available social energy.

With respect to the evolution no less than the dynamics of world politics, functions and structures are analytically as well as actually the necessary, but not sufficient, antecedents to distinctive and defining operations qua process—one that evolves toward and devolves from the ideal-typical norms. The structural manifestations are conveniently conveyed by "s" words in relation to the arena: its structuration, stratification, scope definition, and segmentation—only to end in supersession. Their operational counterparts, relating to agenda, evolve through phases centered on "c" words: initial consolidation, demonstration of continuity by a major realignment, replacement of military with institutionalized diplomatic coalitions in a concert, and late-stage cumulation of crises ending in the collapse of a particular framework of action as either extant or essentially autonomous. The structural and operational planes converge initially and positively in the socialization of collective actors into the roles and rituals of a state system. This system's eventual downturn will be near-inevitably attended by the state being displaced by society as the ostensibly self-sufficient end product of the socialization of concrete and private individuals. The developmental circle closes, while the evolutionary cycle reverts to the proximity of its onset in primitive sedentary or migratory pluralism, in statist-societal and continental-maritime hybrids of regional proportions and community- or empire-like style, prone to lapsing via sublimation of original power drives and simulation of traditional interactions into a state of siege by environing "barbarians."

Variations in this evolutionary progression and regression over time are not ones of kind when it is the Sumer micro-system of Mesopotamian city-states that, after emerging from shapeless pluralism through priest-governed temple communities, was forcibly unified into more empire-than communal-type unification by Sargon's Akkad. And it had been thus displaced before the Near Eastern inter-empire macro-system would evolve comparably through a series of imperially consolidated migrant populations toward supersession in the degeneration-prone Persian Empire resulting, after the Alexandrine interlude, in a triad of amphibiously continental-maritime Hellenistic kingdoms. Nor will a radical caesura intervene when, at this point, the comparably evolved Greek state system slides after the Peloponnesian War, by way of ever less liberalized than trivialized quasi-empires and regional quasi-communities of the league type, into Roman hegemony. Similarly, the barbarian realms and ecclesiastical or populist regimes will evolve in Italy into the second (post-antiquity Renaissance) city-state system, only for the major parties to the initially system-formative competition and midterm realignment and concert schemes to be reduced to a typically terminal meta-systemic condition under Spanish overlordship: warlike Florence (not unlike Athens earlier) as a trade- and culture-centered Grand Duchy of Tuscany, while Venice recedes from primacy in trade and pursuit of regional hegemony into simulation of a balancer role in the wider and mightier "northern" arena. So also, last but not least, the European state system has after a similar course finally expired in a European Union assembling the contrasting images of a post-Peloponnesian Anatolian league, however demilitarized, and a pre-Akkadian temple community, heavily materialized, under the auspices of an American hegemony poised to act through, or contest primacy with, a local quasi-empire in communitarian clothing.

It may well be that the longest-term trend is from the early advantages of genuinely imperial integration, through the ordeals of the statist stage that transform individual states from subjects through stakes into stages of action, to post-statist associations partaking of or pretending to community. It is only possible that such a community's amorphousness may make it lastingly more viable in the sense of resistance to outside shocks and dissolution from within than either of the alternatives and antecedents. Be that as it may, the sequence from before to after the evolutionary statist climax is clearer than any coincidence between the successive real political arrangements and specific economic systems. However, the sublimation-and-simulation of real politics attending the terminal erosion of a state system will coincide with the onset of the materialization process attending the emancipation of society from the state. The economic system that had inclined toward mercantilism's dual face of centralism within and protectionism without as the territorial state took shape will have by then veered toward a more liberal order of economic policies, one due to deviate gradually from aspiration to "freedom" to concern with "fairness" relative to both competing economies and particular economic interests within societies.

Such distinctively and specifically political and economic manifestations of evolution are generically identifiable in terms of materialization (and territorialization) as opposed to immaterialization (and deterritorialization) of both actors and agendas. Along this evolutionary curve, the statist climax exhibits, contrary to either the primitively pluralist proto-

or the institutionalized communitarian meta-stage, the highest degree of territorialization and immaterialization. Concern with strategic role and formal-symbolic status is dominant even though tacitly understood as functionally auxiliary to and operationally interdependent with material resource factors as stakes of contention and payoffs of politico-military performance. Conversely, either pre-territoriality or eventual deterritorialization combines with real politically unmediated materialism in the distinguishing attributes of either primitive or institutionalized progressive pluralism. Finally, as evolution progresses toward and regresses from the statist climax, economic processes and systems relate to the most conspicuous operational (i.e., real political) manifestations of evolution—rise/decline of powers and balance of power—more directly in terms of material capability as the product of particular economic transactions than by virtue of these procedural transactions themselves. This is so regardless of whether the economic processes can or cannot be sequentially ordered in terms of their salient identity from industrial to commercial (or vice versa) and on to financial, or can be compellingly related or reduced to either terms of trade or termini of trade routes.

Just as over a cycle of structural and stylistic manifestations from proto- to meta-systemization, so also in the operational ones toward and past institutionalized concertation, there is a measure of symmetry between start and finish. Initial resistance to one set of "barbarians" (ninth century Europe) progresses to the initiation of the balancing and incidentally state system-crystallizing agenda by the foremost of "civilized" autochthonous powers, only for it to regress to terminal invitation of a later set of extra-systemic or also cultural outsiders into a crisis-ridden state system when the original initiators of the system-formative balancing have renounced the effort to continue this agenda within the bounds of the arena as one capable of perpetuating its autonomy (twentieth century Europe). Following previous Near Eastern resisters to and assimilators of the successive waves of population movements, Egypt's subduing of the "invading" (or, more accurately, infiltrating) Hyksos barbarians set off the former's projection into an activated Near Eastern macro-system susceptible of upgrading the usual pattern of tripartite alliance-wrought crystallization from the Sumerian micro-system. So also, after the decline of the Western Roman Empire, combined impulsion and constraint by the Eastern Roman Empire propelled the fifth-century Ostrogoth and subsequent Frankish rulers and realms into leadership roles in a multipolar quasi-balance of power cum primitive inter-dynastic concert system. Later in Italy, it was more typical for resistance by a semi-formed plurality of polities to a pre-formed rather than markedly predominant actor, the duchy of Milan, just as to kingly France in Europe, to set off the crystallization of a balance of power. Conjointly with the incremental aggregation of polities from their territorial nuclei, this event marked a decisive step beyond premature false starts of evolution through oversized nebular polities such as the Lombard kingdom in Europe's South and the Carolingian empire in the North.

When primitive structure instigates competition, it will sooner or later mutate contention into systemically structured (and systematically waged) conflict. The operationally crucial emergence of a shared territorial stake of contention is concurrently being complemented in a system's constitution by the evidence of both elasticity and continuity: elasticity, as the balancing of power extends from the structural-strategic center of the nascent system toward and into its periphery while the expanding process's center of gravity migrates; and continuity, as previously traditional long-lasting associations break up and parties to them realign with no longer "hereditary" enemies.

As the balancing-of-power process expands and diversifies, the about equally constraining and impelling quantitative structure is amplified into a total one by virtue of the actors' secondary-level differentiation. Essential homogeneity of universally territorial polities yields to secondary existential heterogeneity of actors positioned distinctively in the successively emergent schisms and the cumulatively evolved foreign policy postures reflective of their rise and decline. Although in an organizationally ever more elaborate form, which is an all-inclusive manifestation of evolution in its own right, the attendant functional-institutional differentiation reproduces the different aspects or features of the original, i.e., proto-systemic, radical heterogeneity. Just as the land powers reincarnate sedentary agriculturalists and armed hillsmen, so the sea powers succeed to roving peddlars who in turn prefigure the trading companies: different predators all, capitalizing on either mobility or mass. Similarly, the Mesopotamian compound of priestly governance with military kingship was reborn in the European medieval sacral-military monarchy as the first-generation leading power type, whose replacement, the second-generation maritime-mercantile type of power, reembodied the spirit of the seafaring coastal commercial cities of Asia Minor and the Eastern Mediterranean, such as the Phoenicians, likewise exposed to military pressures from the economically less productive larger hinterland. In sum, the balancing process propels and subsequently manifests evolution in two directions and manners. It homogenizes actors by compelling them to concentrate their resources within definable and defendable territorial bases. And it subsequently conduces to their redifferentiation by encouraging essentially identical polities to maximize their situationally determined particular capabilities or potentials, producing the associated value-institutional superstructures or facades. If this is most pronounced in relation to the land–sea power schism and related differences, this is so because, being the most "pragmatic" of the schisms, it is relatively closest to qualitatively neutral quantitative structure of material capabilities, but it is also most capable of breeding a progressively escalating value-institutional diversity rather than only expressing a preexisting one.

In each of the successive state systems, the combination of land and sea power capabilities will in a major empire-like actor constitute an operational link to the succeeding system: thus Persia from the Near Eastern to the Greek, Macedon from Hellenic to Hellenistic, and Spain from Italian to European—and, say, Germany as stimulus or stake from European to global. But contention between differently constituted land and sea powers will also help thwart attempts at institutionalizing the balance of power in a concert of powers at a system's climax: in the two-power format of an Egyptian-Hatti or the still briefer Spartan–Athenian condominium as much as in the multipower secular-pragmatic counterparts to the Italian "Holy League" or European "Holy Alliance." A concert's pursuit of not so much harmony as demilitarized competition will be thwarted, in a system sufficiently matured to be visibly aging, by contrasts and contentions between new and newly ascendant and relatively declining original or founding members. The "older" members' self-saving tendency to overcontain the "younger" will contribute to precluding the system's stabilization by either a multipower concert that endures because it tolerates re-ranking or a generally endurable one-power coordination by successively preeminent members. Incidentally ruled out is a henceforth dying system's collective and its members' individual entry into the next and typically larger system on the basis of equality with previous outsiders-barbarians, thanks to the power contained system—creatively in its prime (e.g., Milan, France)—becoming the first to call in the barbarians (Milan inviting France, and France the United States) in the system's twilight. An increasingly hard-to-bear strain is concurrently being placed on the concert formula. It grows from one manifest in the concert's routine operation as a diplomatic constellation into the more basic stresses within the associated configuration, made up of parties subject to increasingly disparate basic foreign policy postures.

Successive foreign policy postures and rise-decline and war-peace cycles in evolutionary progression

Sequentially predominant attributes expressed in schisms and generations of dominant types of powers permeate the succession of basic foreign policy postures rather than directing it. For this reason alone, the successive foreign policy postures are not only the most openly manifest features of evolution exhibited by individual actors rather than relations between and within individual systems. They are also most manifestly open to historical intelligence for integration into strategic rationality on the plane of cognition and to statecraft for integrating the organic into the operational dimension on the plane of action. Foreign policy postures are to particular foreign policies what schisms are to specific conflicts: both of the former transcend but are enacted by means of the latter. Unlike the late entrants', the original members' policy postures are necessarily congruent with the environmental structures, because the structures and postures evolve initially toward and subsequently by virtue of reciprocal conditioning. However, the postures can also rely for a degree of autonomy in relation to the environmental structures on some (and, in one instance, critical) correspondence with the domestic structures. For either of these reasons, developmentally significant foreign policy postures are confined to those of the major powers uniquely capable of at once shaping the system and enjoying this requisite latitude, albeit with potentially disruptive consequences and within the limits of an only broadly uniform pattern. This pattern is one of alternating tendencies to expansion and consolidation that exhibit distinctively modifying features at successive stages of both the actors' and the system's evolution.

When an actor has been propelled into potentially enduring existence and significant identity by complying effectively with the laws of struggle for self-preservation, this initial self-affirmation is at once implicit in the risks and impelled forward by the resources latent in the arena. It anticipates the actually formative sequence of the primitive prototypes of generically expansion- and consolidation-directed foreign policies. Closest to the structurally proto-systemic antecedents is an aimlessly open-ended and essentially predatory thrust into a not-yet-crystallized permissive environment. Backed by an elementary functional differentiation and material assets minimally adequate for military use, and by comparatively superior energy-generating psychological surpluses, this originally expansive foreign policy posture will be impelled by pressing other-than-military material scarcities. For a power to be really formed, however, unfocused and undirected expansiveness will soon have to give way to an outward policy posture keyed to consolidating a viable habitat. Oriented toward forces and structures crystallizing in the actor's immediate orbit of so far only potential existence, the implementing policies will be incipiently preclusive of inhibiting if not also paralyzing encroachments from the outside and will be assisted by a modicum of fiscal-administrative management. A thus begun ascent toward adjusting means and ends is also one toward the behavioral norm codifying instrumental rationality. It accelerates thereafter from the consolidative to an exuberant foreign policy posture, different from its expansive antecedent by being now pragmatically as well as adventurously exploratory of vaster horizons. An expanding and henceforth more precisely targeted surplus of energy is mobilized by the onsetting scarcity of domestic outlets for enterprising individuals and groups hemmed in by developing central authority. Pursuit of both material and prestige assets for the community as a whole, including the reigning authority, occurs within an arena that is more tightly and thus discouragingly if not deterrently crystallized at the core than at the consequently all the more inviting periphery. Whereas economic and military resources and rewards are close to being evenly interdependent, internal and external functions of government are about equally important in assuring order at home and access abroad.

Next to be consolidated after prime actors is the arena by virtue of the balance of power-oriented conservative foreign policy posture. Being best suited to mediate not only between once again expanding and relatively stagnating actors but also between the alternately consonant and contrasting rhythms of the arena's spatio-temporal or -transactional expansion and contraction, this conservative posture follows not only logically but also beneficially upon post-consolidation exuberant posture. It is typically the stance of a saturated major actor in an environment sufficiently crystallized at both core and beyond to forestall easy additional gains through territorial expansion and to facilitate adjustment of the rate of transactions, expressed in their density and the requisite reaction times, to the spatial radius over which they extend—and vice versa. Such a power's progressive concentration on domestic improvements as an offset to increased societal mobility exacerbated by continuing functional differentiation will nevertheless require continued successes in foreign policy, apt to frustrate later developing powers and invite their imitation. Because the concert formula is contingent on the major actors clustering closely around the conservative foreign policy posture, the implied menace to it will deepen into a predicament for the system itself when, together with the latecomers gravitating as it were backward to enterprising policies of the expansive or exuberant posture, the founding members are perversely advancing forward to the last, compulsively expansionist posture intended to avert an otherwise seemingly unstoppable and irreversible decline.

At this point, the fiscal foundation of national power again seems to require support from the use of force and governmental authority for greater self-affirmation abroad so as to uphold domestic legitimacy that is on the wane despite functional and administrative hypertrophy. Although aggressive on the face of it, resulting activities are essentially preemptive of dangers that are partly or largely imaginary and unlikely to be mastered by compulsive response in an environment replete with actors covering the full range of ascent and descent. An actor's terminal foreign policy posture is thus also or primarily a refuge from the stress of its antecedents. It entails some kind of withdrawal underneath a sheltering

environment, made up of another power's protective patronage or a stalemate between or among still-vital powers. An accelerated retreat from
external to internal functions of government is not mainly or only for the
sake of expanding foreign trade and investment and preserving residual
diplomatic prestige, but is attended by a wide range of disruptive-to-dis-
integrative societal processes pointing toward the reverse sides of evolution's starting point.

It is along these lines that the passage of the two premier founding
members of the Euroglobal state system, France and England, through
their foreign policy postures set incidentally the pattern for the two main
leading (continental and maritime) types of power, while deformations in
kind and derangements in sequence of their postures' natural sequence
contributed to the system's cumulating crises and ultimate collapse.

The evolutionary scenario began unfolding when France's object-less
expansive foreign policy posture coinciding with the Crusades and its
first, thirteenth-century politico-cultural, hegemony set up the prototype
of the sacral-military medieval monarchy based materially on agriculture
and saturated with the mystique of holy kingship as the compromise formula to mitigate the sacral–secular schism at home and the corresponding
papal–imperial polarity abroad. The culmination of the subsequent foreign policy posture of consolidation (from Philippe Auguste to Louis XI)
overlapped with that of exuberance in and past the invasion of Italy combining late-medieval and early-modern motives and objectives. An eventually less defensively anti-Spain than assertive progression toward a
conservative balance of power phase (from Richelieu to Mazarin) commingled in due course naturally with a climactic bid for preeminence
short of hegemony (Louis XIV) before an again preemptively anti-British
balancing effort for the sake of oceanic parity (from Fleury to Choiseul),
went down in defeat together with the ancient regime itself for lack of the
requisite domestic societal underpinnings. Caught up in the turmoils of
relative demographic and other material declension, France's foreign policy posture recorded thereafter, beginning but not ending with the Revolution and Empire, a checkered career of intermittent compulsive
expansionism-to-hegemonism, each time around less persuasive and more
provocative. Punctuating this posture by relapses into earlier postures
(e.g., the Second Empire's into exuberance in Mexico or for Italian unification) could not indefinitely defer, while increasingly impotent resistance to passive withdrawal finally aggravated, the pain of extrusion from
high foreign polities under successively British and American auspices
beginning with the Third Republic.

As for the British wing of France's Anglo–Saxon nemesis, the defining
moment of its identification with the other leading power type—insular-
oceanic or maritime-mercantile—was the Elizabethan period of foreign

policy exuberance, preceded by the two-phased formative posture: the feudal-dynastic expansiveness associated with the Hundred Years' War and the policies associated with consolidation under the earlier Tudors. Attended throughout by much overseas enterprise, Britain's conservatively balancing policy phase dates in Europe much less from either Henry VIII or Elizabeth than from the Dutch and Hanoverian dynastic imports from the continent anxious to shield their home bases from the French with British power. Favored, unlike contemporaneous France, by concurrently evolving domestic pluralism, this posture faltered in Britain only under pressure from late entrants and then in the direction of compulsive colonial re-expansionism in the late nineteenth and early (pre- and post-World War I) decades of the twentieth centuries, pending withdrawal into an increasingly imaginary special relationship with the former dependency punctuated with relapses into a no more realistic balancing posture relative to a Europe once more in danger of being united under French auspices.[10]

To the extent that anomalies in the postures' sequences inflect peace toward war before, or mar associative efforts with old-style antagonisms after, conflicts that finally terminate the system's autonomy, this malfunction corroborates indirectly the positive effect of the normal sequences: their sustaining evolution and promoting restabilization. Sustaining evolution continuously, most of the time through postures adapting to domestic or external structures, differs from impelling it catastrophically and circuitously through maladaptations. Prominent among them is relapse into an anterior foreign policy posture, which links this particular manifestation of evolution directly and closely to its motor via the crisis that intervenes before progression resumes. Thus also counter-innovation is more catastrophically propellent than innovation when, for instance, an offensive military technology or strategy responds to a previously defensive one rather than vice versa. So are defeat in war rather than victory, resistance to retreat from rather than ascent to primacy or, linked to the antecedent foreign policy setbacks, a revolutionary bid for domestic succession than affirmation of authority or attempt at marginal reform by malperforming incumbents. Overall, catastrophic progression will in such negative cases result from efforts to recover a lost position rather than to move forward to a promising future, not so much to restore equilibrium or even achieve a favorable imbalance as to avert a cumulative disequilibrium.

Just as in the balancing-of-power dynamics, so also in evolution, individual acts undertaken for precise and compelling reasons can and often will produce unintended aggregate results that are on balance or will prove ultimately beneficial for the system without having been envisaged or desired by or being favorable to the agents. Thus the refusal of succes-

sive French statesmen to settle for a conservative balance-of-power posture devoid of preeminence entailed repeatedly a relapse into the
antecedent posture which, while construable as compulsively defensive
against unfavorable overall trends, propelled the consequently convulsed
European state system forward without doing the same for France itself.
This was the case first under the ancien regime, when the latter's ruinous
attempt to roll back British overseas ascendancy on the battlefields for
American independence aggravated the fiscal and other crises of the monarchy beyond the capacity of successive domestic reforms and foreign
policy retrenchments to avert the Third Estate's bid to preside over a
more effective French performance in the external side of succession-cen-
tered politics. And this occurred again subsequently, when the attempt of
Napoleon III to moderate in the second and shorter liberal phase of the
imperial regime the consequences of his earlier efforts to return France to
the position ultimately compromised by his namesake neither did nor
effectively could avert the basically exuberant posture's projection into a
catastrophic military defeat that could not but aggravate the multi-phase
successional struggle between "black" and "red" France—one that exemplified much that was to happen in the rest of Europe with consequences
for its catastrophic evolution and terminal crises in the late nineteenth and
much of the twentieth centuries.

Relapsing into exuberant rather than advancing toward the conservative
foreign policy posture will be most characteristic of a continental founding member. Unlike the expansive posture that is self-sustaining and
-propelling and the consolidating posture that is necessary if the actor is
to continue evolving, efficient conservative foreign policy needs to be
lodged in the dynamic of domestic interest groups, at least some of which
will press for restraint and others for action in any external setting and
situation. Therefore, this posture proved problematic for a France (or
Spain) whose strategically appropriate timing for the passage beyond exuberance to self-constrained conservatism in foreign policy would have
predated the onset of the British (or previously the Dutch) kind of capitalist economic and pluralist societal development. A larger result of the
sensitive domestic dimension for all of the established great powers was
their reluctance to coordinate foreign policies toward the late entrants in
ways capable of promoting their gradual and peaceful assimilation. Instead, opposition of the older great powers to the late entrants' enjoyment
of external outlets and peripheral outreach advanced the key derangement
from the former's conservative phase to the latecomers' developmentally
earlier transition from consolidation to exuberance. After the sterile expansive thrust of the *grossdeutsch* Frankfurt parliamentarians, the problem was typified by united Germany's abandoning Bismarck's attempt to
sidestep the intermediate phase by leaping from consolidation directly to

the conservative foreign policy posture. Direction of the European concert with respect to the day's exuberance-inviting periphery, Africa, would construct simultaneously both the environment (by diplomacy) and the domestic political sphere (by parliamentary tactics) into superficial compatibility with the external German posture. The logic of evolution could not be denied, however, even though the domestic socioeconomic makeup of Imperial Germany was not substantially better prepared to sustain the exuberance of *Weltpolitik* on a partially private or non-public plane than to prop up the European concert on the wholly official plane. This state of things was eventually to explode in the compulsive expansionism of the Third Reich when it followed the Second into a sense of inability to compete indefinitely with the era's global empires on an equal basis by other means. The ensuing withdrawal posture has thereafter been made necessary by the nature of both the anterior challenge and its repulse and rendered possible as well as profitable by the victor's protection and promotion of an open world economy.

The founding members of the European state systems were unable to either hold off the two German Empires or integrate them into Europe at least as successfully as the initial, first or "holy," Germanic empire had co-shaped early Europe from *its* position of status preeminence—one to be passed on to Spain and from Spain to France and on to Great Britain before so far eluding modern Germany. The consequent supersession of the Eurocentric by the only incipiently structured global system kept the United States—like Britain, a combination of territorial actor and lead economy—on its relatively easy path of initially only regional expansion into a comparatively low-pressure environment. This ease was to permit collapsing the expansive and consolidative phases of the formative foreign policy posture into one indivisible manifest destiny, prosecuted under a comparably united ruling-class trusteeship and drawing on an economic base forged, likewise typically, by the necessities and opportunities of a war, that of 1812 to begin with. Likewise far from encountering obstruction, the late nineteenth-century transition to exuberance via the Atlantic and Pacific offshore islands occurred, in the context of interclass transactions and an incipient free trade imperialism, not only in imitation but with the effective encouragement of no longer resistant British faced successively with a less congenial French partner inside and a less acceptable German would-be successor outside the North American continent. Also typically for an insular sea power, America's incremental progression over two world wars toward the conservative balance of power posture, through successful opposition to ever more demonic expressions of continental statism, had been exercised by at least equally significant economic and military means before actual or only apparent lapses in the economic dimension allowed or forced the military branch to play its habitual role in exchanging strategic assets for economic easements by sheltered dependents in spells of formalized protective imperialism, one sufficiently reassuring to delay early (McCarthyite) intimations of a ruling-class trauma to a later day (Vietnam).

The conservative posture is associated with the balance of power and the concert of powers at the intersection of ascendancy with decline of the founding and accommodation with alienation of the late-entering parties. It is, therefore, equally crucial for interaction and evolution although it represents an at least partial exception from the other postures' equal applicability to continental-military and insular-maritime powers and, among the former, Eastern as well as Western (European) powers. This uniformity—and consequent continuity and stability—is greatest when the entry of the habitually disruptive eastern continental powers into the system occurs relatively early in the system's own progression (Russia's, unlike Germany's, no later than the seventeenth century) and their exuberant foray into space (Russia's in Eurasia unlike Germany's overseas) is directed away from the areas of principal concern for the founding members. The situation differed and tension was on the rise when, colliding with America's own late entry into the Eurocentric global system, the Soviet Union's was employed to accelerate the earliest and duplicate the subsequent foreign policy postures of its tsarist predecessor, propelling the sequence past (Khrushchevite) exuberance to (Brezhnevite) unevenly conservative and compulsive phase.

Contrary to the uniformity for other postures, the uniqueness of the conservative phase reflects the disjunction between the logic of consecutive foreign-policy postures and the fact of divergent internal developments of continental and maritime powers. Barring a corrective course or deliberate cultivation of convergence, this divergence grows as the system evolves and reaches its apogee, corroborating the significance of societal structures and their comparative foreign policy-related efficacy in the manifestation of evolutionary progression. A unique prominence for the domestic factor in connection with the conservative posture is only partially at variance with the uniformity of courses (strategies) and outcomes (major wars) attending the recurrent land–sea power triangles regardless of specific as opposed to schism-constitutive generic differences in domestic as well as economic regimes on the part of successive incumbents of the various parts. However, the implicit downgrading of the causal impact of the domestic and economic facets relative to a dominant geostrategic determinant is apt to be less with respect to evolution than interaction. Nor does it annul the advantages of a special kind of hybrid, such as the United Kingdom and the United States, whose dual capacity as a territorial actor and a lead economy exposes it to two distinct evolutionary trajectories of unequal time spans and patterns. Only a facet of the general problem of genuinely political economy, this particular duality confirms the conservative posture's critical location at two intersections: of real politics with political economy, and of interactions comprising the two with evolution.[11]

From convergence of motor-mechanism-manifestations into matrix of evolution to cross-system continuities

Unfolding quasi-cyclically in the real world, the circle of evolutionary progression closes conceptually when energetic motor and conflictual mechanisms engender manifestations that feed back into both of them via the continuing evolution's matrix, which they add up to at any one moment in time. To the extent that the matrix is in effect a momentary receptacle of all the attributes of a total structure, it is static. But it is dynamic as the medium for bringing to bear on contemporaneous processes the compound of rise/decline fluctuations and balance of power interactions, which in the medium run coalesce in foreign policy postures, together with the alteration in the leading types of actor and frameworks of action occurring over the long term. Being both static and dynamic, the matrix is not only objectively actual but also purposively normative as an object of intended change and in both respects subjectively perceptual. As such, the environment is made up of spatial latitudes and temporal longitudes, provisionally stabilizing the corresponding dynamic of spatio-transactional/temporal expansion and contraction. So defined, the matrix presents in both respects either a compressed or a relaxed, constraining or permissive, setting for adjustments and adaptations to disruptive disparities. And it does this in situations wherein the length of available reaction time (temporal longitude) will closely depend on the intensity (transactional density) with which, and the scope of arena within which, the balance of power system is crystallized (spatial latitude). The longitudinous-latitudinous spectrum extends from the relaxed situation attending the dissolution-prone false starts (fifth- to fifteenth-century Europe), through the transactional acceleration in a Europe constricted from the East and expanding westward (late fifteenth to early seventeenth centuries), to the differently relaxed period of consolidation and evolutionary maturity of the founding actors (seventeenth to nineteenth centuries). This relaxation will be subject to reversal under pressure from ascendant late entrants into an acceleration and tightening exceeding the earlier one (e.g., only seventy-five years of Germany's "challenge" from 1870 to 1945 compared with the much longer crisis period of the Ottoman intrusion). Also subject to the spatial and operational environment expanding and contracting periodically and within the longer-term time spans to an extent cyclically, the actors' perception of a momentary situation will be strained further by the segmentation of both arena and agenda between core and peripheral (or central- and regionally sub-systemic) sections. This relatively conspicuous kind of compartmentalization is returned to the opacity of the expansion-contraction dynamic by the less visible lines drawn by the features of the total structure that transcend specific transactions. One set of such features is the several schisms running through actors in the guise of scissions as much as between them. Another is the attitudinal disparities reflecting the distribution of rise and decline attributes among the actors and within the several foreign policy postures.

The ideal-typical norm for the matrix consists operationally of strategically rational behavior within a contiguously crystallized structure, depending for its dynamic on stakes that are uniform for all parties. This norm is consequently met in both principle and practice when the preeminence short of hegemony of one power coexists with a number of near-equal great powers located close to the midpoint of the vertical rise/decline axis and the range of foreign policy postures. Diplomatic constellations are then sufficiently flexible to permit and promote adaptations to both routine discrepancies and disruptions and either functionally or sociopolitically revolutionary transformations. Such a situation is neither that of one power's virtual hegemony such as sixteenth-century Spain's nor a group of powers' radical enfeeblement such as the West European democracies' in the first half of the twentieth century. But it was in evidence in the mid-to-late nineteenth century when conservatively preeminent Britain was surrounded by manageably volatile France, a Russia conservative in Europe and finitely exuberant in Asia, and an inherently conservative Austria (and Austria–Hungary-to-be), compulsively re-expansionist only regionally, while Prussia/Germany was either yet to implement the consolidative foreign policy posture or was only poised on the verge of exuberance. A temporary lull coincided with suspension of the land–sea power schism between a no longer acute Anglo–French–Germanic (Habsburg–or–Prussian) and not yet activated Anglo–German–Russian triangle. No kind of stakes—geopolitical (e.g., the Eastern Question), ideological (liberal-conservative or revolutionary-reactionary), or residually religious (Catholic-Protestant)—was likely to group the five great powers in any more rigid or destabilizing constellation than a 3:2 ratio. Such a configuration will guarantee flexibility through ongoing gains-loss calculations both between (or among) allies and within alliances. And the greater complexity of calculations and lesser cohesion among three than between two allies will direct the equilibrium dynamic toward an equipoise significantly more elastic than the near-static deadlock between equally expansion-oriented parties. The late medieval powers and early-modern European state system conformed to such a deadlock, as did to a lesser extent the mid- to late-eighteenth century contest between France and Britain. Both were equally unable to attract into alliance both of the parties to the intra-German Austro–Prussian stalemate, while would-be compulsively re-expansionist Spain was an unstable and unreliable ally of France when seeking to recover Gilbraltar from the British and Russia was unpredictable as the potentially decisive weight.

Likewise propitious to a stable and stabilizing matrix will be still broader compatibilities such as between the size of major actors, the scope of the arena, and the scale of the total agenda or between diverse kinds of the arena's segmentation, such as by one of the schisms as opposed to regionally sub-systemic routine transactions, with the dominant schism constraining and the schism-neutral situation engendering autonomy for particular contentions. It will help if major-power actors' strategies, subsumed in a foreign policy posture, match the total structure in its capacity as the matrix with respect to the actors' positions on the rise/decline capability curves and fit the momentary condition of a spatial-or-transactional expansion and contraction of the arena itself. This being so makes it more likely that the actors will relate to the arena positively in terms of conflictually determined alignments, configuring the narrowly defined quantitative core of the total structure. By contrast, the matrix will erode—and the particular state system tend to unravel—when the increasing complexity of the matrix of a climactically maturing state system is the cause or only precipitant of two classes of defects. One obtains when heightened complexity is unmatched by the growing capacity of major actors to beneficially invert malignant precedents from the relatively small number of representative crises and cycles of protracted conflicts that punctuate even a long-lasting system. Another obtains when this lack of historical intelligence is compounded by strategic rationality being undermined by all the greater propensity to a preemptively worst-case assessment of and nonrational reactions to hypothetical dangers. As either or both of the defects cause the matrix to erode, appropriately managed transactions recede in favor of an undirected or misdirected organic transformation and a strategic rationality of would-be progressivist but equally overreaction-prone reasonableness. At this point, the arguable presumption of ethical or at least procedural progress within a particular system becomes not uncommonly entangled in the transition to another and possibly different one. It is the attendant, more or less continuous, connections among types of systems—i.e., frameworks of action—of different magnitudes and kinds that constitute the most intriguing because commonly unperceived matrix of any one system's evolution.[12]

A relatively clearly demarcated unequal reciprocal immanence of successive micro- and macro-systems has already been traced from the Sumer via the Near Eastern to the Greek and on to the Hellenistic and from the Italian to the European and on to the (proto-)global. As part of this continuity, the operational immanence of the macro- in the contested micro-systems is superior to the successive transmissions of the smaller entities' jurisprudential, diplomatic, and more inclusively political codes and values to the macro-entities. Weaker than the operational, this value-institutional immanence is nonetheless clearer than when discontinuous micro- or macro-systems overleap the contrary system-size, e.g., the Sumerian and the Greek micro-systems overleap the intervening Near Eastern macro-system, or the Near Eastern and Hellenistic macro-systems overleap the Greek micro-system. What is then at best a reciprocal latency operative at a distance lacks the operational linkage present when the first, pre-Roman Empire Italian proto-system is immediately latent in the defects of the West Mediterranean (Carthaginian–Etruscan–West Grecian) Hellenistic meta-system or the European in the flaws of the late-to-post-Roman Empire all-Mediterranean one. Whereas sequentially orderly links among frameworks of action of different sizes and stages of crystallization constitute only a transcendent matrix of any one system's evolution, the evolutionary logic they have disclosed intimates all the more persuasively the likely future course of progression.

   Implied in the various links is the question whether—and, if so, how and to what extent—the evolutionary climaxes or terminal crises of the successive systems exhibit an upward or downward trend as they gravitate in expanding space over the longest time. Does or does not each system start its developmental ascent from an evolutionary status superior to the preceding? If so, is this mainly or only for reasons of advancing technological civilization or also due to empirically untraceable propagation of institutional craftsmanship or political sophistication? And does either influence assert itself across distances of time and space that exceed those promoting either the value-institutional or operational immanence between consecutive micro- and macro-systems? Finally, did the rate of evolution accelerate over time, or intermittently also decelerate, for either of the basic reasons before seeming to pick up in the present while propelling evolution into a less than ever predictable direction?[13]

Different longitudes and types of history for intertwining statism with pluralism

The less such queries can be meaningfully addressed empirically at present, the more useful is meanwhile a speculative perspective that combines analysis with contemplation and retrospection with projection to produce a factually founded evidence of recurrences and continuities, revolutions and transformations. Armed with the presumption of recurrence and functional equivalence, speculative investigation can combine projection with retrojection of better known present or recent specifics into remoter situations, presumptively analogous because structurally comparable and in no other respect conspicuously divergent. Inquiry may then draw on insights such as the tendency to rationalization of primitive urges, pragmatization of ideological biases, and routinization of military-technological and strategic innovations that predominate at the beginnings of evolution or its major stages, and the continuing readjustments among resources, roles, and risk-related compensations while evolution proceeds. Looking speculatively backward implements a credible shift of vision from uniqueness to uniformities, just as does the inverse projection of vaster and specifically vaguer generic features from the remotest past into one more recent and beyond the present into the future. Quite apart from supplementing knowledge qua information in the realm of cognition, generalizations extracted from the coupling of pro- and retrojection reduce also the analytic salience and, even, the causal significance of time- and space-bound particular factors. Insight from the two mutually reinforcing perspectives deepens as the surveyed time-span lengthens. Adding, therefore, the unconventionally remote to the conventional proximate starting points for such an exploration means extending the latter, in a Western Eurocentric perspective, from such dates as 1945, 1918, 1848, 1815, 1648, to the "fall" of the Roman Empire and on to the Mesopotamian beginnings of recorded history, each combining emergence of specific powers and related configurations with more diffuse processes of evolution.

So to articulate the alternative starting points is not to concede the significance or utility of any sharp periodization but, contrariwise, to underline its impracticability and disutility. As the starting point recedes in time, the range of disclosed salient events or data progressively expands, privileging structures over strategies and functional substitutes over specific functions or instruments as the latter become ever less specific. While emphasis alternates between particular actors and vaster agendas or more impersonal processes and "isms," their successive emergence or dominating salience and reabsorption in the currents of time, and declension behind the horizons of material and immaterial space, become the stuff of seamlessly interdependent reality and its understanding.

Thus, looking back no further than to the mid-nineteenth century (1848)—the traditional starting point, that can be lately advanced to 1918 if not 1945 without promise of much additional insight into longer-term trends—reveals only the separate factors presumed to have led to the first of the two world wars that extinguished the European macro-system. The attention is focused on events such as the German unification and the consequent intensification of inter-great-power antagonisms and on such phenomena as rival nationalisms and imperialisms caught up in and exacerbating a resuscitated real politics. Pushing back the boundary of retrospection to 1815—another commonplace date for considering the evolution of the international system—brings into focus the remoter origins of the just-mentioned events and phenomena. They include the French Revolutionary and Napoleonic impetus to the chain-reacting spread of France-originated nationalism eastward, via Germany; the provisionally culminating gravitation of land-based power in the same direction toward briefly triumphant Russia; and the impulse urbanization and industrialism gave to the sociopolitical and -economic mass mobilization that underlay nationalism and imperialism and supplied the raw materials for rival sociopolitical ideologies as the putative challengers to more prosaically motivated rivalries. Beginning the inspection still further back, the mid-seventeenth century (1648) reveals the rise of the basic politico-administrative framework of the above-named events and processes—the modern secular territorial state, sovereign in law and monopolizing violence in fact. It also reveals the more significant coincident differentiation of these states into land- and sea-oriented and ascending and declining powers, crucial for the operation of a by-then clearly articulated balance of power as well as for the henceforth perceptible recurrent linkages between strategies and structures. It will be reserved for the view encompassing the "fall" of the Roman Empire and its sequelae to identify the gradual and unevenly spaced anterior crystallization of the actors and the arena, critical for the European state system from its earliest beginnings. However, only the longest possible perspective, reaching past the empire and state systems of late antiquity, will penetrate to the most elementary givens that make up the physical, the existentially operative, and the normatively charged, constituents of any and all world politics while embracing also the most elusive interlocks of particular "systems" in their merely sequential or also cyclical connections.[14]

Everything that anticipates within such a vast panorama the indeterminate character of the present neo-medieval hybrid of pluralism and statism enhances the role of historical intelligence relative to strategic rationality's. The balance shifts along paths that lead from functional dispersal to the subversion or only suspension of the structural-strategic type of politics, one that integrates economics into strategics, in favor of the functional-institutional type, which substitutes economics for strategics—and that point from utilitarian economism to ethnoculturally accented ideal "isms." However, this role enhancement also redirects history itself from the vocation of imaginatively intuitive and operationally purposive metahistory to the purposes and utility of mythohistory. In one manner for societies striving to re-become states, such mythohistory is less a rationalization of the state's role in history and more the retrojection of contemporary rationality and strategically rational interests and objectives, associated with modern statehood, into a national past that is only qualifiedly real or actual or actually or really statist rather than essentially or even primitively pluralist. And it works in another manner for advanced societies that are meaningfully states no longer, but anxious to retain or recover selectively the memory of a genuinely statist past wrought by acts judged morally or otherwise repugnant by present standards. This ambiguity about the present and ambivalence toward the past—and, implicitly, also the future—reflects accurately the indeterminate character of the evolutionary progression when evolution, isolated out of the grandest cycle of panhistorical alternations between unevenly statist and diversely pluralist frameworks of action or "orders" encompassed in the proto- to meta-systemic sequences, is confined and in part misapplied to pluralism alone.[15]

Pluralism-defining heterogeneity (and heteropolarity) manifests itself in the haphazard emergence of order out of mere coexistence of only accidentally countervailing opposites rather than a consecutive sequence of stages of evolution, structures, and strategies of competition. The tension incidental to the pluralist mode will be aggravated by premature attempts to convert near-accidental functional aggregation into institutionalized integration by virtue of doctrinal or creedal synthesis. In a statist context, by contrast, similarly activist precipitation will be constrained by developmentally logical linkages among state, (articulated) society, and economy, extending into one between (primitive) society, state, and state system. The first linkage is centered in the state's susceptibility to self-erosion if not -liquidation, to the benefit of society and economy if it meets its constituent functions too successfully; the second linkage in first primitive society's and then the state's operational requisites of self-preservation favorable to systemization. The risk of unconstrained precipitation was signaled, but not exhausted, in Europe by the disruptive effects of the premature thirteenth-century attempt at synthesis of church and state, the local givens and universal aspirations, under either papal (Guelph) or imperial (Ghibeline) aegis. The aftereffects were being contained only by incipient state formation when dynasticism's alliance with popular patriotism was necessary but also sufficient to master the feudal-aristocratic opposition to differently premature attempts at monarchical centralization. The opposite to and antecedent of the sequentially materializing state-centered internal triads—church-state-society and state-society-economy—was in the era enframing the fall of the Western Roman Empire another triad, one less logically than potentially evolutionary although now arguably reappearing. It comprises the coexistence of and chaotically operative partial countervailance among parties to a tripartite, two-tier civilized-barbarian, framework of action at the interface between statism and pluralism. Chaotic primitive pluralism tending to localism coexists with transitionally shaped and precariously consolidated quasi-national statist politics. It is problematically counter-vailed, at the universalist tier, by a decline-resistant preexisting empire (formerly Byzantine, presently American?) and incipiently ascendant authority (then papal, now global-organizational headed by the United Nations?). In the past as in the present, whereas the residually statist universe is the arena of deliberately focused policies, the pluralist one is preeminently that of multi-faceted objective processes, except where the lesser or more primitive polities are propelled into empire-type subordination by deliberate strategy of control or conquest.

The prototype of primitive pluralism of coexistent opposites—sedentary agriculturalists, nomadic pastoralists, and hunters, people of the plains and the hills in Mesopotamia and Asia Minor—has its equivalents and counterparts in the migrant (Dorian, Ionian, etc.) tribes of primeval Greece, unknown pre-Etruscan "peoples" in ancient Italy, and barbarian peoples of post-Roman Empire Europe. They countervailed each other only haphazardly before a measure of institutionalized coherence under wholly religious or also military auspices would be introduced on the way to city-(quasi-)states or larger kingdoms across a range from Sumerian, Minoan, and Mycenaean, Etruscan and Phoenician, Ostro- and Visigothic, Vandal, and Lombard, all subject to imperial sway of one kind or another down the road. The unifying characteristic is the tendency peculiar to primitive pluralism before it carries over into late statism: to relate highly conflicted particularism to a species of transcendent, religio-mythical (quasi-)universalism. The half-conscious object is to mitigate incessant and omnipresent conflict by an ideal accommodation under the auspices of a higher normative power, gods or animistic spirits, all the way from the imagined council of gods at Nippur to the oracles of Delphi and including the religious union of the twelve-hill communities of early Rome.

The blend of inchoate drives and restraints will be existentially reproduced in the successive comminglings of propitiatory priestly with the wartime predatory or protective leadership function at the head of the primitive pluralistic polity, a mix that eventually will evolve into the combination of power balancing with institutionalized arbitration-to-adjudication efforts in modern interstatist organization. Meanwhile, the interfunctional balance will shift from the priestly-sacrificial/administrative civilian to the kingly-defensive/aggressive military functions coincidentally with the increase in material surplus. The attendant secularization will logically—and did actually—lead to ever larger and increasingly statist empire-type polities or city-states with mini-empires. Progressing from

Akkad via Babylon to Persia, Sparta in Peloponnese and Athens in Attica to Macedonia, and Etruscan via the Carthaginian and Western Grecian to Roman, they related to one another in typically triangular configurations fraught with fleeting condominial two-power schemes such as Egypt's with Hatti relative to Mitanni, Sparta's with Athens relative to Persian or potential Greek challengers, and Macedon's with Syria relative to Egypt. The alternative to empire was at all times a larger consensual community, intimated in the Alexandrine concept of intercultural concord (*homonoia*) while actually adumbrated imperfectly in confederative leagues such as the Aetolian and Achaean and Rome's pre-empire phil-Hellenic approach to the faltering Greek meta-system.

Such associations project signs and signals into a future that reincarnates the past in (West) European and Euro–American Atlantic communities. A crucial factor in the course from functional aggregation to a higher degree of integration of either kind was at all times a combination of material surplus, military self-sufficiency, and theologically founded ethos if not also theocratic authority. The requisite of material surplus continues and so does the combination of its availability in growing abundance, with attempts at premature integrative syntheses in the contemporary type of regional community rooted in the sixteenth- and seventeenth-century achievements of Euro–Atlantic economy. A product of the pluralist coexistence-cum-rudimentary countervailance of residually sacral Crown, traditional or post-feudal aristocracy, and premodern middle class, this economy's contemporary form reconciles coexistent contraries in the political cultures and traditions and, up to a point, politico-economic forms of capitalism—to wit, respectively, French statism, German federalism, and Anglo-American societism, as well as neo-feudal German, statist-*dirigiste* French, and freewheeling regulation-adverse Anglo–American economism. The question mark addressed to the future is the long-term capacity of statist-pluralist hybrids of the communitarian (as opposed to imperial-hegemonic) type to dispense with the normatively diversely functioning traditional military (short of militarist) and transcendental (short of theocratic) complements of and counters to an expanding material surplus. Both are precariously propped up and weighed down by an overgrown institutional-administrative component within the circuit of interactive and -dependent functions that historically formed both state-like and state-transcending polities.[16]

Pluralism's indeterminacy makes the related phenomena at least as much a matter of political sociology as of international politics attuned more closely to statism. However, it does not remove them from the purview of realism as a philosophy focused on the study of power in any context and expression, as distinct from a theory focused on power's historical concentration in a unitary state, which sacrifices evolutionary time to conditioning space and buttresses the monopoly of territoriality with ahistoricity. The present era of pluralism's rebirth and only potential and then localized resurgence of classic statism offers but a slender foundation for the attempt to peer into the future at a point that may well prove to have been but one of history's many false starts after a break in antecedent patterns. In any event, meditations about alternative futures must take into account the main features of the statist type of evolution when addressing the associated policy options.[17]

Notes

1. The preceding three sections are excerpted, with changes, from CE 7–30, 338 (2.par.)–346 (end 3.par.); RRA 17(2.par.), 51–57, 108–111.

2. WP 1–3, 227 (1.par.); RWO 165–184 (end 3.par.); WP 227 (2.par.)–229 (end 1.par.), 231 (3.par.)–232 (end 2.par.).

3. WP 60 (2.par.)–66 (end 2.par.), 52 (3.par.)–57.

4. WP 105–108 (end 2.par.).

5. WP 232 (3.par.)–244 (end 2.par.), 244 (3.par.)–257 (end 3.par.), 272 (2.par.)–274 (end 2.par.).

6. WP 326 (3.par.)–334 (end 1.par.).

7. SIE 45 (3.par.)–55 (end 2.par.), 56 (3.par.)–59 (end 1.par.), 66 (2.par.)–67 (end 2.par.); WP 257 (4.par.)–270.

8. WP 271–272 (end 1.par.), 203 (2.par.)–214 (end 1.par.).

9. WP 26 (2.par.)–35 (end 2.par.).

10. WP 339 (3.par.)–350 (end 2.par.), 214 (2.par.)–226.

11. WP 288 (2.par.)–296 (end 1.par.). And ch. 2, n. 1 for references regarding American expansion.

12. WP 302 (2.par.)–308.

13. WP 350 (3.par.)–361 (end 1.par.).

14. WP 361 (2.par.)–363.

15. RR 155–161 (end 1.par.), 10–13 (end 2.par.)

16. RR 115 (3.par.)–129, 141 (2.par.)–145 (end 2.par.), 152 (2.par.)–153 (end 2.par.).

17. RWO 184 (4.par.)–187.

4

Projection Contra Prediction: Alternative Futures and Policy Options

Fully historicizing world politics requires combining exploration of the past by way of evolution with consequently informed connection of the resulting present to a future made meaningful by continuing the past- and present-shaping interactions, while normatively upgrading them wherever possible. Equipping the futuristic with the dialectical dimension, a speculative approach to reality within a further expanded realism becomes an activist-voluntaristic counter to a passive-deterministic theory aspiring to prediction in a scientific mode, without becoming wholly agnostic as to the possibility of unraveling intricate determination. Instead of pursuing through efforts at science-validating prediction a goal inherently inappropriate for the social function of the study of world politics, historicizing realism is committed to empirically-analytically and normatively disciplined policy prescriptions. Unlike a prediction disguising prophecy, prescription of policy rests on the right kind of projections while admitting openly to a prophetic bias. A projection is of the right kind when it corrects for the misleading limitations of a linear mode. It does this when, incorporating both the countervailing interactional and cyclically evolutionary dynamics into trends suggested by its linear variety, projection itself becomes cyclical. Such a correction is not only actually occurring but is also a desirable requisite of historically intelligent and strategically rational policies responding to an actual, on behalf of a normatively preferred, environment under the inspiration from a predictive prophecy intent on straddling the portents of linear and promise of cyclical projection.

A normatively desirable substantive product of such a projection and a genuinely if romantically realistic objective of the resulting policy is the prevalence of accommodation over antagonization short of universal pacification, capable of extending to institutionalized cooperation implement-

151

ing the precepts of realism's progressivist variety. A thus directed policy will express the true facts of the different kinds and motives of expansion as an aspect of both interaction and evolution, without denying those of balancing counteraction and while remaining consistent with the ethically neutral conception of war as a mechanism of reequilibration. As opposed to the substantive objective, the procedural requisite is a systemic kind of thinking, one conforming with the definition of "system" as a complex of interconnected and -acting parts and "thinking" as a dialectically triadic process. Centered on power balancing, such thinking is the operative facet of a speculative system of thought which, adding expansion and evolution to balance-of-power interaction, is in turn the cognitively procedural precondition of a form of thinking more commonly preached than practiced. As a theory-substitute, a system of thought systematizes the many facets of world politics without aiming at or achieving their synthesis, depending on strategy to do the synthesizing in its own motivation and purpose instead of only relating the present inevitably to a future through any kind of action. Connecting all three—system of thought, systemic thinking, and synthesizing strategy—in both analysis and action is a complex of alternative futures. These are to be hypothesized in light of known antecedents and knowable prospective modifiers in the interest of empirically disciplined projection and are to be individually either promoted or prevented in consonance with a prophecy of either positive promise or negative portent.

Expanding the balance of power and realism for connecting systemic thinking with system of thought in policy

Whereas conventional realism is much less of a theory than a philosophy with intimations for policy, neo-realism and poststructuralism pretend to the status of theory with little or no bearing on—or interest in—policy. So far, and for a long time, the only theory world politics could boast of is the balance of power: a depiction of what actually takes place and a guide to policy to make it so. Alone among more ambitious theories it combines explanatory with predictive power or, at least, potential in the only attainable measure: in gross outline over the medium-to-long run. Its intimations are both universal—what happens in principle everywhere—and particular—what happens in practice in a given setting. The only question, creating the space for mixing analysis with imagination, is where the specific locus of its operation is to be found: on what level of the sociopolitical ladder or pyramid and between or among how many and what kind of parties, bearing on the site and type of principal crisis. When the setting is more than usually complex, exhibiting intricate ramifications from the core that constitutes or represents real power, the linkages among several "where's" and "who's" point from a simple or central balance of power to an only structurally multitiered (domestic, regional, global) or also functionally complex equilibrium: a no more than qualifying feature of the concept's and action's elementary simplicity. Absorbing the complexity vindicates the principle's validity (in re theory) and utility (in re policy), due to its root in basic instincts and urges without which at bottom no theorization of so intensely and primitively human and social activity as politics can stand—and, thus founded, survive the bias to oblivion after a moment of academic celebrity.

This being so, it will be only the qualitatively comparable factors pertaining to expansion and evolution that significantly modify elementary balancing of power in ways relevant for both theory and policy. Far from extinguishing the balancing of power like the pretended or would-be technologically, sociopolitically, or normatively identified disqualifiers, and more significantly than its functional and formal-institutional diversifiers, the qualitatively coequal substantive amplifiers expand the scope of the balancing process and its product. They invite strategy to synthesize in action all of the factors, processes, and their products that escape efforts at, and may exceed the grasp of, a generalized condensation in a verbal summation sufficiently succinct to be anywhere near parsimoniously elegant theory formulation.

As one of the equally process- and product-related substantive complements-and-modifiers of the balance of power, expansion is homogeneous with the balance because it is the same in kind—as the other facet of the indivisible drive-restraint or challenge-response complex—and is, as such, complementary as to function. As another modifier, evolution is inherently complementary within the likewise if differently—because less subjectively than objectively—indivisible space/time complex or continuum. The question raised by the two amplifications is whether the balance of power, necessary as both concept and policy guide, is also sufficient in and of itself—i.e., without the two complements—to fulfill the basic purposes of realism-as-philosophical outlook-or-perspective susceptible of subcategorization. That is to say, whether power balancing is in its primitive (i.e., original and elementary) condition sufficient for both understanding *and* policy formulation in principle or fundamentally and for relating past to present practice and beyond futuristically. Integrating the two purposes implies comprehending (i.e., both linking together and intuiting) two crucial facets of dualistic reality and rationality: the former basically as to facts (conveyed through power-related interests) and values (absorbed in norms-related inspirations), and the latter as to strategic rationality (distinctive for real politics qua geopolitics) and historical intelligence (expanding geopolitics into developmentally and normatively expanded geohistoricism).

When internally cleft reality and rationality surface in secondary and in part derivative dualities such as specific conflicts vs. schisms, expansion and evolution present themselves relative to the balance of power in principle and affect practice sufficiently as alternately causes and consequences to confirm their essential homogeneity and existential interdependence. Thus, viewing expansion correctly in light of interactional dynamic and its rational-strategic correlates as alternately or equally a matter of drive or push of actors and pull from or outward-drawing effect of the arena, the state system is a cause of expansion by acting as drive-inviting vacuum or configuration of power in practice, or as ultimate structural as opposed to proximate operational determinant in principle. Conversely, the preservation of this same causally active factor is the actual or aspired-to consequence of the power balancing. Thus also, viewed in terms of evolution and historical intelligence, the state system is the consequence of the first-stage expansive format of the foreign policy posture favoring expansion over consolidation when it is incipiently crystallized as part of resistance to the hypothetical implications of open-endedly diffuse expansiveness (e.g., premature consolidation of a diffuse into an irreversibly compact power structure). Yet as the crystallization of the state system and incidentally the power balance expands from core to entirety of the structure, the latter becomes differently the cause of the exuberant and compulsive formats concurrently with changes in the allocation and configuration of rise and decline factors and actors. Diversely intermediate between the structure-centered pull vs. actor-centered push-related interactional, and foreign policy postures-related evolutionary determinants, are the strategic/systemic, domestic, and economic functional stimuli of expansion as either original or subsidiary and primary or secondary. They are intermediate because neither shortest- nor longest-term in the time spans of their efficacy and neither imperative nor wholly but suggestive in causative effects. As such, the functional stimuli relate to one another directly as, alternately, causes and consequences within the regressive chain of causation, and indirectly in relation to the momentary state of crystallization of the state system and the balancing process. This process is more a consequence in the predatory-drive stage and cause in the preclusive one of the strategic/systemic determinant. And, less distinguishably because of the intervening distances between cause and effect, it is somewhat more cause than consequence in the transactional and traumatic rather than the trusteeship phase of the domestic stimuli and in the formalized-protective and formative-war rather than the informal free-trade imperialism relative to the economic determinant.

The relation between causes and consequences and between primitive

and expanded balance of power and realism is basic to the relationship
between strategic thinking and system of thought. While directed to shaping policies, thinking is systemic when it takes into account the system-
wide ripple effect of any deliberately engendered or spontaneously occurring substantial change. To meet this requirement, this kind of thinking
focuses primarily on the power/interest facets of the power-normatively
formed interactions while reflexively avoiding one-to-one or bilaterally
motivated reactions. The operationally most specific part is the awareness
that any of one power's response or initiative in relation to another actor
will affect the situation and therefore policies of a third party, requiring
consideration of its potential benefits from action undertaken in relation
to the immediately targeted second agent. Thus also, more generally, the
consequence of any act responsive to a prior situation will create a new
situation with second-order consequences to be factored into the first
response to the anterior condition before it is undertaken. This means
that considering the full range of the three-actors-plus reactive responses—embodied in an at least two- and if possible three-link chain
of immediate and ulterior consequences—is as important spatially and
interactionally as the chain of causes is temporally and developmentally.

As part of comprising this causal chain, a system of thought encompasses fully the normative modifier of the balance-of-power dynamic,
converging on values, and the operational modifier by incorporating
expansion and evolution. Doing both helps apprehend, so as to also strategically manage, the historico-evolutionary mutations in the relationship
between equilibration and expansionism, occurring as the representative
actors themselves evolve and expand: from genealogically familistic, tribal
or dynastic, through geopolitically territorial-to-nation statist, to region-
ally-to-civilizationally defined and delimited communitarian polities.
Whether or not expanding physically, actors will diversely qualify as either representative or legitimate in several respects: as at any time "presently" most recent developmentally and also relevant, not least as
potential synthesizers of contrasting sides to contemporaneously dominant schism or schisms; as prospectively optimal in terms of a viable size-
or-scope for operationally effective coherence and sociopolitically or culturally founded solidarity; and, for these reasons, as the legitimate or logical provisional result of evolutionary progression.

The result is both when it conforms to the current state of long-term
development on two levels. One level is from and through an inter-functional circuit, only consummated by a shared corporate ethos, that transforms primitively pluralist into increasingly state-like actors. The other
level concerns transmutations between balance of internally compact
power units and an inter-functionally more complex equilibrium operationalized through a likewise more complicated strategic equation, as part

of an ascent toward or reversion from statism in the direction of institutionalized pluralism. A no more than potential culmination is implicit in the combination of interstatist and pluralist dynamic within a dialectic involving cultures-or-civilizations engaged in ambiguously competitive-cooperative interactions as correspondingly lopsided subjects of values as distinct from power either intrinsically or instrumentally. The resulting regional communities subsume both the balance of power and the strategic equation, both the inherently repellent military-political and at least potentially attractive economic capabilities, in upholding corporate autonomy of the variously enlarged-and-evolved forms of polity that surface from antecedent progression on a no less ambiguously trans-statist or -societal plane.

Implicit in such transfers and transcensions is, conjointly with the change-prone or -capable subjects or incumbents of the pertinent interplay, the hierarchy of individual and collective values. Critical for world politics is the relationship and potential conflict between individual freedom and corporate autonomy in relation to order and authority respectively. This relationship raises the question of the extent to and conditions in which individual freedom may be alienated for the sake of a necessary minimum of order as ultimately preconditional and, therefore, in the last analysis superior, to the exercise of that freedom. Implied in this quandary is one more directly operationally relevant. Is corporate autonomy alienable to any extent and under any conditions, or is it not, regardless of the specific type of a particular order (statist or pluralist) because this autonomy is necessary to preserve moral and legal (or other normatively legitimate and effective) authority—one capable of not only safeguarding the essentials of individual freedom but also setting socially valuable-to-indispensable limits to such a freedom's degeneration into anarchy? If and when the developmentally expanding (because most efficient possible) prime subject-hood of corporate autonomy has settled on regionally delimited community-cum-civilization, the process that comprises many-sidedly interlocking equilibrium, expansion, and evolution gives rise to a particular need and achieves a corresponding capacity for projection. To be projected are factors and facets identified schematically and systematized in an analysis supportive of systemic thinking, into a strategy synthesizing all or most of the wider range of referents of a system of thought. Representative of the ensuing complexity surrounding the balance of power is a problematic choice intrinsic to the power balance itself: between intra- and extra-systemic strategy, i.e., between avoiding and issuing an appeal from autochthonous equilibrium to an outsider, and managing and mismanaging the difference between hegemonic preponderance and mere preeminence. Biased operationally, this choice can be extended in practice and must be expanded speculatively in principle into another choice: between only geostrategically or also philosophico-historically valid strategy. This particular choice is implicit in the fundamental one between only strategically rational systemic thinking or also a historically intelligent system of thought.

One might aspire beyond systematization to synthesis in analysis or to a form of apprehension available to a philosophy of history innocent of real politics. Short of such a synthesis, a system of thought implicit in the speculative approach that introduces expansion and evolution systematically into realism's both indispensable and defining link between understanding and policy does both less and more. It upgrades properly construed in-depth appeasement as a practically valid strategy. Moreover, it can do so without dislodging war, viewed as a normatively neutral mechanism for resolving critically destabilizing discrepancies and conciliating essential continuity with existential change, for the sake of a peace that is unconditionally favored as the normatively supreme alternative to violent conflict because societally, culturally, and ethically cost-free. In lieu of such a peace, appeasement can be vindicated on behalf of the autonomy and authority of a developmentally advanced and spatially enlarged regional-civilizational optimum as a subject of power and values. Instead of merely expanding interstate balance of power mechanically as one revolving around and oscillating in function of internally compact and reciprocally discrete masses of capabilities, a strategy of appeasement achieves also an organic effect by incorporating societally and culturally pluralist features through their dynamic interactions and -stimulations.

Testing theories and categories of realism for capacity to meaningfully aggregate facts with values through policy

Implicit in the potential of the speculative approach are three challenges to—and tests of the validity and utility of—alternative theories of world politics. The latter vary and can be assessed in terms of their capacities to calculate the costs against the benefits of alternative basic strategies, incorporating and transcending apparent or real paradoxes rising to inconsistencies if not also contradictions between power/interest-related facts and norms/values-related fictions and, finally, narrowing if not also closing the gap within world politics between individual acts or intentions and aggregate outcomes. All this is to be done in ways conducive to disclosing significant meanings for the ongoing momentum of dynamic interactions and evolutionary progression, revolving in the last analysis around prevention of forcible unification and promotion of spontaneous unity within expanding orbits.

The costs and benefits of strategies can be confined to the crudest real

political factors of (quantitative) power and (short-term particular) interest, and their calculation can be limited to their distribution among the
several parties to an issue—such as, illustratively but not solely, the appeal
from a suspected hegemony-seeking inside subverter to a presumptive
outside savior of a system's equilibrium. Even when such calculation conforms with the basic law of systemic thinking—embodying the effect of
any one particular change on everything else in an (at least) three-party
spatial setting and three-phase temporal perspective—it will ignore or fi-
nesse any potential conflict between interests and values, not to be confused with formal/legal rights. Thus, protecting the national power of the
appellant can discount the appeal's cost in independence relative to the
outsider while enhancing the latter's power-interest benefit at a corresponding, but presumably unequal, cost to the challenging and the defending insiders. A supporting calculation will combine on the existential,
i.e., real-political, grounds the challenger's primitively construed expansionism with a correspondingly construed balance of power. A conversely
or complementarily normative justification or rationalization will add individual freedoms to be shielded against the values of the adversary (e.g.,
Wilhelmine Germany's autocratic militarism in the context of the Anglo–
French appeal to the United States in World War I), demonized to a degree
commensurate with the implicitly suppressed normative costs in corporate autonomy incurred by the appeal.

The calculation is more complex, and the factor of values (and of extra-
strategic/systemic domestic and economic assets and liabilities) more significant, in and for a strategy that would replace extra-systemic appeal
with intra-systemic accommodation or any other comparable alternative
to a purely or narrowly rational-strategic, reflexively automatic response—i.e., an alternative compatible with expanding the range of system-wide changes, to be taken into account when calculating costs and
benefits, to include degradation of the existing system relative to one positioned to replace it. Such a recalculation implies and may presuppose expanding also, or first, systemic thinking itself in the direction of the
wider-ranging system of thought that incorporates the extra-strategic feature of values. As this amplification unfolds, the interpretation of world
politics in its narrowly power/interest-centered variety associated with a
conceptually primitive balance of power realizes the power-normative
form or essence of politics without necessarily aiming at or being capable
of achieving an overall substantive, rather than only strategy-wrought
procedural, synthesis of the factual and the fictional, transactional and
transcendent, elements—a synthesis that faces up to the issue of ultimate
purpose or meaning of world politics-and-history.

The very notion of a meaning for world politics consummates its fusion
with world history as equally questionable but assuredly inseparable from

the sequentially unfolding and operationally interlocking patterns of evolution. Corresponding to the essential difference between evolutionary momentum and its meaning, the projection from the present to future and "retrojection" from present to past facts in delineating evolutionary progression differs from the only retrospectively possible discernment if not only divination of the meaning of an accomplished historico-political phase or, a fortiori, its prospectively prophetic anticipation at the outset of an only impending phase. Analytically and actually interdependent with the ascending planes of meaningful activities is the amplification of the balance of power as strategy-relevant dynamic by the addition of expansion, evolution, and values. Concurrently occurring is, finally, the structural-functional-normative diversification of the underlying equilibrium dynamic: from compactly multifactoral statist power and the latter's deconcentration through loosely inter-functional and institutionalization-prone equilibrium to a mere dialectic interplay centered on values' often paradoxical relation to power and interests.

At the lowest interstatist systemic level of power/interest-centered action and reaction, concentrated in conflict of actual or self-perceived polar opposites subject to rise and decline, meaning is focused purposively on the prevention of forcible unification by an actually or presumptively hegemony-seeking expansionist, even when this purpose is in fact achieved incidentally to complying with the dictate of individually self-regarding instincts. If this is so, what are the individually corresponding attributes of actually or potentially meaningful processes and their mediation by policies into products occupying the two next higher levels? Prominent among them is, on the second level, the evolution-propelling expression of the equilibrium concept and dynamic in the reciprocal adaptation of subjects of power and values. Involved in schisms transcending particular conflicts, the adaptation is externalized in the very opposites to first-level polar opposition between parties to a primitive balance of power: the interpenetration of changes with continuity in the evolutionary process and the overlaps of specific differences over and above underlying generic similarities if not identities on the part of the schisms. Correspondingly different from the power/interest monopoly are the different assortments of power/interest- and values-centered terms as primary or derivative relative to one another—e.g., values as original and power/interest as derivative for the West–East and the other way around for the land–sea power schism, with the existential-normative universalization of the historically specific sacral–secular as inherently indeterminate. This second-level operational dynamic (and its interpretation) necessarily connects interaction to evolution—the former as the latter's precondition and the latter as the former's propellent—and mandates a strategically sophisticated (i.e., consummately realistic) approach to expansion as a consequence. Its meaning is accordingly raised from the avoidance of forcible unification to advancement of spontaneous unity via an increase in the prospects for appeasement-like accommodation between variably state-like (pre- or post-statist) parties, albeit one to be realized only intraregionally on a pluralist communitarian or quasi-empire-like basis. Operationally, developmentally, and normatively intermediate, this dynamic also points to the third and highest level in terms of not so much interpenetration versus polar opposition as of consummation of previously revealed trends, such as from statism to pluralism or smaller to larger subjects of value, sites of authority-and-autonomy, and scopes of potential combination of diversity with unity and individualities with community.

Traditional realism focuses on the lowest operational level of an "ideally" self-regulating and -perpetuating equilibrium dynamic, susceptible of qualitative distillation into the motions and momentum of political physics. As a mode of interpretation along a scale doing justice to both facts and values, it allows for amplification in the direction of values but will be typically confined to the factual power/interest dimension in regard to action and to rationality in analysis so as to protect its status as theory by limiting the range of included variables. A contrary, and potentially alternative, mode of interpretation is philosophy of history when it centers on values only. Correspondingly opposed to the prevention of forcible unification in pragmatic transactions is, in regard to meaning, the integrally transcendental one of an ultimately necessary, spontaneous or enforced unity that consummates a law-like sequence of cultures and civilizations unequally but increasingly capable or worthy of translating messianic pretensions into a providentially decreed and redemptively unifying order. It is at the intersection of these alternatives that the speculatively articulated romantic subcategory of realism incorporates substantive, cultural-civilizational, and the progressivist subcategory inserts procedural, formal-institutional, values into the historically evolving dynamic of power-centered interests, each brand doing this as neither a theory of politics nor equally pure philosophy of history but in an analytically orderly manner. As a result, a simply-to-simplistically rationalistic action-reaction type causation of real politics, associated with only quantitative conception of structure and either abstraction or Manichean polarization of values, can be encompassed in a more complex fact-value dialectic, and the associated paradoxical expressions of severally dualistic power-normative reality be addressed without submerging real politics in depoliticized history.

This middle way proves its conceptual validity and potential utility for policy when, the conflict between, for instance, freedom of individual Frenchmen and Englishmen and corporate autonomy of France and England as an integral part of such reality gives rise to a theoretical dilemma and a practical policy equation. The tragic poetics-related ethical aspect of neither the dilemma nor the equation is or can be resolved simply in terms of power, either in the sense of compensating the diminution of the collective power of Europe with the accretion of the (American) outsider's or of increasing the collective power of a Europe invigorated by a late-entering insider (Germany) in the pre-World War I setting—and, during and after the Cold War, in the sense of preserving the collective power of the West by favoring China over Russia in analogous capacities. The implications become more complex, but the dilemma somewhat easier to transcend, when viewed in terms of the *Aufhebung*-centered dialectic: Which value can be preserved and which prejudiced if not forfeited in conditions of a necessary choice ruling out the integral preservation of all (sovereign independence or diplomatic primacy of France and England, freedom or privileges of individual Frenchmen and Englishmen, or the power and autonomy of Europe)? And what achievable optimum solution can be obtained within what setting and through which strategy that raises the volume of power-and-influence of the outsider or the intrasystemic challenger within an order that enhances or abridges the sum of values: only formal and procedural ones of the actor's legal-political independence or also the substantive ones pertaining to its cultural-civilizational autonomy? And does either obtain within what spatial scope (national or regional) or also structural shape (statist, pluralist, or mixed hybrid) and what mix of power/interest pragmatic and substantive/procedural normative assets?

Projecting past-present developments into alternative futures to promote or prevent by policy

To inquire meaningfully into the future for the sake of discerning policy options necessitates first organizing the past through an "anti-theory" that unifies propensities governing dynamics with patterns of evolution in a better understanding of the attendant complexities. At the bottom of the complexities are several circularities: an inter-functional (between domestic and systemic, economic and real political factors) pervading political economy, and two inter-motional—one involving interactions in terms of drive and restraint, expansion and equilibrium, and another concerning evolution. Therein, the link between energizing motor and conflictual mechanism gives rise to external manifestations, which at any time constitute the matrix of the interactional dynamic that has stimulated the entire process from the start, beset by its own dilemmas with influence on continuity and change. The circularities will be relaxed and the matrix loosened in favor of radical mutation only when fundamental changes have taken place on the part of key actors and assets, mindsets and motivations, which transform an interstate system into a societally biased pluralistic order—or a mix of the two.

Before a pluralist replaces a statist order, critical sequences will have shaped the pattern of a state system's evolution, manifest most spectacularly in the concurrent crystallization of the powers qua actors and the balance of power qua agenda, the state system's climactic institutionalization in a concert of powers, and its supersession by a successor in the form of another state system most frequently or a different kind of order exceptionally. This terminal crisis will be typically consequent on the system's inability to reequilibrate disturbances from resources available within itself, its own agents and assets, due to a chain of failures by prominent actors to adapt to alternations in capability structures and innovations affecting functions—all of which continue engendering energy-generating crises past their previously productively evolution-propelling potential, channeled into and realized via particular conflicts.

Actors' maladjustment to either intra- or extra-systemic change is automatically transposed into malfunctioning of the arena, triggering pressures for transformations within a system or transference between kinds of system. Role/resource/risk-related generic causes of major wars mediate, meanwhile, the connection between dynamic interaction and evolutionary progression. This happens as the disparities between readily mobilizeable resources and asserted or coveted roles are questionably evened out by assumed, or enlarged by avoided, risks in generating wars as the normatively neutral mechanism of evolution actuated by the rise and decline of major powers and, over a longer cycle, leading types of polity. Staggered entries of early and late participants into connecting interactions with evolution aggravate the dynamics of rise and decline into, and by way of, struggles over succession to primacy, while the rise/decline dynamic is expressed overtly in basic foreign policy postures and covertly in behavioral norms centered on the ideal-typical one of strategically rational means-ends relationship. The root of a system's terminal crisis is in an unmanageably disorderly conjunction of the several sequences, or the objects thereof, which will have given rise to the progressively supplanted founders' inability to withstand the latecomers without assistance from outside the system's boundaries. Which way and how a debilitated system is being superseded will in turn depend on whether its interactional dynamic is only sublimated and muted or virtually suppressed—i.e., meta-systemization is toward regional community or coercive empire—and whether one or the other is within only a sector or the entirety of a system that passes only in space toward a new center or also in time toward a future reproducing an earlier past. When a system is replaced by a different kind of order, a grand political revolution associated with major war will have combined domestic revolutions that engage societies in interclass succession with alterations in forms and magnitudes or types of polities, sufficient in themselves for sequences between micro- and macro- and proto- and meta-systems respectively.

In such an overall actual-and-analytical setting, any attempt at prediction of the future will fall between projection and prophecy before it can vindicate the prediction through the right kind of policy. Limitations affecting prediction convey the impossibility of a methodologically rigorous or scientifically exact international relations theory, while projection and prophecy are in different degrees contingent on no more than a conceptually shaped understanding of world politics. Projecting experienced past and present structures and trends into the future will be subject to their being deflected by counteractive forces and pressures operative on the same basic principle, that of world politics in general and interstate systems in particular. Prophecy will, by contrast, raise the conflicted mechanics of either to the plane and problem of their meaning in that it encompasses values that affect societies and civilizations and inflect their course and conduct as complex organisms. The range of alternative futures is bounded by a limited number of possibilities: the continuance of a basic type of order (statist or pluralist) in its essentials; transition between the types that either moderates or exacerbates the operation of one by the characteristics of the other; and reversion to a previously subordinate or latent type that has been either enhanced by the intervening type of order that it supersedes (representing progress) or subverted by its own tendency to debasement (and represents regression relative to the superseded type). The fact that all three possibilities are commingled in the immediate future of world politics enhances the salience of its antecedents and determines the way of investigating them as the one available basis for meditating on the future via combinations of projection with prophecy. In that looking beyond the present to the future entails more basic choices among the attributes and potentials of projection, prediction, and prescription, it differs from retrospection content to select factors that stimulate expansion or evolutionary progression.

The relatively easiest projection is from structure and related tendencies, such as the tendency of bipolarity to engender multipolarization and, less certainly, for overlarge parties prone to dissolution to be eventually consolidated into smaller but more compact entities as an alternative to total disappearance. Such entities would presently constitute a virtual micro-system when compared with one or both of the superpowers and the scope of a fully globalized and integrated macro-system. As opposed to the virtual, a genuine micro-system such as the Middle Eastern or Southeast Asian can help the recrystallization by eliciting competition among the relatively larger outsiders. But even independently of such a stimulus, a genuine system of states could arise in the post-Cold War future under this projection, comprising the Eurasian and Asian–Pacific powers tending toward midterm institutionalization in a concert of powers implementing the parties' antecedent socialization into such a system's customary conventions. Unlike the relatively straightforward tendency to multipolarization in function of two-power competition, consolidation entails a partially cyclical movement over a longer time span as state systems evolve out of a proto-systemic mix of pluralism and statism only to veer back eventually. Moderately sized statism can, therefore, in large parts of the world be a but brief transition to a more advanced form of pluralism under the auspices of re-enlarged because henceforth regional polities, confirming the twin tendency for optimum size to alternate and evolution to accelerate. A consequently modified and inevitably complicated type of projection identifies less reliably the future center of gravity than the pattern of an emerging order's gradation from initiation to institutionalization prior to eventual supersession by a state system of variable actor magnitudes or a pluralistic alternative to it. Moreover, for this cyclically extended or any other, including linear, projection to integrate historical intelligence fully into policy prescription requires including the recurrent tendency for early ideological biases to yield relatively quickly and soon to pragmatization of basic dispositions and stakes definition, further increasing the difficulty to predict.

Cyclical, unlike linear, projection anticipates reactions to the initial tendency when deputizing for prediction. Its complexities create the basis for prophecy that will incorporate not only the narrowly structural and behavioral tendencies but also broadly cultural factors, and not only formally organizational but also value-institutional constituents of progression. Such normative qualifiers invalidate or at least problematize easy ad hoc projections, and related predictions, from particular past events and complexes of events into future ones on the "back to the future" model. Necessary caution applies to such issues as the Eastern Question (in relation to, say, the Bosnian conflict among South European ministates consequent on the Arab–Israeli conflict) or the so-called Great Game in Asia (regarding, say, competition over Central Asia between post-Soviet Russia and adjacent Islamic states). The technological and organizational facets of narrowly conceived technical civilization, which make up much of empirically manifest progression, reinforce the broadly speaking cultural modifiers that reduce the plausibility of such projections, let alone predictions. Ignoring the modifiers discounts changes in the specific nature of the stakes and the particular methods and instruments employed and employable in their pursuit. This will devalue mechanical projections without necessarily invalidating the resumption of more basic continuities in the evolutionary process to which the reemergent issues testify. Most commonly identified with progress as distinct from progression are the latter's institutional, organizational, and formally (i.e., legally) normative facets that conflate alternating frameworks of action (such as statist and pluralist) within the bounds and under the aegis of an advancing overall organization of world politics. Viewing the future in these meliorative terms—and projecting forward the demonstrable growth of the organizational-normative superstructure—is the easiest approach to the problem and dilemma of continuity versus change. Moreover, commingling thus projection with prediction and both with prophecy is more tempting for the liberal than the conservative mindset's perceptions about cooperation and conflict, and more attractive for the progressivist than the romantic variety of realism. The liberal-progressivist bias becomes especially plausible in periods of a lull between military-political crises, which lull projects either broadly domestic or specifically economic issues and concerns, resources and remedies, into a crisis vacuum inviting or at least responsive to a cooperative approach.[1]

With evolution deflected from a straight path and its rate apparently slowing, previously basic questions cast an all the more necessary bridge between the weakened utility of linear in favor of cyclically extended projection and engender a correspondingly heightened appeal of prophecy. Prophecy's dual quality as promise and portent is in such a setting manifest in the growing tension between utopia and nemesis: the utopia of a world community, revived by the collapse of totalitarian politics and economics before ostensibly triumphant democracy and free market, and the nemesis of too complete a triumph threatening the victorious West no less (and in a new form more) than trials during the late conflict. World community as an end state is contingent on worldwide migration of power centers being completed without arousing recidivist resistance on the part of earlier incumbents. The intervening strategies must meanwhile respond to structures as they emerge out of successive marriages of changing mindsets with innovative technologies without incurring the tyranny of structure by wholly neglecting realization-capable latent for restrictively manifest structure—as important a difference for future prospects as that between only quantitative and qualitatively modified total structures is for any transient present. Mediating between deliverance and doom within prophecy and between contrarily prophetic prognoses and weakly predictive projections becomes essential when manifest structures have become indeterminate while the previously manifest (U.S.–Russian–Chinese) structure has in its currently latent status remained fundamentally unchanged and potentially more than ever determining. Likewise enhanced rather than lessened in and for an era of pluralist-statist heterogeneity is the salience of the two interconnected relationships—between

West and East (and specifically U.S. and Russia) and between the state and society.[2]

Whereas moderate statism is institutionally engaged in confrontation with materialistic society, its procedurally dual (backward temporal and eastward spatial) passing involves it in competition with communitarian pluralism. This agenda has been released from the constraints of a bipolar structure only to be exposed to the ambiguities of alternative dualities (e.g., the "two cities" of the haves and have nots), and from the maritime-continental geostrategic focus of the West–East schism only to face up fully to this schism's originally defining value-institutional essence. The principal great power actors remain substantially the same, but the strategy-relevant attitudes proceed from a substantially modified environment, one tending to recall variously pre-World War I rather than post-World War II conditions without replicating the earlier mindsets due to the intervening dimming of the state's transcendent attributes or merely attributions.[3]

Extended in the amorphous post-Cold War structure together with the evolutionary time frame, the statist-pluralist continuum mirrors the long evolutionary cycle from pluralism to statism and back to pluralism. The heterogeneous forms of political organization and disorganization along the West-to-East (and North-to-South) spectrum constitute presently too indeterminate a structure for it to perform its essential function: to signal appropriately reflective attitudes, agendas, and strategies, including alignments among diversely situated and evolved polities. The result is to problematize defenses or mere deterrents against diffuse sources of a disorder magnified by spontaneous displacements of populations between unevenly favored regions. Preference may in such a setting be plausibly directed to different forms of regionalism, covering a range determined currently more by temporally differentiated evolutionary than by spatially determined factors. A future tending in this direction could integrate the compensatorily strengthened functional-institutional with the temporarily weakened structural-strategic constituent of integral politics in a proportion determined by local/regional conditions and in ways that updated survival-capable (and functionally useful) continuities by incorporating operationally inescapable real changes. A transition from purely statist politics might be mediated, and in the process muted, through two parallel transpositions. While one transposes perennially valuable normative attributes of the state, and potential virtues of the state idea, onto a regional community, the other transposes the existential interstate balancing agenda onto an interregional equilibrium. Such an equilibrium would accommodate also cultural or civilizational differences between regions after safeguarding them against prematurely one-sided attempts at global uniformalization in political and socioeconomic cultures.[4]

Ordering the past-present-future chain by virtue of rebirths and reversions vs. repetitions

When trying to divine the flow of history between past and future, individual events or sets of events treated as uniquely constituted can be aligned chronologically at the risk of rigid periodization. Or masses of data can be more usefully disaggregated into slices of composite events, constellations and contingencies, distinctive-to-typical with respects to an overall configuration as well as to specifics. The present can display characteristics reminiscent of a prior era and arena, or of an earlier transition between eras or kinds of arenas; and several past events attending the transition can be identified as comparable with either differently remote or present ones, and reconstructed in ways highlighting shared salient characteristics. When recurrence of particular events becomes thus a plausible hypothesis, transposing the hypothesis into a practically significant development by either promoting or opposing a previously transpired outcome becomes a credible strategy. The past-present-future chain is operationalized from a proposition necessary for meaningful analysis into a program of possible action and plausible advocacy. And the reconstruction of particulars will serve as a means for a degree of abstraction, preconditional to systematic articulation of the ostensibly chaotic flow of interactions, revealed in events, into the defining incidents of conceptualized and patterned evolution.

The principle of selection by the criterion of present-to-future relevance imposes choices entailing various degrees of simplification. Thus, the data can be assembled in function of the number of key powers or players, from one via two to three and on to more (say five?) as the narrowly quantitative diversifier of structure. Or the scene can be organized according to qualities of key features or attributes that co-shape both structures and strategies while complex compounds of material (trading or industrial economic) and creedal (religious or ideological) factors or features—concentrated in discrete schisms—are identified as comparable over time. Such identification leads to distinguishing complex and volatile arenas and eras from those more settled and crystallized and consequently better managed or manageable by rational strategies. The minimal purpose of identifying discrete situations and attendant clusters of broadly conceived events is to provide a factual-historical basis for abstracting hidden features of dynamic interactions that are significant for evolution. Only when comparable situations have actually recurred, preferably more than once, can their recurrence be a basis for even a hypothetical projection into the future. Such a projection is facilitated by the recognition of the finite-to-small range of discrete cardinal situations and event clusters, reflecting the limited number of issues and institutions central to the dynamics of politics. The paucity of the range does not rule out multiplicity on the part of secondary, conditioning and modifying, features and factors—a fact that complicates the effort to identify comparable situations and the mechanism of transitions from one situation or cluster to the next.

It is difficult to penetrate beyond the generality of an adaptive reequilibration process, instigated by malfunctions as to structures and strategies in the interactional dynamic or asymmetries as to strategies and stages in the evolutionary process. Two facts help a little, but not enough: One, reequilibration is manifest structurally through the tendency for the number of prime actors to alternately expand through the generative effect of competition among very few protagonists or contract through the erosive effect of contentions among the greater number of actors. And two, restoration of balance is attended by the operationally induced trend for real-politically motivated conflicts to alternate between their initial or intermittent exacerbation and the eventual abatement or displacement of their ideologically accented value-institutional features, tantamount to pragmatization. If the object is to articulate alternative futures for the currently extended long run, the momentarily receding structural-strategic model of international politics and momentarily ascendant functional-institutional one serve the purpose all the better for converging in essential respects. Both models involve rebirths of basic forms of polity and structure and returns of policies or strategies, while both display or conceal the potential for reversals and retrogressions that belie different degrees of capacity for real or imputed operational progression or normative progress. Moreover, both supply lessons more likely to be integrated into prescriptions than to actually or immediately ameliorate practices that validate projections.

The structural-strategic variety is best reducible to the number of prime actors representative of quantitative structure, variably modified by the qualitative features that identify particular slices of world history and politics. Presently reemergent is a specific situation, focused tentatively on a single preeminent actor while comprising all of the three constituents of medieval-type pluralism: its consummate manifestation in a transcendent community (Christendom, now a range from the European Union to the United Nations), its intermediate format in the formation of new and reformation of preexistent states, and its primitive shape in chaotic turbulence (small parts of Europe, larger ones elsewhere). The historically attending schism between sacral and secular principles and protagonists is secularized into the normative-existential one, with the U.N. (as before the Papacy) embodying inadequately the normative and the United States (matching the Byzantine Empire and the stronger among the Holy Roman emperors) the existential term. A genuinely one-power, or unipolar or unifocal, structure is sufficiently rare to be unlikely to be repeated in its pure form on a global plane. Imperial China's dominance in a closed regional orbit, extending control by means of cultural superiority and attraction, was reenacted by the Soviet Union with support from enforced ideological conformity. But even imperial Rome's hegemony was constantly and increasingly exposed to external challenges, including long-lasting conflict with Parthia/Persia, that deepened as Rome weakened. Its inactive coexistence with other regional empires such as China's Han does not count in this connnection. Most appropriate as a repeatable—and actually repeated—model is unifocality around the late Western Roman and, especially, Eastern Roman Byzantine empires. As part of it, an essentially manipulative diplomatic statecraft verging on theatrical stagecraft is increasingly commingled with the requisites of an adept siegecraft with respect to investing or also infiltrating outer barbarians. Post-Cold War America becoming the new Byzantium after forfeiting the chance to be the new Rome demonstrates the necessity to differentiate between severe but manageable and marginal but unmanageable outside disorders. The attendant fundamental differences to be recognized and dealt with are those between national and wider imperial interests, between an international order attended by diffuse if not also disruptively chaos-generating modes of behavior without necessitating remedial intervention and a system contingent on articulated structures requiring alert responses to even remote disruption. For the preeminent or any other major power to ignore the differences and work overactively for conflict-free order in the midst of disorder means impeding the conflict-dependent formation or re-formation of essentially orderly interstatist anarchy until consequently unprepared outsiders and dependents have been confronted with the necessity to master their immediate environment on their own.[5]

Historically more common and for the future more significant is a two-power structure and consequently dominant polarizing conflict. Proceeding from antiquity, salient among such structures and conflicts are the Greek–Persian, Atheno–Spartan, Byzantine–Persian, and, in increasingly modern Europe, Spanish–Ottoman, Valois/Bourbon–Habsburg, and in succession Anglo–Spanish, –French, –German, and (secondarily) –Russian. Distinguishing the conflicts centered on relatively if unevenly consolidated powers historically and making them relevant prospectively is the uneven incidence and mix in either of them of West–East value-institutional or cultural-civilizational and continental-maritime features and attributes. Priorities between real political and value-institutional factors in favor of the latter were actually inverted in contentions revolving at least superficially around ideologies and doctrines: between Christianity and Islam, replete with crusades and countercrusades, and Papacy and Empire, enacted through excommunications and depositions. Both were intermittently, and as they unfolded increasingly, reduced to more prag-matic stakes and strategies, allowing for their eventual supersession by contemporaneously more relevant conflicts as the most common substi-tute for a negotiated or otherwise operationally contrived conflict resolu-tion. Most significant in the first category and as instructive for the future as it was ignored in the immediately past U.S.–Soviet conflict, is the Span-ish–Ottoman conflict that bestrode the passage from medieval pluralism to modern statism and commingled the West–East modifier as primary with both powers combining continental and maritime attributes about evenly. Despite propagandistic departures, embodied in "black legends" about the adversary, the rival parties discounted the religio-ideological irritants for recognizing and waging the conflict as one over the geostrate-gic issue of hegemony. Parallels between the rivals were allowed to erode initial polarities pending a measure of substantive convergence arising out of flexible and reciprocal containment strategies. Aided by the eventual divergence of strategic priorities in opposing directions, substantive con-vergence in turn prevented actual or seeming imperatives of implementa-tion to block the requisites of progressive appeasement. Accommodation proceeded pari passu with the erosion of the cultural-civilizational fea-tures by the pragmatic-operational factors and the dispersion of the con-frontation by recognizing third parties in time as equally threatening to both protagonists.[6]

Failure to recognize a common third-party threat is most commonly present in two-power conflicts, beginning with the Atheno–Spartan when a host of relatively weaker third parties was allowed not only to drag the principals into a largely unwanted conflict but also to impede accommo-dation at the conflict's midterm, and continuing when an unnecessarily prolonged Byzantine–Persian conflict opened the way for Islam. A two-power conflict generating a too-long overlooked and competitively en-hanced third party and converting the two- into a three-power structure as a result is a commonplace of history. It is most instructive in situations modified primarily by the continental–maritime disparity. A three-power structure being in any event essentially unstable, the uneven oscillation among three corresponding alliance combinations built into the land–sea power schism and triangle tends to obscure two sources of crisis: one implicit for the sea power in ignoring the long-term threat from a nonpar-ticipant mercantile power in the wings, the other present for long-term stability overall in the unremarked critical role of the ostensibly most passive, rear-continental third party. Whereas the two risks contributed most recently to Japan and China becoming the real winners within the U.S.–Soviet–Chinese triangle, the implied lesson applies presently most to a triangular situation that would have been replicated but also inverted from its West-to-East direction to the opposite spectrum, wherein a "Europe" that includes or excludes Russia becomes the rear-continental party to the U.S.–(or U.S. cum Japan–)Chinese conflict.[7]

The distinction between economic and military-political factors responsible for the just-mentioned risks and implied lessons plays a role in the expansion from a three- into a four- to five-power structure. Associated historically and associable in principle with any of the qualitative modifiers, this multipolarity can be credited with the greatest potential for stability on simply quantitative and numerical grounds. The special case takes place when a triangular political-military conflict is structurally and operationally complemented with a fourth or fifth power as party to a smaller politico-economic triangle: thus adding the Netherlands to the Anglo–French–Germanic, France to the Anglo–German–Russian, and Western Europe and Japan to the U.S.–Soviet–Chinese maritime–continental triangle. In that this feature highlights the tendency for formerly politico-militarily dominant powers to subside into mainly or only politico-economic importance before frequently fading even in that regard, it portends the increasingly significant differences and reciprocal substitutions between mainly or also military-political and primarily or only economic powers. A prospectively growing fungibility of the two kinds of capabilities combines with a growing capacity to manage the economic factor theoretically and practically to a degree sufficient to substantially affect the rise-decline dynamics of world politics and at least potentially diminish its strategic significance while accentuating the priority of the organic over the operational dimension. Incidentally devalued, and much more so than by any military-technological development, would be the difference between land and sea power insofar as it was a function of the sea powers' abruptly meteoric rise and decline and the continental powers' chronically crises-ridden but relatively longer and more level developmental course and curve—without this devaluation nullifying the importance of still more fundamental or eventually emergent new but comparable qualifiers and modifiers.

All the historically evidenced and practically possible structures did and will again combine the basic material-economic and military-political factors, and were and again will be modified by diversely normative creedal factors. The various assortments and combinations constitute particular slices of reality, actually or potentially recurrent over time, including future time. One such slice is the combination of abrupt economic expansion and simultaneous intensification of the creedal factor. Associating the economic effect of an attendant price revolution with the onset of religious conflicts in the sixteenth to seventeenth century, the components of this slice of the total structure reappeared most recently toward the end of the Cold War and extended beyond it as the differently stressful globalization of the economy combined with the residue of the ideological and resurgence of the cultural-civilizational factors. The remoter historical instance coincided with the beginnings of the triangularized land-sea power series when Spain's weakening combination of continental-military and maritime superiority invited challenge by the new Anglo–Dutch type of creedally stimulated economies. The contemporary terminus of the associated Eurocentric conflict series coincides with the American compound of military and mercantile primacy being beset by another rising new, currently Asian, type of power. Relevant for the future is the fact that a significant slice can be constituted analytically by ignoring either quantitatively force-related or qualitatively functions- and values-related component for the sake of overstressing the other, no more usefully than the future will actually unfold in function of either quantitative-structural or qualitatively strategy-determining factors alone. Whereas an only qualitatively or functionally defined environment is too diffuse structurally to be suggestive strategically, an only quantitatively defined structure entails at best a vacantly formal strategic recipe: to try being one of three in a structure of five powers, and a tentative bias: for three countervailing parties aligning against the balance-threatening strongest state, likely to be joined only by a declining-dependent party within the same structure. Neither proposition suggests, let alone indicates, the identities of the interacting parties.

As an agency of transition to a greater or, via erosion, lesser number of powers, functionally neutral balancing becomes deliberate only with the emergence of capacity to consolidate territorial or other gains. Preemptive counterbalancing will then have replaced, as the dominant mode of restabilization, the propensity of loosely pluralist aggregations to near-automatic dissolution. Both dissolution and deliberate counterbalancing differ from the equilibrating effect of near-inevitable diffusion of assets, threatening to maritime-mercantile powers in particular. In this connection, significant for the future is a trend away from statism to pluralism that suggests a return to the primacy—and attendant perils—of strategically unmanageable propensity to dissolution and diffusion as the unreliable avenue to stability, replacing decline and supersession of a unitary statist actor. Patterns and processes such as these can be usefully—and to foster positive and impede negative trends by policies for the future, must be imperatively—identified in the best documented history, that of Europe, before they can be projected onto the global stage, while historical analogy is combined with functional equivalents and the latter with structurally and functionally plausible substitution of future for past incumbents of either continuing or reemergent roles. Thus the twilight of Greece resembled the present when it was marked by an uneven weakening of both the continental and the insular antagonists in a great and prolonged conflict. The debilitation created space for second-degree regional quasi-empires, be they politico-economically liberalized (such as the second Athenian empire, equaling a fourth German and second Japanese) or narrowly based military (Theban, equated by locally limited Russian or Chinese). The real question, however, concerned then as it does now the likelihood and, were it to materialize, the identity of the next continent-wide hegemony. This could be one expanding aggressively from a depleted and divided state system's marchlands (then Macedon or eventually a neo-Czarist Russia) or one sucked in from afar by the state system's or civilization's internal discords (then Rome, prospectively modern China).[8]

Conversely, significant differences will continue to disqualify transposing superficial analogies, such as the Munich analogy, beyond the post-World War II situation onto the future. The principal ignored difference was, in the earlier context and may be again, not one between a bi- and a multipolar structure, but between a healthy and a pathological situation: when capabilities, commitments, and role-status conditions roughly conform and when they do not—as they did not between the wars. Accordingly, antecedent multipolar systems including the Greek and Italian had reappeared in and could be compared with the mid-eighteenth to late-nineteenth century European system—and may echo in the early to mid-twenty-first century Eurasian and global system. But the interwar European situation could not be so compared. Neither would the post-Cold War situation, even though changing from bipolarity to some kind of pluri-centricity, truly reproduce the earlier multipolar situation or situations so long as it suffered from another set of anomalies if not pathologies due to the atrophy of an essentially statist ethos that occasions the employment of large-scale conventional-military capabilities in diplomacy or war. On the other hand, it seemed possible in a structure evolving out of tight bipolarity at the midpoint of the Cold War to anticipate the comparison, more popular after the Cold War, of the respective "presents" with the late-nineteenth century situation of classic diplomacy supported by conventional arms and pursuing specific economic objectives. Finally, and in the long run perhaps most importantly, particular ideal creedal and material economic features of the emergent global international system could be, for some time past, interpreted as reproducing the situation of the creedally divided and economically expanding European system from the sixteenth to the late seventeenth centuries.[9]

The question of whether the complexities attending comparability, recurrence, and continuity are insurmountable is a question especially pertinent to futuristic anticipations that depart from and range schematically while extending sequentially from an order centered on one power and besieged by "barbarians" through contests between two powers, exposed to triangularization, to a multipower situation. Operative as either a constraining setting or background potentiality, such structures are invariably enough permeated by qualitative features to make efforts to integrate particular situations in history and discrete slices of history into its sweep in retrospect and prospect equally compelling as controversial. Schematization of facets and sequences as an avenue to systematization of patterns and processes would ideally culminate in synthesis as a mere intellectual possibility and a wager of philosophical metahistory. Actually, the sequences as an objectively given fact and presupposition of historicizing analysis are contingent on the existence and operation of law-like tendencies that sustain fundamental continuities with practical relevance for historically intelligent rational strategy. These tendencies and resulting continuities favor a basic propensity to system restoration from revolutionary upheavals. Such upheavals constitute relative discontinuities due to schisms-attending sociopolitical revolutions and structural bi- to multipolar variations. The basic difference is between unconsummated tendencies and effected transformations and between an ostensible and a radical transformation which, exceeding while reinforcing a real change, is present when a statist system is at least provisionally replaced at its worst by chaos-prone turbulence uncertainly focalized by a single preeminent power.[10]

The structural-strategic perspective on the future is rooted in the presumptive rebirth of the state systemic structure and order conjoint with its spatial passing from a Euro- to an Asia-centric global setting. Coincidentally returning would be salient strategies, including a directionally inverted replication of the land–sea power triangle globally and an at least partial, spatially graduated, reversion of strategic significance from initially the Anglo–French and eventually also American rimlands of the core West to the Germanic–Slavic heartland. Such modified reversions are threatened by other than simple directional inversions of an antecedent's makeup when the erosion of bipolarity and the concurrent epidemic of interstate peacemaking are attended by increases in unstructured kinds of mainly intra-polity violence. When this form of violence is centered on the growing gap between global haves and have nots, liable to degenerate into a globalized class war, and relatively pacified conflicts among states mutate into animosities between cultures and civilizations, such more or less inversion-prone reversions validate the hypothesis of a constant sum of energy or also violence. Inversion of creedal into material community is especially problematic when normatively slanted futuristic projections are indifferentiable from optimistically salvation-oriented prophecies. Such projections are associated with the functional-institutionally cooperative as opposed to the structural-strategically competitive model of politics, while linear progressivist projections are opposed to cyclical progression-oriented projections and promising predictious to portentous prophecies. A rebirth of medieval pluralism is concurrently attended by intensified attempts to return to multilateralism institutionalized in the international organization of the statist interwar era, conjointly with substituting cooperatively communitarian for both primitively chaos-prone pluralism and empire-type meta-systemization.

Regional empires for order and global organizations for security as past modes or models for the future

As a statist-pluralist hybrid, the institution of empire bestrides the two contrasting models of politics, while equilibrium between empires partakes of the balance of power with a difference shown most recently by the breakup of the Soviet empire. The balance-of-power dynamic is affected most when empires depart from their quality as territorial states in favor of an accidentally-to-artificially assembled pluralist/heterogeneous aggregate invested with a temporally and situationally contingent mission, purpose, or task. This peculiarity translates into an empire's liability to small-scale peripheral and internal assaults by relatively minor forces and its vulnerability to and withdrawal impulse before token or symbolic setbacks in relations with equally major powers. Distinguishing inter-empire from interstate relations, this peculiarity was exhibited dramatically in an ancient setting comparable to the recent one. The collapse of the ambiguously Euro–Asian and continental–maritime (and thus Soviet-like) Syrian empire of Antiochus the Great, after an inconclusive military defeat by Rome, sheds some light on the self-destructive Soviet reaction to failures in the economic growth- and armaments-focused race with the (Rome-like) United States, complementing the Soviet regime's deficient sense of historic statehood in favor of self-perception as primarily a sociopolical system dependent on readily verifiable self-justifying performance. In a wider and longer perspective, these peculiarities weaken somewhat this particular renunciation's negative implications for the future of the state system, predicated on a lastingly precedents-breaking Soviet deviation from normal behavior by great powers qua states. More immediately relevant for the future is the resulting vacuum of ordering authority apt to ensue from the disintegration of either of the competing empires, without clarifying the full long-term implications of the presence or absence of inter-empire status solidarity with respect to the era's ultimate weapon— nuclear in U.S.–Soviet outdoing the "Greek fire" in the Byzantine– Islamic contest.

Henceforth, the always problematic net impact of empires is no more conclusive as to future effect on the balance between conflict and order, due to two contrasting tendencies. One is for the vaster physical and psychological distance between centers of empires than between normal states to mute the contention in favor of class solidarity. The other is for the aggravating effect of competing claims to universality on mutually subversive actual balancing of power to jeopardize the first tendency's positive effect on order. The post-Word War II inter-empire setting dissolved before providing conclusive answers to such queries and resolution of the attendant dilemmas. A longer historical perspective points to the choice between an absolutist solution of either one-sided conquest or shared control, and relativistic compounds of competition and cooperation. Without reaching as far back as ancient Egypt's interplays with the continental empires of Asia Minor, insular Great Britain and the United States as actual empires and, successively, France and Imperial Germany and lately the Soviet Union as prime continental aspirants to empire rather than mere nation-states, highlight the dilemmas and supply some negative lessons without providing a positive blueprint for America's—or Japan's—response to China.[11]

Basic throughout to inter-empire relations—or, alternatively, struggles over empire—is the competitively shared and commonly denatured vision of a both perfect and permanent order. And fundamental to the issue of order is the contention between empire, and thus hierarchy, and equilibrium as alternative approaches to order or its organizing principles. Empire is the obverse of equilibrium qua balance of power that implies constraint on expansion rather than its consummation. However, empire and equilibrium are operationally compatible and may be complementary when the pluralism characteristic of empire does more than displace balancing inward between competing factions. Moreover, heterogeneity associated with pluralism allows for functionally or spatially differentiated sectors to constitute imbalances that are mutually complementary within an overall equilibrium, including the special case of a politicized oligopoly implementing a so-called leadership equilibrium. Heightened American prominence can make leadership equilibrium more reliably relevant for the 1990s and beyond than it was in the late 1960s and the 1970s. Yet even more significant in the long run than any inadequacies in implementing inter-empire equilibrium in the late phase of the Cold War would be the continuing unwillingness of American statecraft, insulated historically from the necessity of choice by the European balance of power, to choose between empire and equilibrium as the two organizing principles of order—or to creatively combine them instead of pursuing a chimeric third alternative of an indeterminate "world order."[12]

As a formula of order, empires are both fundamental and their particular manifestations historically deficient with respect to their development and defense. The development is habitually hamstrung by the difficulty to coordinate central authority with particular autonomies. The defense is jeopardized by the respective shortcomings of the two principal strategies for either elastic in-depth or static perimeter defense. These general liabilities are compounded by the specific problem of an appropriate economy of control that, intertwined with economy of force, avoids both under- and overinvolvement as the organizational counterparts of under- and overexpansion. Such deficiencies are responsible for the empires' propensity to eventual decline in material-economic terms, progressive decay in moral-psychological terms, and ultimate dissolution in power political-organizational terms.[13]

The likely-to-persist generic imperfections raise legitimate questions about the future prospects for order based on the empire formula relative to other formulas differentiated spatially (regional or global), organizationally (degree of institutionalization and control allocation), and normatively (different types of tolerated and penalized disorders). With post-Communist Eastern Europe joining or replacing parts of the post-colonial Third World as the principal area at risk, world order could be implemented regionally by local great powers in ways entailing a measure of global deconcentration; or interregionally and thus globally in a multilateralized setting under the auspices of a preeminent power, presently the United States, in ways entailing various degrees of dilution and concealment of its implied authority and responsibility. Any, including the imperial, order formula can be meaningfully evaluated only in relation to alternative forms just as any U.S.-style shortcomings can be only against the requirements of an accomplished imperial order, made more complex than previously in an environment that has substituted Iraq for Vietnam and, say, Rwanda or Burundi for the Belgian Congo.[14]

Regional empire for control with pretensions to universality is, on the face of it, diametrically contrary to general organization of cooperation for orderly security that is articulated, or is prone to disaggregating, regionally. In fact, the two organisms share a connection with a state of being or condition, that of order, that is in itself problematic. They have in common an at best ambiguous relationship to a dynamic or concept, that of equilibrium. Implementing this paradoxical affinity is an operational tendency. The inability of regional empires to become truly global and impose and maintain order effectively creates space for experimenting with global international organization before its empire-like tendency to dissolution has refocused attention on regionally confined frameworks as stepping stones to world community. In either format, order may be conventionally viewed as the obverse of violence epitomized in war, and thus the opposite of the balance of power when it is perceived as war's chief instigator. Or else forceful intervention is more plausibly seen as necessary for maintaining or restoring order, while a supporting balance of power is viewed as the precondition of efficacy. Finally, order may be equated with law-enforcing organization, despite the substantial differences between order and organization. International organization, just as international law, can be easily defined in terms of (normative) precepts and (operative) procedures, or of purposes and functions. But it is questionably effective. Order is defined more easily by what it is not (e.g., chaos or coercive tyranny) or not yet (e.g., spontaneous community or one-power imperial or authoritative international or world government). But order does intermittently exist, although mostly in procedural terms that favor and facilitate predictability and, thanks to it, prudential moderation. However, it exists then mainly derivatively in that order obtains, if at all, in function of more basic or primary givens, an actual constellation of power and stratification of effective potencies, and in the guise of informal but definite boundaries drawn against behavior consensually perceived as intrinsically illegitimate or momentarily intolerable.

Especially when a major war has reignited the quest for abiding order, it is tempting to treat prospectively emergent norms-implementing institutions as antithetical to detrimentally operative balancing of power. By contrast, the power-normative view of international politics accommodates easily the peaceable coexistence and even useful interdependence of the geopolitical with the institutional principle. They coexist as alternate and interact as concurrent stimulants of action and agencies for their least disputable object: progressive socialization of especially newborn actors. This linkage is achieved in principle by transposing the equilibrium concept and dynamic from deliberately contrived or incidentally resulting balance of power among states onto an international organization as one that is only potentially and therefore differently problematic in equilibrium. How close it is to that condition will depend on how effectively the formal equality of member states is qualified by and reconciled with their unequal capabilities, and commitments with compliance readiness or capacity. It also depends on how effectively the aggregate functions or competencies of a particular organization are adjusted to its potential, and specific assignment to its organs' within appropriate spatial confines. As different combinations of tasks are allocated among diverse organs and organizations, the wherewithals of a functionally complex equilibrium are being institutionalized as an actual propensity or only introduced into order as its normative postulate. When the variably attractive and repellent military-, economic-, and cultural-political strands are insufficiently compressed in national units of power by contentious balancing, the strands' clearer differentiation allows for articulating a strategic equation of stability in organizations that are nonetheless ultimately sustained and shielded against forcible subversion by the balance-of-power mechanism they are supposed to supplant and replace. Amidst such contradictions the organizations function, unequally in equilibrium, to either formalize the accessible degree of moderation for developmental discrepancies or futilely attempt to cancel power differentials.

Provided the guarantee against forceful has been buttressed by provisions for peaceful change, cooperative international organization could be expected to radically transform conflictual international relations. Actually, international organization reflects—and can only marginally contain—political realities so long as the interplay of normative and existential facets is manifest in both its origination and operation. In origination, it is when the latter combines immediately postwar pragmatic objectives relative to ex-enemies adequately with longer-term positive and impartial ones. In operation, it is when mobilizing that the traditional fear of isolation on the part of the greatest of powers supports adequately the desideratum of multilateral action. Opposing the ideal is the operative fact of specificities that persistently hinder mutual adjustments: of an organization's competencies and the actors' compliance with formal commitments, and of this part of the equation with an organization's range of functions that corresponds to broadly perceived real needs and actual feasibility—the equation's second part. Institutional disequilibrium, expressing related frustrations, will be repeatedly responsible for an ultimately depressant evolutionary pattern. It will do so regardless of whether particular displacements from more to less exacting commitments and functions will end in formal dissolution (League of Nations) or only de facto demise of an institution's authority and efficacy (United Nations)—a drift not unlike that of ostensibly contrary control organisms, including empires.

Symptomatic in either case is institutional hypertrophy in performing traditionally essential functions and functional inflation due to multiplying inessential ones. They reinforce one another in the unending search of truly useful functions for effective frameworks of implementation, and vice versa. The search's degree of success defines the ordering cum organizing process and delimits the extent to which a spontaneously complex inter-factor or -functional equilibrium is actually institutionalized at any one time. Identifying the precise extent of this happening becomes as real a challenge to a progressivist but essentially realist theoretical analysis as the institutionalization itself is only a hypothetical danger to traditional real politics. The way the equilibrium concept is formalized in regard to organizational institutionalization represents consequently but one more and highly tentative step beyond the (equilibrium) concept's application to balance of power-type interactions and evolutionary adaptations. In outlining the analytic framework of an international organization's finding (or not finding) itself in equilibrium relative to structure, functions, and geographic scope, the focus is on member capabilities and dispositions. Do they sustain formally stipulated or normatively optimal commitment and performance? Or will lack of conformity between commitment, readiness as either capacity or disposition, and performance, expressed in non-compliance with the commitment, more frequently activate downward pressures on the ideal so as to adjust the ordained to the real-politically viable constitutional arrangements and functional amplitudes? In consequence, do international law and organization as instruments of social control on the negative side of order, and socialization on its positive side, have the potential of implementing a revolutionary transformation of world politics in anything like the medium run? A provisionally negative answer minimizes the immediate implications of the downward trend in specific commitments to genuinely collective security. On the other hand, the fact that the long-term potential does gradually surface, although more slowly than was originally anticipated by the idealists, justifies inspecting the cooperative agencies' and instruments' actual impact through the magnifying glass of a progressivist-realist analysis.[15]

Absent effective collective security, the future of cooperative international organization has been tied to the role of other than security functions in implementing community-fostering interdependence. However, formal-legal covers (such as the domestic-jurisdiction clause) for only gradually yielding resistance to authoritatively institutionalizing the concurrently tightening link between domestic and foreign politics on the global plane have been directing the relevant agenda to particular regions, to the detriment of an ideal regional-global equilibrium. Lack of a stabilizing distribution of complementary functions between the two formats of attempted control, order, and cooperation has underscored the respective shortcomings of the two spatially unequal scopes: the regional one's bias to federalize or founder and the global one's to dilute its purposes or dissolve. Meanwhile, the post-Cold War attempt to revitalize global, including security, organization by means of a U.S.-managed multilateralism has not adequately replaced the globalism implicit in the enforceable precedence of worldwide superpower interests and related strategies over local particularisms and regional organisms. Instead, the attempt reactivated the oscillation between regional and global formats, reflected in measures to coordinate without effectively combining the United Nations' primary (humanitarian) role with NATO's complementary (enforcement) role.

Global-regional interplays and types of regionalism in past and future

The institutional and functional difficulties of coordinating regional with global frameworks are in themselves potent enough when the effort is presided over by one preeminent power. In more normal conditions, the frictions injected into the geopolitical principle by the linkages between structure and strategy do not only underlie, but actually exacerbate, the limitations built into the institutional principle by the asymmetries among competence, commitments, and compliance. Global-regional interplays were under Cold War-time bipolarity effectuated through the two globally active powers competing over access to the several regions and each other's sphere of influence. The problems involved in equalizing the access for two unequally situated powers will not be lessened for the two unequally spacious formats of organization so long as they fail to effectuate a mutually supportive connection, expressing *their* last-resort "class" solidarity. Such a connection occurs only contentiously and over indefinite time spans whenever pre-crystallized smaller (micro-) arena and agenda activate and shape the slower-crystallizing larger (macro-) agenda and arena, only for the former to be integrated into the latter. This being so is one of the ways of filling the gap between subjective-individual intentions and aggregate result. It is present also in a single power's concern about parity with allies more than security vis-à-vis adversaries, but largely absent from attempted institutionalization of a regional-global equilibrium.[16]

Recurrent failure of attempts to both effectively and peaceably interlock global with regional agendas of inter-empire contentions and interagency competencies favors the less ambitious and spacious formats of merely functional aggregation or outright sociopolitical integration associated with regionalism. Within this narrowed orbit, conflictual interactions that constitute a regional sub-system differ from authoritative-to-coercive coordination within great-power spheres, only to ascend via the progressive institutionalization of either modality in a regional order or organization to community-type integration. Whether or not the pertinent patterns and processes relate to the more inclusive inter-regional global setting, confining them within the narrowed spatial compass intimates that which is less clearly visible in the more diffuse wider setting. This is the real-world linkage between progressive rationalization of raw power-centered instincts and the institutionalization of the related interactional dynamic, and between such dynamics and its evolutionary progression.

In keeping with this linkage, a conflicted regional balance-of-power system is the necessary antecedent to any more formal institutionalization of regional order. That such a regional (sub-)system will be formed through opposition to a potential local hegemon or not at all was most recently illustrated on the least developed part of the global ecumene. Consequent local failures of the preliminary crystallization signaled a developmental arrest for some of its least developed regions, previously exemplified in the southern half of the Western Hemisphere. A positive role in the next step, from countervailance-dependent crystallization to a primitive form of organization, can be played by an extra- or an intra-regional great power. The role is enacted by the former when it has a stake in fostering regional cooperation through exclusion of the latter; and by the latter, when it pursues the same basic objective by coordinating lesser powers into a species of international feudalism within its own orbit of influence. Ideologically rationalized normative distinctions between largely consensual liberal and coercively illiberal-to-totalitarian management of such an orbit are realistically reducible to an existential disparity: between an externally pressed and power-politically repellent continental-military power and an externally insulated and more economically if not also culturally attractive than power-politically repellent maritime-mercantile power. Both differentiations are valid, without disclaiming for either reason the generic commonality of this particular method of containing all conduct identifiable as contrary to a core power's conception of order, equated with its total security and implemented through the technique of more or less direct and forcible intervention.[17]

Alternative futures of great power orbits have been intimated differentially by partial concealments and eventual conversion of the U.S. sphere of influence in the Western Hemisphere into a free-trade association and the only partially consented and complete deimperialization of ex-Soviet Russia's geohistorically defined orbit—a transformation that exposes a fledgling democracy and barely incipient market economy to the trials of assimilating Soviet-style Brezhnev to a traditional Russian variety of America's one-time Monroe Doctrine. The related dilemmas for the smaller states of a thus ordered region have disappeared no more conclusively. How is one to reconcile in the future more effectively than in the past a measure of their autonomy with great power centrality if not also authority? And do this in a setting wherein the alternatives of conflicted (re-)crystallization of a regional subsystem and cooperative institutionalization of regional order coexist in principle and interpenetrate productively or destructively in practice? The problem will for some time persist not least for the successively most newly "new" states, currently post-communist after the post-colonial, when military alliances yield overall to political-economic ties but smaller states shy away from associations among themselves and links to regionally major powers, so as not to prejudice the prospect of membership in a preferred association—including alliance—under the more or less direct auspices of a more safely remote than reliably dependable superpower.[18]

When a multi-member regional alliance materializes, it represents a relatively stable midpoint in ordering a region that has contained the dynamics of prior subsystem crystallization and mutes or at least conceals one-power dominance, while stopping short of community. Factors unevenly normative (ideologies), structural (member hierarchy), procedural (consultations and compromises), and substantive (capabilities and pressures) will be variably decisive for the degree of cohesion relative to the measure of member autonomy in either limited- or total-liability and mostly equal or primarily hegemonial alliances. In a changing environment of threats and opportunities, a conventional alliance will be subject to internal strains and stresses emanating from the difficulty of equalizing the disparate gains and liabilities accruing from the only unequal or also unequally developed allies' individual concerns with external security, also or primarily domestic stability, and formal status or also effective role. To forestall the resulting vulnerability if not actual propensity to disruption is a challenge that hangs over an alliance as much as over an empire. And the challenge to make up for the difficulty of displacing the alliance's original to a less demanding alternative purpose or more immediately threatening target-state is one it shares with global international organizations. Both limitations will propel regionalism toward a degree of functional-institutional integration that would reach beyond occasionally coalescing in action and operations to forming an organic community. Thus NATO's capacity to survive its post-Cold War liability to disruption was increasingly contingent on its ability to displace interregional security into intraregional police function (Bosnia). And even before this happened, the conceptual disparity but actually possible overlap between the two alternative roles of a "permanent" modern alliance had been illustrated on the changing perception of the alliance as a mere military-political league of states in the traditionalist geopolitical perspective, or the framework of an Atlantic community from a progressivist institutional perspective.[19]

Both regionalism and globalism can be fostered by either cooperative functional organization or strategically inspired antagonistic alliances, positive community or negative countervailance. The contrast will be narrowed by complementarities in the foundations of efficacy or cohesion as well as the final objectives or ultimate purposes of each format. As the historically more frequently accomplished format, alliances disclose that which is only latent in or preconditional to other forms of organized association, including empires. At the same time, alliances too depend for full efficacy at any time and for a developmental potential over time on functional, cultural, and societal features peculiar to purposively more distinctly community-like organizations. And when a hegemonial alliance brings together highly unequal members, it only mutes the conflicted dynamic of a regional subsystem while merging easily with regional great power orbits, confounding the international with the imperial attributes and the internationalist with the imperialist mindsets. Moreover, to the extent that the process that forms systems is necessarily antecedent to an organizational product capable of channeling the contentious dynamic into developing cooperation, this interlock reveals merely another aspect or feature of the operationally pervasive dependence of cooperation on conflict in interstate relations.

Yet again, whereas the conflict-driven regional balance-of-power system is a mode of aggregation and coordination preliminary to association among states, it is also an extreme boundary case on a continuum of diversified forms and processes. At its other end is integration that directs societal pluralism away from chaotic confusion toward creedal or functional community—now between state-like polities just as previously within inchoate societies on the way to centralized statism. This primitively pluralist-to-statist-to-institutionalized pluralist schematic range and developmental cycle of integrative processes and products of integration does not, for all its continuity, rule out significant conceptual as well as operative differences. An illuminating difference is between a balancer in the power-balancing process and its analogue in the federalizing process. One deliberately separates unequally strong parties or at least keeps them separable as an alternative to forcible merger, making them ideally somewhat more equal or at least independent. The role and possible achievement of the other kind of balancer consists instead in equalizing, to say the least, not so much actors and their capabilities as factors and forces working for and against association so as to allow the integrative process to take off before advancing spontaneously. It is then a matter of choice and circumstance why the principle of institutionalized integration is applied—or integration pursued—within a region: for the sake of a geopolitically conditioned inter-regional balance of countervailing power, or in the interest of cumulating intra- and inter-regional processes with a prospective global terminus, actualizing the potential of only functional or also institutional integration.

Integration exceeds coordination or coalescence but also merely modifies them when pooling competencies rather than abolishing sovereignties. These continuities in structure and process are themselves consistent with applying associative strategies to activities ostensibly contrary to integration such as expansion, war, and power balancing. Owing to elasticity and fungibility of functions despite diversities in operations, this consistency is manifest when integration performs the function of expansion for the strongest partner without expansion's risks and pitfalls; when close federative embrace achieves the object of successful war for even weaker parties by entangling and thus neutralizing the hegemonial thrust or potential of the relatively stronger one; and finally, and most revealingly, when a federal or federalizing balancer's purpose and achievement replace the actually disruptive potential if not also propensity of a particular (insular) type of balancer tout court. Thus the quintessential balancer of the European continent, Great Britain, promoted federative integration in its overseas empire or commonwealth. And the United States or NATO under its leadership has been extending this same function from the federalizing process within Western Europe to Eastern Europe in the wake of success for the balancer's more negative and preventive even if not deliberately divisive purpose globally.

Once the extraneous impulse has exhausted its potential, spontaneous spillover from economic to political and from internal to external functions will halt or regress unless a functionally multiple (i.e., complex) equilibration reaches its policy-shaping climax in forming a corresponding polity. Such is an entity that is integrated both vertically (i.e., institutionally in hierarchically graduated organs) within itself and horizontally (i.e., in concentric or overlapping circles geographically) with comparable polities. A major part of the difficulty in either a national polity or a supra-national region is a duality that only qualifies the essential unity of politics on the conceptual plane, but strains the integrative process operationally on the practical plane: the distinction and difference between the two models of policy, the functional-institutional and structural-strategic. Because each embodies the institutional and the geopolitical principles differently, the former tends to being addressed in terms of a preconceived design, while lacking the latter's association with an implementing strategic concept—a difference associated in Western European unification with the names of Jean Monnet and Charles de Gaulle respectively.[20]

Viewing the interplaying and -penetrating structural-strategic statist (or Gaullist) and functional-institutional communitarian (or Monnetist) modes, prominent in European unification, matches from the unevenly distant past to the present and beyond the gradualist progression from the most conflicted to the most cooperative regional order managed real-politically.

Unifications combined at all times consensually communitarian traits, associated with programmatic designs, unevenly with competitively statist features, associated with strategic concepts. In early medieval Europe, unification processes confined to or extending beyond "national" entities did this with respect to both structures and strategies. Structures were expressed, as they must be, in fairly consolidated sub-units (analogous to those of interstate sub-systems relative to regional organization) and a core unit of power or authority or function around which to assemble (analogous to the great power focus of a regional sphere of influence). Strategies implemented exemplarily an outward thrust beyond spatial confinement by nature or Islam (analogous to the threat of a separate peace in reconsolidating alliances), apt to compel an increase in cohesion and promote a consensual allocation of functions and coordination of competencies of the unifying higher and constituent lower organs. More recent and a lower form of integration is a nineteenth-century informal concert of powers that differs from both a formal concert and a community. It does not aim at structural changes, does not require a prior consensus, and depends on minimal prerequisites, insufficient to achieve the higher form of integration. Thus, the urgency of individual intra-societal improvements is among the incentives, but their achievement is not viewed as contingent on an integrated interactor approach; and the peripheral outlets, requisite to attenuate central conflict, must be combined with sufficiently adversarial diplomatic activism in the central system to energize the statist principle sufficiently for future reactivation.

The medieval communitarian and late modern statist formats of association do not only precede contemporary European unification. They also comprise elements significant for degrees of sought or achieved unity in Europe or elsewhere as a matter of policy. Such a unity would implement the medieval ideal normatively in a secularized mode while reproducing the formation of nation-states on a larger scale functionally by replicating the economic-military-administrative circuit, and institutionally, when sequentially realizing the configuration of executive, judicial, and representative organs. Or this unity would merely advance informal concert among states to their confederative consolidation. The involvement of the two modes of association, reflective of the more basic models of politics, in the integrative process invites analogy with two stages of and antithetical approaches to the first German unification: a liberal-constitutional design-oriented one (the Frankfurt Parliament) and the conservative strategy-oriented one (Bismarck), to be combined eventually in the second German unification and achieve wider applicability. So far, de Gaulle's strategic concept has failed to produce the anticipated result in Western Europe, due in part to the mutually reinforcing insufficiencies of the requisite confinement vis-à-vis the United States and credibility of the French force de frappe relative to the Soviet Union. However, the basic concept remains applicable to all Europe so long as the Monnetist design's update in the Maastricht Treaty fails to inspire decisive progress in the essentially statist domains of national economy (single currency) and foreign policy (joint security). Meanwhile, the statist principle embodied in the confederative formula remains applicable to the state-recreative facet of neo-medievalism in the post-communist half of Europe. Controversies such as those surrounding the alternative tactics of integrative deepening and membership widening are conversely associated with the functional-institutional model, and may or may not definitively crowd out structural-strategic features and perspectives favorable to realignments prior to a measure of disarticulation of Cold War-derived organizations such as the European Union and the Atlantic alliance, as an alternative to retro-gression into adversarial postures.[21]

Actually regressive tendencies would underlie the requisites of integrat-ing geopolitical with economic factors in unifying post-Cold War Europe in its entirety, germane to the strategic concept. The issue is anchored analytically in the distinction between federalism and imperialism, re-flected in the diverse modalities of the Bismarckian and the more recent German unification. It is oriented programmatically to the relationship between the Russo–German Eurasian heartland and the Atlanticist global-oceanic circumference. Operationally prominent are two triangles: one, the cultural-political triangle of a primitive civil society flanked by inter-nal cohesion-fostering national consciousness and internationally disrup-tive integral nationalism; and two, the operationally crucial structural triangle of a functionally and normatively still viable and valuable state exposed, as it is on the nationalism issue, to likewise alternately integra-tive or disintegrative kinds of regionalism. Whereas trans-border micro-regions disarticulate a state functionally, interstate macro-regions reinte-grate local as well as national particularities in a comprehensive entity. Important for achieving the positive effect is a correct sequencing in inte-gration-promoting foreign policy strategies, analogous to the requisite of effective economic reform. The importance of the right sequence grows with the number of factors at work and options present even if not ac-tively pursued.[22]

In its present state and future prospect, regionalism associates the dy-namics of world politics with major problematics of political sociology as to the continuing role of the state relative to society and the reascendance of (ethno-)cultural factors in both intra- and inter-regional real politics. Prominent among the problems are past conversions of nominal value-institutional convergence into effective divergences on both the West–East and North–South axes, as progressive principles diffused from West and North were exposed to Eastern and Southern atavisms. Closely related to this issue is the tendency for the integrative to be confounded with the evolutionary process. Disparate rates and stages of development will inev-itably raise tensions or even create conflict between a sense of historic equity for developmentally delayed or interrupted polities or civilizations and the uniformly modernist urge for economic utility and material pros-perity on behalf of societies. Complicated trade offs between collective ambition and individual aspirations will coincidentally and equally prob-lematically shape outcomes of interrelated processes: pluralistic integra-tion, democratization, and socialization as opposed to, when either or all are not compatible with, the re-formation or merely rehabilitation of unevenly historical and normatively authoritative states.[23]

Facets and features of projection and prophecy reaching beyond conflict to community

A salvationist prophecy linked to international institutions will be belied by failures to respect one difference and one set of similarities. The difference between unequal real capability and attributed formal equality has not ceased to matter in the pluralist environment despite appearances to the contrary. The similarities as to function and inner dynamic of apparently radically different statist and pluralist forms of ordering and organizing world politics, such as regional great power spheres as opposed to communities, withstand meanwhile a real normative difference between them. A real dysfunction follows ignoring the difference, and false starts and misdirected development result from misrepresenting the similarities. Looking for the future through the prism of the functional-institutional model without sufficient discrimination moves gradually, but in the end wholly, from the realm of unavowedly quasi-predictive projections to self-consciously anticipatory and prescriptive prophecy. In the process, structurally conditioned strategies among powers reproducing past configurations in marginally adapted forms are displaced by values-centered solicitation of policies and institutions more fundamentally adapted to the perpetuation and promotion of norms. Regardless of whether it leans toward salvation or doom, prophecy is opposed to linear-mechanical projection because it is imbued with a preemptive at least as much as with a predictive or prescriptive purpose. Its object is to relax the necessities inherent in real politics with the help of intimations elicited from a history which, as a narrative, harbors possibilities before positively prophetic metahistory can enhance them into probabilities.

Relying on metahistory requires identifying the cumulatively shaped central event to which the past ascends as the provisional summation of its dynamics and dilemmas, and with which the future wittingly or unwittingly begins. The Spanish synthesis of continental military and maritime and creedal and pragmatic features can be regarded as such a central event at the point of transition from the Middle Ages to modernity. Were it such actually or plausibly, the logical search would be for its equivalent in the passage beyond modernity: one to be looked for, in the wake of failure to fuse the same features in one power or a combination of powers, in similarly comprehensive regional communities. Thus inspired prophecy deviates from patterns of evolution traced empirically from structures and strategies disclosed in actual politics. Such patterns only imply alternative future prospects impossible to reduce to definite prediction. Not only substantially different from but also transcending the evolutionary patterns, prophetic visions bestriding despair and expectancy plumb the depths of distinct political cultures of leading polities and both wider and deeper cultures indistinguishable from the major powers who share or represent a culture in the makeup of civilizations. Such visions offer the deepest insight into present currents and future trends when a civilization does or seems to undergo a profound moral and psychological mutation, such as one into the post-political mentality increasingly dominating in the West. Intuition infers from such a transformation a crisis unlikely to be resolved by nothing more strenuous than a spontaneous advance from (prototypically feudal agricultural) status through contract (progressively commercial and social) to solidarity (terminally communal) as the successively dominant principles of social organization and political order within and between the three major (western, eastern, and southern) segments of the global ecumene.[24]

Counterposing the portent-and-doom side of prophecy is the qualified promise of a possibility to abstract sufficiently positive meaning from world politics to relativize the negatives of history and position an endangered West on an equal foundation among parallel civilizations, not least by infusing it with the still unexhausted spirit of its historically prejudiced eastern marchlands. A concurrent progression toward a world community by way of an interregional equilibrium would proceed via alternating ascendancies of Western and Eastern, Occidental and Oriental, civilizations on the level of world-historical process and of interstate real and pluralistic societal politics on the level of operative procedures. Cognitively prior to such transformations is a phenomenologically grounded understanding of world political processes capable of ascending levels of meaning beyond the real changes disclosed by the state system in its historical manifestations and mutations to queries addressing the real (in the sense of ultimately valid) purpose of political engagement in the world at large. Abstracting an operationally significant meaning from historically salient events—tendencies and transformations—that might guide future policies would presumably promote the reconciliation of differently remote pasts, and of each such past with reactions to it, in a new departure. In the longest of perspectives, a new system of (up to five-plus) regional civilizations might replace the territorial state in conjunction with the deterritorialization of politics as actual process and desacralization of the state as normative idea. Successive conversions of developmentally disparate subsystems into regional communities would emerge out of a process shaped by the several branches of unevenly classical (Newtonian-Einsteinian-Aristotelian) political physics as a form of meta-systemization both superior and preferred to empires.[25]

Conceptually contravening and effectively quite possibly inhibiting an idealized future of world politics are meanwhile existential phenomena and attitudinal predispositions whose genealogy can be easily traced backward and which cast an equally long shadow forward. Foremost

among them are the newly emergent or at least aggravated dilemmas that
present themselves in ethno-cultural rather than ethical terms and are impossible to resolve by attempts to superimpose the ideal of ethno-cultural
neutrality over heterogeneity—an effort common to both parties to the
Cold War. More elusive but in the longest run possibly more critical is
the bearing of the "two cultures," the scientific and the humanist, on
future foreign policies. In periods of major transitions more than at any
other time, intuitions influenced by culture-conscious social philosophies
enlighten approaches to cleavages such as those between West and East
and North and South more and better than the apparently more precise
calculations of military capability, economic utility, and pragmatic political expediency. Recognizing the tragic nexus that pervades all politics, a
conservatively romantic alternative to wholly future-oriented scientism
is moreover an automatic corrective to liberal-humanitarian meliorism's
tendency to precipitation that ignores the caveats of progressivist realism.

   Meanwhile, the immediately foremost enemy of speculative realism and
historicism is the concretism implicit in ahistorical pragmatism—an aspect of contemporary (macro-systemic) hellenistic schematization cum
codification of the original insights and creations of a preceding (micro-
systemic) hellenic culture. In its U.S.-dominated and -dominating present
form, the quasi-hellenistic deformation is expressed in the combination
of an operationally narrowly mechanistic and normatively Manichean
view of politics to the detriment of a comprehensively mechanical cum
organic and ethical cum esthetic perspective. Simultaneously combining
concretism with pragmatism tends to debase a not unrelated oscillation
between materialism and moralism into a primitively quantitative view of
reality and interpretation of realism. In neither is there room for either the
tragic or the positively prophetic view of interplays among either clashing
polities or dialectically complementary civilizations. Both are caught up
in the consequences of their uneven development in actual fact and in the
confusions of cerebral ideologies and passionately felt isms originating in
correspondingly fallacious perceptions of imaginary "facts"—a combination affecting also governmental responsibilities within unevenly progressed, progressive, and predominant polities.[26]

   Prominent in a unifocal order will be for a time the foreign-policy manifestations of the American brand of conservatism, oscillating easily between isolationism and unilateralism, in contrast with liberalism's
propensity to humanitarian interventionism and strategically objectless
activism. Even more and more uniformly characteristic is America's extreme concretism. It elevates military-technological instruments over politics during a conflict, and elevates the organizational ones for fashioning
national or managing ostensibly multilateral policies over insight into imponderables after a conflict. Following the latest contention, selective uni-

versalism struggles with assertive nationalism in determining the ways of perpetuating liberal internationalism as a supposedly sufficient negation of both isolationism and imperialism. Naive internationalism is consequently invoked more ardently than practiced well beyond continued validity for its conceptual premises and operational presuppositions: the former concentrated in the ideal, and the latter currently undermined by the suspension, of the universal interconnectedness of parties to and agendas within a classic state system that is absent from a hetero-pluralist framework of action.[27]

The oscillating extremes of liberal utopianism and pseudoconservative realism share a deficiency in historical intelligence even as they are proficient in proliferating reciprocally exclusive strategic scenarios in opposition to a coherent concept. Such a concept is to be found, if anywhere, in combining the different requisites of statecraft relative to the ascending "civilized" late entrants from the global East and siegecraft relative to the infiltrating "barbarian" migrants from the global South. It will be no easier to arrive at and implement in the relatively amorphous post-Cold War environment only because it is more necessary and more insistently called for. A consequent casualty will or might well be even the measure of actual continuities in U.S. foreign policy that spanned regions and administrations under the compelling pressures of an acute global conflict. Likely to predominate are henceforth the discontinuities and inconsistencies embedded in the bureaucratic approach to devising foreign policies. This culturally favored approach is incompatible with a comprehensive-and-continuous, systemic and dialectical, mode of thinking because it is governed by a temporally foreshortened perspective in an institutionally fractured setting. Peculiar to a democratically governed society, this kind of policymaking procedure and underlying political culture is not necessarily a present or future improvement on the traditional statist, including dynastic-authoritarian, approach to foreign statecraft practiced formerly in Europe and presently in Asia.[28]

The fact that the state system is subject to an evolutionary logic and can and does periodically, and even cyclically, alternate with an alternative format of action does anything but guarantee that world politics is presently or will prospectively again become internally coherent. Much as the Cold War fits into the logic of the evolution of the Eurocentric state system from two aspiring (papal and imperial) universalisms to the contest between two differently extra-European powers re-exposing this system to the pull between alternate universalisms and a wider range of particularisms, it leaves in its wake a spatio/temporal labyrinth—a world politics of indeterminate structural and operational makeup and evolutionary thrust and direction, initiated by the increasingly only simulated real politics of the late conflict's final stages.

Inasmuch as it entails a transition between statism and pluralism, the ongoing change is radical as opposed to merely real in terms of priorities for the operational and organic facets and external and internal functions. Its bearing exceeds that implicit in late entries into a particular state system or, even, actual or attempted alteration in the leading type of power at any point on its evolutionary course. An either retrogressive trend toward primitive societal pluralism or progressive trend toward its institutionalized community type necessarily entails the passing of the state system and, therefore, of the state itself from its evolutionary peak. In regard to both the state's and the state system's center of gravity, when the passing is mainly spatial—i.e., to another segment of the arena—the principal change can be confined to the combined issues of the balance of power and the rise/decline dynamic among past and present-and-future major powers. This issue will potentially or implicitly reopen the allied one of alternation between micro- and macro-formats implicit in the identity of the seminal (regional) and the segmentation and stratification of the eventually reconsolidated larger (global) state systems. The change goes deeper and ramifies wider when the passing is temporal, backward toward a known past or forward to putative future forms. This issue entails major transformation of both actor (states) and arena (systems)—and, therefore, agendas combining a return to Europe's historic Middle Ages and advance to new types of revolutions in sub- and supranationally oriented versions.

A state is present when a political authority has equipped a functionally integrated territory with sufficient sustenance, physical security, and a combination of order and justice to command a basically willing allegiance. It declines when a functional hypertrophy—a cumulation of nonvital and dispersal of key functions—coincides with normative depletion. A promising candidate is an environment wherein strategically critical territorial delimitations and contiguities, translating into stakes shared with other states, tend to disaggregate into polar extremes along the universalism-localism continuum. Such a spectrum's present extremes are the multidimensional, high-technological "space" for the most advanced and once again one-dimensional, ultra-traditionalist "soil," arable and burial-capable land as opposed to strategy-relevant territory for the more primitive. The state's implicit deterritorialization and desacralization is necessarily passed on to interstate relations; displacement of emphasis from moral authority to managerial administration will attend the prevalence of society over the state with consequences for the heightened status of the economy relative to politics in its narrower, real political to politico-military, connotations. In the developmentally earlier conditions, conjugating the state with the economy in a real politically vital alliance will bear prejudice to society, the third factor in one principally internal or domestic critical triad. Or the organic-or-enforced fusion of the state or state-like authority with society in a totalist, tribal-to-totalitarian, polity will tend to actually or declaratorily downgrade the economic facet to the identification of sustenance with solidarity. In the subsequent phase, the situation is reversed to the detriment of the state as it is supplanted by society's identification with the economy while moral authority gravitates toward, without necessarily settling on, either civil society or trans-statist regional community.

The built-in and, therefore, parallel implications for the other, principally external or systemic, protosociety-state-state system triad entail degrees of sublimation for real politics, a correlate of the state's quasi-sacrality, and its materialization, affecting territoriality. The first-degree sublimation of competition over territory, rooted in elementary drives and instinctual reflexes, is the displacement of competition's stakes to ideal role or status with the aid of strategic rationality. It occurs at the height of the state's sacralization. Depending on one's value judgment, sublimation's second degree downgrades or upgrades interstate military-political conflicts to economic competition among societies, fitted into institutionalized frameworks of cooperation or integration managed by radically pragmatized and problematized, because desacralized, state machineries. Concurrently with the second stage in and degree of sublimation takes place a direct or actual materialization and, inversely, deterritorialization of both polities and politics, actors and agendas. Calculations of utility replace strategic rationality, severing the direct connection between ideal role-status assets of the state and their material payoffs for society. Severance of a link that was tacitly assumed in the official mind and inchoately sensed by popular sentiment under the conditions of first-degree sublimation returns politics close to its pre-sublimation identification with the material stakes such as booty and ransom.

While a depersonalized state endowed with a quasi-sacral aura yields before the material appetites of societies of persons competing over global market shares, the functional and sociopolitical revolutions from above and below are joined by an institutional-procedural "as if" revolution of a regional scope. Such a revolution is propelled as it were or mainly from outside a particular polity by a combination of pressures and opportunities, when it aims at combining and coordinating sub- and supra-state or -national agendas in a comprehensive administration—one that has been altered from means into a self-justifying end and from the state's instrument into what is left of the state in and of itself. Consistent with this reversal are partial ones within the constituents of real change, conducive to radical change. Thus, prior ascendancy of the organic rise/decline dimension relative to strategically rational operations, which are decreasingly linked or can be related to the former, is reversed into the reassertion of transactions, albeit ones henceforth pragmatically utilitarian rather than strategically rational. Concurrently, the ascendancy of internal constructive over external acquisitive functions of government veers back to inter- and supra-nationally cooperative-to-integrative functions and activities. These take shape as part of a cumulative growth of an aggregate of domestic and external functions reflecting and fostering actual or postulated interdependence while aggrandizing the surviving state as a machinery even as it is voided of the mind that integrates mundane functions and the mystique that transcends them.

Denoting the post-Cold War order—or framework of action—as neomedieval implies a mix of continuity and change. A modified rebirth of an antecedent (in this case, pluralist) situation is not its replication but the re-emergence of similarities with a remote past qualified by differences passed on from a more recent (in the present case, statist) past. The ascendancy of society aspiring to the status of community over the state in parts of the world coexists with the re-creation of states elsewhere. This statist urge is similar to a hegemonial drive because just as hegemony is sought, so a state is being created or reconstructed in the psychological context of unrepeatably unique opportunity and fear of irreversible backsliding into permanent extinction. Overall, the interlock between the circuit of military, economic, and administrative functions that forms a state and the concentration if not fusion of such functions in the makeup of capabilities qua power tends in a pluralist environment to the dispersal of such functions or also reversal of priorities among them. This fundamental mutation conduces to the supersession of strategic rationality, focused on cohesive blocks or quanta of power in a concentrated act of will to preserve or enhance security, by the no less compelling but functionally disarticulated concern with multifaceted internal and external stability based on prosperity.

Concurrently disaggregated are internally coherent religio-ideologically accented continental military-political and primarily Eastern, and pragmatic-secular insular politico-economic and primarily Western, types of power. Their sequentially unfolding generational dominance yields to variable composites of corresponding generic traits assembled in the political economies and cultures of residually or resurgently national or regional polities. While functional dissolution converts the aforementioned first-degree into second-degree sublimation of real politics, the operational salience of an active balancing of power responsive to the geopolitical setting is subsumed in looser and less conspicuous strategic equations. Correspondingly diluted is a range of traditionally significant dispositions of which the geopolitical imperative, deactivated into a mostly latent mindset, is only one and, absent a local or temporary resurgence of the so-called security dilemma, most liable to becoming a subordinate one. Both the functional dissolution and the second-degree sublimation entail the actual reversal of priorities in favor of the economic relative to the military-political function and of the organizational and institutional relative to the structurally shaped strategic dimension. This reversal, revealed in the elevation of economics from an instrument of foreign policy into the dominant preoccupation of multilateral diplomacy, finds categorical expression in the bifurcation of world politics into two models or visions of politics differentiated formally in distinctively linear and circular political geometries and achieves the more concrete expression in the bisegmentation of a post-bipolar structure into one between prosperity and poverty materially.

Strategically more directly significant than either the formally different political geometries, functionally and motivationally distinct models of politics, and materially unevenly endowed polities, are the attendant alterations in the classic schisms, headed by the continental-maritime. It is provisionally dormant inasmuch as the near-universal salience of economics—and a fortiori of economics of a certain, free-market, type—undercuts the key disparity among actors, their mindsets, and their assets. Historically responsible for the schism, this disparity is currently resoluble in amphibiously constituted regional associations tending toward the functional-institutional operationalization of the integration-prone and -promoting circular political geometry. Concurrently revalued, the West–East schism has been reduced once again to value-institutional and ethnoculturally creedal facets largely disentangled from geostrategically significant connection with the land–sea power schism. The sacral–secular schism was already secularized previously into one more generally or generically existential-normative. Its range narrows now further into the opposition—or, better, ambiguous overlap—of utilitarian materialism of civil society and pragmatism of demythologized statism, both sufficiently pronounced to instigate a subtly devalued overassertion of the spiritual dimension. As part of it, various kinds of fundamentalist creeds aggravate the transition from pairs of overlapping contraries that make up schisms into outright polarities of opposites, such as conspicuous materialism of the haves and compensatory pseudo-ideal "isms" of the have nots.

Notes

1. FD 1 (2.par.)–4 (end 1.par.), 7 (2.par.)–8 (end 3.par.), 24 (3.par.)–27 (end 1.par.); RUSR 159 (3.par.)–162 (end 3.par.); FD 50 (3.par.)–54 (end 3.par.); RRA 73 (2.par.)–76 (end 3.par.); WP 364–394, 395–426.

2. RRA 204–205 (end 1.par.), 227 (3.par.)–232 (end 2.par.), 221 (3.par.)–222 (end 2.par.), 211 (3.par.)–215 (end 2.par.); RUSR 142–144 (end 1.par.).

3. RR 61–62 (end 2.par.), 14 (2.par.)–17, 99–108.

4. RR 145 (2.par.)–152 (end 1.par.), 110 (3.par.)–115 (end 2.par.).

5. RP 33–36, RUSR 178 (3.par.)–181 (end 2.par.), WO 46–61 (end 1.par.).

6. WP 108 (3.par.)–120 (end 1.par.); RRA 46 (3.par.)–48 (end 1.par.), 59 (2.par.)–60 (end 1.par.), 76 (4.par.)–79 (end 2.par.), 158 (2.par.)–160 (end 3.par.), 132 (4.par.)–133 (end 3.par.), 24 (4.par.)–27 (end 3.par.).

7. RWO 134 (2.par.)–137 (end 1.par.), 138 (3.par.)–140 (end 1.par.).

8. WP 120 (2.par.)–130 (end 1.par.), 388 (end 2.par.)–394; RP 80 (2.par.)–82 (end 3.par.).

9. RRA 35 (3.par.)–39 (end 1.par.), EA 8 (2.par.)–13 (end 1.par.).

10. RRA 28 (4.par.)–34 (end 2.par.), 142 (2.par.)–145 (end 1.par.).

11. IA 12 (2.par.)–18, 46–53 (end 1.par.); QE 39–57.

12. IA 61–64 (end 1.par.); RUSR 127 (5.par.)–130 (end 2.par.); QE xi–xiii (end 2.par.).

13. CE 73–87, 88–102, and chapters 9 and 10.

14. RWO 38–40 (end 2.par.), 99 (3.par.)–102 (end 2.par.); CE 336–338 (end 1.par.), 346 (4.par.)–351; WO 27 (3.par.)–33, 22 (3.par.)–26 (end 1.par.).

15. IE 75 (4.par.)–81 (end 2.par.), 13 (2.par.)–22, and chapter 2.

16. IE 124 (2.par.)–32, 133–142 (end 1.par.); RRA 113 (4.par.)–118 (end 1.par.); RUSR 93 (3.par.)–94 (end 3.par.).

17. SIE 87–96 (end 1.par.); NS 202 (3.par.)–211 (end 1.par.); IE 148 (3.par.)–161 (end 1.par.); RUSR 85 (3.par.)–91 (end 1.par.).

18. RR 84 (3.par.)–88 (end 1.par.); ATW 44–61.

19. NIA 61–115; IE 167 (2.par.)–170 (end 1.par.).

20. IE 162 (2.par.)–167 (end 1.par.), 171 (2.par.)–180 (end 2.par., omitting 177 end 1.par. to 179 end 1.par.); RR 19 (3.par.)–25 (end 1.par.).

21. EA 22 (2.par.)–70.

22. RR 37 (2.par.)–40, 77 (2.par.)–84 (end 2.par.).

23. RR 161 (2.par.)–164.

24. RWO 85–89 (end 2.par.), 109–115 (end 3.par.), 118 (5.par.)–121, 130 (2.par.)–131 (end 1.par.).

25. WP 470 (3.par.)–476 (end 2.par.), 485–496 (end 1.par.).

26. RUSR 182 (3.par.)–187, 152–159 (end 1.par.).

27. RRA 1–11; RWO 115–118 (end 4.par.); RP 58 (4.par.)–59 (end 1.par.), 114 (2.par.)–115 (end 1.par.).

28. RUSR 200 (2.par.)–223; SIE 1–23; RP 21 (2.par.)–22, 34 (2.par.)–35 (end 3.par.).

Part III

Systematizing World Politics-in-World History: Integration and Synthesis

5

System of Thought versus Theory: Integration and Distillation

Schematization that bares the conceptual facets and operational features of world politics with a view to articulating its dynamics and dilemmas is a necessary antecedent to connecting interaction with evolution and, as part of historicizing the present, projecting contemplation of the past into speculation about the future. Only then has the basis been laid for systematizing the component parts of analysis into a comprehensive perspective on a likewise capacious process. An inclusive system of thought can finally aim at reproducing in the mind the measure of actual coherence containing in a meaningful whole the disparities and complexities that beset the subject matter while they externalize its defining essence.

Integrating structure into environment and order

The quantitative combine with the qualitative features in a total structure, configured or temporarily convulsed in close association with strategies that match the structure more or less closely. Related questions arise: which facet conditions what *kind* of world politics in what *way* and to what *degree*? The quantitative features of size and number of actors may be sufficient for setting off routine balance-of-power interactions, although without intimating who aligns with whom. The interplays produce effects that are static when they perpetuate a quantitatively construed structure by strategies that happen to reflect it precisely. Or the effects are subversive when policies, adjusted to the quantitative side of structure only, convulse a total structure that has been correspondingly misconstrued. Headed but not exhausted by the factors shaping the rise/ decline dynamic and constituting the several schisms, the qualitative features link interaction to evolution with effect on the way historically intelligent as well as instrumentally rational strategy achieves an optimum fit with *total* structure. Such strategies are most efficacious because best capable of accommodating continuity as well as change, with beneficial effect on the kind of world politics actually under way. Ignoring or mis-construing the ambiguous character of quantitative and qualitative fea-tures, as ideally complementary in operations but different-to-contrasting in their makeups, will, finally, reduce the degree to which either facet of structure conditions world politics in determining its kind and the way it is shaped.

No less problematic is the other critical relationship that defines struc-ture: one between individual actors and the arena, i.e., between states or societies and the corresponding system or framework of action. This rela-tionship supplements one between cumulatively evolved organic and con-secutively unfolding operational features of politics with that between structure and function within an overall process. The structure of the arena is, at the most elementary level, defined by the size and number of actors within a topographically shaped and strategically configured space. It is secondarily contingent on the inner structure of the actors themselves as divergently cohesive statist or pluralist, aggregated gradually and then lastingly from a solid nucleus or prematurely expanded, contrarily to the cohesive nuclear, into dissolution-prone nebular entities. In regard to functions, actors are formed as military, economic, and administrative functions progressively coalesce, each more primitive in kind or urgency triggering and being consolidated by the more elaborate or comprehen-sive next-in-line other, while spirit in the form of a shared ethos is being added to the functions and galvanizes the resulting structure. As the sev-eral functions are in large and growing part deliberately integrated, with definite effects on the internal structures of actors, the actors themselves perform incidentally a critical function within the arena when they con-solidate and stabilize it incidentally to indulging their drives for self-pres-ervation or self-aggrandizement. While structure and function intermingle in the process of forming actors and stabilizing or transform-ing the arena, an arena's structure is being slanted toward primarily polit-ico-military or economic functions coincidentally with the primacy of one schism or the momentary hierarchy among the schisms.

The rise/decline- and schisms-related qualitative modifiers of the quan-titative features of structure, as well as structure's imbrication with func-tion, are simultaneously the surface expression of the power-normative essence of politics and the root of the main operational problems of world politics: the dynamic of action and reaction and drives and restraints among actors that make up real politics and the dilemmas of comparative salience or causal priority of systemic/strategic, domestic, and economic factors constitutive of the political economy of world politics. In this twofold perspective, one feature raises conflating core essence with operative surface in the structure and configuration of the arena to the status of the overall environment of world politics. This feature is not to be found in the inherently static quantitative facets of the structure, because it is located in the several relationships between qualitatively modified structure and function mobilized in a both dynamically interactive and developmentally consecutive process—one that ranges from functionally contrived formation to structural consolidation of actors and culminates in their inseparably functional and structural transformations.

Actors are formed from within when the primordial force-related military function, linking physical survival with opportunity for tangible material rewards, elicits more elaborately supportive economic functions in a reciprocally stimulating functional circuit which will be continued in administrative coordination of the two core functions centered on physical security and material sustenance so as to engender the essentially sufficient functional cluster. The chief impetus to this functionally effected internal formation of actors emanates from the comparatively primitive structure of the arena representative of the outside—an environment suggestive of threats and opportunities to be mastered on the most primitive level militarily. This inside-outside and function-structure relationship is at a later stage amplified and amended into one of virtual actor-arena parity when actors' propensity to stalemate virtually generates new significant players in an arena successively structured by developing capabilities and configured by associated strategic alignments into a definite polar pattern. This structurally engendered impetus from the outside will instigate significant functional effects within the newcomers in particular, pressed to make up for the disparity between innate resources and extraneously conferred status if not necessarily also role. Elimination of the resource deficit will alone minimize the associated risks and prepare the elevated protégés for their role as the likely future adversary and eventual nemesis of the previously self-interestedly patronizing, because reciprocally competing, promoters.

Actor formation relates any one actor to the arena, and generation of a third actor is typically a product of relations between two competing actors. A three- to multipolar structure will typically be activated into a process not so much in conjunction with the particular military, economic, and administrative actor-formative functions but as a matter of perceptions and operations affecting the actors' unwittingly performed stabilizing or transforming function in the arena. This happens when any two parties relate themselves, as they commonly will, to one another with a view to a third party: what if any cost relative to the latter will be incurred in any benefit sought or entailed in any advantage achieved from an act by any first relative to a second party. Such a tripartite strategic calculation is clearly at issue in a three-power structure and most significantly within a land-sea power triangle. Several sets of such calculations and interactions will be simultaneously at work in a structure exceeding three principal players. When they are in force, the consideration of costs incurred in relation to a third party from profits sought in relation to the second will offset in principle, though only contingently mitigate in practice, the converse process of one or both of the contestants evading stalemate or seeking one-sided superiority by promoting another third party, a promotion that converts procedural elevation in status into generation of a previously nonexistent substantive role together with capability.

Whereas actors are effectively formed functionally mainly from within and can be virtually generated structurally and operationally from the outside, successively structurally and functionally predominant types of actors stimulate one another, combining transformations with eventual supersession of previously salient actor types. Adding long-term evolution to interaction makes for a comprehensive view of structure, just as adding qualitative to quantitative constituents converts a partially defined into a total structure. The two amplifications become one when the qualitative affects the evolutionary feature by way of one of the schisms. Thus the spiritual–secular schism informs the originally both normatively constraining and functionally creative role of organized church in the rise of the state, and the land–sea power schism mediates the interstimulation between the state and society when in this relationship, just as in the church-state relationship, the latter is the former's late-stage product and eventual nemesis: society displaces the state normatively and up to a point functionally after devolving from it in both respects. As reciprocal conditioning consolidates successively salient actor types and as alternate prioritization of some inevitably entails eventual supersession of others, the environment is being shaped over time and its particular condition, or distinctive or dominant structure, determined at any one moment of time. What happens when will depend on the subject of salience and the evolutionary sequence. Thus, the historically repetitive value-institutionally normative and functionally and instrumentally administrative impact of the church or its equivalent on the state or its equivalent in different eras and cultural areas will, prior to the former's relative demotion by if not absorption in the latter, commonly precede a comparable interplay between state and society on a more evenly secular plane.

As part of this interplay, the state provides a church-like normatively disciplining and functionally reinforcing ingredient for an emergent society when this state has itself evolved sufficiently out of elementary-to-primitive intergroup societal structures, such as those of church-related feudalism. When states are being formed, the smallest material surplus is necessary to provide the means for supporting the military and segregating it as a separate function and profession, only for the latter's requisites to necessitate the creation of the economic ingredient and the military's enforcement potential to foster the material ingredient's progressive accumulation. Only subsequently will the military be superseded by the economic function as the state recedes before society and administration mutates from a coordinating instrument into an end in itself, voiding the state of its mystique on the normative plane and converting it into a machinery restricted to the functional plane. So also primitive societal bonds and intergroup succession struggles over the means of physical survival and moral-political superiority had preceded the state before it assumed the authority to constrain a more fully developed (and both slower and longer developing) society on behalf of a viable balance of rights and duties in the distribution of access to material goods. Just as the economic relative to the military factor in the formation of actors, society eventually disempowers the state normatively and absorbs it functionally not only within actors and in denoting the salient actor type but to a degree also in relations among actors with effects on the continuing validity of the state system.

Even as salient actor types succeed one another in the progression from historically medieval and generically pre-statist pluralist to comparatively modern statist polity and back to post-statist societal format, schisms substitute for one another as dominant in interactor relations. This substitution externalizes the tension implicit in the drive for reciprocal subordination between the paired terms of a schism, because it is the tension's course and outcome that determine the identity of the upcoming schism with effects for the successive priority of state or society and state system or alternative framework of action. A technologically or politically deactivated land–sea power schism will raise the standing and transform the thrust of the West–East schism, blunting its geostrategic linkage with the former and reactivating its innate value-institutional and cultural-political implications, lately centered in a greater prominence for society in one of the paired contraries (the maritime West) and the state in the other (the continental East). Similarly, with the church's regression before the state, the sacral–secular schism is devalued or diluted into a generic existential-normative one, and further on into a crudely material-immaterial or -pseudoideological one with the state's retreat before society. The prominence of alternative schisms constitutes a hierarchy among them, apt to structure the arena and agenda conjointly with a hierarchy of conflicts that differentiates a dominant and globally polarizing conflict from diversely subordinate or would-be independent secondary ones.

Just as any particular schism to a specific conflict, so also the two separate but interdependent hierarchies relate to one another paradoxically in terms of transcendence and immanence. A hierarchically ordered, spa-

tially configured, and schisms-reflecting map of conflicts is the most conspicuously galvanizing factor incorporating structure into environment.
This environment's relation to order is shaped not least by the way the
state's relation to society is projected into one between a state system and
an alternative, societally pluralist framework of order. In conformity with
the norm of sequential prioritization, which imparts the indispensable
temporal-evolutionary dimension to interstimulation, a state system
emerges out of a plurality of substantially developed states after its more
primitive condition as a conflicted but structurally indeterminate arena
has decisively conduced to such states' initial constitution. When the societal actor type becomes salient, the state system is automatically liable to
supersession by a more or less extensive, regionally or globally delimited,
and more or less chaotically pluralist (as opposed to anarchically statist),
framework of action.

Both frameworks of action—the statist and the pluralist—derive ultimately from the needs and originate in the activities of physical individuals, embedded in moral personalities. Individuals are increasingly
submerged in the state as it is reified, acts as a thing-like collective agent
with a will and purpose of its own, only for the individuals to be themselves deified in its place as supremely valuable in a setting that has
evolved from chaotic into institutionalized communitarian pluralism. A
static dichotomy opposing a geocentric order centered on the territorial
state to an anthropocentric one highlighting individuals-in-world community is the basis for a more dynamically programmatic opposition between political realism and varieties of utopianisms culminating in the
opposites of particularist totalitarianisms and planetary humanism. Utopias come to life when the environment is agitated by diversely premature
progressivist challenges to the state as it grows stronger, thus when precipitate secularization elicited religious wars giving rise to the absolutist
state and, conversely, when equally premature liberalization provoked
socio-ideological convulsions setting the stage for the totalitarian state as
statism grew weaker. While the sequence from medieval sacral-monarchi-
cal continental military powers to secular-oligarchical insular-mercantile
powers as leading types of power had concurrently anticipated society's
eventual succession to the state, the failure of the attempts to resuscitate
the medieval and reform the modern type of polity in the extreme right-
and left-wing kinds of late-modern totalitarian polity, respectively, has
recreated space for continuing the underlying sequential (church-)state-
society interstimulation. This opportunity points to polities equipped
with state-like laws of motion expressed in the combination of interaction
with evolution and combining a residual element of normative sacralization with a lessened tendency to militant collisions. The new option—or
revived humanist utopia—is a societally pluralist communitarian frame-

work of action that replaces hierarchy of conflicts with a hierarchy of organizational competencies and contains interstatist anarchy within international organization.

Just as structure relates to environment when it is activated, so environment relates to order, actual or potential and only essential or also existentially operative, when the activating dynamic is contained within definite limits. As fact or ideal, order derives either from instinctually driven conflicts arrayed in a de facto hierarchy of central-dominant and peripheral-particular conflicts or from institutionally coordinated cooperation ordained de jure by a hierarchy of ordinances and prohibitions. Only essential or also operatively actual order in a conflict-driven statist setting arises paradoxically out of what formally juridically is anarchy, identified with the absence of rules laid down by a superior legislator and enforced by a shared authority. Contrary to this formalistic perception, essential orderliness is actually implicit in an agenda revolving around shared stakes and enforced by automatic sanctions. Compliance with authoritative rules of law is replaced by the requisite of correspondence between goals or claims of actors and the means or resources they dispose of and engage in the pursuit of self-affirmation—a correspondence that, when observed, is expressed in a match or fit between structure and strategy. A violation of the strategic requisite that generates the rules encounters sanctions in the form of reactions that reestablish the goals-means correspondence, sanctions more automatic and severely punishing than any usually available to constitutionally ordered polities. Spontaneously enforced "rules of the game" anchored in the sanctioning parties' self-interest make states function individually or collectively as agents of an essential order. This kind of order is both inherent in the broadly defined structure of the environment and reflective of the power-normative essence of world politics, and is most of the time actually operative rather than formally ordained.

Deriving essential order as the representation of norm from conflicts that represent power is the defining characteristic and fundamental process of politics among states. Being both, this kind of order contains more specific processes (antagonization, alliance formation, appeasement) that implement more conspicuous phenomena (war and its absence in formal peace) within flexible but definite limits. Moreover, so construed an order is operationally mediated through the drives and restraints that converge in the balancing of power as a mechanism giving rise to a process wherein conflict is moderated by implied constraints but predominates over explicit control. Whereas essential order originates in formal anarchy converted into its opposite by the checks administered by the balance of power, hierarchy that suggests or implies order is in a similarly oblique or perverse manner paradoxically the source of change. Gradations of status and control in the context of normative equivalence for diverse roles and functions define hierarchy as a societally valid if not also ideal norm. In the real world, this compound of actual inequalities and ideal equivalence converts into countervailing motivations and motions of attraction and revulsion in an inter-functional equilibrium more complex or at least less concentrated than the balance of compact power, while the attendant mutations in capabilities and dispositions straining toward equality will actually conduce to re-stratification in terms of capabilities and associated roles.

By contrast with what is true for the balance of power, control predominates over conflict and countervailance in ordering a pluralist or mixed statist/pluralist environment. The prototypical agent of such an order is an empire. It arises out of and is organized to contain heterogeneous sources and agents of conflict by means of more or less centralized and formally institutionalized (i.e., state-like) instruments of order. An empire will commonly activate its statist features as part of the order-creative process when it constrains primitive pluralism or engages in conflictually slanted competitive relations with another empire—albeit typically in ways modified by its special characteristics or pretensions that elevate symbolism over pragmatism and subordinate role to status. Less typical— i.e., historically frequent—than ideal agent or framework of a pluralist order different from empire is community, ranging from regional to global. Actually operative community tends to distribute functions too widely and consequently risks dissipating indiscriminately the bases of its defining characteristic: solidarity. It is, therefore, presently in most places an insufficiently adequate alternative to non-coercive empire-like association and an unreliable foundation for more than only exceptionally effective international organization.

Depending on the mix of pluralist and statist factors in the makeup of environment and either kind or degree of order, a more or less fundamental divorce can occur between the structural and functional ingredients of process severally intertwined in both the actor-arena interactions and evolutionary sequences between actor types. The functional coalesces with the institutional to the detriment of the geostrategically significant structural factor in a pluralist setting focused on political stability and economic prosperity. Conversely, the structural factor retains its association with the geostrategic dimension and military-political function in a security-centered statist setting. Contrary to the functional-institutional, the structural-strategic model performs within the pluralist framework as mainly a residual mindset rather than actual practice. However, the connection between structure and function will be at least partially reestablished in the community-fostering vision of politics when the integrative as opposed to competitive function is being performed and can be achieved only within an appropriately structured and shaped arena. Appropriate are circular areas of integration that actually intersect with other such pluralistically structured areas around strategically situated functions or, more conspicuously, polities. These overlaps are ideally connected to one another by cross-cutting linear axes of mutually reinforcing cooperation within a concentric pattern of smaller and larger orbits of integration. Such connecting straight lines are in this essentially circular political geometry only secondarily significant, unlike the triangulation-prone linear axes of conflict between conflictually interacting statist poles of power, enclosed by the same token within likewise only secondarily significant more or less circular spheres of major-power interests and influence. Implementation of the concentrically circular geometry guarantees order within particular areas of integration more reliably than between them within the total and comprehensive structure and dynamic environment of world politics. The circular communal will therefore in the best of cases continue to coexist with the linear statist political geometry rather than replace the latter fully anywhere and soon.

Integrating political economy into real politics

Power-related statist factors (including external security/supremacy, international stability, and material sustenance) and the polity-related societal factors (domestic political stability and economic prosperity) are integral parts of an inclusively construed political economy of world politics. Domestic stability and economic prosperity share in relation to security-to-supremacy and international stability the quality of the ultimate determinant, inasmuch as achieving stable if not also legitimate authority is the prime object and preserving it the indispensable requisite of a functioning political order while material sustenance rising to prosperity is the prime desideratum of the society involved in that order. By contrast, security-to-supremacy is in relation to this ultimate only a proximate, but operationally mostly salient, determinant. It constitutes an object of policy combining both the internal and external facets of stability and the material sustenance, externalized in capability, to be ensured by the capacity to make war and secure its absence (i.e., peace) on favorable terms—and do this as the necessary and commonly sufficient means to achieving more substantive or positive goals.

Ultimate determination coincides roughly with the organic, the proximate with the operational, dimension of politics: the economic factor qua material capability and the domestic factor qua sociopolitical order susceptible of cohesion being organic, and transactions revolving around economic and political interests operational. A directly related difference is between the short and the longer terms, equipping the theoretical distinctions with practical significance: under environmental stress of any kind, any actor must respond to immediate (short term) pressures with a necessary minimum of efficacy, if only because no regime or order will lastingly survive (long term) in the face of the cumulative failure to do so—hence the salience of the proximate determinant. However, no amount of skill displayed in foreign policy will lastingly compensate for the failure to develop or preserve the incrementally assembled organic assets—hence the ultimate determinant. This practical policy-related short- and long-term feature of the time factor in turn differs from the conceptual ones. One feature is exhibited in the regressive chain of causation wherein the immediately determinant (say, domestic) factor is the consequence of the antecedent (systemic/strategic) factor caused by yet another and more remote (economic) factor; another feature covers the cumulative aggregation of organic givens over time; and yet another, comprising the operational and organic qualities of the other two, is at work in the consecutively primary (strategic, domestic, economic) stimulants to long-lasting major expansion. Sufficiently diverse in themselves, all of the time-related determinants are ambiguously linked to the quasi-spatially differentiated determinants, implicit in the range of possible sites of primary crisis.

Thus, there can be no settled causal hierarchy in a world politics conceived of in terms of a broadly defined political economy. The ensuing complexity warrants identifying the war/peace-related processes with real politics revolving around the balance-of-power dynamic. But it also compels relating this systemic/strategic core—and broadly external facet—of politics to the domestic or internal and economic sustenance/prosperity-related constitutive features. By the same token, genuinely *political* economy is as superior to pure economics and narrowly administrative management of a particular economy, as it is more comprehensive than real politics distilled into its own inner economy. Thus also a multi-functionally complex equilibrium differs from and encompasses its conflictual balance-of-power core, just as power qua psychopolitical control does relative to material capability.

A practical way of addressing the attendant dilemma of circularity in reciprocal determination is paradoxically not the empirically specific one proceeding from particular case to case, defined in terms of events. It is, rather, one only quasi-empirically schematic pointing to one conceptually systematic. Empirically ascertainable facts may or may not support the proposition that economic considerations are more manifestly prominent in domestic than in interactor politics and that domestic politics is in turn prominent depending on the degree of its stability or instability when it mediates the impact of economics on real politics. Only implicit in operationalizing the ultimate causality of the organic domestic and economic factors is the determinative significance of the site or location of salient crisis in the schematizing rather than specifying, but intrinsically still empirical, perspective. Finally, because or so long as the salient crisis is typically located on the strategic-or-systemic level in a state system, this perspective attributes presumptive causal primacy to the real political over the other two constituents of political economy in the process of expanding the schematic (or schematizing) into a systematic (or systematizing) approach to the causal dilemmas. By contrast with a state system, the economic and domestic factors will be a priori presumed to be determinant in a societal-pluralist system—unless, in a crisis situation, contending economic and domestic interest groups being reduced to a common denominator with state-like entities returns causal primacy to the systemic/strategic or real political facet.

Contrarily to ideological simplifications, conceptualizing the dilemma of circular interdetermination combines the subordination of factual inquiry and specific information to implications of and inferences from an overarching system of order—and of thought, arrived at by intellectual processes of distillation of and abstraction from the existential processes of politics. Positioning the mutually determining constituents of political economy in relation to one another both individually (i.e., the domestic and economic factors relative to the systemic/strategic one separately) and collectively (all three interacting in the complex equilibrium simultaneously) sets up an overall perspective for at least a partial and provisional disentanglement of a seamlessly circular interplay between economics and real politics and internal/domestic and external/systemic facets of world politics. This tangled causal web is centered only precariously in the common quality of domestic political and economic material factors as ultimately determinant organic factors. It is expressed operationally in the more pervasively determinative primacy of economics in domestic interclass rather than in interstate politics, a primacy that typically positions and may intermittently impel the domestic agenda to mediate the impact of the economic factor on the systemic component.

Approaching this entanglement with the aid of analytic distinctions militates against the attendant dilemmas and complexities in several ways, but does not resolve or transcend them. Equivocally circular inter-determination among the constituents of the political economy is subject to, and is therefore qualified by, the more univocally conflictual dynamics of real politics, biased causally toward conformity with a determinate environmental structure. Equivocal determination and univocal dynamics can be meaningfully linked—and the lacuna between them bridged—only by virtue of their being reduced to a common denominator. This is to say, structures and processes must be defined with respect to all constituents of political economy in terms of essentially identical units of action con-

cerned with power—be they state-like polities, social classes, or socioeconomic interest groups—subject to comparable general tendencies as
opposed to, say, diffusely communicated public opinion or routine political or economic transactions. The problematic complexities can be otherwise radically but then falsely simplified only through ideologically
dogmatic assumptions and propositions, favoring the causal determinism
of either economics (Marxism and free-market capitalism, when the basic
presumption of the former is not virtually nullified by inserting superstructural co-determinants and the actual thrust of the latter denied by a
contrarily idealized political doctrine), domestic politics (classic-to-so-
cially reformist liberalism, when its external projection is not effectively
nullified by stalemated factionalism), or environmental configurations
(when the plausible basic thrust of traditional conservatism and realism is
radically simplified by quantitatively constricted structuralism).

Less dogmatic than empirically schematic—and, because based on satisfying the requisite of a common denominator, more real or realistic—is
the conceptual clarification of dilemmas besetting the two key relationships: among the several constituents of political economy and between
circular inter-determination and univocally conflictual core dynamics. In
this perspective, the dilemmas are clarified by means of a dichotomy, that
between primarily continental-military and primarily maritime-mercantile powers. This historically actual basis for the systematizing approach
to determination becomes explicit in one way when the sea powers are
correctly construed in terms of their dual identity, as real-political actors
and leaders in a specific type of economy. Depending on the location of
crisis, the sea powers will be determined qua territorial states primarily
extraneously (systemically) and internally (domestically) in their other
capacity. Apart from this peculiarity of one party to it, the schism betwen
land and sea powers as a consistently crises-generating relationship is determinative not only proximately (and operationally) but also ultimately
(and organically). It is the latter because the cumulatively evolved domestic sociopolitical orders of the parties tend to derive genetically from—i.e.,
be conditioned by—the parties' existential situation, being unitary-stat-
ist/authoritarian-conservative on the part of the externally pressured land
powers, and pluralist-societal/liberal-representative on that of the naturally insulated sea powers. Nor do historically evolving particular variations on these basic differences alter significantly, let alone decisively, the
successive manifestations of the triangularized schisms in terms of initiation, course, or consequences. Conversely, the land–sea power divergence
itself originates in spatial-geographic givens (largely land-locked vs. sea-
abutting locations) that entail different material-economic resources and
orientations, i.e., agricultural vs. commercial. However, the ultimate causality of the organic economic factor (qua distinctive capability or order

and entailed trends) does not include particular economic interests and associated transactions, apt to be subordinated to the strategic requisites of the real-political crises inherent in a schism that habitually conduces to a major war. Finally, the fact that the differences in the domestic orders and related social systems actually derive from geographically conditioned types of economy not only circumscribes these orders' and systems' ultimately causative impact as an organic factor but discredits perceiving them as the prime and original operational stimuli of policies responsible for the conflict.

Although closely connected to it, the relationship between war and economics surpasses the land–sea power issue. This relationship is commonly understood as an aspect of the juxtaposition of the competing priorities of power and plenty or "defence and opulence." One way of formulating the causation of wars more concretely can be in terms of long-term economic cycles or alternative economic systems, competing economic interests and resulting transactions, or (most plausibly) clashing because of alternately rising and declining material resources relative to actually exercised or claimed roles. Logically contrary to either determination but actually complementary to the one mentioned last is the particularly uncaused, because autonomously cyclical, alternation of wars with periods of peace that takes place as the stresses or limits on attainable achievements of either pave the way for reactivating the promises or accumulated urgencies of the other. Relatedly alternating are external concerns (related to military-political security-or-supremacy, diplomatic standing, and economic sustenance qua capability) and domestic priorities and preoccupations (concerning sociopolitical stability and economic sustenance qua prosperity). Conjointly prioritizing the location of crisis as the substantively neutral or indifferent determinant is congruent with the normative neutrality of war as the core mechanism of reequilibration in response to the role-resource and related discrepancies responsible for instabilities conducive to war. Finally, there is a mere correlation-capable coincidence contrary to one-sided causation by any one factor, but supplemental to or compatible with cyclical alternations of war and peace and external-systemic and internal-societal crises. Such coincidence may well be that of war-prone and war-resistant situations with unevenly crystallized and constraining domestic or systemic structures, relatively authoritative and permissive types of domestic and economic regimes, or relatively expansionist and conservatively consolidative basic foreign policy postures.

Specific causes of war and conflicted dynamics, circular inter-determination, and either cyclical alternation or merely correlation-capable coincidences relate to one another in ways no more definite than wholly indefinite. So do the attributes that can be postulated for the dual identity defining the maritime-mercantile party to the land–sea power dichotomy:

the three consecutive phases in its evolution as a lead economy or incumbent of economic hegemony (distinctive productive capacity, primacy-to-monopoly in trade, and rise to and dependence on primacy in high finance) and in its evolution as a territorial state (primitively pluralist proto-stage, crystallized-consolidated statist norm-stage, and institutionalized pluralist meta-stage, coincidental with the successive foreign policy postures). Neither sequence either guarantees or rules out causally significant interactions between phases of the two evolutionary processes, even or especially when variable-to-progressively expanding time lags are allowed for. One reason is that the rise/decline curve of the lead economy tends to be irreversible along a trajectory from mercantilist via liberal free trading to fair trade upholding neo-mercantilist policies. Another is that the sequence in typical foreign policy postures is subject to relapses or attempted overleaps on the part of both the sea powers and the continental powers qua territorial states.

Thus qualified, the curve of the lead economy will habitually start rising conjointly with the exuberant foreign policy postures and level off—and begin to decline—with the conservative foreign policy posture of the sea power qua territorial state. This situation is apt to induce the first bid for overseas parity by and thus conflict with the continental power engaged in one of its expansion-oriented postures. When the diffusion or dissipation of its economic assets has weakened the maritime-mercantile power materially and it advances as a territorial state toward a compulsively expansionist foreign policy posture, the challenger's habitual second and—because it aims beyond preeminence to continental hegemony—climactic try for overall continental–maritime parity will respond less to a relative decline that had already materialized (the economic one of the lead economy) and coincide more with one (the continental challenger's) that is only threatening in the real political balance-of-power sphere. Consequently, the origination of wars is a function of interplays between stages in economic cycles of the lead economy (as largely determinant for the world economy overall), the sequential foreign policy postures of both the continental and the maritime-mercantile powers qua territorial states, and the strategic options including alliance choices available to both within a triangle completed by the rear-continental power. An incidental consequence of this intricate causal pattern is a redistribution of principal responsibility for war among the parties to the triangle as well as between pure economics and more complex political economy.[1]

Necessary though they are, analytic distinctions can relieve only partly the dilemmas associated with seamlessly circular inter-determination. They are less easily manageable than the gap between individual-subjective act or incentive and aggregate-objective result or consequence, conspicuous in relation to the balance of power and alliances but narrowed there by policies designed to alternately make the adversary and keep one or several allies manageable at different stages of a contest. A reason for this difference is the clearer one between antagonist and ally and beginning and end of a war in one setting and the less clear one between political stability and economic prosperity in the other. Despite the apparent determinateness of quantifiable economics, its being actually on a par with the domestic factor subject to mass psychological influences makes it in normal circumstances less determinate than strategically rational real politics subject to predictably countervailing and at least superficially distinguishable drives and restraints. Both account for the equations counterposing definite roles and quantifiable resources through the ultimately equalizing calculable risks, assumed more or less effectively in the overall setting of an identifiable hierarchy of interests derivative from the equation's more basic or original constituents. Only explicitly succession-related civil warlike intergroup domestic contentions will reestablish the essential identity of the respective agendas and reduce the practical impact of the differences, while forfeiting the claim to a distinctive form of analysis.

The analytical gap between univocally self-regulating real politics and equivocally inter-determinative constituents of political economy is narrowed when the former actually permeates segments of the latter, subject to unevenly conceptual and operative relationships comprising features and facets of both. Thus the domestic and systemic, or internal and external, factors will affect one another in terms of direct and operative causation, most conspicuously manifest in the large-scale and long-term imperial kind of expansion. Or when mere correspondence or coincidence obtains between domestic and systemic structures and foreign policy postures, and is potentially reinforced by policy for circuitously indirect mutual conditioning of foreign and domestic politics revolving around strategic intentions aimed at one or the other. And finally, when economics and (real-)politics relate to one another symmetrically over a likewise tripartite spectrum, from formal analogy (between mercantilistic politics and economics centered on zero-sum conflict and liberal politics and economics prone to positive-sum cooperation and integration) via conceptual propinquity (the cost-benefit and marginal utility or disutility shared by real politics in general and alliance politics in particular with micro- and macro-economics), to substantively operational causal linkage (economics as instrument in statist politics and impellent of pluralist-societal politics).

Upgrading the inter-determinative circularities to the status of comparative causal primacies of the individual constituents further will rest first of all—and very tentatively—on hard-to-test general hypotheses and propositions positing reciprocal projection or subversion, i.e., extrapolations of domestic stability and economic prosperity into a state of peace, liable to be subverted by domestic political instabilities caused or only precipitated and consummated by economic adversity. Such specific propositions will be relieved of their ideological biases and made more convincing by a schematization that implies a peripatetic, and a temporalization that points to a consecutive, causation. One allows for the migration of causal primacy (or operational salience) among the constituents of political economy in function of the spatial location of dominant crisis or conflict; the other allows for temporal sequences in causal primacy in function of interlocks among the particular factors in their alternating capacity as causes and effects. Such space/time qualifiers of circular causation are at their most graphic in geohistorically conditioned and construed world politics that integrates political economy into real politics both substantively and systematically in conjunction with the continental–maritime schism. This particular schism is the most conspicuous single promoter of the determinative salience of the strategic/systemic factor of political economy—and, thus, of the latter's integration into real politics. It is such because the schism embodies, enacts most consistently, the items denoted by "s" and "c" words that represent the interactional counterpart to their evolution-denoting analogues from structuration via socialization to supersession or from conception via concert to collapse of a state system. They are stakes centered on sustenance, security, or supremacy as conditions of survival mediated by way of successions, in the context of major conflicts and salient crises.

It is true that while this schism comprises all the constituents of political economy and implicitly ranks their original and derivative, primary and secondary, causal impact, its contribution applies only to the periods of its own salience. Moreover, even or especially during such periods, ambiguities obtain relative to both the economic and the domestic constituents/determinants. The distinctive identity of the sea power alone would seem to exemplify the causal primacy of economics centered in the qualitatively distinct character of its and the continental power's or powers' material capabilities. On the other hand, this same power's split personality reaffirms contrarily the causal primacy of the real political factor when the uneven scopes (range or length) and slopes (comparative steepness or flatness) of the trajectories of the sea power's two identities are taken into account. Its trajectory as territorial actor will be typically longer and flatter than the meteorically rising and irreversibly declining curve of a lead economy. This discrepancy will at some point absorb the economic factor in the systemic/strategic facet and propel the sea power toward a materially debilitating forcible defense of both of its hegemonies. More a built-in predicament than self-induced policy error, this contingency can be avoided only at an equally hard-to-endure and -avoid cost to preeminence or, even, effective independence relative to a qualitatively identical mercantile-maritime competitor, one that will be poised to evolve from indispensable ally into inescapable protector relative to the present or future continental challenger.

Next to the economic, a bias in favor of the systemic determinant applies also to the domestic political dimension when an essentially inter-statist land–sea power schism is in force and exhibits continuities in basic inter- and intra-actor structures and strategic options over a sequence of its historical manifestations. Only among the secondary determinants does the domestic political order predominate over the economic in affecting particular transactions. It does so insofar as the uniformly authoritarian continental political systems vary more in their specifics and particulars than either the political systems of the insular powers or the uniformly regulatory economic systems of the continental powers, and freewheeling ones of the maritime powers, at their respective peaks. Moreover, even a mere correspondence between domestic structures and the diverse foreign policy postures across an evolutionary spectrum reflective of the rise/decline of both the land and the sea powers will reserve some—albeit a minimum of—determinative role and effect to the domestic factor. This effect is concentrated in the conservative, balance of power-promoting, posture as one uniquely responsive to the diverse domestic orders of continental and maritime powers. However, even this modest effect will be weakened within the circuitous variety of the domestic-systemic (or internal-external) relationship when one party's policy reverses the domestic factor from efficient cause into hoped-for liberalizing or otherwise positive effect on the rival's part with a view to stabilizing the environment and appeasing a conflict in depth.

On the other hand, the unique role of the continental–maritime schism as a link between political economy and real politics is confirmed significantly in relation to the domestic factor when it substantiates the analytic requisite of a common denominator for inter- and intra-actor real politics. Such a denominator is present when the principal characteristics of not only particular regions within a polity, but also distinctive social classes, that compete over possession of and succession to dominance—i.e., determinative primacy—in defining the distinctive character of the polity, are themselves defined in terms of the schism's contentiously paired constituents. In such a case, trade-oriented coastal maritime and agriculture-related inland regions, and landed aristocracy (as the prototype of conservative-traditionalist) as opposed to mercantile middle class (as that of liberal-progressivist) social groups and elites contend over support by an indeterminate populace, the functional equivalent in revolutionary situations of the ultimately regulatory if most of the time passive rear-continental power in war-prone conditions. Inasmuch as in the intergroup and the inter-region, just as in the interstate, contests it is geography that is the ultimate determinant from which derive first the economic and then the domestic political systems, a consequence follows. The order of original and derivative causal primacy will be reversed when politics is deterritorialized and the state desacralized in a pluralist-societal environment, subordinating incidentally the varieties of realism germane to conflicted real politics in favor of largely inward-oriented prudential Realpolitik and outward-oriented progressivist realism.

Meanwhile, the critical role of the land–sea power schism is confirmed by its association with the other substantive integrator of political economy into real politics: expansion into empire. Only when the environment is wholly indeterminate, is devoid of any discernible schism-related or schism-indifferent structure, will the domestic and economic factors predominate as a rule rather than an exception. However, such a primacy may be only transitional while the resulting structural-strategic ambiguities cause the environment to recrystallize more or less catastrophically. Short of such aberrations, the systemic/strategic factor will predominate also as the original stimulus to an expansion that converts a chaotically pluralist environment into an empire as the prototypical statist-pluralist hybrid. Following the initial fusion of the security and sustenance motive, the primacy of the external impellent is paradoxically underlined by the subsidiary domestic and economic stimuli taking over as separate and distinctive only after the systemic/strategic incentive has become counterproductive in the face of rising external opposition. This contingent priority is manifested in specific ways when the incentives to expansion are related to the land–sea power schism. One way is when the security-related strategic considerations of the would-be amphibious central-continental power relative to the rear-continental one—illustrating the original systemic stimulant—predominate over the concern with material sustenance-to-prosperity (a commonly subsidiary impetus) relative to the oceanic party. Another is when the sea power as a territorial actor applies those same real political priorities to compensate for its declining strength as a lead economy, a situation responsible for the late developmental stage of formalized protective imperialism. Yet another is when actual or assumed strategic requirements are the main propellent behind economically only questionably rewarding new acquisitions at a sea power's evolutionary peak in both of its capacities. This is a situation apt to attend the developmentally climactic informal free-trading imperialism—and will do this without prejudice to the persistence of the particular kind of economy internal to real politics.

Distilling real politics into its internal economy

Decomposing war and peace into processes of antagonization and ap-peasement is a step toward abstracting the power-normative essence of politics from the dynamics of drive and restraint, to be reconnected with both processes and essence through the distillation of real politics into the constituents of its inner economy. As the constituents, political physics subsumes expansion as the propulsive/kinetic and balance-of-power in-teraction as the interactive/dynamic aspects of real politics, and tragic po-etics is dramatized in war as the politics' culmination. Closing thus the circle of speculative reconstitution of world politics reflects its nature as a form of art no less than science, worthy of esthetic appreciation and ethical attribution that remove statecraft from the reach of facile moralis-tic condemnation.

The abstraction of phenomena-decomposing processes into power-normative essence entails a corresponding conception of international politics. It places power as the action-related existential given and opera-tional impellent, associated with or expressed in interests as a key but derivative factor, into a reciprocally offsetting and correcting dialectical relationship with norms as the impellent's and interests' modifier and po-tential restraint, ethical or ideological or institutional—or anything other than strategically rational. A greater, or more explicit, stress on the coun-tervailing normative realm and community-oriented rules than on the laws of power is implicit in emphasis on international institutions rather than real politics, but is fully consistent with a critique of the institutions' tendency to mislead as well as malfunction when divorced from the power factor. An integral part of a consequently amplified progressivist realism is thus distrust of equating the norm side of the equation with qualitative progress identified as the growth of interdependence and cooperation, without for all that denying space to an ethical dimension adapted to both the possibilities and the necessities of real politics. Similarly, conceding the strictures addressed to power as a theoretical concept is consistent with focusing on this phenomenon as offering a uniquely penetrating in-sight into politics of all kinds, which incidentally stimulates inventive the-orizing (as opposed to theory-making) that compensates for the concept's ambiguity if not crudity. Thus also viewing the habitually associated con-cept of national interest as contingent on a subjective appraisal of interna-tional reality translates into a correct interpretation and implementation of this interest as derivative from particular configurations of the total environment and the role sought or attainable within that configuration.

Dealing with such subtleties from the firmer ground of basic predispo-sitions—concerning the identity, place, and role of power and norm in

light of the positive potential of their dialectically creative reciprocal negation—engages a liberal mindset in contention with its conservative counterpart. In principle, a philosophically liberal view ought to confine itself
to the normative and a conservative one to the existential side. Actually,
liberal concession to utopianism can be readily embodied in a progressivist version of realism that struggles over the definition of genuine realism
with the more somberly conservative commitment to the biases of a realism whose philosophical stress on power combines with a call for prudence in its exercise. Inclining toward pessimism (about human nature)
and alarmism (centered on crises and emergencies as the defining feature
of real political dynamics), philosophical realism leans as a result toward
determinism (regarding both processes and potential remedies) and culminates naturally in tragic-mindedness (as a reflection of the ethical predicament of politics and right response to a world permeated by
necessities). A philosophically realist perspective is consequently the basis
for and culminates in the romantic version of realism, which injects historically shaped values-related and ethically exacerbated passional into
strategically rational interests-centered approaches to expansion and balance-of-power interaction in world politics. This particular kind of realism allows uniquely for representing the theater of power qua force
analogically in the metaphor of Newtonian-plus political physics, and
conceiving the arena of the co-active rather than impotently counteracting
normative dimension in that of Aristotelian tragic poetics. Interweaving
political physics and poetics in the inner economy of real politics means
elaborating conceptually on the latter's essence while distilling actually
operative processes into their essentials. Doing so in the perspective of
romantic realism injects a more dramatic than utopian ingredient into too
hopefully progressivist and too soberly philosophical kinds of realism as
well as a humane outlook on politics into pure power politics and a more
inspiring vision of past and future into more timid than prudent Realpolitik.[2]

The dynamics and associated kinetics side of political physics analo-
gizes from the exact science of motion to contingent motives and their
manipulation without allowing science to overwhelm art in the process.
It deals with the essentials: the embodiment of power in bodies politic
qua powers; their responses to the laws of motion; the consequent gravitation of actors, occasioning horizontal constellations (via alliances and antagonisms) and vertical circulation (in function of ascent and decline); and
all this within a field of forces subject to the law-like tendencies ranging
from fairly demonstrable, such as the conflictual responses to vacua of
power in a particular space, to frankly speculative such as the constant
sum of different kinds of conflict within specifiable periods of time.

Kinetics is a special feature—or subcategory—of this dynamic, peculiar to the political physics of expansion as the momentum imparted or neces-sitated by the motion and gravitation of other bodies politic. In actual politics, this means expansion responsive to (i.e., motivated by) the pulls from the environing constellation of forces. Preclusively offensive-defen-sive reactions to such pulls are theoretically as well as practically at least as significant as the predatory push imparted from within the body poli-tic: the drive embedded in the power-dependent survival urge, unlike the draw exerted by the environment. The net surplus of offense over defense, representing expansion, is accordingly the result of a whole complex of incentives that combines recoil from and attraction by or to different magnitudes of power and its functionally diverse constituents. A func-tionally specific application of the physics metaphor extends beyond real politics to political economy when it includes the economic factor promi-nently in the gravitation and migration of centers of preeminent power. This ultimate expression of the dynamics enveloping the kinetics encoun-ters the testing ground of its motivation, motion, and momentum in his-tory—one that qualifies quanta of capabilities acting as forces with attributes of actors behaving as parties to schisms spanning the void that would otherwise open between immaterial spirit and material substance. As much or more than expansion, evolution is integrated into political physics when progression is perceived and represented as a function of not only sociopolitical and functional but also directly power-displacing gravitational revolutions. And when the attendant mutations' graduated velocities in actors and their configurations respond to energy-generating crises acting as the motor of evolutionary momentum.

When manifesting itself in history, the first law of the physics of poli-tics conjugates the denial of indefinitely continuing vacuum with the af-firmation of inertial motion. It holds that, once activated by the attraction of a power vacuum (i.e., inferior power), superior power will keep moving (i.e., expanding) until it has encountered a blocking or deflecting milieu or resistance—for example, intra-actor group conflict or culture-induced inhibition as milieu, and counterforce or system-generated constraint as resistance. That same power will resume motion (i.e., expansion) or re-cover direction only when invested with a new impetus, such as expan-sionist compensation for intergroup domestic struggle or for material deficiency in a dynamic universe. If the above is law number one, law number two postulates that if a vacuum of inferior power attracts, supe-rior power repels that inferior power. The superior power is a threat to the basic law of the inferior power's nature, its tendency to seek corporate autonomy—that is, freely to accept subjection only to the laws of power or politics and not to the dictates of another body politic. Summing up, there are two basic kinds of motion and related laws. One kind of motion is toward a power vacuum or inferior power and is inertial; it responds to the only reliably operative attraction, one exercised by a smaller mass on a larger one. Subsidiary to it is the apparently reciprocal attraction of near-equally strong and dynamic powers converging into virtually un-avoidable conflict over a complete or partial power vacuum, one of them moving or appearing to move forward first and thus attracting counter-vailing power, the other appearing to supply countermovement and coun-terpoise. The other kind of motion is expressed in recoil or flight away from greater power, constituting counterattraction or antigravity.

The two related laws of attraction and counterattraction acting together account for the gravitation of bodies politic. They condition the resulting constellations within a geocentric cosmos, centered upon the territorial state in principle and upon the interactions of such states in practice rather than upon the planet earth itself qua world community. It is possible to postulate additional laws, relating to constant sums—for example, of con-flict or of political energy either present in a system or required for its maintenance over definite periods of time. The object is then to account for other phenomena, such as the expansion of the system and shifts in centers of gravity within the system.

Radically different from the gravitation experienced by bodies politic qua powers is the gravitation of preeminent power qua attributes—the first relative to one another, the second across space. Power as a prime matter permeates the system; it is variably clustered within successive bodies politic, imparting to them specific mass and, with that mass, the capacity to repel or as a function of prior repulsion by one to attract to another actor in consequent relationships. The differential power attri-bute can be seen neutrally as moving or migrating along a path from one place or incumbent to another. The path's direction can be inferred from observable events in history and, if the path and its direction add up to a meaningful pattern, they can be seen as illustrating a historical law. But for such movement to warrant the term "gravitation," responding to a law of motion, it is necessary to identify some kind of direct or derived attraction.

One such gravitation consists in the northwestward, or transoceanic, movement of what was originally economic preeminence from the Medi-terranean to the Atlantic and beyond to the Pacific basin. The direct at-traction accounting for that gravitation can be seen as residing in: (1) the increasing potential implicit in the ever-expanding bodies of water and surrounding land masses; and (2) the successively optimal conditions en-abling individual trade and financial centers—Venice, Antwerp, Amster-dam, London, New York, and points west—to exploit that potential. Assisted by real or apparent historical accidents, the potential and the capacity to actualize it come together and produce the commercial, indus-trial, and related or derived politico-military primacy of corresponding territorial powers. The resulting displacement of preeminent power will commonly institutionalize some kind of functional revolution and will incarnate a cause-effect interplay, as politico-military preeminence perpetuates for a time the economic preeminence that underlay it at an earlier stage. Dynamically supplementing—or operationalizing—the indirect attraction exerted on gravitating power by higher material or organizational potential were the recoils (from threateningly near power) and the derived attractions (by potentially safeguarding remote power) at work between any two of the unevenly maritime-mercantile parties to a land–sea power triangle. The interstate movements promoted or only conditioned the migration of preeminent power and influenced the timing of actual power transfers.

The other, eastward, power gravitation on the Eurasian continent in the modern era occurred comparably, in response to the attractive pull of the vaster potential implicit in successive territorial units: Castile, France, Germany, and Russia so far. Given the expanding shape of the Eurasian peninsula as it stretches eastward, the potential was actualized in ever vaster clusters of national power. Each successive cluster was slower to organize than the preceding one but was more powerful when finally formed. At first, the next-eastern major political space was organized only enough to get preeminent power moving; in the second phase, prepared by the initial displacement, its speed increased as the operationalizing motions— recoil from the previously, if decreasingly, superior contiguous power to the west ending in reciprocal attraction into conflict with it—compelled the rising power to coordinate decisively its so-far only latent resources.

So long, finally, as preeminent power gravitated in early Europe up and down the vertical South–North pathway, the variably attractive magnet resided in the alternative efficacy of the spiritual and the temporal weapons of the two corresponding types of powers, papal and imperial or monarchical. Mediated by recoils from either as a threat, the two kinds of weapons imparted momentary superiority to one or the other power in function of changing secular opportunities or the belief systems of third parties, which conditioned their allegiance and the principal rival's legitimacy.[3]

The abstractions of the physics metaphor take on life in and through the central balance-of-power dynamic revealed through history. Both the analogy and the actuality become progressively more elusive as power balancing moves past the third law of Newtonian mechanics stating that to every action there is a contrarily directed equal reaction. Complexities and related theoretical problems arise with the addition of the third body politic (in lieu of a celestial body) to a system predicated on mutual attraction and gravitation. The analogy applies still rather directly, albeit at the cost of qualifying attraction with revulsion when the smaller third power that recoils from a proximate to a remote bigger power mediates the mutual attraction of the bigger two in that the weak party constitutes a relative power vacuum as well as a stake of contention. Beyond that simplest case, the triangular relationship is modified qualitatively among near-equal continental, insular, and rear-continental parties to the land–sea power schism. It is generalized, and diluted further, into a universal tendency or only desideratum for strategic options being evaluated and enacted in tripartite settings, enjoining upon actor A to avoid any action or advantage relative to B that would cause A greater harm in its relations with C.

Finally, past qualitative diversification and generalized dilution occurs decomposition, associable analytically with postclassical mechanics. It energizes post-statist pluralism after preceding, in a more primitive form, the consolidation of unitary bodies politic and points to the regression of the inter-statist field of forces into the realm of factors and functions. The simple balance-of-power mechanics is superseded by a complex equilibrium, wherein the three-cornered attraction-revulsion dynamic is replaced by a three-factor equation. Therein, the revulsion from the politico-militarily stronger (i.e., more "power-full") party is partially matched by the attraction of the latter's economic potency. And just as the net margin of residual revulsion is or can be offset by cultural-political affinity, so residual attraction will be nullified by culturally founded antipathy—the nonviolent equilibrium-restoring counter of last resort to apolitically motivated capitulation before the economic pull, prone to translating into political servitude.

Although countervailing dynamic is implemented less unequivocally and predictably at each step beyond the simplicity of Newton's third law's operation between two forces, it continues to operate. But it does so ever less through instinct and reflex and more via strategic deliberation or intuition, as part of which the worst-case hypothesis discourages strategic behavior apt to deviate from effective power balancing. At the same time, the connection between the physics, the balancing, and the latter's enactment through war becomes increasingly contingent upon the applied particular strategy in contexts such as the land–sea power triangular one. Or, in the case of pluralist decomposition, the connection itself becomes remote, as the relation between war and stability is inverted from the classic mode of stability reemerging from war as a near constant of power politics into its obverse: stability as the primary object of policy achievable by other means that make resort to war rationally unattractive if not irrational.

Beyond all these nuances, the real-world working of political physics through contentious power balancing is brought home most compellingly in the war-peace (or -stability) context through the implications of the

Einsteinian and Aristotelian varieties of physics when they indispensably amplify the quasi-Newtonian mechanics. The Einsteinian variety does so by highlighting the divergent perceptions of spatially differently situated and temporally evolved actors who, unevenly saturated or satisfied, will deviate from realistic dispositions to utopian perceptions accented either melioristically (liberal progressivism) or mythologically (reactionary conservatism). Because translating such perceptual asymmetries into historical intelligence will accentuate the conflictual bias of interstate politics, only a sharpened awareness of the spatio-temporal relativity will inflect the motion toward conflict in the direction of its appeasement. Both the divergent perceptions and the unevenly relativist appreciations of the predicament and its spatio/temporal relativity-ignoring absolutist denegation have a markedly subjective character. By contrast, the intensification of conflict due to the growth and decline of actors, implicit in the organismic and affecting the purposive tenor of Aristotelian physics, is a comparatively objective given despite its occurring within actors. Actors' degree of saturation, expressed in feeling of satisfaction, and its connection with their position on the growth-decline curve links perceptions to purposes. Consequently, clarifying the reasons behind the saturation will also inject a realistic perception of power-related factors into the purpose. The party satisfied with the status quo will be one at or near, though not commonly past, the peak of growth and will be intent therefore on strengthening the formal-institutional restraints on force and violence in keeping with the melioristic utopia. The obverse will apply to an ascendant power dissatisfied with things as they are and consequently intent on catching up and breaking through normative and other inhibitions by mytho-normativizing reality in favor of historically pristine or mythic violence, relegitimized in a kind of utopia diametrically opposite to that of meliorism.[4]

Such connections link the physics metaphor to more conventional models of politics as regards both perception and purpose. Conversely, purpose alone links political physics focusing on power to political poetics as the ethics of tragedy peculiar to the use of power in international politics. Tragic poetics invests rational promotion of interests with passion in its twofold connotation of emotive exaltation and moral-physical agony. It allows the conception as well as the practice of politics to advance beyond techniques to telos, and impels all-too-conspicuous machinations and manipulations of diplomacy toward the realm of meaning in two complementary ways. One is by transposing the interaction of unequal forces into a collision of values that are intrinsically and may be equally positive when discounted for developmentally and situationally engendered differences among parties. Another is when tragic politics exonerates inordinate hegemony-seeking expansionism as moral heroism impelled by a conflicted system that simultaneously or alternately encourages and punishes attempts to escape its inhibiting constraints and restraints through the most effective possible exercise of self-help.[5]

The power-normative essence of world politics would not connect meaningfully with either Newtonian or Einsteinian physics were it not for the addition of the purposive to the propulsive thrust in the kinetics of Aristotelian physics; nor would the organic blend so seamlessly with the operational dimension. Another correction is necessary in the face of the tendency to melodramatize actual or pretended inequality of values on the part of a mundane—and, specifically, continental—adversary. This is the Einsteinian correction of Newtonian mechanics if the view of tragedy as the defeat of one or both of the parties to a clash of equally positive values is to be plausibly applied to politics. It will be so applied by readiness to discount ostensible differences in the quality or merit of contrasting values by unequally favorable location of parties in space and unevenly advanced development in time. Both qualifiers apply when the values-based definition of tragedy is extended to the revolt against either the specific disparities or the contradictory nature of the system itself, manifested in the bid for hegemony.

The practical significance of the connection of tragic poetics with political physics is best illuminated by applying the equilibrium concept to the war-peace issue. Whereas the tragic nexus between equally positive values tends toward an actual resolution of conflict unequally destructive of both of the agents, the equilibrium principle opens contrary values to reciprocal adaptation over time in conditions of peace. However, the tragic feature also strains the equilibrium dynamic in fact when the tragic hero attempts to break out of the constraints of the dynamic's core in the balance of power by a war-inducing bid for hegemony. The flaw inherent in this excess of ambition is inevitably passed on to the effort's agent and will be partially redeemed through the catharsis attending an equally unavoidable defeat. Moreover, the hubris propelling the bid is exculpated still more fully when it is matched, minus heroism, by that of the moral absolutist's contemptuous neglect of the spatial-temporal relativity. Unaware or dismissive of the extenuating circumstances of the ostensibly "worth-less" aggressor, the apolitical moralist drifts irresistibly toward an also ethically superficial identification of tragedy with war: its consequences in human pain and suffering rather than its causes in the impersonal dynamics and dilemmas of real politics, only subject to misapplication by inept and degradation by unworthy practitioners.

The ethically absolutist position combines the wrong kind of emotionalism with moral and intellectual arrogance in a mix incompatible with political realism of any variety. By contrast, the ethically relativist stance integrating the spatio/temporal factor is fully in keeping with the mundane requirement of realism to put oneself in the place of the adversary when assessing its interests and upholding one's own interests. Without suppressing the statesman's supreme obligation toward his country's vital interests, this stance significantly qualifies it on the plane of public morality—not least because a measure of ethically meritorious compassion for the adversary's predicament that conduces to war will incidentally alleviate the differently tragedy-constitutive inversion of the victor's wartime best into this best's opposite in triumphant peace.

Operationally, the conservative-realist stance will tend to alleviate the drift toward war while treating war itself as a morally neutral functional device of reequilibration from anterior disturbances or disparities, contrary to the liberal utopian's view of war as intrinsically evil. Incidentally relevant is the difference between strategic rationality and commonplace reasonableness that views a conflict as not so much tragic or immoral as criminally foolish. Such a reasonable position links poetics in another fashion to physics as the representation of real politics implemented through a peculiar (i.e., strategic) rationality responsive solely to the postulated laws of power. Thus, the critique of a rationally initiated and conducted conflict in favor of sensible abstention will be shared by the philosophical realist (favoring the minimalist use of theoretically acknowledged and emphasized power in favor of diplomacy, as a matter of principle) and the practitioner or proponent of Realpolitik (who would minimize the ends of policy in recognition of power's diminution or the dangers of overextension). Both are thus allied in effect if unwittingly with the average layman's common sense against the proponent-or-practitioner of the variety of realism identified with power politics as creatively even if forcibly transforming. Conversely, the romantic strain latent in philosophical realism allows for the perception of any, including the Soviet Russian–American contention, in the perspective of a relativized inequality of officially proclaimed ideology of one and glorified civic myth of the other party at one and an acute stage, and of the commonality of spatio-temporally conditioned cultural-political derivation of both parties and their vital interests at another and later stage. Propitious to appeasement, such a view associates strategic rationality with historical intelligence as a pathway to, and precondition of, infusing physics with poetics so as to allow an authentically tragic sense of politics to attenuate the compulsions flowing from its operational necessities while taking them seriously.[6]

At odds with moralism and legalism, the ethical view leaning toward the tragic is fully consistent with estheticism. The esthetics and ethics of statecraft are atemporally united within the tragic mode through a special form of detachment that reconciles esthetic stylization with ethical relativization of climactic real political events, affirming politics in general as a form of art open as such to appreciation at least as much as to adjudication. As a branch of art, politics invites understanding it sympathetically from within at least as much as analyzing it skeptically from without with a scientific rather than esthetic detachment. Being, like art, concerned with the creation of actualities that reveal a reality latent in the corresponding essence, politics is no less legitimately the subject of a form of cognition inaccessible to intellectual processes devoid of intuition.

Never is this truer than when politics migrates from transparent balancing among qualitatively identical states toward rumors of confrontation between cultures and civilizations. Such circumstances highlight the uncertain ability of traditional statecraft to grapple with the problem of developmental discontinuities embedded in state-centered historicist idealism. Is, with its apparent passing, classic statecraft to be bidden farewell for good or only taken leave of conditionally for the time being and in certain places? Perceiving such classic statecraft as a realm of the esthetic covers a wide range—from the virtuosity of routine diplomacy to the tragic dramatics of politics that surround hegemony and make the art of realizing the barely possible one with the science of identifying the necessary. Ethics and esthetics merge not only but not least in statecraft when both justice and beauty can be perceived as equally matters of balance and proportion. A "just equilibrium" connotes an equalization of capabilities and entitlements warranted at least as much by the claim of all to a temporary appeasement as by the gratification of all individual pretensions. A peace proclaimed in the name of equipoise conveys thus, however fleetingly, not only the formal but also the normative creativity of contentions that ostensibly destroy all values, moral and material. Ethics and esthetics seem to differ when esthetic distance, assumed in the interest of stylizing the amorphously actual, rules out descent into either militant or only compassionate speculation about guilt and innocence at the normative core of real politics. However, both perspectives will reaffirm their essential oneness when the detachment of esthetics meets and overlaps with the distaste of politically relevant ethics for facile moralizing. Such an ethics is much too aware of the special poignancy of human striving at the summits of power to share the vain endeavor of a more naive morality to either exculpate or condemn with equal finality. Thus, the ethical and the esthetic dimensions of enacting and understanding "high" politics overlap sufficiently to be ultimately complementary in importing meaning into both statecraft and history from outside the narrowly factual core of either. The poetics of tragedy does better through intuition of the problematically heroic strain in the very excesses of the will to power. An estheticizing vision of the dynamics of contrary forces that constitutes political physics does the same through the imagery that transmutes the raw materials of politics into the patterns of schematic reconstruction.

Were the esthetic and ethical dimensions of classic statecraft as a form of action entitled to corresponding modes of appreciation and evaluation to definitely desert world politics, would this also mark the end of history as a process capable of meaningfully purposive evolution? It would certainly devalue the history of the modern state system and its antecedents as useful for comprehending the present more than superficially, by severing it from that part of the past that occupies the plane of spirit. And it would limit history's meaning to returns and recurrences that bridge continuities in alternately modified structures and variously institutionalized functions. A thus reduced meaning is readily inferrable from the lawlike tendencies and dynamics of power politics, manifest in the rebirth of the process's products. It can be abstracted, although with greater difficulty and a less persuasive result, from the multifarious complexes of historical phenomena or processes in their comprehensive entirety. But the easier inferences and the more difficult reductions are both but a poor social-scientific thing, which can only grossly outline the end of things in terms of actual or imputed purposes and their uncertain fulfillments. They do not disclose the essential drama and the existence-uplifting sense of destiny that interlock in the concerns of statecraft. Yet only when the drama is properly recorded and the idea of destiny made real by philosophically inclined history do the attendant quests and quarrels become fit subjects for the more often and more genuinely tragic than epic poetry, enacted by consummate statesmanship and truthfully represented by more-than-scientific scholarship.[7]

In a complete understanding capable of inspiring esthetically as well as operationally and normatively satisfying statecraft, political physics contributes the sole element of valid science to a real politics capable of constraining while comprising the inter-determinative complexities of political economy by virtue of strategic rationality. Art is by the same token cognitively and operatively associated with intuition contingent on historical intelligence and the sense of the tragic as the necessary supplements to strategic rationality. Consequent understanding and related undertakings will meet the intellectual criteria implicit in the chess metaphor for statecraft and will implement the precepts of underlying geohistoricism through a likewise spatio-temporal perspective, when, considering the implications of any two-power relations for a third party spatially, they will anticipate the ulterior consequences of the immediate consequence of a "present" response temporally. Both three-faceted improvements on ad hoc reflexes encourage and facilitate genuinely systemic thinking—one that assesses any one response or initiative in light of the altered state of the wider arena either will have produced. A rare intellectual feat, systemic thinking is apt to be defeated by the scientific-technological marvels of instant communications and other contributions to functional inflation and organizational hypertrophy. Such are the most striking if essentially sterile and operationally servile improvements on tradition consequent on advances in regions of science and technology more propitious to increases in information than intuition and communication than comprehension of either past or present and, through them, the future.

Integrating the past into the future

Any prognosis of future world politics falls into either projection from actual past or prophecy reaching beyond it. When it postulates progress from world politics toward world community as a process manifestly under way, projective prognosis becomes utopian. The utopia is realistic when it takes into account such a course's and community's operational preconditions. A major one is a completed migration of power among its actual-potential centers of gravity—actors, regions, or civilizations— which has transferred prime concern universally from military-political might to economic matter at a psychologically and ethically sustainable cost to spirit. Moreover, neither the migration of the power center nor the progression along the functional spectrum must have provoked the earlier-matured polities (or regions or civilizations) into self-protective recidivist reactions to the later-entering corporate entities' actually or supposedly prejudicial prominence. This precondition is in turn contingent on strategies of major actors that reconcile the disparate-asynchronic evolutionary stages of successively matured or reborn polities, channeling them toward a generally beneficial and, therefore, universally acceptable terminal state. Achieving such an unconventional outcome by traditional means requires, finally, the strategies being updated to match next to an amply conceived structure also the object of its integral transformation into, say, evenly institutionalized worldwide pluralism. The pessimistic obverse of utopia is prophetically anticipated doom for mankind, ensuing from persistence in the drives and associated strategies that perpetuate the core dilemma of world politics in general and the fatal curse of the state system in particular. A so-primitively constituted and comprehended structure is apt to encourage the pursuit of self-preservation by acts others will plausibly construe as intolerable provocation. The preordained doom will consequently result in a technologically or otherwise increasingly problematic setting from the continuing failure to amend future strategies so as to avoid the worst consequences of conventional responses to historically anterior but recurring structures.

Reflective of the different (intra- and inter-actor and inter-systemic) kinds of manifestations of evolution emphasizing structure, prognoses focused on world community or global catastrophe have symmetrically optimistic-positive and pessimistic-negative or at least problematic-operational counterparts. On the positive side, the progression would not only pass through the evolutionary midpoint and ephemeral climax represented by a concert of powers. It would be indefinitely stabilized there in a configuration combining flexibility of peacefully conflicts-resolving diplomatic constellations and coalitions cemented by their cultural-civilizational neutrality as well as economic utility. War-prone balance of power would yield to an inter-civilizational dialectic reconciling ethno-cultural as much as material and other differences in a cumulatively deepening consensus. To this dialectic open to a spontaneously progressive rather than ideologically forced premature synthesis, the comparatively pessimistic prognosis opposes a statist-societal dichotomy. In this dichotomy, moderated statism open to a wide range of kinds and degrees of association as a way out of the self-preservation-equals-provocation dilemma is superseded by an increasingly materialist society that forces premature aggregations of escalating functions and depreciated values.

Continuing if not also escalating real-political conflict is in the negative operational settings aggravated further in an indeterminate environment subject to the dual—temporal and spatial—passing of a state system. In a situation presently undefined by inter-great power polarity cum triangularity reflective of the statist land–sea power schism, the latter's capacity to fuse geostrategics with geoeconomics is replaced by diffuse cleavages between socioeconomic haves and have-nots. Prosperity incorporating materialism and poverty invoking (pseudo-)idealism means that the parties to this cleavage are less interactive and interpenetrating (as are parties to a schism) than mutually aggravating. Involved in this trend is the reversal of priorities between the East–West and the South–North cleavages and the former's regression to its originating value-institutional disparities conjointly with extension beyond Europe to include Asia. This event has yet to prove the capacity of real politically pragmatic entanglements to temper the implied cultural dissonance as the discords evolve out of what in the absence of traditional risk-embracing means and procedural recourses is only a nominal retrogression or reversion of world politics to traditional regional questions or (sub-)continental "great games." Lastingly more critical than distempers pointing to either siege-like investment of "civilized" West by southern have-not "barbarians" or the replacement of substantive statecraft with theatrical stagecraft in addressing conventional crises is the evolutionary disjunction between a West subject to the temporal passing of the state system back to pluralism and an East exhibiting its passing across space.

Taking off from events of this kind, projection seeks to extrapolate the momentum of future evolution from the presumption of a constant sum

of motion—or of energy related differently to violence-breeding crises—
over finite periods of time, externalized in previous manifestations. Projection ranks consequently below prophecy that seeks to extract the
ultimate purpose or meaning from a profounder understanding of the
interplay between the dynamics of interaction and evolution. Accordingly, prophecy is to projection what meaning is to the motor, mechanism, manifestations, and matrix of evolution—and, specifically, what
schisms are to particular conflicts and foreign policy postures to particular foreign policies: in short, what their transcension is to transactions
that the transcendent levels of action and analysis subsume without suppressing or replacing. Whereas the lower-level transactions integrate
world politics operationally and their analysis empirically into world history and vice versa, the higher-level transempirical postulate of meaning,
toward which all processes and propositions tend and in which they converge, implies an integral fusion of politics with history. Each is mediated
through the other while epistemology (the apprehension of phenomena
through processes) yields pride of place to eschatology (the intuition of
the end, or purpose, of processes and their progression).

   The ascent to prophecy begins from projections originating in two interdependent existential-operational planes. One of them involves past
and prospective inter-great power dynamics. It extrapolates spatial passing of the state system toward the Asian/Pacific area from a developmentally significant mid-sixteenth century configuration attending the
transfer of the center of gravity from the Italy-centered Mediterranean to
Eurocentric Atlantic. At the structural-strategic core of this epochal event
was a combination of stalemate and conflict resolution in favor of one of
the major contestants, favoring Spain over France in Italy and to a lesser
extent over the Ottoman Empire in the Mediterranean. A provisional result of the strategic impasse was a temporary détente (peace of Cateau–
Cambrésis and the post-Lepanto lull, respectively) accompanied by
coordinately homeward- and divergently westward- and eastward-ori-
ented redirection of major actor priorities, conducing to the expansion of
the arena in the West in particular. By contrast, the U.S.–Soviet conflict,
while waged in ways broadly reminiscent of the vaster of the earlier contentions' diverse continental and maritime and northern and southern
theaters, lacked the strategically relaxing and ultimately appeasing two-
directional diversions. In their place was the unbalancing contrast between
the spatial contraction of Europe at the hands of an oriental-despotic (Soviet after Ottoman) invader-expansionist and a repeat of sheltered Western Europe's profitable economic extension farther west. The ensuing
combination of different kinds of expansion and contraction with respect
to space and the density of transactions and mandatory reaction time
along the worldwide West-to-East axis is not unusual. Its presently culmi-

nating in the prospective structural-strategic Asianization-cum-globaliza-tion of world politics is a logical consequence of the preliminary globalization (through extension into the Third World periphery) and Asianization (by the inclusion of first Japan and subsequently China) oc-casioned by a stalemate (in the center of Europe as before in the center of the Mediterranean) and consummated by the Asian great powers' emer-gence as the co-winners of the Cold War.

America's success (just as before the prevalence of Spain) raises the question of whether and when a bipolar conflict can or will, after a period of détente, be succeeded on a statist basis by a multipolar configuration capable of sustaining a progression from a balance toward a concert of powers, henceforth around a Eurasian core of continental powers (pro-spectively German, Russian, and Chinese) flanked by equally insular and unequally Pacific wing powers (the United States and Japan)—and be thus succeeded with more positive result for global stability than was the case for Europe's in the Spain-dominated era. Addressing such queries in depth requires extending the projection from the structural-strategic core, partaking of real politics and its inner economy to the other components of political economy. Substantive transformations in all of them com-bined previously the inflationary expansion of the European into an At-lantic economy with religio-ideological perturbation in ways that established a new range of precedents when they destabilized the domes-tic politics of the major and, especially, the real politically bested powers headed initially by late-Valois and early-Bourbon France. The consequent demonstration of the autonomously cyclical alternation of war with peace and domestic with external conflicts and priorities produced a type of turbulence that substituted lower for higher, less for more state-directed, forms of warfare cresting only in the Thirty Years' War.

Thus diversely revolutionized components of the political economy suspended for a time—subverted before restimulating—the incrementally proceeding aggregation of the key military and economic functions coor-dinated by the administrative and integrated by the creedal ones that had provisionally consolidated the despotic states by the fifteenth century in the wake of the ninth and fourteenth century upheavals. Viewed concep-tually, the actor-formative circuit of functions was thereafter convulsed into an incoherent if not also contentious coexistence of the correspond-ing factors of internally disaggregated "national" power. Unable to recon-verge into compact statist poles of power before the eighteenth century, the prior factoral disaggregation was to be followed by another spell of revolutionary political economy in the late nineteenth century and its in-termittent extension into the late twentieth century under the impetus of a succession of industrial and ideational revolutions. Whereas the former produced an increasingly dominant global economy, most recently under the impulse from resurgent Asian economies and innovative telecommunications technologies (as functional substitutes for American silver and new navigational techniques), the latter spawned post-religious sociopolitical ideologies supplanted eventually by partially pseudo-religiously fundamentalist ethno-cultural and civilizational values disparities. Caused materially or immaterially, the resulting domestic-political upheavals were compounded within the real political segment of political economy by once more radically changing forms of violence. Its lower forms had, after the Napoleonic and a string of limited including national unification wars, been diverted to the non-European world in the colonial conflicts of the nineteenth century before the prolonged suspension of the higher form at the system's core contributed to a conflagration that was to be resumed, following an inconclusive conflict resolution, in the second global conflict, pending reversion to ever lower forms of violence in response to the nuclear stalemate during and pacificatory trends after the Cold War.

Violence-bred and -breeding disaggregation of power and, consequently, polities into agents of individually inflamed and reciprocally subversive economic, military, administrative, and creedal factors—which as functions collaborate in forming the states they subsequently disrupt in a revolutionary setting—does not return the polities either inevitably or uniformly to the chaotic pluralism that preceded their formation. The critical difference is between cumulative coalescence and catastrophic unraveling and entails one between evolution and revolution. In these terms, inter- and intra-factoral disaggregation leading to inter-(micro)regional and intra-(macro)regional disaggregation is, by analogy with earlier Europe, much more a threat to the half-formed great states of Asia, such as China and India, and of great and smaller ones in Eastern Europe, than to, say, Africa with its opposite kind of vulnerability, to structure-less chaos. To the extent that the revolutionary potential is enhanced by precipitate functional and institutional centralization into a unitary state in the East, its counterpart is premature functional aggregation and value-institutional integration in the communitarian-pluralist parts of the West, which undermines a normatively already weakened state before the spatially enlarged regional polity has fully replaced the national framework as a functional and administrative machinery for reasons that are both organizational and organic. The ostensibly diverse dangers have a common root in the difficulty of any political organization to master, as evidence of its efficacy, the implications of the revolutionary economic transformation it has instigated as the societally only remaining valid grounds for its legitimacy. Which format—prospective Eastern statism or Western communitarianism—proves better able to contain the disruptions will determine the global distribution of power, unless both can in developmentally and situationally contrasting settings do their share in projecting world politics beyond the balance of power to diversely amplified equilibrium.

Such a prospect is anything but certain, judging by the reconstitution of the state system in Europe by the third decade of the eighteenth century under the impetus of an ideology-free Reason of State-centered foreign policy, a homogenized (enlightened despotic cum bureaucratic) domestic order and administration, a correspondingly formalized and stylized military deployment and strategy, and, after the seventeenth century correction, a restabilized economy fostered by expanding commerce and subject to improved techniques of management. The attributes of this reconstitution set the pattern for all of the fully unconsummated subsequent moves in the same direction, to be possibly repeated in the Eurasian-Pacific mode in a future not necessarily as removed from the present as the mid-sixteenth was from the mid-eighteenth century.

Such a reconsolidation around a new center of gravity would take off from the fact that the strategic imbrication of (Western) Europe with North America, fully operationalized in the eighteenth-century Anglo–French contentions, had reached a self-sufficient conclusion in the reversal of passive and active, dominant and subordinate, roles of the two branches of the Euro–Atlantic complex. By contrast, the course of the reconsolidation's Eurasian–Pacific extension will be deeply affected by the progression of Russia's geostrategic involvement with Western Europe, likewise effected by the mid-eighteenth century. The eastern power's integral diplomatic-strategic and related cultural-political Europeanization, related to but not identical with its technological-organizational Westernization, is at variance with its more or less complete re-orientalization. This alternative is once again liable to affect among other things the possible redirection of the triangular land–sea power schism from its West-to-East to an East-to-West direction. Centered on China (or a Sino–Russian complex) as the would-be amphibious challenger to a U.S.-Japanese insular would-be oceanic politico-economic hegemon, the orientalized triangle would involve a Europe comprising Russia as the strategically ultimately regulatory rear-continental power factor or Europe minus Russia as the geopolitically irrelevant mercantile-maritime backwater. China itself will have had to escape by then the pitfalls of inter-factoral disaggregation producing micro-regional deconcentration of its territorial integrity while the maritime-mercantile variety of its renascent statism, lodged in the coastal fringe and hospitable to pluralism, prevailed over the centralization-prone continental variety backed by the peasant-agricultural weight of the inland mass—a tacit contest over succession to the political culture and institutions of the Middle Kingdom. Similarly, succession to medieval kingship had in the seventeenth century divided the most China-like European country, France, between Paris-

centered hinterland and the Atlantic coast region with significant implications for interstate relations via the land–sea power schism and negative
ones for France's position and chances in the interstate successorial
sweepstakes.[8]

When the various mixes of conventionally real political and revolutionized sociopolitical and functional components of political economy surface as prime manifestations of evolution, they simultaneously make up
the energizing motor-constituting crises and mechanism-implementing
conflicts that either conduce or are contrary to the reconstitution of a
conventional state system within the matrix of continuing evolution. On
this essentially political and substantive as opposed to technological and
instrumental plane of long-term development, the crucial transitions are
from micro- to macrosystems on the statist level and from the meta- to
the next-following proto-systems as differently and unevenly pluralist sequelae or antecedents respectively to the statist norm and evolutionary
midpoint.

Upon closer inspection, the supersession of the Italian micro- by the
European macro-system and the latter's consequent crystallization required two phases of the larger northern monarchies' involvement, the
initial French invasion and the sustained Franco–Spanish conflict, before
the Italian city-state system definitively lost its autonomy. This fact suggests that in the absence of an enlarged Europe's re-empowerment by a
fully integrated East, (Western) Europe's likewise insufficient reconstitution after the first American intervention will continue being irremediable
after the second, when the superseding global proto-system has begun to
take shape during the U.S.–Soviet conflict over Europe. Only a Europe
strengthened in the East might recover autonomy with effects superior to
those achieved by the Venetian pro-independence "young" party's exem-
plar of lopsided neutralism between the earlier (including Spanish and
Ottoman) and possible future "two hegemonies" of Gaullist memory.
Just as important is the entanglement of transitions between micro- and
macro- systems (including divergently operational and value-institutional
immanence of the former in the latter) with cyclical alternations between
statism and either primitive or institutionalized pluralism (as part of the
likewise lopsided latency of one in the other). Relevant in this connection
is that the Italian city-states had at the critical juncture retained many of
the features of late feudal pluralism and achieved (within their relatively
foreshortened span of development) correspondingly less of the early-
statist attributes than were to go on crystallizing in the larger arena of
longer-lived European polities. A consequently qualified analogy suggests
a continuing difficulty to integrate in a continuously cumulative fashion
developmentally overlapping statist and pluralist features in a regional
community capable of standing on its own feet independently of the

shape of its environment. Thus also, if inversely, the Western European meta-systemically post-statist communitarian and Eastern European more primitive proto-statist and states re-formative pluralisms relate with questionable future effects to one another and, even more important, to the resurgence of classic statism in the Asian/Pacific area. Central to the future in these terms is the relationship between two qualitatively different but equally potent trends: the long-term cycles of pluralism's alternation with statism, exhibiting a historically demonstrated evolutionary logic, and the relatively shorter and only intermittent disruptions of statism through revolutionary inter-factoral disaggregation injected into it from analytically extraneous, prominently including technological and ideological sources and stimuli.

The revolutionary potential if not also propensity of statism matching the two main evolutionary forms of pluralism in decomposing compact power aggregates is a similarity offset by significantly different initial and subsequent thrusts. The disruptive aggravation and dispersal-prone segregation of the several power factors toward conflictual destabilization of interstate relations is typical prior to their reconstitution. By contrast, compressing functions held separate in pluralism's primitive form or phase into factors of national power will precede such factors' transmutation into generic strands in the fabric of interchangeably competitive and cooperative policies in second-stage institutionalized pluralism's transition from linear-statist to integrative-circular political geometry. Outweighing the formal similarity by the material difference actually projects a difference internal to actors, between process and product: between the functional circuit responsible for initial formation and continuing restabilization and structured poles of consolidated power factors, into external relations among actors. Given this outward projection of the combination of similarity and difference, the future of world politics depends in principle on the way the only proto- or meta-statist pluralist and the wholly conventional or revolutionary statist features interrelate on the two conceptually and developmentally equivalent planes. Which one prevails when their operationally divergent thrusts inevitably intersect at some point in time in compliance with pluralism's cyclical alternation with statism and vice versa? Will it be the communitarian facet of the evolutionary potential implicit in modified rebirths of pluralism such as contemporary neo-medievalism lodged in and ramifying out of the West? Or will the East replicate the revolutionary antecedents to a materially and normatively invigorated neo-statism, prospectively impacting a normatively no longer statist European and historically anti- and operationally at best quasi-statist American West?

Two other distinct but operationally similar intermittently linked planes potentially converging over time are the essentially political and the instrumentally technological ones, interchangeably responsible for the multifactoral convulsions of statism and its alternation with pluralisms. One plane involves the means of production or destruction in economically or militarily crucial technologies; the other converts functional into sociopolitical revolutions. The two planes combine in mediating the course of the diverse successions that dramatize the ultimate unity of politics. Should the two planes' gradual convergence eventuate in an intersection favoring the technological plane in areas such as telecommunications and automated data processing with an effect on agendas ranging from rationally managed production and distribution to battlefield operations, world politics would witness a more fundamental succession to the primacy of politics and the revolutionary or evolutionary processes that implement this primacy. A truly new situation would point to a world community and its equally unprecedented predicaments, without the transformation having to pass through the intermediate stages of either interregional and -civilizational communitarian pluralism or reconsolidated postrevolutionary statism clustering regional subsystems around a new center.[9]

Discounting the imminence of a technologically engineered leap from imagination into radically discontinuous interactions highlights a less radical secular alternation between huge and small- or medium-sized, and internally unitary and pluralist, actors as optimally efficient or fatally unsustainable. It is within this range bordered by successively crisis-prone empires and city-states that polities of medium size, as momentarily defined, are intermittently placed in the favorable because technologically and organizationally favored middle. Critical for such alternation's prospectively imminent actual manifestation is the net real change emerging out of two contrary trends: toward predominance of the organic over the operational and the domestic over the external functions of government in the statist setting and this trend's partial reversal in the pluralist setting's favor for outward directed functional connections, a confusing aspect of the latest radical transformation within the long pluralist-statist-pluralist evolutionary cycle. This cycle points currently more or less consistently and compellingly toward a species of meta-systemization: i.e., transition from interstate balance of power (cum potential concert of powers) system toward equilibrium among institutionalized-pluralist regions or regionally circumscribed civilizations. The latter are middle-sized relative to the extremes of nation-states and a global community and as such of optimum size also relative to the requisites of self-dependence at the intersection of the political (or sociopolitically revolutionary) with the technological (or functionally revolutionary) plane.

Ascending from either of the operational levels usable for projections to prophecy, one that assimilates all that enters into projection into implicit or explicit prescription, requires exchanging the existential for a normative plane and the depictions of the motor-mechanism-manifestations aspects of projectable trends for the search of a larger meaning. Such meaning is to be found, if anywhere, in the transactions-transcending constituents of the total structure and, beyond them, in the transcension of their own internal disparities and contradictions. This means the transcension of the land–sea power schism in amphibiously continental-military and maritime-mercantile attributes of regional conglomerates; of the East–West schism and attendant cultural heterogeneity in the inter-civilizational *homonoia* of Alexandrine legacy; and of the sacral–secular or existential–normative schism in both the relocation of the spirit lost to the (national) states to correspondingly larger and more inclusive communities and its concurrent repoliticization and demilitarization. Conjointly with such a process getting under way, disruptions associated with the individual members' or the regional ensembles' divergently expansive and consolidative foreign policy postures would either depart or be significantly muted. As the main reason for this change, the steep rise/decline fluctuations that are the organic basis of these postures would have been flattened in their implications for individual survival, confirming the effect of the two-pronged parting of the ways from the recent classic-statist past. Therein, the shift in emphasis from (national) security to (regional or global) stability in consequence of military-technological revolutions, among others, accords with that from zero-sum mercantilistic concern with economic resources regarding warfare to positive sum-implementing preoccupation with individual and collective prosperity as part of welfare, as a result of improved understanding and practice of the economic factor.

If combined with psychological and ethical correctives to the costs of a mere substitution of materialism for militarism and hedonism for hegemonism, this shift would tend to subsume the distinctive attributes and liabilities of the two successive generations of leading types of powers in a synthesizing third-generation type. Avoiding the excesses of the left- and right-totalitarian would-be syntheses, this alternative would consummate the search for a kind of polity favorably different from both the mytho-normatively authoritarian species, exemplified in medieval continental-military monarchy, and the pragmatically utilitarian kind, reactively inspired by early modern insular-mercantile oligarchy. A search for such a third kind is as unlikely to end as is the quest for a third—neither integrally individualist nor collectivist—way of organizing and managing political economy. Both aspirations are predicated on the possibility of reconciling the ideal attributes of the state and the material achievements and ambitions of society at a next and higher stage of evolution.

A synthesis of ostensibly antithetical entities and phenomena would amount to one more reconciliation of successive pasts with equally con-

secutive reactions to them in a new departure embodying that which has
proven worthy of surviving the confrontations. A metahistoricist perspective of this kind surmounts and, when connected to it by strategically
aware analysis, usefully complements the more narrowly historicist exploration and systematization of linkages between successive micro- and
macro- and proto- and meta-systems. Were the search for meaning to
plumb ever deeper beneath the existential level of projection from structures and operations, it would automatically ascend from the normative
plane of metahistorical intuition to eschatologically inspired analogy with
either cosmologically or theologically oriented interpretation. To the extent that the cosmological interpretation comprises the physical and the
moral-ethical world, an optimistic-positive prophecy depends on the
force of a cumulatively moderating effect of a deepening tragic insight
into the implications of pure political physics. It moves the latter's center
of gravity away from Newtonian mechanics toward a combination of Einsteinian space-time relativity and Aristotelian organismic-purposive finality as the constituents of motion equalling evolution. A like course
toward a pacific but not stagnant, culturally vibrant but not violent, inter-
regional world community can be inferred from a historicist theology or
theodicy predicated on the progression from tribal gods or demons to
monotheistic world religions. In an analogy equating ineffable with mundane progression, both universes partake of a similar process of uniformization and sublimation in the advance from the many and sundry
actualities to one all-encompassing reality.

Notes

1. WP 309–319, 296–302 (see ch. 4, n. 220).
2. IE 1–9 (end of 2.par.); and see Introduction (WP 429–431) for kinds of realism.
3. The preceding five paragraphs are with minor adjustments excerpted from
RWO 145 (2.par)–153 (end 1.par.).
4. WP 182 (2.par.)–189 (end 1.par.).
5. WP 189 (2.par.)–199.
6. RUSR 152–159 (end 2.par.).
7. The preceding three paragraphs are adapted from RR 137 (2.par.)–141.
8. RP 13 (2.par.)–15 (end 3.par.).
9. RP 47–52, 101–102 (end 2.par.).

6

Fractured Actuality and Synthesizing Strategy: Whither Ideal Polity?

Thinking world politics through history and history through world politics is a testimony to their indivisibility in thought that is true to reality. By the same token, actuality is wrought by action which, in politics, is or ought to be shaped by thoughtful policy. To be both thoughtful and effective, a policy needs to be the work of a realism that is more than pragmatic and must be guided by a theory that is less than scientific. For it to be a grand strategy, and steer history within the bounds set by a meaning inferable from its progression, policy needs to marry facts with values and power with purpose, so as to advance the essential form of world politics toward a finality that also resolves its dualities in a meaningful end. And that end, rather than terminating the striving, should redeem the suffering that is the price of a history that, moving in cycles but in a discernible direction, is more than chronology of sterile repetitions disclosing a pathology that exceeds the ills of war and debases the goods of peace. Viewing progression in terms of less interstatist deadlock and more intercivilizational dialectic is to preserve the future of world politics against a form of progress that offers mankind the spiritual blight of a quietistic uniformity. Saving traditional realism also for this reason from amputations inflicted in the service of formal theorization preserves realism as philosophy and balance of power as the actually usable if untidy and expansion-needy theory of world politics for the ages. Finally, keeping open the pathway to integrating philosophy into policy entails a philosophy sufficiently rudimentary to be congruent with the reality it addresses, and a policy genuinely realistic because sophisticated enough to represent a statecraft that is satisfying operationally, ethically, and last but not least esthetically.

As the executive arm of a realistic philosophy of history, synthesizing strategy would ideally conduce to transcending all the tensions besetting world politics. This function of strategy is more than ever vital while the synthesis itself is provisionally hidden by the enigmatically pathological-to-paradoxical character of the actual manifestations of power-normative reality. A confusing compound of reality and actuality is only half-open to a realistic mode of cognition while the course of world politics goes on disclosing the real character of human nature as the ultimate indicator of practically attainable and thus realistically ideal polity—this elusive goal of genuinely realistic policy before it can be the policy's result and reveal the full meaning of world politics at the end of heroic world history.

The central pathology and paradox of statism as a challenge to meaningful history-steering strategy

At the close of the first major war within the West, Thucydides, the progenitor of realism, assumed the burden but also enjoyed the advantage of being the first to outline "for all time" the fundamental dynamics and dilemmas of real politics. It has been since, and is at the presumptive close of the last of modern intra-Western conflicts more than ever, left to his followers to expose—and where necessary and possible adjust—the ages-withstanding insight to intervening events and accumulated experiences. The prime challenge is to do this with the assistance of conceptual refinements that avoid as much as possible the technically (i.e., methodologically) proficient but substantively uncreative quasi-Hellenistic kind of amendments of the great Hellene's vision of the making and thinking of history through politics and politics through history.

The Thucydidian vision is simultaneously upheld and updated through the events contemporaneous with its formulation being confirmed by later ones into enduringly valid basic themes. A prime one suggests that the Greek city-state system was self-destroyed less by internal conflicts than by appeals to civilizationally alien outsiders: to Persia by Sparta against Athens toward the close of the Peloponnesian War and subsequently to Rome when the East Mediterranean Hellenistic survivors of and successors to classic Hellenism, combining loosely or also decadently communitarian and empire-type meta-systemic formations, appealed against one another across the central sea. The appeals were lastingly significant also as an aspect of a continuing Euro–Asian intercivilizational dialectic—one ascending from a fluctuating balance of power between Greece and Persia and among relatively more European and Asian Hellenistic realms, to be consummated after Rome's clashes with Syria and Parthia by an intercivilizational synthesis in the late Roman Empire. Thus also, subsequently in the early-modern Italian and eventually the European context, two successive appeals to and interventions by extra-Italian and -European outsiders were needed to degrade the respective state systems into lower—i.e., less autonomous—forms of ambiguously imperial-communitarian post-statist pluralism. In Italy, this happened once again in the context of a civilizationally shaped interplay updating the Crusades and counter-Crusades involving the West with Islam in the form of a Euro–Asian, Hispano–Ottoman balance of power—the original Crusades to be reenacted by colonialism and post-colonial reaction in a developmentally comparable, globally proto-systemic, setting and the balance of power to be potentially replicated in the U.S.- or Western–Chinese one. The tendency toward stalemate had been, and may again be, attended by elements of convergence or at least parallel developments before the balance of power tilted in the earlier instance to the not necessarily irreversible real- and cultural-political advantage of the Western civilization, provisionally immune to extra-systemic and -civilizational appeals with minor exceptions such as France's or the German Protestants' appeals to the Ottomans.

Likewise prefigured in Thucydides and subsequently only corroborated is the root cause of the pathology affecting an interactional-and-evolutionary momentum when it is diverted from self-sustaining natural progression. This root is implicit in the Greek's simple-to-simplistic indictment of Athenian expansionism as the ultimate cause rather than only proximate precipitant of the war. Attributable to a partisan-personal bias of a kind destined to be perpetuated over time, this failure to examine more objectively the wider grounds and multiple qualifiers of the indicted hubris weakened also the tragic character of the war, and its proffered interpretation, in that it assigned guilt to only one party while by implication exonerating the other party's subsequent willingness to be indebted to Persia for the material means of victory. Consequently misconstrued, not for the last time, was the potential of strategy to mediate dilemmas and relieve paradoxes. Again unqualifiedly indicting the Sicilian expedition required ignoring the difference between strategic necessity (as the only available way out of a military impasse reflecting the underlying tragic knot responsible for the war) and its tactical/operational mismanagement, while widening rather than trying to narrow the chasm between low-grade (domestic-political) pragmatism if not opportunism and potentially elevating inescapable predicament.

Such and similar fact-value paradoxes have ever since jointly added up to the central pathology of world politics, revealed in the terminal crisis of successive state systems. They are equally implicit in facts alone, engaging the relationship between the balance of power and the state system, and in the facts' relation to values. When the state system causes expansion by raising draw above drive, pull above push, and structural over operational determinants, it self-destructively engineers its supersession

by defending itself against forcible unification through the agency of a
balance of power conceived primitively, applied reflexively, or directed
self-interestedly by a presumptively disinterested balancer. It only adds
to the paradox that this self-destructive act will coincide with the extraneously assisted defeat of the supposedly or actually would-be hegemon
who has rebelled, in principle even when not in practice, on behalf of all
against the system's operational contradictions. Implicit in the conflict
between the requirement of self-help and the limitations placed on its
extreme expression, the contradiction is the consequence of the impossibility to realize through spontaneously achieved unity a nominally ideal
and universally desired remedy. The pathos of the incidentally engendered war and the price paid by its material consequences are overshadowed when the operational immanence of the superseding macro-system
in the antecedent micro-system and the latter's shadowy survival in the
former through its formal-procedural/diplomatic values—both associated
with the intervening outsider or outsiders—entail the sacrifice of the latter's substantive-cultural/civilizational values and consequent depletion
of their sum overall.

As for the value component of the fact-value relationships, it emerges
fully and in part again paradoxically through the original fact of the initially emergent state as itself an ideal value, superordinating its corporate
autonomy to any other value, including individual freedoms, not only
explicitly in authoritarian but under stress both operationally and logically necessarily in all political systems. Only at a later stage of the state's
relative decline will the defense of its procedurally valuable independence
through the devices of a primitive balance of power, defined in terms of
interests alone, tend to entail the forfeiture of the autonomy of an entire
system of states and the associated civilization. The consequent destruction of a higher or at least more inclusive substantive value than vested in
the (dynastic or national) state itself as an original fact is in turn part of a
developmentally associated subsidiary fact: the translation of the state's
decline in power into the rise of society as the more natural site of the
primacy of the individual over the collective in terms of the former's freedom and the latter's autonomy and, implicitly, priority of material-economic over ideal-political values, reflecting the intricate relationship
between historicist idealism prioritizing the role-status of the territorial
state and historicist materialism that repeatedly reasserts material resource in an extra-territorially societal setting.

When the facts- and fact/value-related paradoxes converge in causing
the pathology of a state system revealed in the terminal loss of both corporate autonomy and collective power, this pathology surfaces yet another—and, in a way, central—paradox. The state is created by the
balancing of power dynamic as a fact prominently embodied in its ma-

chinery at the interstimulating beginnings of both. But it is eventually destroyed as a value, incarnate in mystique, at a later stage for both the (balancing) process and the (statist) product conjointly with the latter being superseded by its own creation: society. Stated in the generic terms of the actor-arena relationship, the creative impact of an elementary but earlier-crystallizing arena on state-like actors-to-be passes through the developmental climax of balance or equilibrium between them to post-mature actors' would-be reforming impact on the arena. It is at this point that the relationship translates operationally into the fatal recourse of the indigenous actor or actors to the presumptively normatively cognate but in fact culturally and civilizationally alien outsider.

Whereas the interpretive scope of theoretically more rigorous-parsimonious methodologies is too narrow to engender understanding of this dilemma, geohistoricism itself is not immune to misconceiving the drive-restraint dialectic in a way that perverts the power-normative essence of politics into a fact-value paradox: a declining particular power saving itself for a time at the cost of lasting destruction of a universal value that is anything but diminishing. So deep-reaching a paradox complicates immeasurably the ostensibly self-evident and -sufficient dynamics of normatively neutral or neutralized real politics and exceeds the dilemmas of political economy related to the dynamics' causation. Suspending in the face of such complexities the quest for the meaning of world politics past the discernible intermediate stages of evolution augments the risk of overlooking the ultimate paradox when focusing attention on the particular ones. Surfacing in the pathology of the state system, the latter are as much the objective facet of the subjectively experienced tragic predicament of world politics as the differently super-statist modes of overcoming the pathology in primarily pluralistic modes are the exact opposite of the tragic heroism of the aspirant to hegemony. The supreme paradox is correspondingly implicit in the fact that attenuating conflict within a pluralistic universe that inevitably expands the number of active participants has the effect of degrading the constant sum of energy to the detriment of the amount of useful energy. Were this to be happening within a conflict-free world community representing qualitative progress, the attendant expulsion of the ethics of (Aristotelian) tragic poetics from the political physics originally responsible for tragedy's emergence into (Thucydidian) consciousness would depress classic statecraft under pressure from physics' less classic (post-Newtonian thermodynamic) branch to the lower, pragmatically transactional side of the chasm that defines it on the operational plane. Such progress would, supremely paradoxically, signal an end of not only world politics but also world history as a sum of dialectically—that is, also conflictually—created and positively creative events, capable of harboring meaning. It would be conclusively shown

how comparatively unimportant it is whether such a meaning is retrospectively discernible, and as such psychologically reassuring in that it
shields against hysteria born of an ahistorical sense of unprecedented
uniqueness, or is postulated prospectively and as such invigorates morally
as a challenge to be faced and met with the combined resources of historically intelligent real politics and strategically rational philosophy of history.

Linking the two depends on reconciling power/interest-related fact
with realistically conceived value in a framework of action that perpetuates the productive flow of energies, while diminishing dependence on
channeling crises through violent conflict. The difficulty as well as longer-
term necessity of overcoming the otherwise inherent pathologies of the
state system is implicit in the contrary—but reciprocally potentially re-
demptive?—emphases and limitations?—of traditional realism's defining
exemplars. In respect of the fact-value dilemmas, Thucydides stands in
principle for the affirmation of value expressed through the tragic vision.
However, his inferable practical preference for prudence over defiance
(for Diodotus over Cleon or Alcibiades), implying one for conciliation
over collision, is as inconsistent with the core logic of pure tragic poetics
as it is with that of political physics. Machiavelli's correction downgrades
transcendent value in favor of fact absolutized in the self-sufficiency of
propellent energies and motivating effects as the constituents of pure political physics, only implying the tragic factor in the contrary inversion of
willed purposes, intentions, and consequences. Instead of the Athenian's
sympathy for prudence over defiance, the Florentine values *virtù* over any
other kind of politically expedient virtue and power driven by interest
over apolitically normative precept. His error is failure to plumb the contradiction between this kind of clinically pure physics and Italy's particular de facto tragedy, which his preferred politics is least likely to remedy
in the existing power configuration and diplomatic constellation.

Thucydides fails to resolve the fact-value paradox by depreciating the
capacity, and indicting the pretension, of Athens as alone able to marry
power and culture in ways capable of preserving or reenergizing Greek
civilization as one autonomous toward both Persia and Rome. In terms
of a postulable ultimate purpose if not otherwise, Machiavelli comes
closer to relating the realistic facts of political physics to the romantic
value of a unified Italy, correctly perceived as solely capable of affirming
the corporate autonomy of renascent neoclassic civilization at the point
of transition from a micro- to a macro-system and from residually feudal
pluralism to reascendant statism. The confrontation of unequally imperfect resolutions of the fact-value problematic, tending toward the status
of paradox fraught with pathology, suggests both negative and positive
conclusions. The dilemma will not be resolved by raising moralism as an

expression of apolitical values over realism as the exaltation of values-neutral pragmatism. Therefore, traditional realism has to be expanded beyond facts to values, but can be so expanded realistically only in ways valid historically as well as ethically and normatively as well as operationally. This means that the value or values have to be representative of a historical stage or context in one (the historical) respect and of the historical context-reflecting merger of political nature, standing for fact, with practically political culture, embodying value, in the other (normative) respect. This will, or plausibly can, mean the statist value enshrined in spirit or mystique, as supplement to material capability or machinery, in the evolutionary transition beyond primitive pluralism, and the value of regionally delimited corporate autonomy of a receding and implicitly endangered civilization in the progression from an actual or (relative to the emergent) virtual micro- to a macro-system. A compound of culture and power, this civilizational value, as a spatially expanded and developmentally advanced adaptation of the statist one, is both contrary and potentially a counter to equally unqualified pragmatism and moralism, radical individualism and repressive collectivism, in general and is applicable to the Euro–American regional relative to prospectively Asia-centric global arena in particular.

Questionably corrective flaws in societal economism and pluralism on the way out of statism

It trivializes but also concretizes enigmas more tempting to the historico-philosophically biased prophetic than to the would-be predictive theoretico-scientific mindset, that so much—perhaps everything—has come to depend on the staying power of a relatively prosperous and progressively expanding world economy promoted by the latest of the functional revolutions in the curiously misnamed "knowledge" area. Like any other such revolution, the informational one mainly reinforces the foreign policy effects of related sociopolitical revolutions, lately attendant on the variable combinations of and linkages between democratic populism and ethnic nationalism—both in turn intertwined in a cause-effect relationship with the fortunes of industrial-capitalist economism as the engine of social mobilization. As between the two, the transformative impact of the democratic (and, more inclusively liberal-democratic) tendencies on international politics, notably where typically coexistent with the decline of major continental powers from their evolutionary peak, may well exceed that of the more directly cultural trend. This is so because nationalism of any including the integral or messianic kind has historically imparted to offensive-defensive postures associated with some form or phase of territorial statism, including expansionist objectives and techniques, nothing more substantial than an extra psychological impetus in the form of an aggravating irrationality on the mass level or more frequently popularly plausible rationalizations on the official decision making level. This fact reduces the effect of both nationalism's eclipse and its more recent revival in the variously degenerative forms of an ideal counterpart to an either no longer sufficiently psychologically satisfying or not yet productively efficient materialism. Across a still wider range of polities, the conversely moderating apparent effect of democracy on assertive foreign policies is the more positively expressed creedal-institutional and broadly political manifestation of this same economic progression and is, as such, only more widely and potentially disruptively contingent on the economy's productive and distributive underpinnings.

As a result, the collapse of the global economy is the only predictable cause of a relapse of world politics into traditional power politics in two extreme formats. One is a systematic inter-regional balancing of power factors consolidated within and more or less coercively around regionally reassertive powers anxious and able to minimize the domestic consequences of the economic dislocations. Mainly the continental one or ones would consequently be open to charges of global hegemony-seeking expansionist ambition. Another is an intra-regionally chaotic interplay of contentiously disaggregated factors of national power, attendant on revolutions while subject to evolutionary processes of reaggregation in entities revealed experimentally as viable. Either format is the logical negative alternative to the positive multi- or inter-functional option of an interregional complex equilibrium cum inter-civilizational dialectic within an economically stable-to-prosperous environment.

Rooted in politico-economic givens and determinants, either the progressively (inter-)functional or regressively (inter- or multi-)factoral bias is at least as organic in its foundations as it is operationally subject to the effects of deliberate high policies responsive unequally to spatio-temporally conditioned geostrategic givens. Ideally determining the policies are fundamental assumptions about matters such as the forthcoming centrality of China and relatedly Sino-Russian relations in the Eurasian heartland, and Russia's significantly greater immediate and prospective accessibility to external influence and thus malleability by policies shaped—in compliance with the requisites of systemic thinking—by concern for or about third parties and for the ulterior consequences of the immediate or direct consequences of present-day policies by, say, the United States. Proceeding from this currently preeminent power on the West-to-East spatial axis, more or less constraining or permissive American policy toward Germany or Germany-centered European Union in the short run, governed by Atlanticist rather than Eurasian–Pacific priorities, will immediately either help integrate Russia fully into Europe or isolate it within and alienate from Europe in the midterm. The still longer-term consequences for Russia's posture toward and relations with China will in turn affect Japan's with both China and Russia in cooperation with or gradual separation from increasingly Pacific-oriented America in the longest run, but in a similar manner as applies to the Russo–Chinese relationship: to wit, in favor of a confident or compliant, cooperative or countervailing, pro-Western or Oriental-style, relationship with China or a diversely lopsided Russo–Chinese combine, with eventually westward-gravitating consequences for U.S.–Western European relations. As the policy-controlling focus shifts, together with the presumptive spatial passing of the state system or its center of gravity toward Asia, while the chain of unevenly antecedent and proximate consequences works itself out, sets of successively most critical two- and three-power plus relationships change accordingly, crystallizing into a multi-power configuration conducive to accommodation or antagonization among the core powers—and such powers' relationship with the lesser states adjoining or interposed between them and having progressively diminishing effect on the ultimate results.

Capturing temporally staggered and spatially interlocking activities in genuinely systemic thinking is still—if newly contingently—the operational core of a more inclusive system of thought. It is up to the latter to test expressions of the power-normative essence in the phenomena-decomposing processes for the newly critical ability to reconcile national power with more comprehensive values and individual interests with wider corporate autonomies. To this end, the apparently eastward-migrating interstatist geostrategic facet of world politics will have to be prudently coordinated with the inter-functionally integrative pluralist-societal (as opposed to revolutionary violence-breeding inter-factorally disintegrative power-political) facet in scenarios for a future capable of combining rebirth with reform.

Actual prospects are uncertain and the outcome does not hinge on deliberate choices by even the major participants while world politics seems to be receding from—or rises above?—prevention of forcible unification by a hegemon toward the associated negatives' transcendence in spontaneous unities sufficiently short of uniformity to avoid static immobility. Resolved conjointly with the interplay between disruptive drives and offsetting restraints in overt conflicts might and ideally would be the essential power-normative as well as the existentially operative dualisms. Illustrating the transcension of the former, the latter's resolution in amphibiously continental-maritime regional communities would rest on support from equally valued because valuable Eastern and Western, and Northern and Southern, cultural identities. An inter-regionally converging if residually competitive global community might then evolve beyond the balancing of articulated politico-military capabilities, focused on security, while pointing further on beyond the differently flawed present conditions of stability. In a stability that is nothing more than stalemate between inter-functionally integrative and multi-factorally disaggregative tendencies, an only locally and containably disturbed surface quietude has thus far reflected nothing so much as reluctance or impotence. Exhibiting both are formally directing but in terms of moral authority questionably or conditionally legitimate elites, unwilling or unable to incur, in the face of a conflict-weary Zeitgeist, the risks involved in defying the status quo on behalf of the less circumspect appetites of their fundamentally no more adventurous or audacious constituencies. Yet systemic inertia punctuated unproductively with sporadic localized turbulence can substitute only transiently for a more deeply lodged stability, one grounded next to geostrategically meaningful and materially solid also in normatively sustaining foundations. Only such stability can effectively replace socio- and quasi-religiopolitical utopias that are no longer widely believed or intrinsically believable.

Presently absent are both plausible statist or sub- or supra-statist ideals among the prosperous and a sufficient capacity of the destitute to propagate exacerbated substitutes more than locally. That which is thus being tested, but remains indeterminate at the psychological center of world politics, is more significantly than anything else the true nature of homo sapiens. At issue is humanity's capacity not so much to bring about and maintain but to be content with and endure vertically as well as horizontally expanding consumption of material goods and physical mobility of persons, of the well-to-dos for distraction and of the have-nots for satiation. The resulting experiment is historically novel, because the expansion is in principle possible and in practice potentially successful. Sociopolitically, the experiment's success hinges on the lasting sufficiency of substitutes for normatively stimulated and psychologically appeasing conflict in the form of a range of moral substitutes for war, not least but not only in a wide range of simulations of combat in the arena of routine politics no less than of more overtly gladiatorial antics. In terms of high policy, revitalized statecraft at the prosperous core will have to devise effective siegecraft relative to a periphery impelled after centuries once again into mass migration by the experiment failing or taking too long to succeed—a statecraft, incidentally, that does not at the core's quasi-imperial center have to depend for respite on ever more necessary but decreasingly credible stagecraft.

Cyclically unfolding progression verges on qualitative progress when deliberately purposive policies refine the outward expression of natural urges or instincts without being severed from this vital impulse. This being so, the future—because the quality—of real politics depends on its ability to functionally perpetuate but operationally humanize traditional practices in danger of eroding or being discarded as no longer sufficiently persuasive normatively or imperative materially. Identifying while updating the indispensable practices is the task looming at the very heart of a process that solicits inquiry into past-present-future temporal and local-regional-global spatial facets of geohistoricism in the area stretching between two extremes: superstructurally most transforming technologies and most revision-resistant mentalities. New technologies point at the outermost surroundings of the globe to ever-newer new frontiers inviting henceforth peaceful conquests. The "old Adam" is in his innermost recesses uncertainly willing to transcend violent conflict in equally fulfilling and creative competition, while the vicissitudes of world politics and world history continue to reveal his own defining character. Contrasting expressions of humans' perhaps only self-flatteringly postulated dual, physical-metaphysical or animal- and god-like, nature will meanwhile impede the definitive clarification of this most recondite schism that ultimately determines all of its manifestations.

Confronting enigmas with functional revolution and realistic cognition

Anticipating an ever-receding but eventually perhaps inescapable disclosure of who we are by means of evidence of what can make us truly peaceful as well as genuinely productive within individual selves and societies as well as externally between them is the wearisome, not to be shortened, prelude to a veritable end of history. Waiting for the revelation will meanwhile be attended—and extended—by evolutionary cycles and determinative circularities that reflect the enigma of continuity versus change as the temporal counterpart to one opposing power and norm or norms in spatially located configurations and contentions. Both enigmas objectify the central mystery of the nature of humans and meaning of history mediated through world politics. Critical in a futuristic perspective, the continuity-change enigma will be meanwhile exposed to presently multiplying descriptions of many-sided change while it remains open to analytical devices capable of distinguishing valid from false historical analogies—that is to say, devices capable of projecting and weighing functional revolutions against functional equivalents, organizational against strategic innovations, and seemingly incomparable against alternating capability structures.

Complementing the problem of human nature at the core of the power-normative essence, the issue of the nature of knowledge permeates the continuity-change dilemma and the associated enigmas. Alternative perceptions vary in this connection between one existentially significant, because bearing on operations directly, and one epistemologically more problematic that bears on operations only indirectly by way of preliminarily clarified mode of cognition. Directly concerning the more practical kind of knowledge, one favoring tradition-reflecting intuitions over an allegedly revolutionizing increase in informations, is the paradoxical relationship between functional revolutions and functional equivalence. The former obscure the latter on the surface, but sustain it as a precondition in elementary logic. When analysis projects equivalence against revolutions and the other way around, it treads a problematic but only passable two-way street to plausible projection. Likewise indispensably will historicist schematization, leaning on an equally appropriate mode of cognition, reduce the infinitely variable individualization of polities and processes by sociological and institutional peculiarities to manageable ranges, while abstracting from conventional narratives of facts and events.

In present fact, functional revolutions converge and climax in an equally problematic relation and balance of significance between essentially military and civilian, i.e., peaceably politico-economic, revolutions. Both kinds seem to underpin the triumphalist optimism of late-capitalist post-industrialism. But they do so unequally when the gravity center of the continuity-change dilemma is being displaced from the nuclear via a post-classic conventional military revolution to the economic one, attributed to the displacement of conventional knowledge through unprecedented volumes and techniques of information cum communications. As this happens, the strategic issue of defense versus deterrence in the domain of alternative forms of action for an immediate present moves on to that of information versus intuition in relation to different kinds and objects of knowledge used or usable less for linking the past to the present than de-linking both from the future.

Actually, revolutionizing the source and kind of knowledge risks defeating tradition with greater ease and worse effects than revolutionary military technology could do and has done. Arguing for intuition informed by strategic rationality and historical intelligence against speedily and widely distributed information is the source of only uncertain and provisional comfort when the quality of statecraft declines relative to its quality in conditions requiring weeks or months for the exchange of messages between a very small number of makers and executors of state policies. Thus also on the soft power issues that multiply and may predominate in the societally pluralistic environment, communicating stressful events pictorially en masse can still fail to either inspire statesmanlike remedies or inspirit public responses fraught with risks and costs on behalf of a normatively reshaped and elevated order. Over time and

space, military revolutions have alternated between, and their consequences proceeded through, quantitative changes in numbers of combatants susceptible of effective command and control and qualitative ones in
types of weaponry and associated strategies. The informational revolution
conspires with the latest of the qualitative military ones when they accentuate the debilitating effect of the diversely commerce-shaping, pre- and
post-industrial, economic revolutions on the territoriality of world politics in terms of both the short or long radius and overland or seaborne
medium of trade. Equally common to the converging functional revolutions have been their ultimately critical real- or sociopolitical implications
for the perennially many-sided issue of succession. Prominent in assort-
ing sheer migration of centers of power with the latter's transformation,
the military revolutions needed conjunction with the civilian ones to add
alternations in the tone-setting types of powers to the migration. Substantive consequences of this conjunction for the normative sacrality of polities and the territoriality of entailed politics have exceeded, and will
critically shape, the consequences of the wholly or largely but procedural
functional revolutions.

Near-invisibly hidden behind the operationally significant quality of
knowledge—intuition vs. information—but ultimately controlling for the
interpretation of essential reality and projection from present actuality
are epistemologcally accented or refined types of cognition. In regard to
projection, stressing continuities highlights the residual survival of antecedents into developmentally following—or also dialectically formed—
states or conditions that emerge subsequently and are provisionally
ulterior rather than in any sense ultimate. Contrary to this imbrication is
the separation of anterior from posterior states of being through either a
fixed date or a dramatically turbulent event, identified for the sake of
investigating all the more exhaustively a thus individuated and isolated
time span. The preference for continuities or changes has either a subjacent non-rational cause or is the methodologically imposed consequence
of the kind of contemplated inquiry affecting interpretation. One, prefer-
ring continuity, merely accepts or defiantly postulates the objective reality
of a substantively defined subject matter, its agents as well as agendas, and
related strategic or operational priorities and practices, as reported by
conventional historiography. Preference for change will distrust and deny
objective givens in favor of preconceptions engendered in less than consecutively ordered temporal and coherent ordering-capable spatial settings. The cognitively more daring or hazardous objectivism is or intends
to be realist. It relies more confidently than the comparatively nominalist
opposite on consensually evolved and conditionally accepted tradition as
to both facts and their causation. It does so in order to be able to build
upon a consequently construed essential reality a temporally conditioned

reconsideration of past and present with relevance for the future. Rejection of any such tradition in favor of contingent social construction, and of any essence for the denial of any foundational entity or concept, will inevitably elevate method and procedure over substance and shaping discourse over complexly shaped development.

Replacing speculatively construed with socially constructed reality has ideological implications when contemporaneously crypto-revolutionary or just radically reformist strain with class-based or comparable bias takes over from a conservative outlook, one that is no less sensitive to socio-revolutionary transformations but mainly in the historical perspective and for long-term futuristic projection. The difference is narrowed when a "presentist" historiography or historical intelligence interprets the past in light of contemporary problems and thus to a degree subjectively. But it reappears when the socially conditioned construction of the present as much as of the past and desired future takes precedence over the analytic decomposition of objectively given and recurrent phenomena into like processes as the prevailing epistemology. A conjunction of cognitive with operational realism is consequently in danger of degenerating into de facto pragmatism if not also strategic nihilism that avoids substantive issues in deference to radical skepticism. To the extent that this happens, an only nominally historicist perspective merely employs sophisticated philosophy to deepen the primacy of methodology in ahistorical social science, exemplified by behaviorism's revolt against the alleged and in part actual theoretical poverty of traditional realism.

The twin revaluation of knowledge combines one in favor of information against intuition incongruously with another in favor of creating over comprehending reality. An inorganic junction of the two perspectives threatens meanwhile to defeat a geostrategically self-conscious philosophy of history and exchange it for a study of world politics stretched between two kinds of proceduralism. One is in the form of operative institutionalism reminiscent of the interwar period, relegating analytically as well as actually fractured real politics to the domain of academic-type journalism. The other is in the guise of an open-ended formalistic preparation for a return to substance when it has been armed with methodologically superior investigative strategy. A nineteenth-century historicism, rediscovered for uses in interpreting the world politics of the twenty-first, remains meanwhile suspended between the ease of conceptually critiquing and the burden of substantively deepening the inadequate theorization of world politics by conventional realism.

Historicism's signposts to ideal polity via counter-utopian universalism

A productive historicism will resist limiting the effect of any kind of functional revolution—presently illustrated in the informational one—to essentially procedural or managerial aspects, sidetracking the revolutions' implications for the location of migratory power and identity of the dominant type of polity. Proceeding otherwise inhibits projection and discredits even less reliably founded optimistic predictions. However, also a comparatively more projection-capable, because integrally politicized, historicism is diminished in this potential when, highlighting individualities, it does not subject time-bound particulars contingent on momentary organization and technology to some kind of universals and the associated specifics to generic categories. Foremost among such universals and categories are the few truly basic functions actually performed and to be performed in society generally and in either a statist or a pluralist-societal setting of world politics in particular. Being few, the basic functions are hospitable to functional equivalence when they are superficially altered by functional revolutions while the revolutions are being assimilated into the limited range of persistently operative processes and available policy options. Such assimilation devalues the revolutions operationally relative to the consequences they ought to have in logic or common sense in view of their defining, revolutionary character.

Precisely reflecting the limited range of available-and-feasible basic functions is the narrow range of plausible strategies. Both narrow ranges comprise and may well center in the legitimation of domestic authority through external activities susceptible of enhancing this authority's efficacy in performing its core functions in matters of security and sustenance. The two specific functions are intertwined—and in a way further circumscribed—not least by equating acquisition or maintenance of material substance and security-promoting formal status in a way most likely to ensure an actor's irreducible measure of autonomy consistent with the era's conventions and expectations. Heading the many particular instances of functional equivalence while expressing the obvious one between differently rationalized-institutionalized kinds of balancing is that between forms of expansion: the territorial cum militarily conflictual (and typically continental-statist) kind and the trans-territorial and economically competitive (insular-societal) kind. Significantly connected with this equivalence is a key exception from its persistence, the absence of an efficient or even plausible functional substitute for war in comparably effective procedures of peaceful change. This deficiency points to the previously likewise identified real change within the structurally radical one between statism and societism: the shift of emphasis to internal over external functions of government, implementing that to organic over against operational form and effects of governmental activity among polities.

In an intricately continuous and changing environment, it has been one thing to diagnose the present by linking past-present-prospective conditions of stability and unity to humans' yet fully unrevealed identity as the

root determinant of politically significant corporate identities and essential reality. It is another approach to the same problem to shape the present into an analytically ordered geohistoricist perspective resting on
functional equivalence of functionally revolutionized structures and processes evolving cyclically. More questions are raised by either kind of diagnosis than can be confidently answered with help from either kind of
knowledge. But juxtaposing en route to coalescing both might eventually
supply clues to the principal queries: Does the present represent a radical
melioration expressing heightened economic productivity and embodied
in predominant sociopolitical stability warranting progressivist optimism? Or, alternatively, is the present but one more cyclical return to
or rebirth of comparable interludes between less attractive predominant
patterns? Such an alternation has most recently been evidenced in the
upswing from the upheavals of the sixteenth to the seventeenth centuries
into the relative orderliness of the subsequent, economically intensified
(mercantilist) and politico-militarily moderated (interstatist or state-systemic), order of the late seventeenth and most of the eighteenth centuries.
The latter could be and contemporaneously actually was vaunted as a
decisive break with not only religio-politically revolutionary but also territorially expansionist imperialistic politics and eras: the empires of antiquity such as the Roman and the imitative late-medieval aspiration to (or
exaggerated fear of?) universal monarchy such as the Habsburg.

Comparably optimistic assessments of the present state of things follow
upon a more sixteenth-to-seventeenth than eighteenth-century type of
situations and statecraft, culminating in the mid- and late-twenieth th century. Discounted in both the past and the present upbeat views is the
merely relative character of the highlighted innovation. The asserted radical difference between imperialism and balance of power was in the earlier
context actually but one between two kinds of expansionism: territorial
into contiguous areas and mercantile overseas. Expansion was less plausibly replaced qualitatively by rationalized balance-of-power statism within
the commercial facet of the new diplomacy and political order than displaced geographically outside Europe as an aspect of this same balancing.
Actually replaced with operationally less fundamental consequences was
something else: the subsistence requisite of relatively primitive urbanism
with the functionally equivalent requisite of primitive mercantilist capitalism. Whereas the former was dependent on extraneously located sustenance of city-bred social parasitism, the latter depended on exports as
the presumptively no less indispensable source of assets for the military-
political promotion of incipient industrialism.

Just as previously, so also the presently vaunted progress is being attributed to a broadly comparable movement from military-political to economic techniques of expansive self-assertion. Moreover, it has the same

particular cause or origin when pioneered by victors in either antecedent or concurrent military or quasi-military engagements. Somewhat less than auspicious for the future are, however, once again the neither unrelated nor reliably erased fault lines in the new economic order, the presumed stabilizer of a beneficial systemic change. It failed already once when, reverting to the antique cum pre-Enlightenment state of things, land-hungry empire-type actors discarded ancien regime strategic rationality in favor of old-style territorial rapacity by resuming the search for spatially contiguous protection against the vicissitudes of a discredited neo-mercantilist early capitalism.

The alternatives remain wide open—while a choice between them is apparently posed—in a setting that is functionally revolutionary in terms of new instruments and technologies as well as replete with functional equivalents. Both continue to implement their paradoxical relationship within the finite range of practical or practicable modes for meeting the political imperative of linking domestic politico-economic stability to an effective external outreach. The linkage can be overtly forcible or ostensibly pacific, and prone to generate competition if not also conflict of different kinds, depending on at least two factors. One is the identity of the most efficient mode of assuring a regimes-legitimizing minimum of material sufficiency as defined by a society's place in space and, consequently, evolutionary stage. Another is the precise quality and thus strategic implications and functional priorities of either an interstatist rational conflictual or confusedly multi-functional pluralist stalemate. Either type remains possible while the filling up of the capability gaps at the structural core of Europe, co-responsible for the earlier displacement of expansionist drives beyond and past it, spreads to one-time peripheries. Nothing is less certain in these conditions than the reversal of the earlier cycle or cycles into the radical alternative of open-ended linear progress. On the face of it, such progress implies the end of equally state-systemic and empire-type high politics, centered on the issue of hegemony, in favor of militarily-politically neutralized and developmentally matured economism, promising universal prosperity. In actuality, trans-territorial modes of expansionism have been separately and selectively relatively benign only in the short run, and will only ideally converge in ways productive for all in the longer run.

Viewed realistically, the quality and complementary of the variously mitigated or only relocated expansionisms will depend as ever and only more than ever on two substantive improvements. Intellectually, they will depend on an improved diagnosis of the expansionist phenomenon itself, its motivation and susceptibility to accommodation—a matter of cognitive realism, counterposing evolution to innovations. Equally significant practically is the ability to sustain the economic growth rate at the effi-

cient center and to localize disruptions at the fringes—a matter of operative realism combining an economically updated kind of statecraft with
the rediscovery of ancient siegecraft. Both will be necessary to shield the
core against either spontaneous diffusion of weakness from the most ret-
rograde parts of the periphery or reactivation of the will and capacity of
old or new major central players to exploit the local negatives for the
enhancement of their central-systemic assets or positives. A restored
great-power game will, in either case, testify to the imperviousness of
an immemorial predicament to passing whims behind routine politics,
transient contingencies of geoeconomics, and humankind's perennially
self-attributed but never seriously tested longing for peace over war
amidst uniformly shared stability and prosperity.

Against such an ambiguous and partially contradictory background, it
is only possible that geohistoricism will have correctly identified, or even
shown a way to, the ideal polity for the immediate future in the guise of
regional communities. Pitting the positive against the negative prophecy
of doom makes such communities appear to be the most promising agents
of a remedial transcendence of pathology-constitutive paradoxes of statism and the flaws, reflecting a developmental momentum, inherent in the
transitional forms of contemporary pluralism. A favorable developmental
momentum would affect all of the main parties to the implied dilemmas:
the state, expanded as to scope and partially preserved as to its spirit in
differently statist/pluralist post-imperial regional sphere-composing or
community-constituting actors capable of projecting power under stress,
not only representative of but typically coterminous with a civilization;
and the balance of power, differentiated functionally in ways integrating
culturally defined and determined affinities and antipathies with economic and real-political features in a complex equilibrium. This first-degree transcendence of the dilemmas to be consummated on the inter-
regional plane can presently only foreshadow their second-degree transcendence in the form of an inter-civilizational dialectic conducive to,
only to be contingent on, the substantive synthesis of the widest possible
range of factors and processes, facts and values. All can be intimated by
prior schematization and integrated by subsequent systematization, but
their synthesis can be achieved only in principle by a speculative approach
that is susceptible of summation as to its precepts and principles capable
of inspiring a synthesizing strategy.

A beneficial or any other future cannot be anticipated outside intimations from a composite past, one that can be interrogated speculatively
with the fairest degree of achievable cognitive realism and theoretical utility for synthesizing strategy. Drawing on projections tainted with prophecy allows appeals to history to mediate and, eventually, adjudicate the
problematic relationship between nature and culture: the power/interest-

driven core nature of politics and values-enshrining particular cultures within civilizations. Poised to replace discredited ideologies, the surviving major civilizations do not leap out of nowhere to unchallenged prominence amounting to terminal extinction of either statehood or statism. In whatever association with community-type societal pluralism, their new prominence betokens instead mere transformation in the balance between mystique and machinery within the territorial—more importantly than national—state as polity and statism as policy. Incorporating history, nature, and culture in ways yet to be disclosed, civilizations may, but need not, newly interrelate enduring facets of reality within a dialectic productive of a felicitous end of history and of world politics as known to history. Whether they do will depend on this dialectic engendering the subsequent mutation in keeping with the habitually less consonant than contrary rhythms of territorialization and deterritorialization of human-driven politics and sacralization and desacralization of human-made polities.

Synthesizing strategy for outward projection of power-normative essence into practice and of past into future

A mere systematization of antecedent analytical schemata into a system of thought is sufficient for melding the dual aspects of reality into an intuitive comprehension of the total geohistorical process without wholly effacing the lines of analytic differentiations. While sufficient, this approach is also necessary in a setting that exhibits the characteristics of an ambiguously pluralist-statist global proto-system accelerating its expansion out of the Eurocentric core eastward toward Asia and the Pacific after fully consummating the westward extension across the Atlantic by a completed transfer of the center of gravity.

By the same token, if schematization is antecedent to a system of thought, individual policy options corresponding to alternative futures are prior to synthesizing strategy that draws intuitively on the full range of potential futures weighted differently according to their probability and desirability. A probable future is one likely to result from foreseeable reactions to an initial thrust implicit in unimpeded linear projection from an existing situation. Envisaging the direction of the more plausible, i.e., cyclical, projection extends systemic thinking beyond interactional present into the future over at least a medium run. A synthesizing strategy applying this kind of thinking actively to a conformable system of thought is geohistorically realistic, because it combines interaction with evolution. And it is realistically progressivist without being utopian when aimed at a plausible future that is also desirable in terms of a normatively

enhanced environment and operationally moderated agenda. Both qualities apply, because the strategy modifies instinctually balancing restraints
with expansionist drives construed as incorporating the pull as much as
the push factor with respect to the arena and the comparatively defensive
(i.e., decline-resisting compulsive) as well as the relatively offensive (i.e.,
ascent-attending expansive-or-exuberant) foreign policy postures relative
to the actors.

While mediating progression, a correctly intuited and implemented
synthesizing strategy will promote a momentarily achievable variety of
progress when it fosters the advance from operationally catastrophic to
cumulatively organic transformations and, through them, evolution. A
linear projection offers scarce safeguards against the perpetuation of the
pathologies and malignant propensities of either statism or pluralism. The
target of a synthesizing strategy focused on contrarily cyclical projection
and systemic rather than reflexive thinking is plausibly—and within the
range allowed by the basic tenets of realism melioratively—an environment and agenda constrained normatively toward lessened coercion and
normatively inspirited toward an intensified sense and expanded scope of
corporate identity and autonomy. Along these lines, regional polity will
ideally counter the deficiencies of statism with the assets of institutionalized pluralism and vice versa. Each will allow for developmentally appropriate local modes of operations combining features from the full range
of regional formats of politics, from competitive sub-systems via great
power-centered associations to more fully integrated communities, within
correspondingly adapted and evolving forms of inter-regionally coordinating global organization.

In tracing the projection from the future-relevant past of Europe to the
past-reflecting speculation about the West and its relation to the Asian
East, two perspectives open up for the promotion or prevention of moderation by synthesizing strategy. The more straightforward one projects
purely or primarily statist alternatives and trends, centered on the balance
and concert of powers, into a genuinely global state system re-triangular-
ized in function of a geographically inverted land–sea power schism extending from a maritime Pacific East to a henceforth rear-continental
European West. Equally or more plausible is a projection incorporating
pluralist features of both the empire- and the community-type systematically into the statist perspective. Suggestive in this perspective is the record of the European state system across a trajectory taking off from the
proto-systemic antecedents of sixteenth-seventeenth century statecraft
and shaped by the strategic implications of the alternative strengths and
weaknesses of an ambiguously statist-pluralist continental-oceanic Spanish imperial conglomerate, a comparatively compact and medium-sized
statist France, and, realized in the Netherlands, an economically promi-

nent micro-regionally configured community of quasi-independent provinces. By the early twentieth century, this Europe was defined essentially along the statist (French) mode on the continent to the eventual detriment of France itself while preserving and further developing the Dutch mode in its insular-oceanic Atlantic extension and inconclusively relegating the Spanish mode to the (Russian) East. Europe was thus defined only to reach a decisive turning point for any state system and its civilizational identity. Such a point toward which both the system and the civilization ascend and from which they emerge regenerated or fatally weakened is one of the confluence of three transitions: from a preeminent power to the next, from the system's salience and autonomy to the preservation or forfeiture of either or both, and from one type of system or framework of action to another.

This decision point arrived for Europe when the French beneficiary of one-time Milan's appeal from the Italian balance of power outdid its latter-day British diplomatic patron in appealing to the United States from the European balance of power in fact—and on behalf of continued system-paralyzing dominance of declining actors against the continuing autonomy of an arena-defining civilization in effect.

At this point—when a meta-system is willy-nilly operationally linked to the next-following proto-system—the manifestations of evolutionary progression at or near its climax propel the appeasement potential of interactional dynamic to the strategic foreground. Is this potential to be actualized by circuitously purposive or denied by reflexive foreign policies that integrate strategic rationality with, or isolate it from, historical intelligence? And that do the integrating or the isolating when either allowing for or suppressing concern with wider stability relative to immediate security and with long-term domestic and socio-political effects relative to immediate and narrowly real-political external consequences? Specifically at issue in such queries is the particular evolutionary phase of the power against and of the balance of power from which an appeal to the outside "barbarian" is or is not to be issued. Critical with respect to the crucial actor is the precise identity of the ascendant power's rise/decline-related foreign policy posture of the expansion- (vs. consolidation-) oriented category: object-lessly unfocused expansive, peripherally targeted exuberant, or centrally oriented compulsive. With the first being unlikely to endanger overall stability and the second inherently satiable without fatal detriment to the central balance, the most problematic is the third posture aimed at averting irreversible decline before achieving resource-role parity as much as if not more than consolidating irresistible dominance. As such it is also most appeasable within an area that has been to this end appropriately expanded in fact or perception. Correspondingly at issue with respect to the state systemic arena's power distribution

is its configuration, shaped by the still wider range of differently equilibration-prone and -capable foreign policy postures of the unevenly
evolved, rising or declining, major powers.

Both size and structure of the arena will ideally arbitrate between abiding by the immediately short-term national interest and including it as
but an element of a wider systemic or civilizational interest. Whereas the
former prompts recourse to extra-systemic reinforcements in the absence
of intra-systemic ones, the latter incorporates into this imperative of strategic rationality the historically corroborated intelligence of such an appeal's unavoidable consequence for all of the members of the system,
including the appellants. Consequently withstanding structural compulsion for the sake of creating the strategic latitude for an intra-systemic
readjustment of role-and-status relations means taking into account not
only ever-evolving power differences and the present characteristics of
both the suspected expansionist and the arena. To be also and especially
considered is the historically proven capacity of the arena to evolve not
only despite but actually because of a succession of preeminent original
and later-entering powers at the fulcrum of quantitative power balancing.
Respecting this dynamic will reconcile the essential autonomy requisites
of individual member states with provisional relegation of typically oversized outsiders—more difficult to assimilate than the disturber is to integrate—to a sufficiently prolonged period of preparation. This deferral
evolves from earliest perception of the range of significant outsiders' strategic relevance for an appeasement strategy in the long run to gradually
escalating participation in actual diplomacy, before the ultimately critical
outsider qualifies for an active-to-military role in an arena whose scope
corresponds to the median size of core-systemic and peripheral, original
and later-entering, principal actors.

The operational immanence of a macro-system in the contest over a
micro-system and the latter's value-institutional perpetuation in the former are about equally near-automatic or, at least, historically recurrent.
A succeeding proto-system's latency in the antecedent meta-systemic
phase is by contrast anything but automatic or habitual on the grounds
of either operations or values—of the actually adopted strategy or national versus systemic/civilizational interests. It is neither, regardless of
whether the only quantitatively evaluated structure points to a strategically rational countervailing response or a qualitatively expanded total
structure and purposively sought normatively upgraded environment
provide an arguable rationale for an accommodating strategy. When, finally, the critical transition moves from that between preeminent powers
and a historical system's continuing or abridged autonomy to one between a state system and a pluralist framework of action, the issue of both

immanence and latency involving statist systems is expanded correspondingly.

Henceforth, the critical dilemma and dynamic come to comprise and be ultimately focused on the relationship between the empire- and the community-type format: the former's scope, center, and astringency and the latter's spontaneity, self-dependence, and cultural identity. This transition and related developmental and strategic alternatives transpose prime significance from appropriate response to an actual or pretended bid for hegemony (as opposed to mere preeminence), in relation, to inter-state equilibrium, to the problematically statist/pluralist character of empire (as opposed to community) in relation to order. This becomes a matter of wider than formerly intra-European significance when projected into a spatially extended West–East dimension of a global proto-system. An empire's identity, as a both structurally and normatively statist-pluralist hybrid, is reflected in its developmental ambiguity, as a function of the evolutionary trajectory of its environment: an empire's propensity to being relatively pluralistic in the early proto-systemic (generally pre-statist) phase, and comparatively more unitary-centralized statist in the late (generally post-statist) meta-systemic phase. Unlike Asia before and after the Roman Empire and its encroachments into Europe, post-Roman core Europe escaped the centralized empire-type variety of the meta-systemic phase after the proto-systemic pluralist empire-type conglomerates from the Frankish–Germanic to the Spanish had inspired sufficient individual and increasingly coordinated collective resistance to forward multi-statist crystallization typified by monarchical France. The concurrent unraveling of the antecedent aggregation of continental-maritime resources in Spain under pressure from the Anglo-Dutch maritime powers had by then engendered one possible meaning for the evolutionary momentum of the world historical cum political process. This meaning could or would be revealed only retrospectively by such aggregate's eventual reproduction in a developmentally progressive, enlarged and constructively updated, integration of the previously destructively competing land- and sea-based elements. Meanwhile, an essentially statist central event will contend with the Spain-centered futuristic prospect and associated historical perspective over comparative weight in imparting a wider than parochial meaning to Europe's travails through an advance toward amphibiously equipped and culturally amalgamated trans-national/statist regional communities. Concerning the tension between consolidated individuality and wider unity differently, this alternative is focused on France and defined, beginning with the papal-imperial contest, by successively intimated (or imputed) "hegemonical" aspirations to Rome-like unity and the impossibility of achieving it under universally acceptable because ethically or otherwise value-neutral auspices.

Imparting a historically factual substance to the ideal of wider unity in the interest of its counter-utopian character points to the combination of the typological triad with a three-generational sequence of types of polities or powers, aggregating pluralism with statism and functional diversification-to-polarization with integration. Thus, in the developmentally many-sidedly seminal sixteenth-seventeenth-century slice of European history associated with incipiently multi- and residually heteropolar structure, Spain represents the late-medieval form of pluralist unity. It updated the anti-papally imperialist to supra-nationally dynastic principle or ethos and was supported functionally by the integration of continental-military and more effective maritime than mercantile assets and efficacy verging on primacy. At the other corner of the typological triangle, France's early-modern compact statism embodied internal unity while prefiguring the impossibility to combine it with larger or wider unity on an interstatist basis: a fact demonstrated as conclusively by the indisposition of Louis XIV to aspire beyond the preeminence of a foremost monarch to Charles V's hegemonial "universal monarchy" as by the inability of Napoleon I to found European unity on the basis of enlightened rationalism, bureaucratic and other, after forfeiting the thrust of revolutionary universalism to the benefit of French nationalism. Contributing to the divisive effect of structure-related interstatist fragmentation, the functional polarization between France's continental-military and England's oceanic mercantile priorities served to highlight the advantages of the alternative pioneered by the Dutch: functional integration of decreasingly political-military, including naval forces, and increasingly economic and maritime commerce-directed features within a pluralistic community.

As a species of typological synthesis, contemporary West European communitarian pluralism is the nearest approximation to the Dutch model. A partial reversion to the functionally comprehensive integrative Spanish and incomplete departure from the normatively statist French model would less contradict than complementarily complete and confirm the triadic typological with a third-generational evolutionary synthesis of features defining the first generation sacral-military medieval monarchy and second-generation maritime-mercantile oligarchy. As a matter of historical logic and radical scarcity of basic developmental alternatives, such a synthesis was—after the defeat of radically unitary totalitarian statism's climactic bid for and pretension to such a succession—most likely to occur in the supra-statist pluralist manner of reincarnating attributes validated historically but individually no longer viable in their original forms. Such a succession's legitimacy and efficacy alike is, in terms of the several antecedents, contingent on an ethnically/culturally neutral basis of unity over and above compatible diversities buttressing institutionalized interfunctional integration. A continuing development of the "Napoleonic" rationalist/bureaucratic features currently embodied in the European Commission under mainly French influence is contingent on expanding the reach of the only inter- or trans-provincially or -microregionally unifying "Dutch" economic factors from essentially societal and primarily economic functions to the distinctively statist ones related to foreign policy and defense. The "Spanish" dynastic facet of supra-ethnicity or -nationality is manifestly absent in the European prototype of possible future regional components of and antecedents to an inter-regional cum -civilizational order. A substitute will have to be transposed from the medieval religio-mythical and transitional dynastic patriotism, and the developmentally climactic (and typologically generic) statist mystique, into a quasi-statist communitarian ethos and patriotism—one that evolves from merely offsetting ethnic diversities and particularistic economic utilities and priorities to also transcending both in crisis situations. This alone will redress somewhat the contemporary Western Europe-style inversion of the medieval community's transcendentally spiritual universalism and economic localism into its present opposite while combining the scattered positive elements and attributes of the statist heritage with the reascending pluralist ones.

For the processual-evolutionary dynamic illustrated in Europe to be duplicable on the inter-regional and -civilization plane, it would have to meet the genuinely conservative requisite of maintaining diversity within organically growing unity, and it would have to do this within an institutional framework expanding in terms of both optimum scope and real needs-fulfilling feasible functions. To this end, the mandate for strategy is to mediate progression among historical phases and across spatially conditioned differences as the prime, or only available, synthesizing agent capable of integrating the converging illuminations dispensed by strategic rationality and historical intelligence. A correspondingly geohistorically oriented speculation may be also called upon, if only as an illustration of a both theoretically and practically viable merger of (subject-)matter with method, to tentatively advance beyond schematization and systematization toward substantive synthesis. This move requires a climactic if problematic feat of imagination, performed by ascending the levels of meaning and layers of understanding of the world historical-cum-political process from the conflictually real politically interstatist lowest or primary toward higher ones.

Beyond the European space but in keeping with the European experience, the statist and the pluralist perspectives on the contemporary global proto-system intersect in the consequences of the Anglo–French two-stage appeal to American arbitration from a real or imagined, actual or imputed, centralized (German-based) empire of the meta-systemic kind, which enlarged the Euro- into a Americano-centric West. The consequences project the (quasi-Spanish) empire-related vs. (quasi-Dutch) community-related problematique into the future along the West–East axis—and do so within only Euro–Atlantic macro-regional or inter-regionally global confines. A relatively pluralist rather than centralized (meta-systemic) format of empire-type order might have materialized within the narrower scope conjointly with appeasing the confrontation and simultaneously relaxing internal structures in a de facto U.S.–Soviet condominium. It may still eventuate intra-regionally in the form of a U.S.–Germanocentric West European–Russian triangle of quasi-imperial great power spheres disguised as common markets or free trade areas. This basic format is susceptible of globalization in the form of a U.S.–Russocentric all European–Chinese (or Sino–Japanese) equivalent. Both triangles would reproduce in different shapes and combinations the unevenly centralized imperial and statist politico-military and pluralist communitarian politico-economic types of polities encompassed in the earlier Spanish–French–Dutch typological triad.

A major proviso in relation to both the intra-regional and inter-regionally global confines, referring back to the hegemonial statist dilemma, is that failure to subordinate a narrowly defined U.S. national to a wider Western systemic-civilizational interest has not alienated Russia by means including but not limited to a countervailing appeal to China, displacing the former into the camp of the contemporary wider range and more immediately disruptive kind of outside "barbarians" to the one-sided advantage of Asia's automatically invigorated statism.

Consistent with or also complementary to avoiding so questionable a triumph of strategic rationality over historical intelligence for contrarily disarmed narrow-Western societism is associating China and Japan with the quasi-imperial-to-communitarian type of order along an extended West–East axis. Such an association would optimally perform the function of the earlier pluralist empires when acting (the medieval Germanic) as a seedbed of more consensually community-like integration or more effectively (the early-modern Spanish) as a stimulus to reactively state-like re-articulation of the arena. Within the narrowest of Occidents excluding Russia, finally, a centralized meta-systemic U.S. empire might develop in response to internal stresses of diversely post-statist character and external pressures from overassertive Asian statism. It is both less likely and less desirable than a merely quasi-imperial American preeminence—unlikely though the latter is to have sufficient stimulus potential for extending re-crystallization of resistant (West) European into wider Western statism on a multipolar basis, or substantially more of the seedbed potential for wider-regional communitarian integration on a cumulatively continuous basis. In this respect, America's phantom hegemony is more likely to be engaged for some time inconclusively but in the long term most decisively with the communitarian type of meta-systemization in two discrete and not necessarily coherent or compatible ways and degrees: externally with the clearly post-statist pluralist form in Western and Central Europe (European Union), and internally or intra-regionally with an ambiguously statist-pluralist format in North America or also Eastern Europe. In the former, this would take place in function of the trend toward only deconcentration of federalism in favor of state rights and functions (the United States) or also micro-regional disaggregation-to-disintegration along cultural and economic lines (Canada); in the latter, as part of macro-regionally confederative or only functionally (re-)integrative tendencies in response to post-centralized empire-based pressures on independently uncertainly viable polities.

Decisive for the issue of an inter-regional and -civilizational world order will, in either case, be the kind and intensity of corresponding linkages: Whether and, if so, how and to what extent the structural-functional-institutional alternatives and tendencies could or would link an either residually exclusionist and quasi-statist or outward-extended pluralistic North America with Europe and Asia, and a correspondingly shaped, integrally Euro–American or one-sidedly U.S.-centered, West with the global East. The course and outcome would hinge on the ways of developing the differently statist and pluralist tendencies in the two hemispheres: largely separately and independently from one another if not also adversarially and reactively to each other, or in two-directionally reciprocal integration through functionally and structurally overlapping pluralisms. A promotion of the latter option sufficiently timely to be protective of the autonomy of both of the dialectically interrelated civilizations is in turn apt to be contingent on being operationalized real politically—by geostrategic devices such as a supportive network of mutually reassuring great-power security guarantees of critical intercultural or -regional boundaries, pending their gradual erosion on the way to the inter-regional-to-global community-type order. Strategically promoted, institutionally sustained, and historico-philosophically meaningful structurally-functionally pluralist integration, interacting positively with residually statist coordination of the concert-of-powers type, conjugates the tenets of conservatively romantic with the precepts of liberally progressivist realism. The somberly prophetic alternative is qualitative bifurcation and structural-strategic polarization of West and East: between differently non- and post-statist pluralist societal entities in the West and resurgently if not also retributively statist East. If combined with adequate economic performance, statism's greater power-political potency would in such a case transfer the power of the critical choice from the Eurocentric onto an Asia-centered universe. The choice between narrowly rational-strategically inspired national interests and historically ratified systemic-civilizational stakes is concretized in the option of either a West–East balance of power that has been restored from its late pro-Western to an antecedent contrary imbalance or an inter-regional equilibrium devoid of the burden of historically rooted reprisals or only the cosmic tedium of mechanistic repetitions around alternating centers of gravity.

Searching for counter-utopian meaning reconnecting trivial pragmatics with tragic predicament within an ideal polity

Substantive values, even when accorded priority in the longest-term perspective, can be ignored in the short-term optic or only marginally injected in the midterm one, before the eschatologically prophetic meaning focused on the end of things achieves parity with the unevenly (purely or normatively amended) real political subjects of meaning related to means more than ends. In so complex a power-normative setting, a paradoxical relationship exists between power/interest-related facts and norms-representing values (or figments of imagination and rationalization), questionably fused in authentic or contrived national or wider identities and likewise prone to degenerate into two opposing terms of a frustrating chasm—that between a values-implicating tragic predicament, writ large in the rise and fall of great principalities and powers revealing the precarious fate of nations and civilizations, and an interests-fixating pragmatic politics, liable to shrinkage into the most commonplace of routine transactions. This kind of gap between the highest politics, prone to culminating in war and revolution, and the lowest, liable to rising at best to concern with inert stability or disturbances-minimizing level of prosperity, is susceptible of substantive closure only speculatively and at the close of each major evolutionary phase retrospectively. It can meanwhile be narrowed actively, albeit always provisionally, by a strategy that discriminatingly balances facts against values, values against facts, and the insights of historical intelligence against the imperatives of strategic rationality. On both counts, such a gap is more difficult to bridge than the only contributory secondary gap—that between individual stimuli and aggregate result peculiar to the conventional balance of power and implementing alliances, which tends to narrow if not also close automatically under the impetus of strategically rational imperatives alone.

It is in keeping with the dialectical relationship between the defining and differentiating features of the several levels of actually or potentially meaningful activities—and corresponding modes of interpretation and consequent layers of achieved or achievable understanding—that the levels themselves are similarly connected. Accordingly, the level encompassed by the combination of romantic with progressivist realism absorbs the conventionally realistic balance-of-power dynamic and ethically like-wise neutral war as joint obstacles to forcible unification. But it adds the existential dimension of ambiguously motivated expansion and the nor-mative dimension of valuation-worthy corporate autonomy of progres-sively expanding subjects susceptible of appeasement within intra-regionally integrative community. It is this valuation that incidentally ele-vates, more than anything else, the simple operational collision of power/interest-centered agents past its tragic potential into an unquestionably tragic confrontation between equally positive values: a national actor's and a wider (systemic or civilizational) regional actor's or arena's power/interests and autonomy, and between corporate autonomy and individual freedom. Repeatedly manifest up to this (national vs. regional) point, the absorption-and-elevation transpires only hypothetically on behalf of a prophetically postulable terminal evolutionary stage and its meaning on the highest, inter-regionally global, plane capable of spontaneous unifica-tion.

In the presently plausible context of an extended West–East schism, this plane is subject to being activated on the supposition that a prior sacrifice of the power and autonomy of Europe for the national interests and individual freedoms of the West Europeans will have unwittingly ex-panded the relevant orbit from Europe to the Euro–American West. Con-jointly transposed would presumptively be not only the multi-factorally compacted balance of power, characteristic of statism, as it evolved into a functionally diversified and intra-regionally pluralist equilibrium (and related strategic equation), centered less instinctually on action and reac-tion than on a considered orchestration of revulsion (from superior power), attraction (by economic efficiency), and their mediation and equalization by individually or mutually shared affinity or antipathy in terms of cultural values. A regionally confined complex equilibrium might be eventually also transposed via an inter-regional one into a dialec-tic interplay between regionally delimited Euro-American and Asian civi-lizations. An equally power/interest- and values-centered reciprocal negation, inherent in a dialectic relationship, would tend toward recipro-cally modifying and moderating differences or outright contraries such as Western societal economism by Asian statism and vice versa to mutual advantage. Supportive of such a process would optimally be the prior resolution of the land–sea power schism in the shape of amphibious re-gional communities capable of adjusting the sacral–secular schism to fit the expanded actor's normative next to existential requisites. The globally expanded inter-regional West–East schism would simultaneously project its defining value-institutional disparity into commonly derivative real political competition, although one that has been pragmatically moder-ated conjointly with the attenuation of the values-related differences.

The lower levels of activities being absorbed in evolutionary momentum, one that associates the meaning of world politics integrally with that of world history, points to the possibility of eventual inter-civilizational appeasement that is positive both operationally and normatively. To the extent that this appeasement-capable dialectic represents and potentially consummates a transcendence of the tragedy-constitutive conflict between positive values, it represents an advance over conventional modes of resolving a simply power/interest-based conflict. As part of being emphatically contrary to the Manichean opposition of an ideal self to an evil other in principle, this dialectic preserves a presumptively receding war as less an evil than an ethically neutral, if ultimately tragic, last-resort device for eliminating disparities (such as between an actor's disposable resources and claimed role) that represent a negative value when destabilizing a statist or pluralist arena. The prospectively most promising exit from the implied paradoxes is through an actually or only perceptually expanded arena and diversified agenda. Such an amplification is, therefore, also contrary to preemptively intra- or prematurely extra-systemically initiated countervailing containment of conceptually misconstrued and actually stimulated, if not effectively provoked, expansion on behalf of a both conceptually and perceptually contrarily narrowed primitive balance of power. The arena itself is expanded perceptually (rather than actually) when it is addressed by the strategist as comprising no more than potential reserve power, whose prospective incorporation is ideally to be activated only incidentally to the de facto invigoration or energetic expansion of the original arena itself, wrought by a newly ascendant insider being offset by intensified countervailance or assimilated by concessions, each reflecting the acceptance of its provisional preeminence. Both modes of reempowerment from within are consistent with the arena's autonomy, while both the perceptually expanded existing environment and the purposively promoted subsequent environment are consistent with including the previous outsider in a relationship of parity with either the newly salient insider alone or the combined capabilities of the old core of the new system/arena, allowing preeminence to settle progressively on whomsoever without detriment to anyone's corporate autonomy—or individual freedoms.

When the arena has been expanded and both power and balance have been decentralized-to-disaggregated in regard to factors structurally, diversified functionally, and problematized normatively, a synthesizing strategy encounters conditions wherein it can complete the work of amplification. Complementing the conversion of a both diversified and amplified balance of power from univocally conflictual into a more ambiguously constituted dialectic interplay are the special qualities of both culture and civilization and their sociopolitical counterpart or embodiment in community. As the consummate form of societal pluralism, community differs from statism most specifically in regard to either's territoriality, materiality, and sacrality, variably prominent and unevenly interrelated in combinations that attend the state's rise to and declension from its developmental climax between primitive and institutionalized pluralisms—a difference that can, as has been shown in context, be conceptualized in terms of historicist idealism and materialism. It is pertinent in this connection that civilization differs from culture and relations between civilizations from either warlike frontal collision or harmoniously pacific fusion as much as the state differs from society and the latter from community—and, because of their actual complementarity and developmental consecutivity, as little. When it is not diluted into any and all habitual ways of behaving, a culture's defining expression in religion and art is primarily a matter of mind, aspiring to an internally coherent symbolic representation of the world. By contrast, civilization—which spans the range from collectively shared and inter-collectively projected but unevenly evolved techniques or technologies to least tangible formalized rituals observed inter-individually—is also integrally a matter of power translatable into graduated status-and-role ranking of parts in a whole.

Regardless of which more prominently engenders the other, culture and civilization can intimately blend in the mystique or spirit of a state-like polity, unlike a society deficient of community. Conversely, the feature that differentiates civilization from culture most is the power factor: only a diffusely pervasive relationship of control, manifest in super- and subordination between participants in a civilization or between civilizations themselves, or more tellingly a capability concentrated in a great power representative of a civilization. In either case, the key relationship is not likely to be one of mutually enriching interpenetration prior to reciprocally challenging interaction, as it may be between qualitative ranking-resistant cultures. A civilization is, therefore, unlikely if not unable to abdicate the use of raw power for the sole purpose of allowing the refinement of mores to be plausibly proposed or experienced as the highest or defining expression of "civilized" conduct. Nor is, however, this inter-civilizational dialectic a matter of frontal clashes of a kind peculiar to narrowly territorially based and strategically focused quasi-spiritually sacralized states typical of the lower plane or planes of action.

It is part of the correspondingly accentuated paradoxical nature of the fact-value relationships that, for it to preserve the meaning of world politics on the lower levels, the end postulated on the highest plane and pursued by intuitively synthesizing strategy must not be utopian. It cannot credibly stand for surcease from both individual and corporate predicaments in harmonious cooperation of either regional or global scope, one representing unity bereft of diversity and community minus individuality.

It can, consistently with the beginning in natural laws of social intercourse and human disposition, only transpose predicaments onto a different and only conditionally progressive plane. This can be so with respect to facets such as schisms, transposed to altered terms and parties to them or (more likely) less contrarily overlapping and actually conflictual relations between their constituents; or facets such as rise and decline, transposed to either steeper or (preferably) flatter fluctuations among its subjects; or features such as cyclical trajectory of any one factor or alternation among several factors, transposed to such cycles' less violently or forcefully propellent stimuli and persistently change-resistant termini. All this is possible or at least conceivable within spatially vaster or narrower scopes, temporally shorter or longer reaction times, and diversely salient or only subsidiary functional and institutional constituents.

If this kind of end entails corresponding transposition-to-transformation in the makeup of evolutionary progression, it is likely with respect to the motor and mechanism no less than the manifestations and matrix of evolution. The implied supposition is that a qualitatively diversified structure and correspondingly revised conception of expansion favor mitigation of crises and conflicts attending a shift from determinative tyranny of narrowly quantitative structure and primitive balancing over reflexive strategy in the direction of a greater leeway for foreign policy. A correspondingly emancipated, but in no way arbitrary, strategy can in such a case target also the domestic politics of the actually or potentially rival side more effectively than otherwise, proceeding circuitously by such means as deliberate concessions of parity for reasons intimated by the plausible-to-desirable direction of the circuitous approach's objective signposts, cyclically construed projection and realistically practical political economy. It may be supposed further that such an end entailing the elevation and expansion of nation-states to regionally delimited cultures and civilizations is in keeping with the admittedly regressions-rich overall tendency—i.e., the recurrently reversed and resumed trend—toward larger polities as the most crises-resistant optima. However, since supposing this expansion is not the same as positing the results' frictionless fusion in a maximally expanded and invariably peaceful world community, this projection short of prophecy meets the requirement of continuing dramatic tension even while modifying the balance of power to the point of transforming it dramatically.

Conclusion: Expanding Realism into Geohistoricism

Summed up in the inclusive term "geohistoricism," a correspondingly expanded realism remains fully within a long and enduring tradition. For tradition to become enduring, it must be satisfying esthetically and ethically: it must allow and account for the drama of existence and provide for its valid object in a meaningful destiny. It must represent a world that both intrigues and inspires agents with sufficiently dynamic movement to necessitate and reward activity that is practical in the sense of useful and in some way morally elevating. Realism fulfills these conditions as the reservoir of incrementally accumulated and repeatedly corroborated intuitions of a general philosophy tested for validity across the ages. Standing as such for continuity, realism accommodates change, including changes that affect its basic postulate of identifiable power capable of rational manipulation. For it to be a tradition for all seasons, however, realism must be capable not only of accommodating change abroad but of also assimilating development and growth within itself without degenerating into a momentary academic fashion.

The realist tradition upholds the balance of power as the only practicable theory of world politics and the main provider of the dramatic quality that, however, leaves the larger issue of purpose or destiny untouched. Expanding this theory into a system of thought and stretching the tradition to cover all past and possible future seasons entails, therefore, modifying or amplifying primitive—original or elementary—balance of power by developing the dramatic and adding the purposive facets. The dramatic is developed by providing for the antecedent to the operation of the balance of power, i.e., expansion, and for alternatives to its defining but impermanent condition, i.e., compact power, in the form of its disaggregation into positively institutionalized functions and negatively revolutionized factors. The purposive is added by extending the central emphasis on space as the theater and conditioning milieu of its operation to time, interaction to evolution, geopolitics into geohistoricism, and relativity beyond physical location to a broadened concept of situation.

Amplifying the reach of realism in this fashion enriches its esthetic quality by the disclosure of only mutually compatible or also symmetrical ranges of complexities vindicating the quality of politics as more art than science. And injecting the ethical dimension through purpose in the shape of teleology and predicament in the guise of tragedy incidentally engenders the compulsion to address the expanded insights' practical utility. Consequently, the conceptual amplification of the traditional realism of primitive power balancing translates in principle automatically into a practicable strategy capable of combining legitimate self-assertion with maximum possible accommodation. By synthesizing all the components of the system of thought, itself incapable of or resistant to any such premature consummation, such a strategy enables realism to extend itself in the direction of practicable utopia while remaining hostile to the dogmatic simplifications of realism's hereditary counterparts: moralism and morality's travesty in formalized legalism.

Systematizing the components of the speculative approach to the interactional-evolutionary unity of politics

Projecting the past speculatively toward the future requires anchoring transcendental historico-philosophical meditations in transactional real politics, in keeping with the dualistic character of reality encompassing particular relationships such as between schisms and conflicts and foreign policy postures and particular policies. Doing so means forgoing meta-historical synthesis devoid of strategic specificity in order to preserve the practical, including social, utility of both retrospection and projection. Meditating in this fashion about the course of the ages with significance for the direction of the present toward the future associates historicist empirical analysis with appropriate ontological and epistemological facets and understanding reality with a centralizing concept.

Geohistoricizing world politics accordingly differs radically from wholly ahistorical theorizing and significantly from identifying conceptually significant differences between historical eras. An individualizing approach will be historicist when viewing events and entities genetically in terms of their origins and development. But, while sharing these concerns with geohistoricism, its commitment to historical individualities in the widest range of their attributes and determinants differs from the generalizing approach that reviews particular eras or any other object of interest as an incident to searching for structural and functional continuities with a view to identifying significant uniformities. It will do this at a level that combines the methodological necessity of abstraction with the historiographical requirement of substantive concreteness, and not only because geohistoricism explicitly adds the geopolitically significant spatial to the historically temporal dimension.

At a related plane of differentiation, the individualizing approach will tend to be academic in the sense of being only indirectly, if at all, concerned with immediate and long-range policy implications. Generalizing geohistoricism is by contrast activist and involved, although in a fashion different from any possible interest of the ahistorical theorist in policy and policy implications when its practitioner abandons the rigorous theorist's ultimate ambition to predict and adopts the would-be statesmanlike philosopher's desire to enlighten and, when prescribing, draws out the logical policy implications of previously delineated structures and processes. If the implied call for a historically intelligent statecraft to incorporate the temporal-evolutionary dimension into analysis of space-centered action has an academic quality, the activist corrective requires criteria of policy relevance that are stricter than many an ahistorical theorist's. Utilized concepts and either phenomena or processes to which they are applied must, in this view, be meaningful to the practicing statesman in terms of a perception of reality that is not only ideally desirable but also practically conceivable in terms of aspects affecting the main problems, pressures, and patterns encountered in statecraft. Being meaningful in terms of perceptions, the speculative approach must address the statesman's conventional predicaments in a fashion that is intellectually as well as operationally manageable. That is, one that can be translated from concept into conduct by allowing for the integration of strategic rationality pertaining to dynamics into historical intelligence, germane to evolutionary progression, as well as vice versa; and that, respecting the qualitative difference between the long term and the sum of the short runs, facilitates the creative reconciliation of the two discrete and uneven temporalities in the practice of an exceptional and thus historically rare but because exceptionally occurring actually conceivable category or quality of statecraft.

An empirical avenue to understanding actuality, geohistoricist interpretation is directly the temporal and derivatively the value-institutional associate of romantic realism, the ontological facet of the speculative approach concerned with reality. Its evolutionary dimension equips realism with an elementary philosophy of history, or metahistory, that aims at transcending chronologically ordered factual data of the past in a search for their significance in the present and for the future. Taking history systematically into account means theorizing it independently from theorizing politics with a view to joining the two in a more complete understanding of both real politics and the ideal polity—an apprehension delving past the identification of patterns and sequences to degrees of transformation and beyond to a sense of the either only positive or also purposive meaning of both process and its intermediate and conceivable ultimate products.

This kind of understanding will be won only at ever less empirically manifest levels of reality. Inquiry must, therefore, reach beyond the routine transactions of Realpolitik and integrate the reflexively actuated action-reaction core of the dynamic into intellectual constructs of its contexts. Having operational significance and being empirically plausible, the reality behind such constructs is perceivable only over time and in historical perspective while co-shaping nonetheless both the interactions and, even more, their outcomes. These transactions-transcending aspects of reality exceed a mere actuality that can be readily dissected analytically and is commonly managed operationally on a day-by-day or short-term basis concerned with immediate problems and prospects. They are nonetheless of a kind that fulfills the above-mentioned requirement of essential meaningfulness for the policy maker and operational manageability by policies. Among them are positions of actors and attributes of arenas and agendas reflecting the organic rise/decline fluctuations and related evolutionary trajectory; variably ascending and receding (sacral–secular or existential–normative, land–sea power, and West–East) schisms and the alternately expansive and consolidative foreign policy postures closely related to both the fluctuations and the trajectories. All are engaged in amplifying structures of material capabilities with qualitative attributes and mobilizing them into process, be it within state systems or an alternative framework of action that progress toward or regress from an optimum point of development.

Distinguishing and integrating the primitively transactional and the plausibly postulated transcendental aspects of reality are a key part of the approach to knowledge engaging the epistemological facet of the speculative approach. The defining procedure is the decomposition of phenomena into processes en route to identifying the essential form. The phenomena of war and peace and of stability and prosperity, critical for real politics and political economy, are, together with the corresponding processes, encompassed in the overarching phenomenon, the changing composite environment or setting of world politics. Such an environment's second-degree abstraction, beyond dynamic interaction into evolutionary progression, breaks down further into specific processes. These are in part identical with those of interactional dynamics as to their kind, the conflictual mechanics. But they add to them changeable sources of propulsion—the energy-generating motor—and the critical factor of movement over time, disclosed in the manifestations of evolution. Thus also when the operational dimension is not in effect superseded in evolution by the organic one, it is more crucially supplemented by it in evolution than in interaction. These differences in emphasis coalesce in one between forms of action (and reactions) and states of being that crystallize unevenly persistent and varying results and outcomes of such actions.

A related and similarly elusive contrast applies to the essential form of the relation between phenomenon and process. It opposes continuity and change within evolution to power and norm in interaction. Any historicist perspective will expand the boundaries of the norm beyond narrowly legal or ethical to diversely value-institutional and cultural factors. Meta-historicism is the record, just as the reality it seeks to understand is the receptacle, of temporally varying and variable values and associated institutions and cultural artifacts that are secreted by routinely reflexive politics—itself an intrinsically unchanging process subject only to diverse kinds of rationalization, from intellectual and teleological to instrumental and technological. It follows that in the imbrication of continuity with change the factor of power as the existential impellent in the essential (power-normative) form of the dynamic represents, without exhausting, the facet of continuity in the evolutionary dimension while the normatively accented value-institutional factor, biased toward restraint in the dynamics, is primarily responsible for change without, again, exhausting its sources.

Such alterations are superstructural and cover a wider spectrum than does structure in the strict sense of a space-bound distribution of capabilities susceptible of particular configurations. By the same token, the instruments employed to implement conduct and promote its objectives occupy as functionally oriented devices a wider range of historically changing possibilities than does the functional side of either conduct or configuration that directs behavior or process toward an end or purpose by appropriate means only including instrumental ones.

Values and institutions are the crucial modifiers within a narrow definition of structure (as to what is or is to be created), of functions (i.e., actions of actors viewed from the vantage point of structure with a view to what is or is to be done within a structure or for its sake), and of process (as to what is coming to be or is to become from structure's imbrication with function). The values and institutions modify the primitive constants within a narrow range of consequently recurring configurations and strategic alternatives. Whereas the configurations distribute and interrelate the qualitatively diversified capabilities, merely coexisting in time/space for the purposes of structure, in a particular fashion with the aid of diplomatic constellations and politico-military coalitions, the strategic alternatives formalize and rationalize behavior patterns as responses to rather than intrinsic components of structures or configurations. Relatively constant basic objectives in regard to structure are pursued and corresponding acts are performed by actors, consciously for their own sake and implicitly as a functional requisite of maintaining a system or order: its being perpetuated if it is not to be fundamentally altered to the advantage of an alternative framework of action and, from the actors' subjective viewpoint, an actual or potential rival.

Such a perception of progression by way of process warrants, and the postulate of sequentially patterned evolution presupposes the validity of, corresponding devices of analysis pertinent to action. Foremost among them are the functional equivalence of formally different entities and structurally-functionally conceived and perceived analogies as distinct from chronological antecedents. Both the equivalents and the analogies tend to discount the extent of change apparent in surface events, outward forms of institutions or agencies, and key functions-performing instrumentalities.

Thus construed, prevalence of continuity over change fits perfectly with the fourth and final attribute of the speculative approach, the unifying concept. Equilibrium is now viewed as a process of continual adaptations, or its opposite a circuitously achieved product of maladaptations, to different kinds of change or changes tending to eventually restabilize a previously disturbed environment. With respect to discrepancies that are more or less substantial within the context of changes that are more or less real and a continuity that is more or less cyclical, a reequilibration comprises a mix of the status quo ante and the disturbance in a new state of being that scales down the peak of change implicit in the disturbance or aimed at by the disturber. This mitigation corresponds to a cyclical pattern that exhibits less than positive repetitions, enacting nothing more than the inessentially but still significantly modified recurrences of events, rebirths of a structure, or returns to a strategy. Thus understood, recurrence combines cyclism with a linear attribute implicit in the overall progressive or regressive direction of qualitatively neutral evolutionary progression, distinct from progress as some kind of improvement.

As an in and of itself teleologically neutral process, endowed by progression with a qualitatively or normatively neutral direction compatible with the attribution of meaning, evolution draws on equilibrium-like adaptation that entangles continuity with change to do two things: one, reflect or replicate the anatomy of a revolution consisting of moderately reformist antecedent, violent climax, and conservative restoration; and two, illustrate the historical process-illuminating dialectic of thesis, antithesis, and provisional synthesis. Their conjunction is concretized, via a major war, most strikingly in the power politics of a balance of power disrupted by the bid for hegemony, only to be reconstituted after absorbing the defeated and consequently altered challenger in the next defensive coalition associating different parties in an essentially recurring setting for a functionally identical purpose.

Shaping the evolutionary dimension of world politics in ways and by means of intellectual categories pertaining to its dynamics contributes to the presumption of the unity of politics around a finite number of issues and related processes. A thus-molded speculative approach looks to informed understanding to replace scientific rigor with intuitive sympathy for the dilemmas of an actor—polity or policy maker—who, caught up in the multiple circularities between internal and external, politico-military and economic factors that affect if not determine one another, is inescapably exposed to the resulting environmental and operational complexities. One way to analytically simplify the task is to break up such a reality into the several facets of a composite held together by a coherence that is ultimately (and paradoxically) rooted in the very causal circularities and cyclical reversions clustering around and centered in equalization-prone balances between the two "primitive" motivational and existential givens: drives and restraints, mutually reinforcing one another in the central dynamic of both interaction and evolution. The aim is a schematic rendering of the total qualitatively differentiated structure and related interactional and evolutionary process at a level of abstraction and generality that allows for systematization but preserves enough substantive contents in terms of historical and contemporary data to be significant with respect to particular operations without surrendering a sense of the whole to the proliferation of heterogeneous specifics. The ongoing thrust and progressively intimated meaning of a correspondingly process-driven progression can be only inferred from thus ordered events without being invalidated by the inference's tentativeness. By the same token, the several categories that either transcend or constrain particular transactions—poles of power, triangles, and center-periphery dualities, along with schisms, structures- and rise/decline-related policy postures—in terms of which the events reflecting action and reaction are ordered, can be in part only imputed to multifaceted actuality, but without abrogating the validity or authenticity of a thus construed core reality. Making this reality intellectually manageable and intuitively plausible through historically evinced manifestations does not rule out the possibility or even likelihood relative to the transcending categories. Thus the more pragmatic variety of an originally normative schism such as the statist–societal of the sacral–secular one can and progressively will yield to or be only subsumed in even more broadly generic but functionally equivalent dualities when the normative-existential is further reduced to the immaterial-material one in the context of historicist idealism-and-materialism. Nor is even thus relaxed a view of reality inconsistent with assisting the operational management of actuality. This is especially true when both the visible features of an actor's perceived actuality and the inferred or imputed attributes of the interpreter's postulated reality constitute complementary aspects of an objective given at any one time and in a particular place, as well as at a comparable stage in the flow of evolutionary progression recurring in various places over time.

Thus also, for the sake of full apprehension and wholly effective action, whereas meaning may be largely only inferred and reality intuited, the relationship between action and its setting—an environment constitutive of a type of order—may have to be inverted. This will be particularly so when the external environment is not sufficiently determinate as to its structure and specific as to configuration to determine strategies—i.e., assist in inspiring and shaping them more, and more consistently, than any other factor. Environment is then inverted from an existential given into a normative goal or purposive object of strategies that, set free by the environmental void, are raised to the status of transitionally original factors so as to constitute a more determinate environment as a future actuality in improved consonance with the essential reality inferred from the historicist investigation of world politics.

A structure-reconstitutive strategy, deriving a realistically utopian vision of the future from the historically progressing and regressing formation of qualitatively nuanced total structure, represents the obverse of two deformities. One is enshrined in a view of international politics that would have a narrowly, i.e., only quantitatively, conceived uni- to multipolar structure reproduce itself automatically and indefinitely by dint of strategies wholly determined by a structure defined so narrowly as to appear to be unambiguously determination-capable. This view effectively rules out change in practice after failing to provide for it in theory. Another deformity is implicit in the postulate of not only perpetual but also structurally wholly ambiguous and, therefore, analytically incomprehensible transformations in and of the environment. Inherently less flexible, strategies are then persistently and inescapably at variance with—i.e, lack a minimum of the necessary fit with—a qualitatively overdifferentiated structure. Absent either deformity, an intrinsically avoidable disruption takes place only when and because the strategist has failed to interpret the constituents of a manageably articulated total structure with sufficient historical intelligence to avoid the pitfall of grossly oversimplified strategic rationality.

Failure to incorporate the qualitative modifiers and transcendent constructs into strategy will produce a crisis; an analysis lacking the modifiers will make the crisis incomprehensible. An approach that places crudely defined structure at the center of analysis is no more revealing than one that, concentrating on behavior alone, leaves the objective factors that condition strategic behavior in the shadowy margins of analysis. Acknowledging complexities and admitting circularities is the necessary consequence of rejecting both primitive structuralism and methodologically oversophisticated behaviorism as alternatives to speculative geohistoricism. This approach sacrifices conceptual parsimony in favor of interpretive potency without wholly surrendering to either the circularities or the complexity. The inter-determinative circularities between internal and external, politico-military and economic factors and concerns are relaxed by injecting progression into interaction for two reasons. One, the evolutionary perspective prolongs the regressive chain of causation that is or can be investigated. Two, structurally or functionally comparable events can be and, in fact, will have to be identified across time differentials to establish continuities and differences. Thus, if the most immediate cause of a broadly defined event is economic, it may very well and often will be revealed as being the consequence of, say, an antecedent military-political event or process—and vice versa. The same is true for the relation between internal and external factors as either cause or effect when, as often happens, apparently determining domestic circumstances arise out of preexisting systemic ones. When the causal primacy or relative potency of X and Y is inconclusive, a comparison across time of the overall contexts—i.e., the aggregation of potentially causative factors and the identification of either as the principal locus of energy-generating crisis will at the very least discredit false, ideologically or otherwise inspired, presumptions of causality. This process of elimination will identify if not the overall causal primacy of X or Y then the conditions and constellations under which either of them is apt to predominate.

An example arises in connection with events attending the land–sea power triangles and discrete phases of large-scale and prolonged expansion. Whereas causal circularities can thus be partly disentangled, the complexities are somewhat simplified—relaxed though not resolved—by anything that establishes the direct operational connection between dynamics and evolution, between the propensities at work in the former and the sequences articulating the latter. Rooted in the instinct of self-preservation and responding to power structures, the propensities actuate law-like tendencies that shape the dynamics; the sequences are elevated to process by their connection with identifiable propellents and procedural modalities of the attendant transformations. Whereas the sequences articulate evolution, socially revolutionary expressions or functionally revolutionary instruments of the propellents behind the propensities punctuate the adaptive process of reequilibration. This profoundest of determinative circularities—between interaction and evolution—is conceptually enshrined in the matrix qua environmental setting of evolution. Therein, the political physics-implementing balance of power dynamics functions underneath the complex manifestations of evolutionary progression as the near-invisible but ultimately decisive regulator of action and agenda. The more visible or only ostensible features manifesting the state of evolutionary progression at any one moment are, as it were, frozen conceptually within the matrix and are only potentially—and when actually, only temporarily—stabilized operationally around the balance of power acting as a crucial part of the adaptive facet of the equilibrium process.

Systematizing the relation between interaction and evolution by way of the time/space continuum

Operationally, the crucial linkage occurs most flagrantly in the conflict-centered mechanics of evolution and is only implicit in this mechanism's motor-like impellents, centered in or originated by a range of crises. This same connection of interaction with evolution is conveyed formally by the postulate of ideal-typical norms of the behavior of actors and structure of the arena, representing in one way or another the fully rational strategic implementation of the balance-of-power dynamic. The norms equal—are most likely to be actualized in and through—balance of power-centered interaction among internally consolidated, politically stabilized, economically empowered, and spatially contiguous or actionally interlinked parties. Such actors are both capable and strongly motivated to project power abroad over issues centered on a universally shared and thus conflictually unifying stake, one defined substantively in terms of territory or territory-related assets and purposively as security or primacy if not supremacy in role or status. And these actors will do this militantly even when not militarily in a fashion that is more variably than radically impeded by normatively or organizationally constituted constraints. Advance toward such a norm will occur by way of manifest events attendant on the largely, but far from wholly or perennially, concurrent crystallization of the actors and the arena liable to peak in a moderate institutionalization of power balancing and to recede amidst a series of escalating crises.

A terminal crisis is apt to engender the demotion of the system- or order-founding actors and the supersession of the arena as constituted within its preexisting scope and boundaries. So long as the typical polity is a species of state and the consequent order partakes of the attributes of a state system, the supersession will entail most prominently differences in size. When the succeeding actor or arena is more potent or bigger in scale and size than the antecedent entity, the transition relates to the predecessor as a matter of evolutionary process rather than mere sequence when the successor is operationally immanent in the predecessor because the supersession and its beneficiaries originate in contests over or with the demoted or displaced entities. As part of the same process, the superseded smaller (micro-) actors or arena commonly survive or even prevail normatively in the bigger (macro-) ones through the mainly procedural values or institutions transferred one way or another to the succeeding actors or arena. Such transfers constitute another, less immediately conspicuous though lastingly and cumulatively more significant, link between interaction and succession and between continuity and change than is the formative contest of the bigger actors over the smaller arena viewed in isolation from the cultural diffusion.

Alternations in sizes—e.g., between Hellenic and Hellenistic, Italian and Italianate European systems—extend over time differences in political cultures and behavior. These are manifest when supersession entails either suppression of an autonomous state system or only the sublimation of the power drives that define it. Different degrees of suppression are implicit in a one-actor dominance ranging from a "mere" hegemonial alliance to a coercive empire. Both are apt to combine pluralist with statist features while replacing countervailance with control as the guiding principle of order and practice of policy. Suppression exceeds, but will often succeed to, a mere sublimation of the conflictually manifested power drives that will ideally set a state system on the road toward confederative associations or community-type institutionalization. Institutionalized community retains at its best the residues of the ethically normative features that distinguish statism, whereas an empire actually introduces that latter's operationally disciplinary features into pluralism. Pluralism's institutionalization represents the opposite end of a developmental trajectory from developmental arrest when it is incurred by primitive pluralism on the road to state formation. Much as the sublimation of power drives is liable to degeneration into a not only post-statist but radically order-resistant situation, an amorphously heterogeneous structure of primitive-to-chaotic pluralism will invite empire-type consolidation more often and more typically.

Thus preliminarily identified and differentiated proto- and metasystemic polities precede and follow, as their inversely shaped deviations, the structural and behavioral norms that comprise but are not coterminous with the ethically normative attributes of statehood. The preparatory format is capable of evolution if not also pregnant with further development by reason of the intrinsic impermanence and inner incoherence of primitive pluralism's heterogeneous constituents. The progressivist bias peculiar to the community type of post-norm is differently inhospitable to the rationally implemented self-help requisites that define the behavioral and shape the structural norm represented by the territorial state. Since this norm entails perfect congruence between available means and envisaged ends with respect to behavior, deviations from it necessarily imply the

prevalence of ends over means in the pre-norm and of means over politically feasible objectives in the post-norm phase. These asymmetries corre-
spond with the predominance of material scarcities and surplus of driving
energy in the former and the opposite ratio of material to psychological
surplus and scarcity in the latter deviation. Similar reversals apply to
structure when pre-norm entails fragmentation relative to the norm-rep-
resenting actor or arena (a consolidated unit of a contemporaneously optimally manageable size) and post-norm the substantial enlargement of
either into regional community or empire.

The interrelated norms converge and will be compounded in a behavioral and structural composite whenever there is a direct, objectively given
and subjectively perceived, connection between two principal general objectives of policies and issues of politics: one is the performance-based
and -reflecting standing or status of the state-like or pluralist polity, another the material subsistence of its wards, be it citizens or subjects. This
connection translates into minimum legitimacy when it is realized and
fosters strategic rationality when aimed at. It is at its closest in, and the
compound norm is exemplified by, a state system at its evolutionary climax and operational optimum while the deviations are diversely societal
and pluralist.

Viewing the proto- and metasystemic deviations with respect to structures as corresponding grosso modo to the behaviorally defined pre- and
post-norm, is not a matter of formal symmetry only or primarily. Doing
so conveys the real connection between the alternative structures and the
predispositions and attitudes of the parties to such structures, translating
into behavioral tendencies. Strategic rationality encouraged by a firm
structure is distinct from both its approximation in reflexively instinctual
responses characteristic of primitive pluralism and from this particular
rationality's only residual survival if not complete submersion in its utilitarian variety within, and largely between, institutionalized communities
and empires. An alternative mindset is directed more to prosperity than
power in communities and to stability than security in empires, the former being centered on an overmature political culture and the latter on
centralized coercion in the last resort.

The norm-defining dynamic centered on the balance of power permeates the transitions between both the small-sized micro- and bigger-sized
macro-actors and arenas and the contrary, antecedent and posterior, deviations from the structural and behavioral norms. This same dynamic is
even more directly, and consciously, involved in the sociopolitical and the
functionally instrumental revolutions. Both kinds of upheavals do more
than mediate the evolutionary sequences when they transform them into
a process by virtue of drives informed by two basic purposes of either a
social class or state-like actor. The primary concern being to adapt to

threatening alterations of any kind for the sake of continued existence, the derivative object is to succeed in prominence to a materially or functionally weakened incumbent. The manner of implementing the consequent balance of power dynamic is influenced by, and the dynamic itself activates, both kinds of revolutions. Successive functional revolutions in the military, economic, and administrative or organizational instruments associate with pressures and inducements implicit in the most primitively structured an arena in instigating the crystallization of actors even before a progressively rationalized balancing had involved them in systematic relations with other parties. As part of the same dynamic, the sociopolitical revolutions revolve around the discovery, diffusion, and counter-innovative neutralization of functional-instrumental innovations, although less directly and consciously than around interactor succession compounding a social class's or power's ascension, stalemating, and dispossession.

The role of balance-of-power dynamic in the two kinds of revolutions is most conspicuously related to evolution when they converge with a major war as either incentives to its initiation (by way of a party's functional innovation) or consequences of the war's result in the defeat of one party (due to sociopolitical revolution). An intermittently climactic grand political revolution combines inter- and intra-actor upheavals in the radicalization-restoration pattern of any revolution and the antagonization-appeasement process associated with the war phenomenon or only potential of a war-threatening contention. This combination materializes in routine transactions that, implemented through intergroup coalitions and interstate alliances, conceal behind conspicuous precipitants and operationally proximate determinants the ultimately decisive causal impact of transactions-transcending structural or organic givens—the aforementioned schisms, organic rise-decline fluctuations, and spontaneously expansive-to-exuberant, conservatively preservationist, and compulsively reexpansionist foreign (or, for social classes, domestic) policy postures anterior to final withdrawal from active self-assertion. All these givens are diversely conducive to the war- and revolution-breeding disparities and disjunctions: the revolution-related ones between a class's claimed or actually occupied status and its socially requisite function in war or peace, or the war-engendering ones between the role and status and disposable resource of state-like actors, bridged in either case more or less effectively by the risks a resource- or function-deficient actor is prepared to run and able to turn to its advantage.

Concretizing the complexities of interactional-evolutionary world politics' unity with world history

Viewing the integration of the evolutionary into the interactional dynamic in terms of analytically separate but actually intersecting dimensions of time and space is the conceptually basic way and preliminary step. This perspective will be concretized somewhat when such imbrications are seen as constituting a particular slice of actuality that can be identified in terms of a sufficiently distinctive and recurrent salient feature to be compared and contrasted with other slices. Doing so with respect to an analytically manageable representation of actuality will assist in disentangling the interlock between motor- and mechanism-representing impellents and manifestations of progression within evolution's momentary matrix. A conceptual category that completes a speculative representation of complexity, this matrix can more than any other be grasped only intuitively and be empirically unraveled only at a cost to a more complete apprehension of reality.

The salient feature identifying a slice of actuality is at its simplest, quantitatively structural level, subject to an expanding roster of modifying qualifiers. Thus, moving up or down from unipolar to a two- and three- to a five-power structure, the included modifiers can (and for verisimilitude must) comprise next to the features pertaining to the several schisms the other transcendental categories or attributes. By the same token, the ideal-typical features defining the behavioral and structural norms differentiate state systems that actually approximated them (e.g., mid-eighteenth century European and mid-twentieth century only quasi-global) from anomalously pathological ones (interwar European and, differently, post-Cold War quasi-state system). Or, with increasing difficulty for analysis, reflecting rising complexity and declining determinateness of the environmental setting, the features coalescing in a distinct slice can be not so much structural and strategic and, therefore, inter-subjectively operational, as functional and processual and objectively therefore even more impersonal. A recurrent slice of this kind will compound pragmatically significant economic transformations (e.g., inflationary or deflationary monetary revolutions) and normatively creedal (religious or socio-ideological) convulsions. At its beginning, the crisis may well be more independent from the setting defined by the number and size of the poles of power than from the state of health of the affected (declining or rising, continental and maritime) polities. However, the turmoil's distinctive features will eventually be subject to absorption and the disaggregated factors of power to reaggregation in response to compulsions emanating from a reconstituted polar setting. The latter's eventual recovery of a conventional shape will entail a reassertion of the pragmatizing effect of routines on the creedal component of the crisis and of the real-politicizing effect on the economic constituent.

Simplifying the complex interactional-evolutionary imbrications by confining them within a slice or specific composite permits exposing the basic premise of the speculative approach to a reality check: the recurrence over time of comparable configurations subject to identifiable mutations. Both recur within finite ranges of variation while each is subject to the developmentally significant difference between completed transformation and an unconsummated tendency, one that points toward the change in principle or potentiality but is insufficient to effectuate it in practice and actuality. Identifiable mutations comprise multiplication and reduction of the number of actors in slices defined by polarities, insofar as two-power interactions automatically engender additional and multipower ones erode and may not replace extant parties. Slices differentiated in terms of creedal features will be dominant at the beginnings of or transitions between evolutionary phases or structural reconfigurations. They will register a tendency to pragmatization just as slices exhibiting the causal primacy of economic factors will experience its disappearance when a temporary lull in real-politically defined conflicts has passed in part as a result of the economic turmoil. Likewise typical and essentially predictable is the tendency of a state system to generate discrepancies that are only concentrated in the disjunction between assumed role and available resource of major actors, responsible for the pathological conditions of a state system. The remedial tendency is to subsequently correct the discrepancies by means of the course and outcome of the warlike or socio-revolutionary convulsions the disjunction has caused.

The most comprehensive object of mutation and subject of alternations is the overall environment or type of order that not only overtops but also conditions all the other possible particular slices of agenda in world politics. The difference between the two environmental settings or frameworks of action unevenly determinate in structure and therefore determining of action (the multi-member statist plural and the pluralist societal) is not absolute. It is attenuated insofar as the pluralist order satisfies two requisites. First, it must be essentially political in that it is shaped by the concern with power on the part of parties to it, however distinguished they may be otherwise from states. They will differ insofar as they are insufficiently homogeneous in type, organizationally unitary and normatively unified internally, and firmly based or contiguous territorially to project their capabilities abroad into contention over sufficiently well defined and uniformly shared stakes to constitute a system—one imbued with even if not reducible to immaterial spirit expressed internally in ethos and externally in concern with status. Such nonstate polities occupy instead a shifting point along a spectrum of variably ordered coexistence exhibiting variable degrees of patterned interaction and essential predictability of structure-reflecting actions as they advance to or recede from the statist norm. The other requisite of an attenuated contrast is that such an order exhibits the potential to evolve toward either an interstate system or, at least, be institutionalized within a community or empire approximating the normatively disciplining attributes of statism and precluding the lapse into chaos as a merely possible starting point of development toward the more accomplished framework. Consequently, the two typological opposites are also complementary developmental constructs marking diverse stages of evolution with respect to an ideal-typical norm. The difference between them is resolved to the extent that the specific operational dynamism among parties to a state system (a matter of a particular way of doing enshrined in actor strategies) connects with the developmental dynamism toward the statist norm latent in parties to the pluralist framework. The latter will be meanwhile defined by multiple foci or stakes of interaction and overlapping circles of association open to parties to such an order (a matter of alternative forms or states of being in relation to the structure of the arena).

Medieval pluralism and modern statism differ radically while the multipolar interstate system in the eighteenth century and bipolar one in the twentieth century differ only relatively. Related contrasts in forms of behavior and consequent interactions responsive to the different structures are codified in unequally specific conventions or rules. Comparing and contrasting the responses and the rules will suggest nothing more far-reaching than behavioral tendencies, implementing subjective propensities of the actors. Specifying the particulars of the latter's relationship with the conditioning structural setting will refine the understanding of political dynamics by clarifying intersubjective tendencies that inform objective or aggregate processes—i.e., upgrade individual propensities and subjective tendencies to processual ones. Either kind of these two kinds of tendencies constitutes only an evolutionary potential, one that at the very best substantiates the presumption of evolution as a necessary incident to interaction. It will require a sequence of discernible alterations in structure and related behavior within a particular space and over a bounded period of time to disclose the fact of evolution and its pattern for one such area, in terms of a state system and the alternative framework of action. Phrased differently, identifying the sequence will confirm the presumption of evolution, inferred from the tendencies, as an actual event with a plausible pattern (e.g., one prior and posterior to a behavioral or structural norm), to be refined and confirmed by recurrence in situations comparable in terms of structure, evolutionary stage, and principal strategies or strategic options.

When a thus identified pattern recurs in different time and space settings (e.g., in the modern Italian after the antique Greek state system) and does so in ways that combine parallels in the overall pattern with comparability of particular stages that make up the pattern, the result is a plausible presumption of repetitive evolutionary trends that meaningfully aggregate particular, subjectively behavioral and objectively processual, tendencies. However, it will require a third recurrence (in the European state system) to rule out the possibility of only accidental similarity and confirm the presumption as to the developmental trends. Converting a plausible presumption into a positive proposition about state systems comes close to a theory of evolution as a continuous process susceptible of both generalization and particularization in degrees of rationalization and institutional elaboration or differentiation of basic functions, constitutive of progression either within individual or between only successive or also operationally interlocking state systems. Moreover, inasmuch as the evolution is closely linked to the balance of power and this form of interaction is implemented through alliances, the implied convergence and interdependence are confirmed rather than confounded by critical distinctions. Thus, whereas a subjectively behavioral tendency is to seek association with another subject against a threat implicit in a structure of power, the related objectively processual tendency is for such alliances to dissipate with the threat's disappearance. And the two interlocking tendencies ascend over time to the evolutionary trend for offensive alliances to yield to preclusively defensive ones and alliances to community-like leagues or other form of association as a state system evolves into its meta-stage.

Two significant differences apply in this connection. One is that between the number of repetitions and the degree of their identity, because essentially identical entities can recur over time with actual but inessential differences. For instance, the chaotic-or-institutionalized two-faceted pluralist cum quasi-statist because either proto- or post-statist order can occur in antiquity, the European Middle Ages, and in the post-Cold War present; or the fifteenth-century Italian and the eighteenth to mid-twentieth century European interstatist system can anticipate the late-twentieth century Middle Eastern one. Such recurrences, or rebirths, demonstrate continuity because of essential similarity, but also evolutionary progression because of actual modifications: thus, for primitive and advanced pluralisms, the relative primacy and extent of sway and scope of creedal-mythical and material-pragmatic preoccupations, and for statist micro-systems, the degree of their autonomy relative to coexistent or only latent macro-systems and, therefore, ready and unobstructed recourse to war.

The other difference concerns the direction of the temporal perspective. When the perspective is reversed from one connecting past to present to one extending the present to the future, the structure-related behavioral and processual tendencies that have been seen as constituting only an evolutionary potential and thus a presumption of evolution become the basis for similarly conditional and contingent prevision, in the form of mere projective extrapolation from present into the future. Far from constituting specific prediction of either an event or its timing, a projection yields

only a priori presumptions as to impending structures and broad guide-
lines for continuing to apply the strategic rationality previously responsible for transmuting wide ranges of possible behavior into discernible
tendencies variably responsive or unresponsive to a given structure. A
higher form of anticipation and forethought than projection will require
combining strategic rationality with historical intelligence that supplements the awareness of particular (subjective and objective) tendencies
with the sense of evolutionary trends and particular stages of development of both actors and arenas, which aggregate the tendencies in sequentially ordered patterns of an already transpired and presumptively
continuing progression. Only thus can a grossly and often misleadingly
predictive projection be supplemented with a prescription of strategy
that, synthesizing geohistoricist correctives to primitive balance-of-power
pragmatism or chaos-prone pluralism, upgrades a response to an existing
with the production of an alternative environment that is more determinate or more closely in line with previously transpired evolution.

Projection from structures and structure-related tendencies is but a
weak alternative to and basis for prediction of particular events, apt to
consummate tendencies or at least corroborate their existence. However,
dialectically sophisticated (cyclical) projection forms an indispensable, albeit only partial, empirical basis for prescription if the latter is to possess
an empirical basis for the normative purpose of implementing the intent
of prophecy to substitute future promise for present predicament and
timely deliverance for impending doom. A structurally indeterminate environment, typified by a pluralist or mixed statist-pluralist format, makes
even projections difficult. It is this difficulty that intermittently transfers
the primary determining role to strategies inspired by a mere vision of
the framework of action most apt to reestablish a measure of predictability that, combined with a more definite structure, will constitute the essentials of both procedural and substantive order.

Interrelating world history with world politics in both backward- and
forward-looking perspectives has two basic requisites. The wide range of
historical events must be reduced to features that, while transcending particular real political transactions because they escape control by any one
individual actor, do nonetheless meaningfully relate to such transactions
objectively and can in principle be integrated into actors' policy-related
perceptions. This criterion is fulfilled not only by the features that connect the organic rise/decline side of interactions with particular policies
(via the more fundamental foreign policy postures) and the capabilities of
actors with their dispositions (via the various schisms and variably leading
or representative types of actors). The criterion of pertinence will also be
met by not only specifically political but also broader cultures insofar as
the latter, in their distinctive persona as civilizations, represent distill-

ations of power political processes or mirror the standing of component polities within structures and hierarchies of power. That is to say, the cultures or civilizations must do more than concentrate a body of ideas and norms that, as part of the intellectual history of mankind, follow independent laws of their gestation and interconnections only remotely related to real political processes and situations when not posing as such processes' prime determinant in their own right.

The other requisite—or the same requisite stated conversely—is that the amorphous mass of historical data is integrated into evolution in a way that corresponds to its character as a definite process that implies propellents, procedures, and patterns but lacks substantive contents or particulars. Outside such sociological generalities as functional differentiation or biosociological analogies of growth and decay, history alone can supply substantive contents to evolution and substantiate its relation to politics. But it will do so on condition that the historical record is addressed both selectively and systematically with this object in mind. History will, in such a case, provide the means for supplementing evolution with an intimation of its direction and ideal end. Direction is implicit in the concept of qualitatively neutral progression capable of a propensity, as distinct from progress, that is suggested inter alia by tentative instrumental alterations and operational accommodations corresponding to a more fundamental real change. A hypothetical goal is implicit in the postulate of meaning, one to become apparent only progressively through actual developments and be fully revealed, if ever, only retrospectively at history's end or from a transhistorical vantage point.

Articulating world politics for easy fit into world history (Part I) and integrating world history into thus construed world politics and individual policies (Part II) covers the same ground from two complementary perspectives or only emphases in a speculative joining of the dynamic of one in space to the movement in time defining the other (Part III). This joining implies a distinctive system of thought devoted to eliciting a vision rather than producing a description passing for analysis or pretending to the status of theory. For thinking world politics through world history to be systematic and the resulting thought to constitute a system, both the process and the product must center on a unifying concept just as a state system does or must on a unifying stake: that of equilibrium in its dual, countervailing and adaptative, application. In applying the concept, its representation expands from a hard core of instincts and reflexes representing human nature at its most basic and immutable to extrapolations into strategically progressively rationalized and historically sophisticated behavior. Conducive from the outset to real politically significant configurations of structures reflecting capabilities and strategies devoted to their management on one level, thus upgraded instincts (and amplified human nature) rise to value-institutional sublimations thereof on another level, embodied in cultural artifacts. Such artifacts raise the product of the basic activity above its survival-related original function and immediate significance to a point sufficient to realize the procreative potential of the tension between primitive and trivial actualities and transcendent and tragic reality—a tension that defines and shapes world politics and history alike while confronting both with the dilemma of conspicuous changes coexisting with fundamental continuities.

Currently, basic real change, in favor of the organic over the operational dimension, coincides perfectly with the ascendancy of internal over external functions of government. But it also translates into the problematic enhancement of the state as a machinery to the detriment of its mystique, debased in its quality as substance-transcending spirit. Consequently affected is the traditional connection between the role and status of a state and society's access to material sustenance, as well as the link between prestige as the equally intangible supplement to material capability and physical security. Eroding thus the immaterial aura of the inner core of actual capacity does more than weaken a power's temporary shield against the effects of transient debility: it creates a normative vacuum to be filled by an alternative subject of the value of corporate autonomy that constitutes a polity into a higher-than-pragmatically founded object of loyalty and the wider-than-operational incumbent of cultural identity and political independence.

One of two simultaneously convergent movements associates political economy ever more intimately with real politics, while the other channels cycles within and between statist and pluralist formats toward the latest expansion from smaller into larger, more than ever secular but normatively newly conspicuous, incumbents of socially valuable autonomy. The two movements' net result entails more than a mutation from force-based conflict into a values-centered "mere" dialectic within the compass of evolutionary progression. It represents the possibility of qualitative progress as a realistic alternative to the utopia of inherently anti-conflictual cooperative organization, one superseding real politics and its conflict-centered inner economy completely with support from societal dispositions bred by the material conditions of an economy that is only nominally "political." As a matter of fact, a significant shift from mere progression toward actual progress remains contingent on developments within both the nature and the culture of world politics. In regard to power/interest-related nature, and its link to specifically political culture formalized in major-power status, the issue is how much and for how long the status-associated drive for a hegemonic or only preeminent role will continue to be optionally, or under environmental pressures necessarily, associated with material prosperity, translating into political stability and regime legitimacy either generally or in a particular region? In regard primarily to values coalescing in a wider-than-political culture, the related question is whether critically significant corporate autonomy can or will be transferred—and perceived as validly extended—from a nation-centered state to a regionally expanded civilization as the site of spirit best qualified to counteract the growing attractions and deepening pitfalls of societal materialism.

At issue is a middle ground between two historically experienced extremes: the extinction of individuality and a radical erosion of community—the former within an all-absorbing polity ranging from ritualized kinship groups through antique polis to the modern totalitarian state, the latter through the subversion of normatively potent collectivity by unchecked individualism extending from heroic self-affirmation in chaotic-barbarian pluralism to hedonistic self-indulgence in institutionalized societal pluralism. Were a sense of regionally defined and shared civilization to allow equally for the psychic urges and normative imperatives of both individuality and commonality, it would constitute a provisionally "natural" cultural framework for implementing the real changes transpiring in world politics. Translating this cultural optimum into operative policy norms militates against policy-related counterparts to the values-related extremes of unchecked individualism and collectivism. Ruling out appeals to an extra-civilizational power against culturally cognate polities on behalf of narrowly national power or individual rights and freedoms, a balanced policy stand is equally contrary to no less narrowly self-regarding denials of such a power's special concern with and responsibility for regional stability as present preconditions of eventual community. Connecting both imperatives and related interdicts means implementing the requisites of an informal concert of powers within an appropriately modified expansion-constraining balance of power. And it means achieving this in the global interest of regional and eventually inter-regional orders evolving along the developmentally tested spectrum from the dynamic of power-balancing through hierarchically structured spheres of great-power influence to functionally aggregated-to-institutionally integrated community.

In contemporary actuality, the perhaps only temporary subsidence of West-centered triangular land-sea power conflicts works in favor of their potentially moderated East-centered inversion, centered on the tripartite Sino-Russian-German continental heartland and extending to the Pacific basin in the maritime-mercantile sphere. Even as a mere possibility, this prospect calls for synthesizing the diverse policy options, corresponding to the wider range of alternative futures, within a strategy that reflects the realistically plausible—and, on balance, optimum conceivable—evolutionary transformation.

One future, characterized by the romantically realist preoccupation with residually surviving but spatially migrating normative statism, implies a policy that reverses this particular statism's decline in the West and constrains its resurgence in the East. A corresponding adjustment would retard the rush from already disempowered into an increasingly disempowering communitarian pluralism in the West, so as to gain time and strategic space for managing the eastward extension of the ongoing race between receding old-style hegemonicism and advancing new-style hedonism over the longer run. This perspective affects immediate policy attitudes toward a Euro-Atlantic community generally and NATO specifically with an eye on incidental effects of alternative approaches on the relationship of forces between Russia and China and the two Eurasian heartland powers' cultural- or also real-political predispositions. In the progressivist-realist vision of the future, which prioritizes formal organization of collective security, the prime concern is for a viable balance of regional and global frameworks. It affects such contemporary issues as the Middle Eastern and North or South Asian balances of power and their activation in local wars such as the Persian Gulf War or wider conflicts. It suggests a policy that would no more rush into penalizing "aggression" by lesser powers for ostensibly formal-legal or immediately salient material reasons than it would allow cultural conceit of a major power to translate into unbounded real political license. Instead, policy would see merit in only policing, but then as forcefully as necessary, the outer limits of the actual or suspected "hegemonial" aspirant's historically valid-to-indispensable role in the progressive articulation of a regional and interregional global order stabilized indigenously by a competitively internalized sense of achievable gains and tolerable costs and risks. A strategy that synthesized these and alternative policy options would plausibly pursue the fusion of statist and communitarian values in developmentally differentiated regional structures and operational norms, capable of progressive convergence under the impetus of an inter-civilizationally shaped dialectic with both differentiating and mutually propitiating purposes and effects. At the present juncture, such a strategy comes closest to living up to an all-encompassing requisite of combining strategic rationality with historical intelligence in that it integrates a historically evolving reality into a correspondingly historicized traditional realism.

To encompass such complexities while continuing to address their core, traditional realism has had to be expanded toward an updated reality's twin attributes of historicity and normativity. Realism becomes explicitly and distinctively normative in both its romantic and progressivist modes when the former stresses emotively impacting values such as statist mystique or civilizational autonomy and the latter allows for procedurally progressive institutional or juridical norms. Neither enhancement of realism would be operationally meaningful—i.e., be conventionally realistic—rather than utopian, or would reflect the existential power side equally with the normative facet of the power-normative essence of world politics, were it not for its operational basis in the more fully developed idea and apprehended practical relevance of evolution, expressing historicity, and revised concept of expansion, affecting strategic rationality. Both modify significantly the central concept of equilibrium: in terms of adaptation in regard to evolution, and assimilation in regard to acts and agents of expansion, the two aspects converging in a balance of power that integrates the change from the primacy of the operational to that of the organic factor in mature world politics. Aggregating these modifications in corresponding notions of reality (quasi-ontology) and rationality (quasi-epistemology of cognitive realism wedded to processual decomposition of speculatively construed real phenomena within a strategic rationality incorporating historical intelligence) results in a realism that reflects and accommodates real change while preserving fundamental continuity as the precondition of any and all possible meaning of world politics/history and an avenue to more than superficial understanding.

List of Author's Works
and Abbreviations

ATW   *Alliances and the Third World* (Baltimore: The Johns Hopkins University Press, 1968).

AW   "Arnold Wolfers as Theorist and Policy Analyst: Remembrance and Reappraisal," in *Discord and Collaboration in a New Europe: Essays in Honor of Arnold Wolfers*, ed. Douglas T. Stuart and Stephen F. Szabo (Washington, D.C.: The Johns Hopkins Foreign Policy Institute, 1994).

AW2   "The Third World," in *America & the World: From Truman Doctrine to Vietnam*, ed. Robert E. Osgood et al. (Baltimore: The Johns Hopkins University Press, 1970).

BK   *Beyond Kissinger: Ways of Conservative Statecraft* (Baltimore: The Johns Hopkins University Press, 1970).

CE   *Career of Empire: America and Imperial Expansion over Land and Sea* (Baltimore: The Johns Hopkins University Press, 1978).

EA   *Europe Ascendant: The International Politics of Unification* (Baltimore: The Johns Hopkins University Press, 1964).

FD   *Fallen Dominions, Reviving Powers: Germany, the Slavs, and Europe's Unfinished Agenda* (Washington, D.C.: The Johns Hopkins Foreign Policy Institute, 1990).

IA   *Imperial America: The International Politics of Primacy* (Baltimore: The Johns Hopkins University Press, 1967).

IE   *International Equilibrium: A Theoretical Essay on the Politics and Organization of Security* (Cambridge: Harvard University Press, 1957).

MvM   "Morgenthau vs. Machiavelli," in *Truth and Tragedy: A Tribute to Hans Morgenthau*, ed. Kenneth Thompson and Robert J. Myers (Washington, D.C.: New Republic Book Co., 1977).

NIA   *Nations in Alliance: The Limits of Interdependence* (Baltimore: The Johns Hopkins University Press, 1962).

NS   *New Statecraft: Foreign Aid in American Foreign Policy* (Chicago: The University of Chicago Press, 1960).

QE   *Quest for Equilibrium: America & the Balance of Power on Land & Sea* (Baltimore: The Johns Hopkins University Press, 1977).

RE   "The Third World: Regional Systems and Global Order," in *Retreat from Empire?: The First Nixon Administration*, ed. Robert E. Osgood et al. (Baltimore: The Johns Hopkins University Press, 1973).

RP   *The Restoration of Politics: Interrogating History about a Civilization in Crisis* (Lanham, Md.: Rowman & Littlefield, 1996).

RR   *Return to the Heartland & Rebirth of the Old Order: Reconceptualizing the*

Environment of Strategies for East-Central Europe & Beyond (Washington, D.C.: The Johns Hopkins Foreign Policy Institute, 1994).

RRA   *Russia and the Road to Appeasement: Cycles of East-West Conflict in War & Peace* (Baltimore: The Johns Hopkins Press University, 1982).

RUSR *Rethinking US-Soviet Relations* (Oxford, U.K.: Basil Blackwell, 1987).

RWO   *Russia & World Order: Strategic Choices & the Laws of Power in History* (Baltimore: The Johns Hopkins Press University, 1980).

SIE   *States in Evolution: Changing Societies and Traditional Systems in World Politics* (Baltimore: The Johns Hopkins University Press, 1973).

SR   "The Heroic Decade and After: International Relations as Events, Discipline, and Profession," *SAIS Review*, Summer 1966.

WO   *War and Order: Reflections on Vietnam and History* (Baltimore: The Johns Hopkins University Press, 1968).

WP   *The Ways of Power: Pattern and Meaning in World Politics* (Oxford, U.K.: Basil Blackwell, 1990).

WPJ   "Continuity and Change in International Systems," *World Politics*, October 1963.

Index

actors: factoral disaggregation of, 232, 235; formation of, 113, 128, 134–36, 148–49, 185, 194, 200–203; relation to arena of, 44–45, 86, 113–15, 162, 200–201, 204; representative legitimacy of, 155–56; 232; socialization of, 178; successively dominant types of, 119–20, 133, 202–4, 221, 237; typological triad of, 262–64. *See also* the state; structure

adaptation: as condition of continuity, 162; as evolutionary facet of equilibrium, 111–12, 122, 168, 276–77

alliances and alignments: cohesion and disruptive of, 60, 183; dynamics and alterations of, 79, 287; and foreign policy postures, 142–43; as format of regional organization, 182–83; and incidence of wars, 62–66, 69; and politics of economic assistance, 77–79; relation to balance of power of, 58–61, 213; relation to regional community of, 183. *See also* balance of power

anarchy: vs. chaos, 43, 166, 169, 232; contradiction implicit in, 57; vs. essential order, 45, 205; formal vs. actual, 43; relation to individual freedom of, 156. *See also* hierarchy

antagonization. *See* war

appeasement: as alternative to antagonization, 63–64, 151–52, 157, 272; and autonomous war-peace cycles, 122; and meaning of world politics, 160, 244; modes and modalities of, 68–70, 124, 169–70, 244, 248–49, 259–60, 268–70; as object of foreign policy, 81, 108, 157, 270; is, peace as absolute value, 157; and tragic poetics, 225

arena. *See* actors; structure

autonomy, corporate: and extra-systemic appeals, 158, 160–61, 234, 240–41, 243, 244–45, 259–60, 268; as value relative to individual freedom, 156, 160–61, 219, 242, 267

balance of power: actual operation of, 51–52, 54, 156–57; and catalytic vs. cathartic conflicts, 123–25, 127; common misunderstanding of, 50–51, 56, 57, 59; evolution of, 83–84, 131–32, 146, 172; and foreign policy postures, 140–42; functional disaggregation of, 20, 55–56, 178; and idealized balancer, 51, 58, 184–85, 242; institutionalized manifestations of, 52–54; needed expansion of scope of, 82, 153–55, 159, 242, 256, 271–72; as only practical theory of world politics, 152–53, 139; and political physics, 217–23; relation to expansion of, 96–97, 99–101, 106, 108; relation to international order

201–2; relation to system-founding actors in effect on evolution of, 32–33, 114, 118, 124, 133, 135, 138–40, 141; and terminal crisis of system, 162. *See also* schisms, and kinds of (land vs. sea powers); schisms, relation to empire of; schisms, relation to particular conflict wars of; schisms, relation to political economy; schisms, West-East (North-South) vs. continental maritime

meaning, of world politics-and-history: and esthetic dimension of statecraft, 226; levels of, 159–60, 189, 266–67, 269–70; vs. momentum of evolution and interaction, 158–59, 227, 230, 243–44; relation to diplomatic machinations of, 223; relation to eschatology (vs. epistemology) of, 230, 238, 243–44, 266; as subject of prophecy, 163, 188–89, 237

models (visions) of politics: identification of, 27; recurrences of, 168, 174–75, 185–87; relation to political economy and geometry of, 75–76, 146, 195, 207; relation to types of order of, 206–7

Morgenthau, Hans J.: realism of, compared with Arnold Wolfers's, 6

neo-medievalism: current state of, 146, 168, 174–75, 186, 192, 194–95; forms of, 17

neo-realism. *See* realism

order, international or world: alternative formats and frameworks of, 177, 206, 281; vs. balance of power, 177, 178; conditions and definition of, 177–78, 205; and empires, 175–77, 281; relation to global international organization of, 178–80; relation to (normative vs. existential) environment of, 205–7, 278, 288. *See also* international organiza-

tion; regional order and organization

pluralism, societal: and causal determinants, 77–78, 87–88; and foreign policy posture, 83–84; and historicist materialism, 18, 131, 242; implications for real politics vs. political economy of, 73, 75–76, 194–95; and interstate system, 1, 27, 35, 120, 128–30, 146–48, 243, 285–86; kinds of, 1, 16, 18, 27, 192; modification of political physics by, 222; problematic present rebirth of, 150, 166; vs. statism, 16–17, 149–163, 194–95; untidy development of, 167–69, 184. *See also* society

political economy: core dilemmas of, 18, 24, 70, 208–10, 212–13, 243; evolutionary facet of, 121–22, 125; interdetermination vs. varieties of causation in, 24, 71–90, 200, 207, 227; and organic vs. operational dimensions, 71–72, 76, 81, 85, 157, 207–8; and politics of economic assistance; 77–80; relation to political geometry of, 17, 75–76; relation to real politics of, 70–71, 75, 85, 208–9, 213–14; specific to alliances, 78–80; variably "political," 19, 207–8. *See also* causation; economic factor

political geometry: as function of radical change, 17, 195, 235; linear vs. circular, 19, 27, 75–76, 207

political physics: as element of "science" in world politics, 227; and fact-value dilemmas, 244; kinds of and their interrelation, 218, 221, 223–34, 238; laws of, 219–220; manifestations in history of, 220–21, 243; and political economy, 219; relation to balance-of-power interaction and evolution of, 217, 218–23

power: alternative poles of, 36–37; as central concept of realism, 50, 149, 217, 271; disaggregation vs. aggregation of, 231–33, 246, 271; gravitation of, 220–21, 228; and "national interest," 260, 271; values- vs. interest-centered features of, 17–18, 41, 157–58, 159–61

power-normative duality and essence: as defining feature of political reality and dynamic; 16, 153, 217; and fact-value paradoxes, 241, 242, 243, 244; manifestations and deformations of, 17, 200; relation to ethical and esthetic value component of statecraft of, 225–28, 242, 245; relation to inner economy of real politics of, 217, 224; relation to power/interest-related facts of, 18, 157, 159–61, 244, 266; synthesis-resistant expressions of, 240; as ultimate source of order, 205. *See also* system of thought

prediction. *See* projection

progression: conflict-centered mechanism of, 110–11, 113, 118, 122–25, 234, 274; crises-centered motor of, 110, 113–14, 116–22, 234, 274; cyclical pattern of, 112, 125, 132–33, 167, 276; inter-determinative circularity of, 125, 161; manifestations of, 112, 113, 123, 125–33, 274; matrix of, 112, 113, 141–44, 279–80; as past-present-future chain of structures and events, 167–80, 182, 189, 230–38, 257–59, 261, 288–89; vs. progress, 24, 25, 74, 109, 114, 118, 143, 165, 168, 239, 248–49, 255, 269–70, 289; and regional-global interplays, 180–84, 185; and regression, 168, 187, 192. *See also* evolution

projection: as approach to understanding, 145–46, 159, 163, 167–95, 229–38, 253, 254, 256–57, 258–59, 287–88; and hypothetical futures, 163, 167–95, 228–38, 258–66; kinds of, 163, 164–65, 257; and policy prescription, 151–52, 163–64, 167, 168, 237; vs. prediction, 151–52, 163–65,

174, 287–88; and prophecy, 151–52, 159, 163, 164–65, 174, 188–89, 228–29, 236–38; relation to meaning of world politics-history, 159, 189

prophecy. *See* projection

quasi-epistemology. *See* reality
quasi-eschatology. *See* meaning; projection
quasi-ontology. *See* reality; projection

rationality, strategic: concern with security vs. stability of, 194, 282; deterioration of, 143; development of, 125–26; ideal-typical norm of, 162; and intuition vs. informations, 250; kinds of, 34, 153; vs. reasonableness, 225; vs. utilitarian calculations, 193–94, 282. *See also* historical intelligence

real politics: ethical vs. esthetic dimension of, 225–28; evolution of, 23, 130, 131; hypothetical effect of world economy on, 246; institutionalization of, 179–80, 181; internal economy of, 208, 217–25; vs. "new" international politics, 74, 192; and philosophy of history, 157, 160; pragmatization of ideological manifestations of, 168–70; relation to political economy of, 22, 70–71, 75, 208–9, 212, 214; sublimation vs. materialization of, 193–94, 194–95, 237; values-related modification of, 243, 274

realism, traditional: characteristics and applications of, 4, 5–6, 7, 149, 152, 240, 271; constriction in neo-realism of, 5–6, 8, 149–50, 152, 160, 210, 239; critiques of and alternatives to, 5–9, 279; vs. "hellenistic" (U.S.) concretism, 190–91; and historicism, 7, 109, 151, 173–74, 190, 252, 272; vs. idealism or utopianism, 5, 7, 18, 75, 126, 165, 180, 204–5, 223, 278; and liberal and conservative social philosophies, 6, 56, 74–75, 190–

tionary dynamic of, 128–33, 148–
49, 162, 204, 214, 230–33, 285–87;
evolutionary links between kinds
and sizes of, 127–38, 133, 143–44,
146–47, 158, 163, 234, 242, 280–81;
vs. international society, 43; paradoxes and pathology of, 241–43,
242–43, 244; passing (temporal and
spatial) of, 1, 25–26, 45, 162, 174,
175, 192, 229; relation to pluralism
of, 1, 27, 35, 120, 129, 204. *See also*
statism
system of thought: as alternative to
"scientific" theory, 3–4, 5, 10, 151,
191, 239; as anti-theory, 161, 225–
26, 289; constituents of, 10–11, 15,
21–22, 33, 34–35, 151, 156, 158, 199,
256–57, 272–83; and synthesizing
potential of strategy, 152, 153, 158,
239, 241, 257–58, 263, 269–70, 272,
292; and systemic thinking, 33, 152,
155, 156–57, 158, 227–28, 230, 246–
47, 257. *See also* realism, traditional;
theories of world politics

territory: and arena segmentation,
142–43; as material aspect of power
and the state, 18, 193, 220–21; vs.
soil, 192; and territorialization vs.
deterritorialization of politics, 18–
19, 130–31, 189, 193, 216, 251, 257.
See also spatio-temporal dimension
theories of world politics: and the balance of power, 152–53; condition of
validity of, 153, 157; speculative theorizing vs. scientific theories, 3–4, 5,
8, 10–11, 34, 151–52, 217, 226–27,

239, 272–73, 277; varieties and evolutionary pattern of, 5, 7–9, 252. *See
also* system of thought
tragic poetics: aspects of, 223–24; and
fact-value paradoxes, 243, 244; vs.
pragmatic politics, 266; relation to
ethical and esthetic dimension of,
226, 227; relation to political physics of, 218, 223–25, 243

values. *See* cultural-civilizational factor; institutional principle; power-
normative duality; tragic poetics

war: absence of functional substitute
for, 253; and autonomous war-
peace cycles, 122, 211; causation of,
62–66, 66–69, 121–22, 162, 211–12,
241; and constant-sum-of-violence
(and energy) hypothesis, 64, 121,
174, 218, 243; effect of nuclear variety of on world politics, 64, 67–68;
vs. lower forms of turbulence, 231–
32, 248; as neutral mechanism, 157,
211; prevention of, 70; relation to
stability vs. security of, 222; relation
to tragic poetics of, 224–25, 241;
utility for evolution of, 69, 162
Wolfers, Arnold, realism of, compared
with Hans J. Morgenthau's, 6
world politics: academic approaches to,
2–4, 6–7, 8; hypothetical futures of,
163–66, 182, 189–95, 228–38, 241,
246–49, 254–66, 290–93; identity
with world history of, 23–24, 28,
32, 158, 230, 239, 249, 273, 288–93;
problematic meaning of, 158–60,
189, 230

About the Author

George Liska retired on his 75th birthday as the Distinguished Service Professor of the Johns Hopkins University and the Paul H. Nitze Professor of the university's Nitze School of Advanced International Studies.

This is the concluding work in a long series of books on formative processes and institutions of international politics, extending over four decades and most recently including *The Restoration of Politics: Interrogating History about a Civilization in Crisis,* also published by Rowman & Littlefield (1996).